Practical Cookery

VICTOR CESERANI M.B.E.
The School of Hotel Keeping and Catering,
Ealing College of Higher Education

RONALD KINTON
Institute of Education, Garnett College,
London University

Fourth Edition

EDWARD ARNOLD

© VICTOR CESERANI and RONALD KINTON 1974
First published 1962
by Edward Arnold (Publishers) Ltd.,
41 Bedford Square, London WC1B 3DQ

Second edition 1967
Reprinted 1968, 1969, 1970
Third edition 1972
Reprinted 1972
Fourth edition 1974
Reprinted 1976
Reprinted 1977, 1978, 1979

ISBN: 0 7131 1853 9

Printed in Great Britain by
Western Printing Services Ltd., Bristol

Contents

NOTE: *Each relevant section begins with an index of the recipes to be found within it.*

Introduction to Fourth Edition

The object of this book is to provide a sound foundation of professional cookery for students taking City and Guilds of London Catering Examinations 705 (441); 706 (147, 151), the Ordinary National Diploma in Hotel and Catering Operations, the Higher National Diploma in Hotel and Catering Administration and the Membership examinations of the Hotel and Catering Institute Management Association. We also think that it will assist students of catering other than those taking these examinations.

Cookery is an art, and we feel very strongly that there should be ample scope for individual interpretation from basic principles. The student must realise that although most basic principles are adhered to in the kitchen, variations in method and recipes are commonplace, and that this is accepted by all practising cooks. Therefore, although for some recipes we have given alternative methods, the student must still expect further variations from teachers and professional cooks.

In preparing this fourth edition we have decided to increase the number of recipes. Previously our choice of recipes had been influenced to some extent by the examination requirements of the City and Guilds courses but as the practical examination constraints have been considerably modified this leaves the student able to study and practice over a wider area of work. In view of the ever increasing cost of food we would strongly advise all students to make themselves aware of the prices of all commodities and to keep up to date with price fluctuations.

Unless otherwise stated the recipes are given for four portions.

LARGE-SCALE METHODS

We have received requests to consider the inclusion of large-scale quantities and methods in this book. However, after much consideration we are of the opinion that to attempt to cover the differences between small-scale and quantity food production in one book would make recipes and explanations less clear for the student.

The basic principles of good food preparation apply to both small and large quantities; however, when large quantities of food are being prepared, then large-scale equipment should be used, which may cause slight variations in methods of work.

Students should be aware that most establishments catering for large numbers, e.g. School meals, hospitals, ICI, Sutcliffe Catering Company, will have their own standard recipes which are frequently costed to meet the requirements of the particular establishment.

iv

METRICATION

On the advice of the Metrication Board we are using the basic module of 25g. This module is not intended to equate with 1 oz but is being used because it is easily multiplied for larger metric quantities.

CONVENIENCE FOODS

We have not included any specific recipes or instructions for the use of convenience foods as the changes in the types of products are so numerous.

Owing to circumstances such as insufficient skilled labour, shortage of labour, cost of labour, inadequate space, cost of space and lack of time is it often expedient or convenient to use various forms of pre-prepared foods. Different terms are used to describe such foods— for example, convenience, ready, instant, pre-portioned. Examples of convenience foods include pre-portioned meats, poultry, fish, made-up dishes, dried potatoes and vegetables, tinned potatoes and vegetables, soups, sauces, coffee, milk, pastry and pudding mixes and frozen foods of all kinds.

Craftsmen and persons concerned with purchasing and controlling of food should be fully aware of all types of convenience foods available. Comparison should be made of the merits of the various brands, as should comparison of convenience foods with fresh, unprepared foods.

When assessing the merits of convenience foods it is advisable to compare the various makes of the same product before making comparison with fresh products.

Factors to be considered in comparison should include quality, price, cost of labour, time, space required, equipment required and disposal of waste. Under the factor of quality should be included flavour, appearance, consistency, colour, texture and smell.

It is useful to use a five-point scale when making assessment, for example: 5—very good; 4—good; 3—satisfactory; 2—poor; 1—very poor.

In order to use convenience foods to the best advantage, the manufacturer's instructions should always be followed implicitly. The craftsman can then modify, improve or use the product to produce a food as he wishes. For example, pea soup with the addition of cream and garnished with peas; dried potato with the additions of chopped ham and butter; dried, sliced vegetables added to stews; meat extracts added to sauces.

The student of catering, when studying the craft of cookery and its traditional processes, should, at the same time, make himself aware of all convenience foods and begin to form opinions as to when and in what circumstances one or the other (traditional or convenience) or possibly a combination of both, should be used. Convenience foods are not new and in a limited way they were being used in high-class cookery many years ago. There are today many more ready-prepared convenience foods on the market and the wise caterer makes a thorough study of all types available and if and when they are suitable to his particular line of business, incorporates them into his work.

Perhaps the most important factor when considering the use of convenience foods is the same as for traditional foods. For whom is the food intended? What price are they able to pay? Having considered these points it is necessary to decide whether the consumer will accept, or reject, convenience foods or possibly even prefer them.

We recommend the use of the following books: *Le Répertoire de la Cuisine* by L. Saulnier; *The Larder Chef* by Leto and Bode; *Guide to Modern Cookery* by A. Escoffier.

V. C.
R. K.

OVEN TEMPERATURE CHART

	Electric		Gas
	Degrees F	Degrees C	Regulo 1–9
Slow (cool)	250–300	120–150	1–3
Moderate	300–400	150–200	3–4
Moderately hot	400–450	200–230	4–6
Hot	450–475	230–250	6–8
Very hot	475–500	250–270	9

METRIC EQUIVALENTS

	Approx. equivalent	Exact equivalent
$\frac{1}{4}$ oz	5 g	7·0 g
$\frac{1}{2}$ oz	10 g	14·1 g
1 oz	25 g	28·3 g
2 oz	50 g	56·6 g
3 oz	75 g	84·9 g
4 oz	100 g	113·2 g
5 oz	125 g	141·5 g
6 oz	150 g	169·8 g
7 oz	175 g	198·1 g
8 oz	200 g ($\frac{1}{4}$ kg)	227·0 g
9 oz	225 g	255·3 g
10 oz	250 g	283·0 g
11 oz	275 g	311·3 g
12 oz	300 g	340·0 g
13 oz	325 g	368·3 g
14 oz	350 g	396·6 g
15 oz	375 g	424·0 g
16 oz	400 g ($\frac{1}{2}$ kg)	454·0 g
2 lb	1 kg	898·0 g
$\frac{1}{4}$ pt	125 ml	142 ml
$\frac{1}{2}$ pt	250 ml ($\frac{1}{4}$ litre)	284 ml
$\frac{3}{4}$ pt	375 ml	426 ml
1 pt	500 ml ($\frac{1}{2}$ litre)	568 ml
$1\frac{1}{2}$ pt	750 ml ($\frac{3}{4}$ litre)	852 ml
2 pt (1 qt)	1000 ml (1 litre)	1·13 litre
2 qt	2000 ml (2 litre)	2·26 litre
1 gal	($4\frac{1}{2}$ litre)	4·54 litre

METRIC ABBREVIATIONS

g = gramme
kg = kilogramme or kilo
m = metre
cm = centimetre
cm^2 = square centimetre
cm^3 (ml, cc) = millilitre

1
Methods of Cookery

THE OBJECT OF COOKING FOOD

The object of cooking food is to make it pleasing to the eye and receptive to the palate in order to help stimulate the digestive juices, thereby creating an appetite; to render food more digestible, by physical and chemical changes and by alteration of the texture, thereby assisting mastication, and to ensure the destruction of harmful bacteria and parasites.

METHODS OF COOKING FOOD

1 Boiling
2 Poaching
3 Steaming
4 Stewing
5 Braising
6 Pot roasting (Poêlé)
7 Roasting
8 Baking
9 Grilling
10 Frying (deep and shallow)
11 Paper Bag (en papillotte)
12 Microwave

BOILING

This is cooking in a liquid, usually water or stock.

Meat and Poultry
Boiling is restricted to the first few minutes in order to seal the pores, thus helping to retain the natural juices. After this, gentle boiling must take place, otherwise known as simmering. Rapid boiling or over-cooking causes the protein to harden and the connective tissues holding the meat fibres together to dissolve. Only just sufficient liquid should cover the article to be cooked. To retain the flavour in the joint, plunge into a boiling liquid and allow to reboil and then to simmer. If a well-flavoured stock is required, start slowly in cold water, then bring to the boil and simmer. Salted or pickled meats should always be started in cold water.

No exact rules can be given as to the time required to boil meat and poultry as age, size and quality must be allowed for. The approximate cooking times are 25 min per ½ kg (1 lb) for beef, mutton, pork, bacon and ham. For poultry, allow approximately 30 min per ½ kg (1 lb), but the age of the bird has a great bearing on the time required.

Vegetables
Vegetables grown above the ground are cooked in boiling salted

water; vegetables grown below the ground are started in cold salted water, with the exception of new potatoes. When cooking vegetables such as turnips and cauliflower boiling should be gentle otherwise the cellulose breaks down and the vegetable becomes mashed.

Fish
Whole or sliced fish are covered with the liquid and allowed to boil very gently.

POACHING

Poaching is cooking slowly in a minimum amount of liquid which should never be allowed to boil, but which should reach a degree of heat as near as possible to boiling point. It is usually applied to fish and fruit, but one exception is poached eggs.

STEAMING

This is cooking in moist heat by steam either:
(*a*) by placing the article in a perforated container or on a covered plate over a saucepan of water; or
(*b*) in a steamer with a minimum pressure of $1\frac{1}{4}$ kg/cm² (2 lb 8 oz per in²).

Vegetables
Certain vegetables are sometimes steamed, e.g. potatoes (particularly when required for sauté potatoes) and beetroot.

Puddings (Meat and Sweet)
These must be protected with greaseproof paper or foil and if possible a cloth or foil, to prevent water getting into the pudding.

STEWING

Stewing is gentle simmering in the smallest quantity of water, stock or sauce. The food is always cut up, and both the liquid and the food are served together.

This method has economical and nutritional advantages, as it will render tender and palatable the coarser, older and cheaper types of poultry or meat which would be unsuitable for grilling or roasting. The success of cooking such food depends on not allowing the liquid to reach too high a temperature. In the slow process of cooking by gentle heat the connective tissue is converted into gelatine so that the meat fibres fall apart easily and become digestible. The protein is coagulated without being overhardened and the soluble nutrients and flavour pass into the liquid, all of which is served.

All the cheaper cuts of meat and certain fish dishes, e.g. bouilla-baisse and matelote, which are fish stews, and certain vegetable dishes, e.g. marrow provençale and petits pois à la francaise, are cooked by this method.

BRAISING

This is a combination of roasting and stewing in a pan with a tight-fitting lid (braisière or casserole) to prevent evaporation so that the food retains its own juices together with the articles added for flavouring, e.g. bacon, ham, vegetables, herbs, etc.

Meat
The meat should be sealed by browning on all sides, placed on a lightly-fried bed of roots, and the stock, jus-lié or demi-glace two-thirds of the way up the joint, and flavourings then added.

It is covered with a lid and allowed to cook gently in the oven till the meat is very tender. If the joint is to be served whole, the lid should be removed approximately three-quarters of the way through cooking, the joint is then frequently basted in order to glaze it. Certain joints, e.g. venison and beef, are sometimes marinaded with red wine, vegetables and herbs for a few hours.

The braising of sweetbreads varies, and the necessary information is on page 206.

Vegetables
Certain vegetables are frequently braised, e.g. celery, cabbage, lettuce, onions and endive. The recipes for these are given in the Vegetable section.

POT ROASTING

This is cooking on a bed of root vegetables in a covered casserole or pan, using butter for basting. Only good-quality meats, game and poultry are used in this way, the chief advantage being that most of the flavour and goodness is retained in the joint. After the joint is removed the vegetables and juices are used with a good stock to form the basis of the accompanying sauce or gravy.

ROASTING

(A) *Spit Roasting* is cooking by direct (radiated) heat with the aid of fat in the form of basting (the spit must constantly revolve). It is applied to first-quality joints of meat and game and poultry. It is the original form of roasting, but because of many disadvantages in practice, oven roasting has developed in its place.

(B) *Oven Roasting* is cooking in an oven with the aid of fat and is applied to first-class meat and poultry and certain vegetables.

Meat and Poultry
Joints should always be raised out of the fat by means of bones or a trivet (with small joints, even halves of raw peeled potatoes are used) to prevent the meat from frying and becoming hard.

Joints should always go into a hot oven in order to seal the pores —exposure to a high temperature for the first ten minutes rapidly coagulates the surface albumen and prevents the escape of meat juices—heat is then reduced according to the size of the joint. Frequent basting is essential.

	Approximate cooking times	*Degree of cooking*
BEEF	15 min per ½ kg (1 lb) and 15 min over	Underdone
LAMB	20 min per ½ kg (1 lb) and 20 min over	Cooked through
MUTTON	20 min per ½ kg (1 lb) and 20 min over	Cooked through
VEAL	25 min per ½ kg (1 lb) and 25 min over	Cooked through
PORK	25 min per ½ kg (1 lb) and 25 min over	Thoroughly cooked
POULTRY	(See chapter on Poultry)	

Vegetables
Potatoes and parsnips may be roasted; the recipes are given in the Vegetable section.

BAKING

This is cooking by dry heat usually in an oven, in which the action of the dry heat is modified by the presence of steam which arises from the food whilst cooking. Bread, cakes, pastry and potatoes (Pomme au four—baked potato in its jacket) may be cooked by this method.

GRILLING OR BROILING

(A) Over heat—on grill bars.
(B) Under heat—salamander or grill.
(C) Between heat—between electric grill bars.

A   *Over heat*—Grill
This is cooking on greased grill bars, with the aid of fat over direct heat, Only first-class cuts of meat and poultry and certain fish may be used.

The grill bars which may be heated by charcoal, coke, gas or electricity should be made hot, brushed with oil to prevent the food sticking. The bars should char the article on both sides to give the distinctive flavour of grilling.

Most foods are started on a hot part of the grill and then moved to a cooler part to complete the cooking. The thickness of the food and the heat of the grill determine the cooking time, which can only be learnt by experience.

Grills are typical à-la-carte dishes and are ordered by the customer to the degree of cooking required.

Degrees of Cooking Grills

Rare	—	au bleu
Underdone	—	saignant
Just done	—	à point
Well done	—	bien cuit

B *Under heat*—Salamander
This is cooking on grill bars or on trays under direct heat. Steaks, chops, etc., may be cooked on the bars, but fish, tomatoes, bacon and mushrooms are usually cooked on trays.

The salamander is also used for browning by gratinating and glazing certain dishes, e.g. macaroni au gratin, filets de sole bonne-femme.

C *Between heat*
This is grilling between electrically-heated grill bars and is usually applied to meat.

FRYING

This is cooking in fat, either shallow or deep.

a) *Shallow frying* is cooking in shallow fat in a frying or sauté pan, or on a griddle plate. Any fats or oils may be used and as a general rule the presentation side should always be fried first. Poultry, meats, fish, vegetables and pancakes are foods which may be cooked in this way.

All foods are turned and cooked on both sides, but in certain cases, e.g. potatoes (pommes sautées), they are tossed in the pan and the French term 'sauter' is here used in one of its forms.

Sauté
Another use of this term is when applied to the cooking of poultry and meats of first-class quality in a sauté or frying-pan. When using a sauté pan the food, when cooked, is removed, the fat poured off and the pan swilled out (déglacé) with stock, wine, etc., this process forming an important part of the finished sauce.

It follows therefore that when the term 'sauté' is used for a dish of meat or poultry, e.g. Rognon sauté; Poulet sauté; Bœuf sauté, the meat should be completely cooked, the sauce finished and the two only combined for serving.

Obviously only first-class foods can be used and misunderstanding and misuse of the term have come in because inferior meats have been used which needed stewing. Therefore the term 'ragoût' should be used when the meat and sauce are stewed together. A common example of this error is Sauté de bœuf, using stewing beef, when it should be called Ragoût de bœuf.

b) Deep-frying
This is cooking in a friture in deep clarified fat. It is important that the fat selected can be raised to a high temperature without burning. Olive oil is the best, but because of its high price it is uneconomical; a good quality vegetable oil, e.g. cotton-seed, palm-oil, etc., or a first-class dripping or vegetable fat is generally used.

GENERAL POINTS

1   A friture should not be more than half to three-quarters full.
2   Fat should not be allowed to smoke, as this is a sign of burning.
3   The normal frying temperature is between 175° and 195°C. (350° and 380°F) and this is indicated by a slight haze rising from the fat.
4   Do not fry too much food at one time.
5   Allow the fat to recover its heat before adding the next batch of food.
6   A frying basket and a spider must always be at hand as a safety precaution.
7   Any wet foods, e.g. potatoes, should always be well dried before being fried.
8   Fat should always be strained after use.

Meat and Poultry
This is usually applied to made-up dishes, e.g. rissoles, cromesquis, chicken cutlets, which are coated either with pastry, batter or egg and crumbed.

Fish
Many fish may be deep fried, either whole (sole, whiting), filleted (plaice, haddock), in pieces, usually indicated 'en goujon' (sole, turbot), and as a made-up dish (fish-cakes). Fish should always be coated before being deep fried, so as to protect the fish from burning and to prevent the fish from absorbing fat or oil in which it is being

fried. It also prevents moisture from the fish going into the fat and spluttering.

Vegetables
Potatoes are fried in numerous ways, e.g. fried potatoes (pommes frites), croquette potatoes. Aubergine and cauliflower are sometimes deep fried.

Fruits
Apples, bananas, pineapples, etc., are coated in batter, deep fried and known as fritters (beignets). There are also cheese fritters, which are usually made from choux paste combined with cheese.

MICROWAVE COOKING

Microwave is a method of cooking and heating food by using high-frequency power. The energy used is the same as that which carries television from the transmitter to the receiver but is at a higher frequency.

The waves disturb the molecules or particles of food and agitate them, thus causing friction which has the effect of cooking the whole of the food from the inside, whereas in the conventional method of cooking heat penetrates the food only by conduction from the outside. Food being cooked by microwave needs no fat or water and is placed in a glass, earthenware, plastic or paper container before being put in the oven. Metal is not used as the microwaves are reflected by it.

The advantage of microwave cooking is its speed; for instance a 1.5 kg chicken takes only seven minutes' cooking time.

When using microwave ovens for cooking food certain factors should be considered.

1   The food is not coloured, e.g. with the cooking of a small chicken the outside of the bird would not colour. However if using a microwave/convection oven coloration does occur because the equipment includes traditional heating elements.

2   The thickness of the item to be cooked is related to the cooking time, e.g. penetration of the microwaves into food is only a short distance (7.5 cm) Whilst a chicken will cook satisfactorily because of the bone structure, a thick item of food such as a leg of lamb for instance, would not cook through satisfactorily.

3   The more uniform items of food are in shape the better they cook. Uneven shaped items cook unevenly, e.g. a baked potato cooks well, but a leg of lamb does not cook evenly because of its irregular shape.

4   Metal containers of any kind, including foil containers, must not

be put into the oven because the magnetron will be damaged by the reflected rays.

5   Apart from cooking foods, the microwave oven is used for re-heating frozen cooked foods, e.g. cottage pie, cod mornay, etc.

Further information: *Understanding Cooking*, Edward Arnold; *Guide to Microwave Cooking* by L. Napleton, Northwood Publications.

CONVECTION AND MICROWAVE

In some comparatively new cookers convection and microwave have been successfully combined within the one unit (illustration page 99 'Theory of Catering'). Either the microwave or convection can be used separately but are normally used simultaneously. Unlike the microwave oven metal pans and trays can be used in these units which therefore lend their use to more traditional methods of cookery.

Further information: Mealstream (U.K.) Ltd., 24 Cornwall Road, London, S.E.1.

2
Culinary Terms

Abats	Offal, heads, hearts, liver, kidneys, etc.
Abatis de volaille	Poultry offal—giblets, etc.
Acrolein	Product from burning fat which has an acrid smell
Aile	Wing of poultry or game birds
à la	In the style of
à la française	In the French style
à la carte	Dishes prepared to order and priced individually
Aloyau de boeuf	Sirloin of beef
Amino acid	The basic materials from which protein is built up
Appareil	Prepared mixture
Aromates	Aromatic herbs, spices
Arroser	To baste as in roasting
Ascorbic acid	Known as Vitamin C found in citrus fruits and blackcurrants. Necessary for growth and maintenance of health
Aspic	A savoury jelly mainly used for decorative larder work
Assaisonner	To season
Assorti	An assortment
Au bleu	When applied to meat it means very underdone
Au four	Baked in the oven
Au gratin	Sprinkled with cheese or breadcrumbs and browned
Au vin blanc	With white wine
Bacteria	Single-celled micro-organisms some of which are harmful, e.g. cause food poisoning. Others are useful, e.g. in cheese-making Bacteria—plural Bacterium—singular
Bain-marie	(i) A container of water to keep foods hot without fear of burning (ii) A shallow container of water for cooking foods in order to prevent them burning (iii) A deep, narrow container for storing hot sauces, soups and gravies
Barder	To bard. The covering of the breasts of birds with thin slices of bacon
Barquette	A boat-shaped pastry tartlet
Beignets	Fritters, sweet or savoury
Au beurre	With butter
Beurre manié	Equal quantities of flour and butter used for thickening sauces
Beurre noisette	Nut-brown butter
Beurre noir	Black butter
Beurre fondu	Melted butter
Bat out	To flatten slices of raw meat with a cutlet bat
Blanchir	To blanch (a) To make white as in the case of bones and meat (b) To retain colour as in the case of vegetables

	(c) To skin as for tomatoes
	(d) To make limp as for certain braised vegetables
	(e) To cook without colour as for the first frying of potatoes
Blanquette	A white stew cooked in stock from which the sauce is made
Blanc	A cooking liquor of water, lemon juice, flour and salt. Also applied to the white of chicken
Bouquet garni	A faggot of herbs: parsley, thyme and bay leaf usually tied inside pieces of leek and celery
Bombe	An ice-cream speciality of different flavours in bomb shape
Bouchées	Small puff paste cases
Bouillon	Unclarified stock
Brine	A preserving solution of water, salt, saltpetre and aromates used for meats, e.g. silverside, brisket, tongue
Brunoise	Small dice
Calorie	A unit of heat or energy
Casserole	An earthenware fireproof dish with a lid
Calcium	A mineral required for building bones and teeth. Obtained from cheese and milk
Canapé	A cushion of bread on which are served various foods, hot and cold
Carbon dioxide	A gas produced by all raising agents
Carbohydrate	This is a nutrient which has three groups, sugar, starch and cellulose. The first two provide the body with energy
Carte du jour	Menu for the day
Cellulose	The coarse structure of fruit, vegetables and cereals which is not digested but used as roughage
Clarification	To make clear, e.g. fat, stock, jelly
To cook out	The process of cooking the flour in a roux, soup or sauce
Chaud-froid	A demi-glace or creamed velouté with gelatine or aspic added, used for masking cold dishes
Chauffant	Pan of hot salted water for reheating foods
Chapelure	Crumbs made from dried bread
Châteaubriand	Head of the fillet of beef
Chinois	A conical strainer
Chlorophyll	The green colour in vegetables
Civet	A brown stew of game, usually hare
Clostridium Welchii	Food poisoning bacteria found in the soil, vegetables and meat
Clouté	Studded, e.g. clove in an onion
Coagulation	The solidification of a protein which is irreversible, e.g. fried egg, cooking of meat
Cocotte	Porcelain or earthenware fireproof dish
Collagen and Elastin	Proteins in connective tissue, e.g. gristle. Found in large quantities in tough cuts of beef which, when braised or stewed, is tenderised.
Court-bouillon	A well-flavoured cooking liquor for fish
Compôte	Stewed fruit
Concassée	Coarsely-chopped, e.g. parsley, tomatoes
Correcting	To adjust the seasoning, consistency and colour

Consommé	Basic clear soup
Contrefilet	Boned sirloin of beef
Côte	A rib or chop
Côtelette	Cutlet
Cordon	A thread or thin line of sauce
Coupé	Cut
Coupe	An individual serving bowl
Crêpes	Pancakes
Croûton	Cubes of fried bread served with soup, also triangular pieces with spinach and heart-shaped with certain vegetables and entrées
Cuisse de poulet	Chicken leg
Croquettes	Cooked foods moulded cylinder shape, egg and crumbed and deep fried
Dariole	A special mould
Darne	A slice of round fish on the bone
Demi-glace	Equal quantities of espagnole and brown stock reduced by half
Déglacé	To swill out a pan in which food has been fried, with wine, stock or water in order to use the sediment
Dégraisser	To skim fat off liquid
Désosser	To bone out meat
Duxelle	Finely chopped mushrooms cooked with chopped shallots
Drain	To place food in a colander
Dilute	To mix a powder (custard, arrowroot, cornflour, etc.) with a liquid
Doily	A fancy dish paper
Dish paper	A plain dish paper
Emulsion	A mixture of oil and water which does not separate on standing, e.g. mayonnaise, hollandaise, homogenised milk
Escalope	Thin slice
Estouffade	Brown stock
Entrecôte	A steak cut from the boned sirloin
Espagnole	Basic brown sauce
Egg wash	Beaten egg
Farce	Stuffing
Feuilletage	Puff paste
Fines herbes	Chopped parsley, tarragon, chervil
Flake	To break into natural segments (fish)
Flan	Open fruit tart
Fleurons	Small crescent-shaped pieces of puff pastry
Frappé	Chilled
Friandises	Petits fours
Fricassée	A white stew in which the meat or poultry is cooked in the sauce
Friture	A pan that contains deep fat
Fumé	Smoked
Garnish	Garniture—the trimmings
Gâteau	A cake of more than one portion

Gelatine	A soluble protein
Gibier	Game
Glace	Ice or ice-cream
Gluten	This is formed from protein present in flour when mixed with water
To glaze	(a) To colour a dish under the salamander, e.g. filet de sole bonne femme (b) To finish a flan or tartlet (c) To finish certain vegetables, e.g. carottes glacées
Haché	Finely chopped or minced
Hors d'oeuvre	Appetising first-course dishes
Jardinière	Vegetables cut into batons
Julienne	Cut into fine strips
Jus-lié	Thickened gravy
Larder	To insert strips of fat bacon
Liaison	A thickening or binding
Lardons	Batons of bacon
Macédoine	(a) A mixture—fruit or vegetables (b) Cut in $\frac{1}{2}$ cm ($\frac{1}{4}$ in) dice
Magnetron	The device which generates microwaves in a microwave oven
Marinade	A richly spiced pickling liquid used to give extra flavour and to assist in tenderising
Marmite	Stockpot
Petite marmite	A small earthenware pot in which soup is made and served
Menu	Bill of fare
Micro-organisms	Very small living plants or animals, e.g. bacteria, yeasts, moulds
Mignonette	Coarsely-ground pepper
Mill pepper	Pepper from the pepper mill
Mirepoix	Roughly-cut onion, carrots, celery and a sprig of thyme and a bay leaf
Mineral salts	These are mineral elements, small quantities of which are essential for health
à la minute	Cooked to order
Mousse	A dish of light consistency, hot or cold
Mise en place	Basic preparations prior to serving
Mono-sodium glutemate	A flavouring added to meat products to increase flavour
Napper	To coat or mask with sauce
Navarin	Brown stew of lamb or mutton
Niacin	Part of Vitamin B found in liver, kidney, meat extract, bacon
Noisette	A cut from a boned-out loin of lamb
Native	A menu term denoting English oysters
Nutrients	These are the components of food required for health (protein, fats, carbohydrates, vitamins, minerals salts, water)
Piqué	Studded, clove in an onion

Pané	Passed through seasoned flour, beaten egg and white breadcrumbs
Pass	To cause to go through a sieve or strainer
Paysanne	To cut into even, thin pieces, triangular, round or square
Paupiette	A stuffed and rolled strip of fish or meat
Persillé	Garnished with chopped parsley
Parsley butter	Butter containing lemon juice and chopped parsley
Picked parsley	Sprig of parsley
Petits fours	Very small pastries, biscuits, sweets, etc.
Phosphorus	A mineral element found in fish. Required for building bones and teeth
Ph value	A scale indicating acidity or alkalinity in food
Piquant	Sharply flavoured
Plat du jour	Special dish of the day
Printanière	Garnish of spring vegetables
Protein	The nutrient which is needed for growth and repair
Prove	To allow a yeast dough to rest in a warm place so that it can rise and expand
Pulses	Vegetables grown in pods (dried)
Ragoût	Stew
Refresh	To make cold under running cold water
Reduce	To concentrate a liquid by boiling
Riboflavin	Part of Vitamin B known as B2. Sources—yeast, liver, egg, cheese
Rissoler	To fry to a golden brown
Réchauffer	To reheat
Roux	A thickening of cooked flour and fat
Sabayon	Yolks of eggs and a little water cooked until creamy
Salamander	This is a type of grill heated from above
Salmonella	Food poisoning bacterium found in meat and poultry
Staphylococcus	Food poisoning bacterium found in the human throat and nose also in septic cuts
Seasoned flour	Flour seasoned with salt and pepper
Strain	To separate the liquid from the solids by passing through a strainer
Singe	To brown or colour
To sweat	To cook in fat under a lid without colour
Shredded	Cut in fine strips, lettuce, sorrel, onion
Set	To seal the outside surface
Sauté	(a) To toss in fat, e.g. pommes sautées (b) To cook quickly in a sauté or frying pan (c) A brown stew of a specific type
Soufflé	A very light dish, either sweet or savoury, hot or cold
Sodium	Mineral element in the form of salt (e.g. sodium chloride). Found in cheese, bacon, fish, meat
Starch	A carbohydrate found in cereals, certain vegetables, farinaceous foods
Syneresis	The squeezing out of liquid from an overcooked protein and liquid mixture, e.g. scrambled egg, egg custard
Terrine	An earthenware dish used for cooking and serving pâté
Tourné	Turned, to shape in barrels or large olives

Table d'hôte	A meal at a fixed price
Thiamine	Part of Vitamin B known as B1, it assists the nervous system. Source—yeast, bacon, wholemeal bread
Timbale	A double serving dish
Tranche	A slice
Tronçon	A slice of flat fish on the bone
Vol-au-vent	A large puff pastry case
Velouté	(a) A basic sauce
	(b) A soup of velvet or cream consistency
Vitamins	These are chemical substances which assist the regulation of body processes

3
Stocks and Sauces

STOCKS

Stock is a liquid containing some of the soluble nutrients and flavours which are extracted by prolonged and gentle simmering (with the exception of fish stock) which requires only 20 minutes; such liquid is the foundation of soups, sauces and gravies. Stocks are the foundation of many important kitchen preparations; therefore the greatest possible care should be taken in their production.

1   Unsound meat or bones and decaying vegetables will give stock an unpleasant flavour and cause it to deteriorate quickly.
2   Scum should be removed, otherwise it will boil into the stock and spoil the colour and flavour.
3   Fat should be skimmed, otherwise it will taste greasy.
4   Stock should always simmer gently, for if it is allowed to boil quickly, it will evaporate and go cloudy.
5   It should not be allowed to go off the boil, otherwise, in hot weather, there is a danger of its going sour.
6   Salt should not be added to stock.
7   When making chicken stock, if raw bones are not available, then a boiling fowl can be used.

8   If stock is to be kept, strain, reboil, cool quickly and place in the refrigerator.

THE STOCKS	LES FONDS
1 **White beef stock**	Fond blanc or fond de marmite
2 **White mutton stock**	Fond blanc de mouton
3 **White veal stock**	Fond blanc de veau
4 **White chicken stock**	Fond blanc de volaille

Uses of the above: white soups, sauces and stews.

5 **Brown beef stock**	Fond brun or estouffade
6 **Brown mutton stock**	Fond brun de mouton
7 **Brown veal stock**	Fond brun de veau
8 **Brown chicken stock**	Fond brun de volaille
9 **Brown game stock**	Fond de gibier

Uses of the above: brown soups, sauces, gravies and stews.

10 **Fish stock**	Fond de poisson or Fumet de poisson

Uses of the above: fish dishes.

11   **General proportions of ingredients for all stocks except fish stock**

4 litre	water	1 gal
2 kg	raw bones	4 lb
½ kg	vegetables (onion, carrot, celery, leek)	1 lb
	bouquet garni (thyme, bay leaf, parsley stalks)	
	12 peppercorns	

General method for all white stocks (except fish stock)
1   Chop up the bones, remove any fat or marrow.
2   Place in a stock pot, add the cold water and bring to the boil.
3   If the scum is dirty then blanch and wash off the bones, re-cover with cold water and re-boil.
4   Skim, wipe round sides of the pot and simmer gently.
5   Add the washed, peeled, whole vegetables, bouquet garni and peppercorns.
6   Simmer 6–8 hours.
7   Skim and strain.

During the cooking, a certain amount of evaporation must take place, therefore add ½ litre (1 pt) cold water just before boiling point is reached. This will also help to throw the scum to the surface and make it easier to skim.

General method for all brown stocks
1   Chop the bones and brown well on all sides either by:
(*a*) placing in a roasting tin in the oven, or
(*b*) carefully browning in a little fat in a frying-pan.

2 Drain off any fat and place the bones in stock pot.
3 Brown any sediment that may be in the bottom of the tray, déglacé (swill out) with ½ litre (1 pt) of boiling water, simmer for a few minutes and add to the bones.
4 Add the cold water, bring to the boil and skim.
5 Wash, peel and roughly cut the vegetables, fry in a little fat till brown, strain and add to the bones.
6 Add the bouquet garni and peppercorns.
7 Simmer for 6–8 hours.
8 Skim and strain.

For brown stocks a few squashed tomatoes and washed mushroom trimmings may also be added to improve the flavour.

Fish Stock   *Fumet de Poisson*

4 litre	water	1 gal
2 kg	white fish bones (preferably sole, whiting or turbot)	4 lb
200 g	onion	8 oz
50 g	margarine or butter	2 oz
	1 bay leaf	
	juice of ½ lemon	
	parsley stalks	
	6 peppercorns	

1 Melt the margarine in a thick-bottomed pan.
2 Add the sliced onions, the well-washed fish bones and the remainder of the ingredients.
3 Cover with greaseproof paper and a lid and sweat for 5 min. Remove greaseproof paper.
4 Add the water, bring to the boil, skim and simmer for 20 min, then strain.

GLAZES

12 Meat Glaze   *Glace de Viande*

13 Fish Glaze   *Glace de Poisson*

These are made by boiling steadily white or brown beef stock or fish stock and allowing them to reduce to a sticky or gelatinous consistency. They are then stored in jars and when cold kept in the refrigerator.

They are used to improve the flavour of a prepared sauce which may be lacking in strength.

SAUCES   *LES SAUCES*

A sauce is a liquid which has been thickened by a) roux, b) cornflour, arrowroot or fécule, c) beurre manié (kneaded butter), d) egg yolks.

All sauces should be smooth, glossy in appearance, definite in taste and light in texture, that is to say the thickening medium should be used in moderation.

14 The Roux

A roux is a combination of fat and flour which are cooked together. There are three degrees to which a roux may be cooked, namely (i) white roux, (ii) blond roux, (iii) brown roux.

A boiling liquid should never be added to a hot roux as the result may be lumpy and the person making the sauce may be scalded by the steam produced. If allowed to stand for a time over a moderate heat a sauce made with a roux may become thin due to chemical change (dextrinisation) in the flour.

White Roux
Uses: Béchamel sauce (white sauce), soups.

Equal quantities of margarine or butter and flour cooked together without colouring for a few minutes to a sandy texture.

Blond Roux
Uses: Veloutés, tomato sauce, soups.

Equal quantities of margarine or butter and flour cooked for a little longer than a white roux but without colouring, to a sandy texture.

Brown Roux
Uses: Espagnole (brown sauce), soups.

200 g (8 oz) dripping to 250 g (10 oz) flour per 4 litres (gallon) of stock, cooked together slowly to a light-brown colour. Overcooking of brown roux causes the starch to change chemically (dextrinise) and lose some of its thickening property. This will cause the fat to separate from the roux and rise to the surface of the soup or sauce being made. It will also cause too much roux to be used to achieve the required thickness and will give an unpleasant flavour.

15 Other Thickening Agents for Sauces

Cornflour, Arrowroot or Fécule
Uses: Jus-lié and sauces.

These are diluted with water, stock or milk, then stirred into the boiling liquid and allowed to re-boil for a few minutes.

Beurre Manié
Uses: Chiefly fish sauces.

Equal quantities of butter or margarine and flour kneaded to a smooth paste and mixed into a boiling liquid.

Egg Yolks
Uses: Mayonnaise, hollandaise and custard sauces.

Refer to the appropriate recipe as the yolks are used in a different manner for each sauce.

Blood
Use: Jugged Hare (see page 238)

BASIC SAUCE RECIPES FOR 1 LITRE (1 QUART)

Basic Sauces: Béchamel; Velouté; Espagnole; Demi-glace; Sauce tomate; Sauce hollandaise.

16   White Sauce   1 litre (1 quart)   *Béchamel*

This is the basic white sauce made from milk and a white roux.

1 litre	milk	1 qt
100 g	margarine	4 oz
100 g	flour	4 oz
	1 studded onion	

1   Melt the margarine in a thick-bottomed pan.
2   Add the flour and mix in.
3   Cook for a few minutes over a gentle heat without colouring.
4   Gradually add the warmed milk and stir till smooth.
5   Add the onion studded with a clove.
6   Allow to simmer for 30 min.
7   Remove the onion, pass the sauce through a conical strainer.
8   Cover with a film of butter or margarine to prevent a skin forming.

SAUCES MADE FROM BECHAMEL
(Quantities for ½ litre (1 pt) 8–12 portions)

	Sauce	*Served with*	*Additions per ½ litre (pt)*
17	**Anchovy** Sauce Anchois	Poached or fried or boiled fish	1 tbspn anchovy essence
18	**Egg** Sauce aux Œufs	Poached fish or boiled fish	2 hard-boiled eggs in small dice
19	**Cheese** Sauce Mornay	Fish or vegetables	50 g (2 oz) grated cheese, 1 yolk. Mix well in boiling sauce, remove from heat. Strain if necessary but do not allow to reboil
20	**Onion** Sauce aux Oignons	Roast mutton	100 g (4 oz) chopped or diced onions cooked without colour either by boiling or sweating in butter

Sauce	Served with	Additions per ½ litre (pt)
21 Soubise Sauce Soubise	Roast mutton	As for onion sauce but passed through a strainer
22 Parsley Sauce Persil	Poached or boiled fish and vegetables	1 tbspn chopped parsley
23 Cream Sauce Crème	Poached fish and boiled vegetables	Add cream or milk to give the consistency of double cream
24 Mustard Sauce Moutarde	Grilled herrings	Add diluted English mustard to make a fairly hot sauce

25 Velouté (Chicken, veal, fish, mutton) 1 litre (1 quart)
This is a basic white sauce made from white stock and a blond roux.

100 g	margarine or butter	4 oz
100 g	flour	4 oz
1 litre	stock (chicken, veal, fish, mutton) as required	1 qt

1   Melt the margarine in a thick-bottomed pan.
2   Add the flour and mix in.
3   Cook out to a sandy texture over gentle heat without colour.
4   Allow the roux to cool.
5   Gradually add the boiling stock.
6   Stir until smooth and boiling.
7   Allow to simmer approx. 1 hour.
8   Pass through a fine conical strainer.

A velouté sauce for chicken, veal or fish dishes is usually finished with cream and in some cases, also egg yolks.

SAUCES MADE FROM VELOUTES

26 Caper Sauce   ½ litre (1 pint)   *8–12 portions*   *Sauce aux Câpres*
Use: served with boiled leg of mutton.
This is a velouté sauce made from mutton stock with the addition of 2 tbspn capers per ½ litre (1 pt) of sauce.

27 Supreme Sauce   ½ litre (1 pint)   *8–12 portions*   *Sauce Suprême*
Uses: served hot with boiled chicken, vol au vent, etc., and also for white chaud-froid sauce.
This is a velouté made from chicken stock flavoured with well-washed mushroom trimmings.

½ litre	chicken velouté	1 pt
25 g	mushroom trimmings (white)	1 oz
60 ml	cream	⅛ pt
	1 yolk	
	2–3 drops lemon juice	

1   Allow the velouté to cook out with the mushroom trimmings.
2   Pass through a fine strainer.
3   Re-boil.
4   Mix the cream and yolk in a basin (liaison).
5   Add a little of the boiling sauce to the liaison.
6   Return all to the sauce.
7   Mix, finish with lemon juice and correct the seasoning.

28   Aurore Sauce   ½ litre (1 pint)   *8–12 portions*   *Sauce Aurore*

Uses: boiled chicken, poached eggs, chaud-froid sauce, etc.
Proceed as for sauce suprême, add 1 tbspn tomato puree to the
sauce. This should give a pink and slightly tomato-flavoured sauce.

29   Mushroom Sauce   ½ litre (1 pint)   *8–12 portions Sauce aux Champignons*

Uses: boiled chicken, sweetbreads, etc.
Proceed as for sauce suprême, add 100 g (4 oz) well-washed, sliced,
white button mushrooms. After the velouté has been strained simmer
for 10 min and finish with yolk and cream.

30   Ivory Sauce   *Sauce Ivoire*

To the sauce suprême add a little meat glace to give an ivory colour.
Used with boiled chicken.

Uses of veal velouté
An example of veal velouté is the sauce prepared in a blanquette of
veal.

Uses of fish velouté
Refer to fish section (pp. 99–129)

31   Brown Sauce   1 litre (1 quart)   ✳   *Sauce Espagnole*

50 g	good dripping	2 oz
60 g	flour	2½ oz
1 litre	brown stock	1 qt
25 g	tomáto purée	1 oz
100 g	carrot	4 oz
100 g	onion	4 oz

1   Melt the dripping in a thick-bottomed pan.
2   Add the flour, cook out slowly to a light brown colour, stirring
    frequently
3   Cool and mix in the tomato puree.
4   Gradually mix in the boiling stock.
5   Bring to the boil.
6   Wash, peel and roughly cut the carrots and onions.
7   Lightly brown in a little fat in a frying-pan.

8   Drain off the fat and add to the sauce.
9   Simmer gently 4–6 hours.
10   Skim when necessary. Strain.

Care should be taken when making the brown roux not to allow it to cook too quickly, otherwise the starch in the flour (which is the thickening agent) will burn, and its thickening properties weaken. Over-browning should also be avoided as this tends to make the sauce taste bitter.

32   Demi-glace Sauce   1 litre (1 quart)   *Sauce Demi-glace*

This is a refined Espagnole and is made by simmering 1 litre (1 qt) Espagnole and 1 litre (1 qt) brown stock and reducing by a half. Skim off all impurities as they rise to the surface during cooking. Pass through a fine chinois (conical strainer), re-boil, correct the seasoning.

SAUCES MADE FROM DEMI-GLACE
(Recipe for $\frac{1}{4}$ litre ($\frac{1}{2}$ pint))

33   Bordelaise Sauce $\frac{1}{4}$ litre ($\frac{1}{2}$ pint)   *4–6 portions*   *Sauce Bordelaise*

50 g	chopped shallots	⎫	2 oz
125 ml	red wine	⎬ reduction	$\frac{1}{4}$ pt
	pinch mignonette pepper		
	sprig of thyme		
	bay leaf	⎭	
250 ml	demi-glace		$\frac{1}{2}$ pt

1   Place reduction in a small sauteuse.
2   Allow to boil until reduced to a quarter.
3   Add the demi-glace.
4   Simmer 20–30 min.
5   Correct the seasoning.
6   Pass through a fine strainer.

This sauce should also include poached beef marrow either:
(*a*) in dice poached and added to the sauce; or
(*b*) cut in slices, poached and placed on meat before being sauced over.

Usually served with fried steaks, e.g. Entrecôte Bordelaise.

34   Chasseur Sauce $\frac{1}{4}$ litre ($\frac{1}{2}$ pint)   *4–6 portions*   *Sauce Chasseur*

50 g	sliced button mushrooms	2 oz
25 g	butter	1 oz
10 g	chopped shallots	$\frac{1}{2}$ oz
250 ml	demi-glace	$\frac{1}{2}$ pt
100 g	tomatoes (concassée)	$\frac{1}{4}$ lb
	chopped parsley and tarragon	
60 ml	white wine (dry)	$\frac{1}{8}$ pt

1   Melt the butter in a small sauteuse.
2   Add the shallots and cook gently for 2–3 min without colour.

3   Add the mushrooms, cover with a lid, gently cook for 2–3 min.
4   Strain off the fat.
5   Add the wine and reduce by half.
6   Add the tomatoes.
7   Add the demi-glace, simmer 5–10 min.
8   Correct the seasoning and add the tarragon and parsley.

Usually served with fried steaks, chops, chicken, etc., e.g. Noisette d'Agneau Chasseur.

---

35   Devilled Sauce   ¼ litre (½ pint)   *4–6 portions*   *Sauce Diable*

50 g	chopped shallot or onion ⎤	2 oz
5 g	mignonette pepper ⎥	¼ oz
	tbspn white wine ⎬ reduction	
	tbspn vinegar ⎥	
	cayenne pepper ⎦	
250 ml	demi-glace	½ pt

1   Boil the reduction and reduce by half.
2   Add the demi-glace.
3   Simmer 5–10 min.
4   Season liberally with cayenne.
5   Pass through a fine chinois.
6   Correct seasoning.

May be served with grilled or fried fish or meats e.g. Jambon Grillé, Sauce Diable.

---

36   Poivrade Sauce   ¼ litre (½ pint)   *4–6 portions*   *Sauce Poivrade*

50 g	onion ⎤	2 oz
50 g	carrot ⎥	2 oz
50 g	celery ⎬ mirepoix	2 oz
	1 bay leaf ⎥	
	sprig of thyme ⎦	
25 g	margarine	1 oz
	2 tbspn white wine	
	2 tbspn vinegar	
5 g	mignonette pepper	¼ oz
250 ml	demi-glace	½ pt

1   Melt the margarine in a small sauteuse.
2   Add the mirepoix and allow to brown.
3   Pour off the fat.
4   Add the wine, vinegar and pepper.
5   Reduce by half.
6   Add the demi-glace.
7   Simmer 20–30 min.
8   Correct the seasoning.
9   Pass through a fine chinois.

Usually served with venison.

37   Italian Sauce   ¼ litre (½ pint)   *4–6 portions*   *Sauce Italienne*

50 g	chopped mushrooms ⎫ duxelle	2 oz
10 g	chopped shallots ⎭	½ oz
25 g	margarine or butter	1 oz
25 g	chopped lean ham	1 oz
100 g	tomatoes (concassée)	¼ lb
250 ml	demi-glace	½ pt
	chopped parsley, chervil and tarragon	

1   Melt the margarine in a small sauteuse.
2   Add the shallots and gently cook 2–3 min.
3   Add the mushrooms and gently cook 2–3 min.
4   Add the demi-glace, ham and tomatoes.
5   Simmer 5–10 min.
6   Correct the seasoning.
7   Add the chopped herbs.

Usually served with fried cuts of veal or lamb, e.g. Escalope de Veau Italienne.

38   Brown Onion Sauce   ¼ litre (½ pint)   *4–6 portions*   *Sauce Lyonnaise*

100 g	sliced onions	4 oz
25 g	margarine	1 oz
250 ml	demi-glace	½ pt
	2 tbspn vinegar	

1   Melt the margarine in a sauteuse.
2   Add the onion, cover with a lid.
3   Cook gently till tender.
4   Remove the lid and colour lightly.
5   Add the vinegar and completely reduce.
6   Add the demi-glace, simmer 5–10 min.
7   Skim and correct the seasoning.

May be served with Vienna Steaks or fried liver.

39   Madeira Sauce   ¼ litre (½ pint)   *4–6 portions*   *Sauce Madère*

	2 tbspn madeira wine	
250 ml	demi-glace	½ pt
25 g	butter	1 oz

1   Boil the demi-glace in a small sauteuse.
2   Add the madeira, re-boil.
3   Correct the seasoning.
4   Pass through a fine chinois.
5   Gradually mix in the butter.

May be served with braised ox tongue (Langue Braisé au Madère).

40   Sherry Sauce ⎫ are made in the same way   *Sauce Xérès*
　　　　　　　　　⎬ as Madeira sauce, using dry sherry
41   Port Wine Sauce ⎭ or port wine as indicated.   *Sauce Porto*

42 Piquant Sauce ¼ litre (½ pint) *4–6 portions* *Sauce Piquante*

50 g	chopped shallots	2 oz
60 ml	vinegar	⅛ pt
250 ml	demi-glace	½ pt
25 g	chopped gherkins	1 oz
10 g	chopped capers	½ oz
	½ tbspn chopped chervil, tarragon and parsley	

1 Place vinegar and shallots in a small sauteuse and reduce by half.
2 Add demi-glace, simmer 15–20 min.
3 Add the rest of the ingredients.
4 Skim and correct the seasoning.

May be served with made-up dishes, e.g. Durham Cutlets with Piquant Sauce.

43 Robert Sauce ¼ litre (½ pint) *4–6 portions* *Sauce Robert*

50 g	onions	2 oz
10 g	margarine	½ oz
60 ml	vinegar	⅛ pt
250 ml	demi-glace	½ pt
	1 tbspn English mustard	
	¼ tbspn castor sugar	

1 Melt the margarine in a small sauteuse.
2 Add the finely chopped onion.
3 Cook gently without colour.
4 Add the vinegar and reduce completely.
5 Add the demi-glace, simmer 5–10 min.
6 Remove from the heat and add the mustard diluted with a little water and the sugar, do not boil.
7 Skim and correct the seasoning.

May be served with fried pork chop, e.g. Côte de Porc, Sauce Robert

44 Charcutière Sauce ¼ litre (½ pint) *4–6 portions* *Sauce Charcutière*
Proceed as for Sauce Robert and finally add 25 g (1 oz) sliced gherkins.

May also be served with pork chop.

45 Reform Sauce ¼ litre (½ pint) *4–6 portions* *Sauce Réforme*

25 g	carrot ⎫	1 oz
25 g	onion ⎬ mirepoix	1 oz
10 g	celery ⎪	½ oz
	½ bay leaf	
	sprig of thyme ⎭	
10 g	margarine	½ oz
	vinegar	
	½ tbspn redcurrant jelly	
	few peppercorns	
250 ml	demi-glace	½ pt
50 g	julienne of cooked beetroot, white of egg, gherkin, mushroom, truffle, tongue	2 oz

1 Fry off the mirepoix in a sauteuse.
2 Drain off the fat.
3 Add the crushed peppercorns and vinegar and reduce by two-thirds.
4 Add the demi-glace.
5 Simmer for 30 min.
6 Skim.
7 Add the redcurrant jelly.
8 Re-boil and strain through a chinois.
9 Add the garnish cut in julienne.

Served with lamb cutlet, e.g. Côtelette d'Agneau Réforme.

MISCELLANEOUS SAUCES

46 Curry Sauce $\frac{1}{4}$ litre ($\frac{1}{2}$ pint) *4–6 portions* *Sauce Kari*

10 g	fat	$\frac{1}{2}$ oz
	$\frac{1}{4}$ clove of garlic	
10 g	flour	$\frac{1}{2}$ oz
25 g	chopped apple	1 oz
	1 tbspn chopped chutney	
5 g	desiccated coconut	$\frac{1}{4}$ oz
50 g	chopped onion	2 oz
5 g	curry powder (approx)	$\frac{1}{4}$ oz
5 g	tomato purée	$\frac{1}{4}$ oz
375 ml	stock	$\frac{3}{4}$ pt
10 g	sultanas	$\frac{1}{2}$ oz
	salt	

1 Gently cook the onion and garlic in the fat in a small sauteuse without colouring.
2 Mix in the flour and curry powder.
3 Cook gently to a sandy texture.
4 Mix in the tomato puree, cool.
5 Gradually add the boiling stock and mix to a smooth sauce.
6 Add the remainder of the ingredients, season with salt.
7 Simmer 30 min.
8 Skim and correct the seasoning.

This sauce has a wide range of uses, e.g. with prawns, shrimps, vegetables, eggs, etc.

For poached or soft-boiled eggs it may be strained and for all purposes it may be finished with 2–3 tbspn cream.

47 Roast Gravy $\frac{1}{4}$ litre ($\frac{1}{2}$ pint) *4–6 portions* *Jus Rôti*

200 g	raw bones	8 oz
50 g	onion	2 oz
25 g	celery	1 oz
50 g	carrot	2 oz
250 ml	stock or water	1 pt

For preference use beef bones for roast beef gravy and the appropriate bones for lamb, veal, mutton and pork.

1   Chop bones and brown in the oven or brown in a little fat on top of the stove in a frying-pan.
2   Drain off all fat.
3   Place in saucepan with the stock or water.
4   Bring to boil, skim and allow to simmer.
5   Add the lightly browned mirepoix which may be fried in a little fat in a frying-pan, or added to the bones when partly browned.
6   Simmer 1½–2 hr.
7   Remove the joint from the roasting tin when cooked.
8   Return the tray to a low heat to allow the sediment to settle.
9   Carefully strain off the fat, leaving the sediment in the tin.
10   Return to the stove and brown carefully, swill (déglace) with the brown stock.
11   Allow to simmer for a few minutes.
12   Correct the colour and seasoning.
13   Strain and skim.

48   Thickened Gravy   ¼ litre (½ pint)   *4–6 portions*   *Jus-lié*

200 g	raw veal or chicken bones		8 oz
25 g	celery	mirepoix	1 oz
50 g	onion		2 oz
50 g	carrot		2 oz
	½ bay leaf		
	sprig of thyme		
5 g	tomato purée		¼ oz
10 g	arrowroot or cornflour		½ oz
500 ml	stock or water		1 pt
	mushroom trimmings		

1   Chop the bones and brown in the oven or in a little fat in a sauteuse on top of the stove.
2   Add mirepoix, brown well.
3   Mix in the tomato puree and stock.
4   Simmer 2 hr.
5   Dilute the arrowroot in a little cold water.
6   Pour into the boiling stock stirring continuously until it re-boils.
7   Simmer 10–15 min.
8   Correct the seasoning.
9   Pass through a fine strainer.

49   Bread Sauce   ¼ litre (½ pint)   *4–6 portions*   *Sauce Pain*

375 ml	milk	¾ pt
25 g	breadcrumbs	1 oz
10 g	butter	½ oz
	small onion studded with a clove	
	salt, cayenne	

1   Infuse the simmering milk with the studded onion for 15 min.
2   Remove the onion, mix in the crumbs.
3   Simmer 2–3 min.
4   Season, correct the consistency.
5   Add the butter on top of the sauce to prevent a skin forming.
6   Mix well when serving.

Served with roast chicken and roast game.

50   Apple Sauce   ¼ litre (½ pint)   *4–6 portions*   *Sauce Pommes*

400 g	cooking apples	1 lb
25 g	margarine	1 oz
25 g	sugar	1 oz

1   Peel, core and wash the apples.
2   Place with the sugar, margarine, a little water in a saucepan
     with a tight-fitting lid.
3   Cook to a puree.
4   Pass through a sieve.

Served with roast pork, duck and goose.

51   Cranberry Sauce   ¼ litre (½ pint)   *4–6 portions*   *Sauce Airelles*

400 g	cranberries	1 lb
60–100 ml	water	⅛–¼ pt
50 g	sugar	2 oz

Boil together in a suitable pan (not iron or aluminium) until soft, sieve if required.

Traditionally served with roast turkey.

52   Tomato Sauce   ¼ litre (½ pint)   *4–6 portions*   *Sauce Tomate*

10 g	margarine	½ oz
	½ clove garlic	
10 g	flour	½ oz
375 ml	stock	¾ pt
25 g	tomato purée	1 oz
	salt, pepper	
10 g	bacon scraps ⎫	½ oz
50 g	onion ⎪	2 oz
50 g	carrot ⎬ mirepoix	2 oz
25 g	celery ⎪	1 oz
	½ bay leaf ⎪	
	sprig of thyme ⎭	

1   Melt the margarine in a small sauteuse.
2   Add the mirepoix and brown slightly.
3   Mix in the flour and cook to a sandy texture. Allow to colour
     slightly.
4   Mix in the tomato puree.
5   Cool.

6   Gradually add the boiling stock, stir to the boil.
7   Add the garlic, season.
8   Simmer 1 hr.
9   Correct the seasoning.
10   Pass through a fine chinois.

This sauce has many uses, e.g. served with spaghetti, eggs, fish, meats, etc.

53 Melted Butter   ¼ litre (½ pint)   *4–6 portions*   *Beurre Fondu*

200 g   butter   8 oz
          2 tbspns water

Method I   Boil gently together till combined, then pass through a fine strainer.

Method II   Melt the butter and carefully strain off the fat leaving the water and sediment in the pan.

Usually served with boiled fish and certain vegetables, e.g. blue trout, salmon; asparagus and seakale.

54 Hollandaise Sauce   ¼ litre (½ pint)   *4–6 portions*   *Sauce Hollandaise*

200 g   butter   8 oz
          salt, cayenne
          2 egg yolks
          6 crushed peppercorns ⎫
          1 tbspn vinegar   ⎬ reduction

1   Place the peppercorns and vinegar in a small sauteuse and completely reduce.
2   Add 1 tbspn cold water, allow to cool.
3   Mix in the yolks with a whisk.
4   Return to a gentle heat and whisking continuously cook to a sabayon (this is the cooking of the yolks to a thickened consistency, like cream, sufficient to show the mark of the whisk).
5   Remove from the heat and cool slightly.
6   Whisk in gradually the melted warm butter until thoroughly combined.
7   Correct the seasoning.
8   Pass through a muslin, tammy cloth, or fine chinois.
9   The sauce should be kept at only a slightly warm temperature until served.
10   Serve in a slightly warm sauceboat.

The cause of Hollandaise sauce curdling is because the butter has been added too quickly. Or because of excess heat which will cause the albumen in the eggs to harden, shrink and separate from the liquid.

Should the sauce curdle, place a teaspoon of boiling water in a clean sauteuse and gradually whisk in the curdled sauce.

Served with hot fish (salmon, trout, turbot), and vegetables (asparagus, cauliflower).

55   Béarnaise Sauce   ¼ litre (½ pint)   *4–6 portions*   *Sauce Béarnaise*

200 g	butter	8 oz
10 g	chopped shallots	½ oz
	1 tbspn tarragon vinegar	
	sprig chopped chervil	
	3 egg yolks	
5 g	tarragon	¼ oz
	6 crushed peppercorns	

1   Make a reduction with the shallots, peppercorns, tarragon stalks and vinegar.
2   Proceed as for hollandaise sauce.
3   After passing add the chopped tarragon leaves and chervil.

Usually served with grilled meat and fish, e.g. Châteaubriand Grillé, Sauce Béarnaise.

HARD BUTTER SAUCES

56   Parsley Butter   *4 portions*   *Beurre Maître d'Hôtel*

50 g	butter	2 oz
	juice of ¼ lemon	
	¼ tspn chopped parsley	
	salt, pepper	

1   Combine all the ingredients
2   Shape into a roll 2 cm (1 in) diam.
3   Place in wet greaseproof paper.
4   Harden in the refrigerator.
5   Cut into ½ cm (¼ in) slices.

May be served with grilled meats and fish and fried fish (Sole Colbert).

57   Anchovy Butter   *4 portions*   *Beurre d'Anchois*

50 g	butter	2 oz
	salt, pepper	
	few drops anchovy essence	

Proceed as for parsley butter.
May be served with grilled and fried fish.

COLD SAUCES   *LES SAUCES FROIDES*

58   Mayonnaise Sauce   ¼ litre (½ pint) *8 portions approx. Sauce Mayonnaise*
This is a basic cold sauce and has a wide variety of uses, particularly in hors d'œuvre dishes. It should always be available on any cold buffet.

If during the making of the sauce, it should become too thick, then a little vinegar or water may be added. Mayonnaise will turn or curdle for several reasons:

1   If the oil is added too quickly.
2   If the oil is too cold.
3   If the sauce is insufficiently whisked.
4   If the yolk is stale and therefore weak.

The method of rethickening a turned mayonnaise is either (*a*) by taking a clean basin, adding 1 tspn boiling water and gradually whisking in the curdled sauce, or (*b*) by taking another yolk thinned with ½ tspn cold water whisked well, then gradually whisking in the curdled sauce.

250 ml	olive oil	½ pt
	2 tspn vinegar	
	salt, ground white pepper	
	2 egg yolks	
	⅛ tspn English mustard	
	1 tspn boiling water (approx.)	

1   Place yolks, vinegar and seasoning in a bowl and whisk well.
2   Gradually pour on the oil very slowly, whisking continuously.
4   Correct the seasoning.

59   Andalusian Sauce   ¼ litre (½ pint)   *8 portions approx.*   *Sauce Andalouse*

Add to ¼ litre (½ pt) of mayonnaise, 2 tbspn tomato juice or ketchup and 1 tbspn pimento cut in julienne.

May be served with cold salads.

60   Green Sauce   ¼ litre (½ pint)   *8 portions approx.*   *Sauce Verte*

50 g	spinach, tarragon, chervil, chives, watercress	2 oz
250 ml	mayonnaise	½ pt

1   Pick, wash, blanch and refresh the green leaves.
2   Squeeze dry.
3   Pass through a very fine sieve.
4   Mix with the mayonnaise.

May be served with cold salmon or salmon trout.

61   Tartar Sauce   ¼ litre (¼ pint)   *8 portions approx.*   *Sauce Tartare*

250 ml	mayonnaise	½ pt
25 g	capers ⎫	1 oz
50 g	gherkins ⎬ chopped	2 oz
	sprigs of parsley ⎭	

Combine all the ingredients.
Usually served with deep fried fish.

62   Remoulade Sauce   ⅛ litre (¼ pint)   *Sauce Remoulade*

Prepare as for Tartar sauce adding 1 teaspoon of anchovy essence and mixing thoroughly.

This sauce may be served with fried fish.

63   Tyrolienne Sauce   ⅛ litre (¼ pint)   *Sauce Tyrolienne*

30 ml	oil	¼ pt
5 g	shallots	¼ oz
50 g	tomatoes	2 oz
⅛ litre	mayonnaise	¼ pt
	¼ bay leaf	
	small sprig thyme	
	½ tspn parsley, chervil, tarragon	

1   Finely chop the shallots.
2   Cook without colour in the oil.
3   Concassé the tomatoes.
4   Add to the shallots.
5   Cook until soft and dry.
6   Pass the tomatoes and shallots through fine sieve.
7   Allow to cool.
8   Mix in with the mayonnaise and chopped parsley, chervil and tarragon (fines herbes).

This sauce may be served with fried fish or cold meats.

64   Horseradish Sauce   ⅛ litre (¼ pint)   *8 portions*   *Sauce Raifort*

25 g	grated horseradish	1 oz
	1 tbspn vinegar	
	salt, pepper	
125 ml	lightly whipped cream	1 gill

1   Wash, peel and re-wash the horseradish.
2   Grate finely.
3   Mix all the ingredients together.

Served with roast beef.

65   Mint Sauce   ¼ litre (½ pint)   *8 portions*   *Sauce Menthe*

	2–3 tbspn mint	
	1 dsspn castor sugar	
125 ml	vinegar	1 gill

1   Chop the washed, picked mint with the sugar.
2   Place in a china basin and add the vinegar.
3   If the vinegar is too sharp dilute with a little water.

Served with roast lamb.

66 Cumberland Sauce ⅛ litre (¼ pint) *8 portions*

100 ml	redcurrant jelly	¾ gill
5 g	chopped shallots	¼ oz
	juice of ¼ lemon	
	2 tbspn port	
	juice of orange	
	pinch of English mustard	

1 Warm and melt the jelly.
2 Blanch the shallots well and refresh.
3 Add the shallots to the jelly with the remainder of the ingredients. Cut a little fine julienne of orange zest, blanch, refresh and add to the sauce.

May be served with cold ham.

67 Oxford Sauce

As for Cumberland sauce, using chopped blanched orange and lemon zest instead of julienne of orange.

CHAUD-FROID SAUCES AND ASPIC JELLY

Chaud-froid sauces are derived from béchamel, velouté and demi-glace to which aspic jelly or gelatine is added so as to help them to set when cold. They are used to mask fish, meat, poultry and game, either whole, or cut in pieces, for cold buffets. They are usually decorated and then coated with aspic.

Aspic is a savoury jelly used on the majority of cold egg, fish, meat, poultry, game and vegetable dishes that are prepared for cold buffets so as to give them an attractive appearance. For meat dishes a beef or veal stock is made; for fowl, chicken stock; and for fish, fish stock.

68 Chaud-froid Sauce (White) 1 litre (1 quart)

1 litre	béchamel or velouté	1 qt
50 g	leaf gelatine	2 oz
125 ml	cream (if necessary to improve the colour of the sauce)	1 gill

1 Soak the gelatine in cold water.
2 Bring the sauce to the boil.
3 Remove from the heat.
4 Add the well-squeezed gelatine and stir until dissolved.
5 Pass through a tammy cloth.
6 When the sauce is half cooled mix in the cream.

Chaud-froid Sauce (Brown)

| 1 litre | demi-glace | 1 qt |
| 50 g | leaf gelatine | 2 oz |

Proceed as above, omitting the cream.

69 Aspic Jelly 1 litre (1 quart)

1 litre	strong, fat free, seasoned stock (as required poultry, meat, game or fish)	1 qt
75 g	leaf gelatine (approx. 24 leaves)	3 oz
	2–3 whites of eggs	
	2 sprigs tarragon	
	1 tbspn vinegar	

1 Whisk the whites in a thick-bottomed pan with $\frac{1}{4}$ litre ($\frac{1}{2}$ pt) of the cold stock and the vinegar and tarragon.
2 Heat the rest of the stock, add the gelatine (previously soaked for 20 min in cold water) and whisk till dissolved.
3 Add the stock and dissolved gelatine into the thick-bottomed pan. Whisk well.
4 Place on the stove and allow to come gently to the boil until clarified.
5 Strain through a muslin.
6 Repeat if necessary using egg whites only to give a crystal-clear aspic.

4
Hors d'Oeuvre

Hors d'œuvre may be divided into two categories:

(*a*) a single food, e.g. caviar, smoked salmon, oysters, etc.

(*b*) an assortment of well-seasoned dishes.

SINGLE FOOD HORS D'ŒUVRE

1 Oysters   *Les Huîtres*

The shells should be tightly shut to indicate freshness. The oysters should be carefully opened with a special oyster knife so as to avoid scratching the inside shell, then turned and arranged neatly in the deep shell and served on a bed of crushed ice on a plate. They should not be washed unless gritty and the natural juices should always be left in the deep shell.

Accompaniments—brown bread and butter and lemon. It is usual to serve six oysters as a portion.

2 Caviar   *Caviar*

This is the prepared roe of the sturgeon, a very expensive commodity usually served in its original tin or jar, in a timbale of crushed ice. One spoonful, 25 g (1 oz), represents a portion.

Accompaniments—toast, butter and lemon.

3 Smoked Salmon   *Saumon Fumé*

Before being carved a side of smoked salmon must be carefully trimmed so as to remove the dry outside surface. All bones must be removed; a pair of pliers will be found useful for this. The salmon is carved as thinly as possible on the slant and neatly dressed overlapping on an oval silver flat dish, decorated with sprigs of parsley 25–35 g (1–1½ oz) per portion.

Accompaniments—brown bread and butter and lemon.

Other smoked fish served as hors d'œuvre include eel, conger eel, trout, mackerel, herring (buckling), cod's roe, sprats.

4 Plovers' Eggs
Œufs de Pluvier

These are considered a great delicacy, but because of difficulty in maintaining supplies they are often substituted by gulls' eggs. They are hard-boiled, then served cold, and should be dressed on a bed of mustard and cress on a silver flat dish. It is usual to serve two per portion.

Accompaniments—brown bread and butter.

5 Foie Gras
Foie Gras

This is a ready-prepared delicacy made from goose liver, and it should be served in its original dish or pastry case. If tinned, it should be thoroughly chilled, removed from the tin and cut into 1 cm ($\frac{1}{2}$ in) slices.

Serve on a silver flat dish and garnish with a little chopped aspic jelly.

6 Liver Pâté (*Recipe 1*)   *4 portions*
Pâté de Foie

This is a home-made preparation often seen on the menu as Pâté Maison. A typical recipe is:

25 g	butter	1 oz
50 g	fat pork	2 oz
50 g	lean pork	2 oz
100 g	liver (chicken, pigs, calves, lambs, etc.)	4 oz
10 g	chopped onion	$\frac{1}{2}$ oz
	$\frac{1}{2}$ clove garlic	
	sprig of thyme	
	sprig of parsley	
	sprig of chervil	
	salt, pepper	
25 g	fat bacon	1 oz

1 Cut the liver in 2 cm (1 in) pieces.
2 Toss quickly in the butter in a frying-pan for a few seconds with the onion, garlic and herbs.
3 Allow to cool.
4 Pass with the pork, twice through a mincer.
5 Season.
6 Line an earthenware terrine with thin slices of fat bacon.
7 Place in the mixture.
8 Cover with fat bacon.
9 Stand in a tray half full of water.
10 Cook in a moderate oven for 1 hr.

When quite cold cut in ½ cm (¼ in) slices and serve on lettuce leaves on a silver flat.

Usually accompanied with toast.

Liver Pâté (*Recipe 2*)   *12 portions*

250 g	liver (chicken, pigs, calves, lambs, etc.)	10 oz
100 g	larding fat	4 oz
150 g	ham, bacon or pork fat	6 oz
50 g	lard	2 oz
25 g	sliced onion	1 oz
	1 clove garlic	
125 ml	choux paste (page 293)	¼ pt
60 ml	double cream	⅛ pt
	sprig of thyme	
	1 bay leaf	
	salt	
	mill pepper	

1   Line a two-pint earthenware dish with thinly sliced larding fat, allowing an overlap for the top.
2   Lightly fry the ham, bacon or pork fat in the lard with the onions, garlic, thyme and half of the bay leaf.
3   Add the seasoned liver, fry quickly for a few seconds.
4   Pass all the ingredients twice through a fine mincer then through a fine sieve.
5   Add the choux paste and the cream and mix thoroughly.
6   Place mixture into the lined dish, cover the top with the overlapping fat, place the other half of the bay leaf on top.
7   Cover with a lid, place in a bain-marie and cook in a moderate oven for one hour.

7 and 8   Salami and Assorted Cooked or Smoked Sausages   *Saucisson*

These are ready-bought sausages usually prepared from pork by specialist butchers. Most countries have their own specialities, and a variety of them are exported. They are thinly sliced and either served individually or an assortment may be offered. Mortadella is an example of this type of sausage.

9   Potted Shrimps

These are a bought prepared dish consisting of peeled shrimps cooked and served in butter. They may be served on their own or with smoked salmon.

10   Grapefruit   *Pamplemousse*

These are halved, the segments are loosened with a small knife, then they are chilled. Serve with a maraschino cherry in the centre.

The common practice of sprinkling with castor sugar is incorrect, as some customers prefer their grapefruit without sugar.

Serve half a grapefruit per portion in a coupe.

11 Grapefruit Cocktail

Allow ½–1 grapefruit per head.

The fruit should be peeled with a sharp knife in order to remove all white and yellow skin. Cut into segments and remove all the pips. The segments and the juice should then be dressed in a cocktail glass or grapefruit coupe and chilled. A cherry may be added.

12 Grapefruit and Orange Cocktail

Allow half an orange and half a grapefruit per head.

Prepare segments as for grapefruit cocktail and arrange in a coupe. A cherry may be added. Serve chilled. Sometimes known as Florida Cocktail.

13 Orange Cocktail

As for grapefruit cocktail, using oranges in place of grapefruit.

14 Florida Cocktail

This is a mixture of grapefruit, orange and pineapple segments.

15 Fruit Cocktail

Allow ½ kg (1 lb) unprepared fruit for 4 portions.

This is a mixture of fruits such as apples, pears, pineapples, grapes, cherries, etc., washed, peeled and cut into neat segments or dice and added to a syrup (100 g (4 oz) sugar to ¼ litre (½ pt) water) and the juice of half a lemon. Neatly place in cocktail glasses and chill.

16 Melon Cocktail

Approximately half a melon for 4 portions.

The melon, which must be ripe, is peeled, then cut into neat segments or dice or scooped out with a parisienne spoon, dressed in cocktail glasses and chilled.

17 Chilled Melon   *Melon Frappé*

Approximately half a honeydew or cantaloup melon for 4 portions.

Cut the melon in half, remove the pips and cut into thick slices. Cut a piece of the skin so that the slice will stand firm and serve on crushed ice.

Castor sugar and ground ginger are served separately.

18   Charentais Melon   *Melon de Charente*

1 melon per portion.

1   Cut a slice from the top of the melon to form a lid.
2   Remove the seeds.
3   Replace the lid and serve chilled.

19   Charentais Melon with Port   *Melon de Charente au Porto*

As for previous recipe adding ½ glass of port to the inside of each melon approximately 15 min before service.

20   Charentais Melon with Raspberries   *Melon de Charente aux Framboises*

As for recipe 18 adding 50 g (2 oz) picked and washed raspberries. (Strawberries may be used as a variation.)

21   Fruit Juice

Pineapple, orange, grapefruit.

This is usually bought ready prepared, but may be made from the fresh fruit.

22   Tomato Juice   *Jus de Tomate*

¼ kg (1 lb) tomatoes for 4 portions.

Fresh ripe tomatoes must be used. Wash, remove the eyes, then force through a sieve or strainer. The juice is then served in cocktail glasses and chilled.

23   Avocado Pear   *l'Avocat*

Allow ½ a pear per portion.

The pears must be ripe (test by pressing gently, the pear should give slightly).

1   Cut in half lengthwise.
2   Remove the stone.
3   Serve garnished with lettuce accompanied by vinaigrette (page 244) or variations to vinaigrette.

Avocado pears are sometimes filled with shrimps or crabmeat or other similar fillings.

24   Shellfish Cocktail;   *Cocktail de Crabe;*
Crab; Lobster;   *Homard; Crevettes;*
Shrimp; Prawn   *4 portions*   *Crevettes Roses*

125 ml	shellfish cocktail sauce	¼ pt
	½ lettuce	
100–150 g	prepared shellfish	4–6 oz

1   Wash, drain well and finely shred the lettuce.

2   Place about 2 cm (1 in) deep in cocktail glasses.
3   Add the prepared shellfish.
    (*a*) crab (shredded white meat only).
    (*b*) lobster (cut in ½ cm (¼ in) dice).
    (*c*) shrimps (peeled and washed).
    (*d*) prawns (peeled, washed, and if large cut into two or three
      pieces).
4   Coat with sauce.
5   Decorate with an appropriate piece of the content, e.g. prawn
    on the edge of the glass of a prawn cocktail.

Shellfish Cocktail Sauce   ⅛ litre (¼ pint)

Method I

  Mayonnaise

    1 egg yolk
    salt, pepper, mustard
    3 tbspn tomato juice
    1 dsspn vinegar
    5 tbspn olive oil

Make the mayonnaise as in Recipe 58, p. 31.
Combine with the tomato juice.

Method II

    5 tbspn lightly whipped cream
    3 tbspn tomato juice
    salt, pepper
    few drops of lemon juice

Mix all the ingredients together.
Fresh or tinned tomato juice or diluted tomato ketchup may be
used for both the above methods, but the use of tinned tomato puree
gives an unpleasant flavour.

25   Dressed Crab

Allow 200–300 g (8–12 oz) unprepared crab per portion.

When buying crabs, care should be taken to see that they have both
claws and that they are heavy in comparison to their size. When
possible they should be bought alive to ensure freshness.

Place the crabs in boiling salted water with a little vinegar added.
Allow to boil for approx 15–30 min according to size; these times
apply to crabs weighing from ½–2½ kg (1–5 lb). Allow to cool in the
cooking liquor.

To dress:
1   Remove large claws and sever at the joints.
2   Remove the flexible pincer from the claw.
3   Crack carefully and remove all flesh.
4   Remove flesh from two remaining joints with back of spoon.

5   Carefully remove the soft under-shell.
6   Discard the gills (dead man's fingers) and the sac behind the eyes.
7   Scrape out all the inside of the shell and pass through a sieve.
8   Season with salt, pepper, Worcester sauce and a little mayonnaise sauce, thicken lightly with fresh white breadcrumbs.
9   Trim the shell by tapping carefully along the natural line.
10 Scrub the shell thoroughly and leave to dry.
11 Dress the brown meat down the centre of the shell.
12 Shred the white meat, taking care to remove any small pieces of shell.
13 Dress neatly on either side of the brown meat.
14 Decorate as desired, using any of the following: chopped parsley, hard-boiled white and yolk of egg, anchovies, capers, olives.
15 Serve the crab on a flat dish, garnish with lettuce leaves, quarters of tomato and the legs.

Serve a vinaigrette or mayonnaise sauce separately.

26   Soused Herring or Mackerel

	2 herrings or mackerel	
25 g	carrots	1 oz
	½ bay leaf	
	6 peppercorns	
25 g	button onions	1 oz
60 ml	vinegar	½ gill
	sprig of thyme	
	salt, pepper	

1   Clean, scale and fillet the fish.
2   Wash fillets well, season with salt and pepper.
3   Roll up with the skin outside.
4   Place in an earthenware dish.
5   Peel and wash the carrot and onion.
6   Cut into neat thin rings.
7   Blanch for 2–3 min.
8   Add to the fish with the remainder of the ingredients.
9   Cover with greaseproof paper and cook in a moderate oven for 15–20 min.
10 Allow to cool, place in a dish with the onion and carrot.
11 Garnish with picked parsley.

ASSORTED HORS D'ŒUVRE

27   Anchovies   *Anchois*

Remove from the tin and dress in raviers, pour over a little oil and decorate if desired with any of the following:

capers, sprigs of parsley, chopped hard-boiled white and yolk of egg.

28 Sardines

Sardines à l'huile

Remove carefully from the tin, dress neatly in raviers and add a little oil. The sardines may be decorated with picked parsley and lemon.

29 Tunny

Thon

Remove from the tin, dress neatly, cut or shredded, in raviers, decorate as desired.

30 Egg Mayonnaise

Oeuf Mayonnaise

To cook hard-boiled eggs.
1   Place the eggs in boiling water.
2   Re-boil and simmer for 8–10 min.
3   Refresh until cold.

If eggs are cooked for a long time, iron in the yolk and sulphur compounds in the white are released to form the blackish ring (ferrous sulphide) around the yolk.

(i) *As part of a selection for hors d'œuvre*
Cut the hard-boiled eggs in quarters or slices, neatly dress in raviers and coat with mayonnaise.

(ii) *As an individual hors d'œuvre*
Allow one hard-boiled egg portion, cut in half and dress on a leaf of lettuce, coat with mayonnaise, garnish with quarters of tomatoes, slices of cucumber.
Dress neatly on silver flat dishes.

(iii) *As as main dish*
Allow two hard-boiled eggs per portion, cut in halves and dress on a plate, coat with mayonnaise sauce. Surround with a portion of lettuce, tomato, cucumber, potato salad, vegetable salad, beetroot.

31 Stuffed Eggs

Œufs Farcis

	2 hard-boiled eggs	
	4 tbspn mayonnaise	
25 g	butter	1 oz
	salt, pepper	

1   Quarter or halve the eggs.
2   Remove the yolks and pass through a sieve.
3   Mix the yolks with butter and mayonnaise and correct the seasoning.
4   Place in a piping bag with a star tube.
5   Pipe neatly back into the egg whites.
6   Dress in a ravier.

For variation add a little tomato ketchup, spinach juice, duxelle or anchovy essence, to the egg yolks.

32 Shellfish Mayonnaise

Shrimp, prawn, crab, lobster
As an hors d'œuvre allow 25–35 g (1–1½ oz) prepared shellfish per portion

	1 lettuce	
100–150 g	prepared shellfish	4–6 oz
125 ml	mayonnaise sauce	¼ pt
	capers, anchovies	
	parsley for decoration	

1 Shred the lettuce finely and place in a ravier.
2 Add the shellfish cut as for shellfish cocktail.
3 Coat with mayonnaise sauce.
4 Decorate as desired.

This may also be served as a main course in which case the amount of shellfish is doubled and the other ingredients are slightly increased.

33 Potato Salad *Salade de Pommes de Terre*

200 g	cooked potatoes	8 oz
60 ml	mayonnaise	½ gill
	1 tbspn vinaigrette, salt, pepper	
10 g	chopped onion or chive	½ oz
	chopped parsley	

1 Cut the potatoes in ½–1 cm (¼–½ in) dice, sprinkle with vinaigrette.
2 Mix with the onion or chive, add the mayonnaise and correct the seasoning.
3 Dress neatly in a ravier.
4 Sprinkle with chopped parsley.

34 Potato and Egg Salad *Salade de Pommes de Terre Aux Œufs*

As for recipe 33 with the addition of 2 chopped hard-boiled eggs.

35 Vegetable Salad *Salade de Legumes*
(*Russian Salad*) (*Salade Russe*)

100 g	carrots	4 oz
50 g	peas	2 oz
60 ml	mayonnaise	½ gill
	1 tbspn vinaigrette	
50 g	turnips	2 oz
50 g	French beans	2 oz
	salt, pepper	

1 Peel and wash the carrots and turnips.
2 Cut into ½ cm (¼ in) dice or batons.
3 Cook separately in salted water.

4   Refresh and drain well.
5   Top and tail the beans.
6   Cut in ½ cm (¼ in) dice, cook and refresh.
7   Cook the peas and refresh.
8   Mix all the well-drained vegetables with vinaigrette and then mayonnaise
9   Correct the seasoning.
10   Dress neatly in a ravier.

36   Fish Salad

Salade de Poisson

100 g	cooked fish (free from skin and bone)	¼ lb
	1 hard-boiled egg	
	¼ lettuce	
	chopped parsley	
50 g	cucumber	2 oz
	salt, pepper	
60 ml	vinaigrette	½ gill

1   Flake the fish.
2   Cut the egg and cucumber in ½ cm (¼ in) dice.
3   Finely shred the lettuce.
4   Mix ingredients together, add the parsley.
5   Correct the seasoning.
6   Mix with the vinaigrette.
7   Dress neatly in a ravier.
8   May be decorated with lettuce, anchovies and capers.

37   Fish Mayonnaise

Mayonnaise de Poisson

The method is the same as for shellfish mayonnaise (page 45) but using cooked flaked fish in place of shellfish.

38   Meat Salad

Salade de Viande

200 g	cooked meat	8 oz
50 g	tomatoes	2 oz
5 g	chopped onion or chives	¼ oz
50 g	cooked French beans	2 oz
25 g	gherkins	1 oz
	chopped parsley	
	vinaigrette	
	salt, pepper	
	3 tbspn oil	
	1 tbspn vinegar	
	1 tbspn French mustard	

1   Cut the meat and gherkin in ½ cm (¼ in) dice.
2   Cut the beans into ½ cm (¼ in) dice.
3   Skin tomatoes, remove seeds.
4   Cut into ½ cm (¼ in) dice.
5   Mix with remainder of the ingredients.
6   Correct the seasoning.

7   Dress neatly in a ravier.
8   Decorate with lettuce leaves, tomatoes and fans of gherkins.

Well-cooked braised or boiled meat is ideal for this salad.

39   Beetroot   *Betterave*

Wash and cook in the steamer or in gently simmering water till tender (test by skinning), cool and peel. Cut into $\frac{1}{2}$ cm ($\frac{1}{4}$ in) dice or $\frac{1}{2} \times 1$ cm ($\frac{1}{4} \times \frac{1}{2}$ in) batons. It may be served plain, with vinegar or sprinkled with vinaigrette.

40   Beetroot Salad   *Salade de Betterave*

200 g	cooked beetroot	8 oz
	chopped parsley	
10 g	chopped onion or chive	$\frac{1}{2}$ oz
	4 tbspn vinaigrette	

1   Combine all the ingredients.
2   Dress neatly in a ravier.
3   Sprinkle with chopped parsley.

41   Cucumber   *Concombre*

Peel the cucumber if desired; cut into thin slices and dress neatly in a ravier.

42   Cucumber Salad   *Salade de Concombres*

$\frac{1}{2}$ cucumber
chopped parsley
4 tbspn vinaigrette

1   Peel and slice the cucumber.
2   Sprinkle with vinaigrette and parsley.

43   Tomato   *Tomate*

If of good quality the tomatoes need not be skinned.
    Wash, remove the eyes, slice thinly or cut into segments. Dress neatly in a ravier.

44   Tomato Salad   *Salade de Tomates*

200 g	4 tomatoes	(approx. 8 oz)
10 g	chopped onion or chive	$\frac{1}{2}$ oz
	chopped parsley	
	$\frac{1}{4}$ lettuce	
	4 tbspn vinaigrette	

1   Peel tomatoes if necessary.
2   Slice thinly.
3   Arrange neatly on lettuce leaves.
4   Sprinkle with vinaigrette, onion, and parsley.

45   Tomato and Cucumber Salad   *Salade de Tomates et de Concombres*

> ¼ cucumber
> 4 tbspn vinaigrette
> 2 tomatoes
> chopped parsley

1   Alternate slices of tomato and cucumber.
2   Sprinkle with vinaigrette and parsley.

46   Rice Salad   *Salade de Riz*

100 g	cooked rice	4 oz
100 g	2 tomatoes	4 oz
	salt, pepper	
50 g	peas	2 oz
	4 tbspn vinaigrette	

1   Skin and remove seeds from tomatoes.
2   Cut in ½ cm (¼ in) dice.
3   Mix with the rice and peas.
4   Add the vinaigrette and correct the seasoning.
5   Dress neatly in a ravier.

47   Celeriac   *Céleri-Rave*

200 g	celeriac	8 oz
	1 tbspn diluted English mustard	
	salt, pepper	
	½ lemon	
60 ml	mayonnaise or cream	½ gill

1   Wash and peel celeriac.
2   Cut into julienne.
3   Combine with lemon juice and remainder of the ingredients.
4   Dress in a ravier.

48   French Bean Salad   *Salade d'Haricots Verts*

200 g	cooked French beans	8 oz
	4 tbspn vinaigrette	
	salt, pepper	

Combine all the ingredients and dress in a ravier.

49   Niçoise Salad   *Salade Niçoise*

200 g	cooked French beans	8 oz
10 g	anchovy fillets	½ oz
5 g	capers	¼ oz
	4 tbspns vinaigrette	
100 g	tomatoes	4 oz
10 g	stoned olives	½ oz
100 g	cooked diced potatoes	4 oz
	salt, pepper	

1   Peel tomatoes, remove seeds.
2   Cut into neat segments.
3   Dress the beans, tomato and potato neatly in a ravier.
4   Season with salt and pepper.
5   Add the vinaigrette.
6   Decorate with anchovies, capers and olives.

50   Haricot Bean Salad

Salade de Haricots Blancs

200 g	haricot beans cooked	8 oz
	4 tbspn vinaigrette	
	chopped parsley	
10 g	chopped onion or chive	½ oz
	salt, pepper	

Combine all the ingredients and dress in a ravier.

51   Raw Cabbage

A good crisp cabbage such as a savoy cabbage is ideal for this.

200 g	savoy cabbage	8 oz
	4 tbspn vinaigrette	

1   Trim off the outside leaves.
2   Cut the cabbage into quarters.
3   Remove the centre stalk.
4   Wash the cabbage, shred finely and drain well.
5   Dress in a ravier.
6   Serve vinaigrette separately.

52   Cole Slaw

125 ml	mayonnaise	¼ pt
200 g	white cabbage	8 oz
50 g	carrot	2 oz
25 g	onion	1 oz

1   Trim off the outside leaves of the cabbage.
2   Cut into quarters.
3   Remove the centre stalk.
4   Wash the cabbage, shred finely and drain well.
5   Mix with a fine julienne of raw carrot and shredded raw
    onion.
6   Bind with mayonnaise sauce.

53   Sweet Corn

Mais

This is usually bought tinned. The corn having been cooked is
removed from the can and bound with a light cream sauce.

54 Radishes   *Radis*

The green stems should be trimmed to about 2 cm (1 in) long, the root end cut off.

Wash well, drain and dress in a ravier.

HORS D'ŒUVRE À LA GRECQUE

All vegetables cooked à la grecque are cooked in the following liquid:

250 ml	water	½ pt
60 ml	olive oil	⅛ pt
	juice of 1 lemon	
	½ bay leaf	
	6 peppercorns	
	6 coriander seeds	
	salt	

55 Artichokes   *Artichauts à la Grecque*

1   Peel and trim six artichokes.
2   Cut the leaves short.
3   Remove the chokes.
4   Blanch the artichokes in water with a little lemon juice for 10 min.
5   Refresh the artichokes.
6   Place in the cooking liquid.
7   Simmer 15–20 min.
8   Serve cold in a ravier with a little of the unstrained cooking liquid.

56 Onions (Button)   *Oignons à la Grecque*

1   Peel and wash 200 g (8 oz) button onions.
2   Blanch for 5–10 min.
3   Refresh.
4   Place onions in the cooking liquor.
5   Simmer till tender.
6   Serve cold with unstrained cooking liquor.

57 Cauliflower   *Chou-fleur à la Grecque*

1   Trim and wash one medium cauliflower.
2   Break into small sprigs about the size of a cherry.
3   Blanch 5–10 min.
4   Refresh.
5   Simmer in the cooking liquor 5–10 min. Keep the cauliflower slightly undercooked.
6   Serve cold with unstrained cooking liquor.

58 Leeks   *Poireaux à la Grecque*

1   Trim and clean ½ kg (1 lb) leeks.
2   Tie into a neat bundle.

3   Blanch for 5–10 min and refresh.
4   Cut into 2 cm (1 in) lengths and place in a shallow pan.
5   Cover with the cooking liquor.
6   Simmer till tender.
7   Serve cold with unstrained cooking liquor.

59   Celery   *Celeri à la Grecque*
1   Wash and clean two heads of celery.
2   Blanch in lemon water for 5–10 min.
3   Refresh.
4   Cut into 2 cm (1 in) pieces.
5   Place in a shallow pan.
6   Add the cooking liquor, simmer till tender.
7   Serve cold with unstrained cooking liquor.

60   Hors d'œuvre à la Portugaise

All the vegetables prepared à la Grecque may also be prepared à la
Portugaise. They are prepared and blanched in the same way then
cooked in the following:

	1 tbspn olive oil	
	1 clove garlic	
	salt, pepper	
	½ bay leaf	
	1 chopped onion	
400 g	tomatoes	1 lb
	chopped parsley	
	sprig of thyme	

1   Sweat the onion in the oil.
2   Skin and remove the seeds from tomatoes.
3   Roughly chop.
4   Add to the onion with the remainder of the ingredients.
5   Correct the seasoning.
6   Add the vegetable and simmer till tender, with the exception of
     the cauliflower which should be left crisp.
7   Serve cold with the unstrained cooking liquor.

61   Cocktail Canapés or Canapés à la Russe

These are small items of food hot or cold which are served at cocktail
parties, buffet receptions and may be offered as an accompaniment to
drinks before any meal (luncheon, dinner or supper). Typical items
for cocktail parties and light buffet are:

1. Hot savoury pastry patties of lobster, chicken, crab, salmon,
mushroom, ham, etc.

2. Hot sausages (chipolatas), various fillings, such as chicken
livers, prunes, mushrooms, tomatoes, gherkins, etc., wrapped in
bacon and skewered.

3. Savoury finger toast to include any of the cold canapés. These may also be prepared on biscuits or shaped pieces of pastry. On the bases the following may be used: salami, ham, tongue, thinly sliced cooked meats, smoked salmon, caviar, mock caviar, sardine, eggs, etc.

4. Game chips, gaufrette potatoes, fried fish balls, celery stalks spread with cheese.

5. Sandwiches, bridge rolls open or closed but always small.

6. Sweets such as trifles, charlottes, jellies, bavarois, fruit salad, strawberries and raspberries with fresh cream, ice creams, pastries, gâteaux.

7. Beverages, coffee, tea, fruit-cup, punch-bowl, iced coffee.

A full range of cocktail canapés and forcemeat preparation may be obtained from *The Larder Chef* (Leto and Bode).

Canapés are served on neat pieces of buttered toast or puff pastry or short pastry. A variety of foods may be used, slices of hard-boiled egg, thin slices of cooked meats, smoked sausages, fish, anchovies, prawns, mussels, etc. They may be decorated with piped butter and are usually served coated with aspic jelly.

The size of a canapé should be suitable for a mouthful.

62   Bouchée Fillings

These are numerous as bouchées are served both hot and cold. They may be served as cocktail savouries, or as a first course, a fish course or as a savoury. All fillings should be bound with a suitable sauce, e.g.:

Mushroom	— chicken velouté or béchamel
Shrimp	— fish velouté or béchamel or curry
Prawn	— fish velouté or béchamel or curry
Chicken	— chicken velouté
Ham	— chicken velouté or béchamel or curry
Lobster	— fish velouté or béchamel or mayonnaise

63   Savouries using Barquettes and Tartlets

There are a variety of savouries which may be served either as hot appetisers (at a cocktail reception) or as the last course of an evening meal. The tartlet or barquette may be made from thinly rolled short paste and cooked blind.

Examples of fillings:
Shrimps in curry sauce.
Chicken livers in demi-glace or devilled sauce
Mushrooms in béchamel, suprême or aurora sauce
Poached soft roes with devilled sauce, e.g. Barquette Méphisto

Poached soft roes covered with cheese soufflé mixture and baked, e.g. Barquette Charles V.
The cooked tartlets or barquettes should be warmed through before service, the filling prepared separately neatly placed in them, garnished with a sprig of parsley. Service should be on a dish paper on a silver flat.

5
Soups

SOUPS   *LES POTAGES*

Soups may be classified as follows:

Consommé, Broth, Potage or *Soupe, Purée, Velouté, Cream*

They are served for luncheon, dinner and supper.

A portion is usually between 200–250 ml ($\frac{1}{3}$–$\frac{1}{2}$ pt), depending on the type of soup and the number of courses to follow.

Consommé—a clear soup prepared from a beef, chicken or game stock.

Broth—a good stock (beef, mutton or chicken) garnished with brunoise of vegetables, diced meat or chicken and rice or barley.

Potage or Soupe—these terms cover a wide variety of soups.

Purée—a passed soup, thickened by the dried or fresh vegetable of which it is chiefly composed.

Velouté—a thick soup made from white stock and a roux, finished with a liaison of yolks and cream.

Cream—a soup of creamy consistency which can be made in several ways:

(*a*) velouté finished with cream,
(*b*) half béchamel and half vegetable purée,
(*c*) purée soup finished with cream or milk.

1   Consommé (Basic Recipe)   *4 portions*

200 g	chopped or minced beef	8 oz
1 litre	cold, white or brown beef stock	1 qt
	bouquet garni	
	3–4 peppercorns	
100 g	mixed vegetables (onion, carrot,	4 oz
	celery, leek)	
	1 egg white	
	salt	

1   Thoroughly mix the beef, salt, egg white and $\frac{1}{4}$ litre ($\frac{1}{2}$ pt) cold stock in a thick-bottomed pan.
2   Peel, wash and finely chop the vegetables.
3   Add to the beef with the remainder of the stock the bouquet garni and the peppercorns.
4   Place over a gentle heat and bring slowly to the boil stirring occasionally.
5   Allow to boil rapidly for 5–10 sec.
6   Give a final stir.
7   Lower the heat so that the consommé is simmering very gently.
8   Cook for $1\frac{1}{2}$–2 hr without stirring.
9   Strain carefully through a double muslin.
10   Remove all fat, using both sides of 10 cm (3 in) square pieces of kitchen paper.
11   Correct the seasoning and colour, which should be a delicate amber.
12   Degrease again, if necessary.
13   Bring to the boil.
14   Serve in a warm soup tureen.

    A consommé should be crystal clear. The clarification process is caused by the albumen of the egg white and meat coagulating, rising to the top of the liquid and carrying other solid ingredients. The remaining liquid beneath the coagulated surface should be gently simmering.

    Cloudiness is due to some or all of the following:

(*a*)   poor quality stock
(*b*)   greasy stock
(*c*)   unstrained stock
(*d*)   imperfect coagulation of the clearing agent
(*e*)   whisking after boiling point is reached whereby the impurities mix with the liquid
(*f*)   not allowing the soup to settle before straining
(*g*)   lack of cleanliness of pan or cloth
(*h*)   any trace of grease or starch

    Consommés are varied in many ways by altering the stock, e.g. chicken, chicken and beef, etc. Also by the addition of numerous garnishes. Certain consommés are also served cold and are popular in very hot weather for luncheon, dinner or supper.

2   Royale—a royale is a savoury egg custard used for garnishing consommé, it should be firm but tender, the texture smooth, not porous. When cut no moisture (syneresis) should be apparent, when this happens it is a sign of overcooking.

1 Whisk up 1 egg; season with salt and pepper and add the same amount of stock or milk.
2 Pass through a fine strainer.
3 Pour into a buttered dariole mould.
4 Stand the mould in a pan half full of water.
5 Allow to cook gently in a moderate oven until set, approx. 15 min.
6 Remove when cooked, when quite cold turn out carefully.
7 Trim the edges and cut into neat slices 1 cm ($\frac{1}{2}$ in) thick, then into squares or diamonds.

3 Consommé Royale

1 Prepare royale as above.
2 When ready for service place the royale in the tureen and pour the boiling consommé on top very carefully.

4 Consommé Julienne

Basic consommé with a garnish of 50 g (2 oz) carrot, turnip and leek cut in 3 cm ($1\frac{1}{2}$ in) long fine julienne which has been previously cooked in a little salted water, then refreshed to preserve the colour. The garnish must be added to the consommé at the last moment.

5 Consommé Brunoise

Basic consommé with a garnish of 50 g (2 oz) carrot, turnip and leek cut into 2 mm ($\frac{1}{16}$ in) dice, cooked as for julienne. Add to the consommé at the last minute.

6 Consommé Célestine

Basic consommé with the addition of fine 2 cm (1 in) long julienne of pancake. The pancakes are made from basic pancake mixture, seasoned with salt and pepper and chopped parsley, tarragon and chervil are added. Add to the consommé at the last moment.

7 Consommé Vermicelle

Cook 25 g (1 oz) vermicelli in boiling salted water until tender. Refresh and wash well under a slowly running water tap. Drain in a strainer and add to the consommé at the last moment.

8 Consommé aux Pâte d'Italie ou Alphabétique

Cook 25 g (1 oz) special alphabet-shaped Italian paste as for vermicelli.

9 Consommé Tapioca

Cook 25 g (1 oz) of seed tapioca in boiling salt water until transparent. Pour into a fine strainer, wash under running water, drain well and add to consommé.

10 Consommé Sagou

As for tapioca using sago.

11 Consommé aux Profiterolles

Use 30 ml ($\frac{1}{8}$ pt) choux paste, place in a piping bag with a 3 mm ($\frac{1}{8}$ in) plain tube. Pipe out pea-sized pieces on a lightly greased baking sheet. Bake in a moderate oven approx. 5 min. Add to the consommé at the last moment. (Do not add sugar to the choux paste.)

12 Cold Consommé   *Consomme en Tasse*

This is a basic consommé lightly jellied and served in cups. The basic ingredients should be strong enough to effect the jelling, failing this a little gelatine must be added.

13 Consommé Madrilène (cold)

This is a basic consommé well-flavoured with tomato and celery and served with a garnish of neatly cut 3 mm ($\frac{1}{8}$ in) dice of tomate concassé.

14 Petite Marmite   *4 portions*

This is a double-strength consommé garnished with neat pieces of chicken winglet, cubes of beef, turned carrots and turnips and squares of celery, leek and cabbage. The traditional method of preparation is for the marmites to be cooked in special earthenware or porcelain pots ranging in size from 1–6 portions. Petite marmite should be accompanied by thin toasted slices of flute, grated parmesan cheese and a slice or two of poached beef marrow.

1 litre	good strength beef consommé	2 pt
	4 chicken winglets	
50 g	lean beef (cut in 1 cm dice)	2 oz
100 g	carrots	4 oz
100 g	turnips	4 oz
100 g	leeks	4 oz
25 g	cabbage	1 oz
50 g	celery	2 oz
	8 slices of beef-bone marrow	
50 g	toasted slices of flute	2 oz
25 g	parmesan cheese (grated)	1 oz

1   Trim chicken winglets and cut in halves.
2   Blanche and refresh chicken winglets and the squares of beef.
3   Place the consommé into the marmite.

4   Add the squares of beef and bring slowly to a simmer on the side of a solid-top range.
5   Allow to simmer 1 hour.
6   Add the winglet pieces, turned carrots and squares of celery.
7   Allow to simmer 15 min.
8   Add the leek, cabbage and turned turnips, allow to simmer gently until all the ingredients are tender.
9   Correct seasoning.
10 Degrease thoroughly using both sides of 6 cm square pieces of kitchen paper.
11 Add the slices of beef bone marrow just before serving.
12 Serve the marmite on a dish paper or a round flat dish accompanied by the toasted flutes and grated cheese.

15   Turtle soup   *4 portions*   *Tortue Claire*

An original recipe for preparing this soup from live turtles can be found in *Guide to Modern Cookery* by A. Escoffier. In Britain probably the only organisations that prepare turtle soup today according to the original recipe are food manufacturers. Good trade practice should be to use a real turtle soup purchased from a reliable manufacturer, however the following method is sometimes used.

1 litre	good strength consommé	2 pt
50 g	dried turtle meat	2 oz
25 g	arrowroot	1 oz
	1 sachet turtle herbs	
60 ml	dry sherry or madeira	$\frac{1}{8}$ pt

1   Soak the turtle meat in cold water for at least 24 hours.
2   Remove the turtle meat from the water, place in a little white stock and allow to simmer until tender.
3   Cut the turtle meat into 1 cm dice.
4   Bring the consommé to a gentle simmer.
5   Add the turtle herbs ensuring that they are securely wrapped in a piece of cloth.
6   Allow the turtle herbs to infuse for 5–10 mins, then remove.
7   Dilute the arrowroot in a little cold water.
8   Slowly add the diluted arrowroot to the gently simmering consommé stirring continuously until the consommé reboils.
9   Strain the consommé into a clean pan, reboil, add the diced cooked turtle meat and pour into a hot soup tureen.
10 Add the sherry or madeira and immediately place the lid on the soup tureen.
11 The turtle soup should be accompanied with cheese straws and quarters of lemon.

Turtle herbs are bought ready prepared and usually comprise a blend of basil, sage, thyme, coriander, marjoram, rosemary, bay-leaf and peppercorns.

16 Scotch Broth *4 portions*

1 litre	white beef stock	2 pt
25 g	barley	1 oz
	bouquet garni	
	chopped parsley	
200 g	vegetables (carrot, turnip, leek, celery, onion)	8 oz
	salt, pepper	

1 Wash the barley.
2 Simmer in the stock for approx. 1 hr.
3 Peel and wash the vegetables and cut into neat 3 mm (⅛ in) dice.
4 Add to the stock with the bouquet garni and season.
5 Bring to the boil, skim and allow to simmer until tender, approx. 30 min.
6 Correct the seasoning, skim, remove the bouquet garni, add the chopped parsley and serve.

17 Mutton Broth *4 portions*

200 g	scrag end of mutton	8 oz
25 g	barley	1 oz
	bouquet garni	
1 litre	water	2 pt
200 g	vegetables (carrot, turnip, leek, celery, onion)	8 oz
	chopped parsley	
	salt, pepper	

1 Place the mutton in a saucepan and cover with cold water.
2 Bring to the boil, immediately wash off under running water.
3 Clean the pan, replace the meat, cover with cold water, bring to the boil, skim.
4 Add the washed barley, simmer for 1 hr.
5 Add the vegetables, cut as for Scotch Broth, bouquet garni and season.
6 Skim when necessary, simmer till tender, approx. 30 min.
7 Remove the meat, allow to cool and cut from the bone, remove all fat, and cut the meat into neat dice the same size as the vegetables, add to the broth.
8 Correct the seasoning, skim, add the chopped parsley and serve.

18 Chicken Broth *4 portions*

	¼ of a boiling fowl	
25 g	rice	1 oz
	bouquet garni	
	salt, pepper	
1 litre	water	2 pt
200 g	vegetables (celery, turnip, carrot leek)	8 oz
	chopped parsley	

1   Place the fowl in a saucepan, add the cold water, bring to the
     boil and skim. Simmer for 1 hr.
2   Add the vegetables, prepared as for Scotch Broth, bouquet
     garni and season. Simmer until almost cooked.
3   Add the washed rice and continue cooking.
4   Remove all skin and bone from the chicken and cut into neat
     dice the same size as the vegetables, add to the broth.
5   Skim, correct the seasoning, add the chopped parsley and serve.

19   Green Pea Soup (with dried peas)   *4 portions*   *Purée St. Germain*

200 g	green split peas	8 oz
50 g	carrot (whole)	2 oz
	bouquet garni	
25 g	green of leek	1 oz
1½ litres	stock or water	3 pt
50 g	onion	2 oz
50 g	knuckle ham or bacon	2 oz
	salt, pepper	
	Croûtons	
	1 slice stale bread	
50 g	butter	2 oz

1   Pick and wash the peas.
2   Place in a thick-bottomed pan, cover with cold water or stock.
3   Bring to the boil and skim.
4   Add the remainder of the ingredients and season.
5   Simmer until tender, skim when necessary.
6   Remove the bouquet garni, carrot and ham.
7   Pass through a sieve.
8   Pass through a medium conical strainer.
9   Return to a clean saucepan, re-boil, correct the seasoning and
     consistency. Skim if necessary.

Serve accompanied by ½ cm (¼ in) diced bread croûtons shallow
fried in butter, drained and served in a sauceboat or special dish.

20   Cream of Green Pea Soup (fresh peas)   *4 portions*   *Crème St. Germain*
Basic Recipe

250 ml	peas (shelled)	½ pt
	sprig of mint	
25 g	onion	1 oz
60 ml	cream	⅛ pt
500 ml	water	1 pt
	bouquet garni	
500 ml	thin béchamel	1 pt

1   Cook the peas in the salted water with the onion, mint and
     bouquet garni until soft.
2   Remove the mint, bouquet garni and onion.
3   Pass firmly through a sieve.

4   Add to the béchamel, re-boil and simmer for 5 min, correct the
     seasoning.
5   Pass through a medium strainer.
6   Return to a clean pan, re-boil, skim, correct the seasoning and
     consistency.
7   Finally stir in the cream.

21 —   *Crème Lamballe*

As above with a garnish of 25 g (1 oz) cooked and washed tapioca
added at the same time as the cream.

22 —   *Crème Longchamps*

Crème St. Germain garnished with 25 g (1 oz) cooked and washed
vermicelli and julienne of sorrel cooked in butter.

23 Yellow Pea Soup (dried peas)   *Purée Egyptienne*

Proceed as for Green Pea Soup using yellow split peas and omitting the
leek. The carrot need not be removed and can be sieved with the peas.

24 Lentil Soup   *Purée de Lentilles*

200 g	lentils	8 oz
50 g	onion	2 oz
	bouquet garni	
	salt, pepper	
1 litre	stock or water	2 pt
50 g	carrot	2 oz
50 g	knuckle of ham or bacon	2 oz
	1 tspn tomato purée	
	Croûtons	
	1 slice stale bread	
50 g	butter	2 oz

Method of cooking and serving as for Green Pea Soup.

25 Haricot Bean Soup   *4 portions*   *Purée Soissonnaise*

200 g	white haricot beans	8 oz
50 g	carrot	2 oz
50 g	knuckle of ham or bacon	2 oz
50 g	onion	2 oz
	bouquet garni	
1½ litres	stock or water	3 pt
	salt, pepper	
	Croûtons	
	1 slice stale bread	
50 g	butter	2 oz

Method of cooking as for Green Pea Soup.

26 Potato Soup *4 portions*   *Purée Parmentier*

25 g	butter or margarine	1 oz
50 g	white of leek	2 oz
1 litre	white stock	2 pt
	salt, pepper	
50 g	onion	2 oz
400 g	peeled potatoes	1 lb
	bouquet garni	
	chopped parsley	
	Croûtons	
	1 slice stale bread	
50 g	butter	2 oz

1 Melt the margarine in a thick-bottomed pan.
2 Add the peeled and washed sliced onion and leek, cook for a few minutes without colour with a lid on.
3 Add the stock and the peeled, washed, sliced potatoes and the bouquet garni and season.
4 Simmer for approx. 30 min.
5 Remove the bouquet garni, skim.
6 Pass the soup firmly through a sieve then pass through a medium conical strainer.
7 Return to a clean pan, re-boil, correct the seasoning and consistency.
8 Pour into a warm soup tureen at the last moment before serving.

Sprinkle on a little chopped parsley. Serve croûtons separately.

27 Potato and Watercress Soup   *Purée Cressonnière*

1 Ingredients as for Potato Soup plus a small bunch of watercress.
2 Pick off 12 neat leaves of watercress, plunge into a small pan of boiling water for 1–2 sec. Refresh under cold water immediately, these leaves are to garnish the finished soup.
3 Add the remainder of the picked and washed watercress, including the stalks, to the soup at the same time as the potatoes.
4 Finish as for Potato Soup.

28 Vichyssoise *4 portions*

25 g	butter or margarine	1 oz
50 g	white of leek	2 oz
1 litre	white stock	2 pt
	salt, pepper	
50 g	onion	2 oz
400 g	peeled potatoes	1 lb
	bouquet garni	
	chopped parsley	
	chopped chives	
125–250 ml	cream	$\frac{1}{4}$–$\frac{1}{2}$ pt

1   Melt the margarine in a thick-bottomed pan.
2   Add the peeled and washed sliced onion and leek, cook for a few minutes without colour with a lid on.
3   Add the stock and the peeled, washed, sliced potatoes and the bouquet garni and season.
4   Simmer for approx. 30 min.
5   Remove the bouquet garni, skim.
6   Pass the soup firmly through a sieve then pass through a medium conical strainer.
7   Return to a clean pan, re-boil, correct the seasoning and consistency.
8   Finish with cream and garnish with chopped chives, raw, or cooked in a little butter.
9   Chill and serve.

29 Tomato Soup   *4 portions*

50 g	butter or margarine	2 oz
1¼ litres	stock	2½ pt
25 g	bacon trimmings	1 oz
	bouquet garni	
50 g	flour	2 oz
100 g	onion	4 oz
100 g	carrot	4 oz
50 g	tomato purée	2 oz
	salt, pepper	
	Croûtons	
	1 slice stale bread	
50 g	butter	2 oz

1   Melt the margarine in a thick-bottomed pan.
2   Add the bacon, rough diced onion and carrot, brown lightly.
3   Mix in the flour and cook to a sandy texture.
4   Remove from the heat, add the tomato puree.
5   Return to heat.
6   Gradually add the hot stock.
7   Stir to the boil.
8   Add the bouquet garni, season lightly.
9   Simmer for approximately 1 hr. Skim when required.
10   Remove the bouquet garni.
11   Pass firmly through a sieve then through a fine conical strainer.
12   Return to a clean pan, correct the seasoning, and consistency. Bring to the boil.
13   Serve ½ cm (⅛ in) dice fried croûtons separately.

30 Cream of Tomato Soup   *Crème de Tomates*

1   Prepare soup as for tomato soup using only 1 litre (2 pt) stock.
2   When finally re-boiling the finished soup add ¼ litre (½ pt) of milk or ⅛ litre (¼ pt) of cream.

31 Tomato Soup (using fresh tomatoes)

1 Prepare the soup as Recipe 29, using 1 litre (2 pt) stock.
2 Substitute $\frac{1}{2}$ kg (1 lb) fresh tomatoes for the tomato purée.
3 Remove the eyes from the tomatoes, wash them well and squeeze them into the soup after the stock has been added and has come to the boil.
4 If colour is lacking add a little tomato purée soon after the soup comes to the boil.

Cream of Tomato Soup with Rice *Crème Portugaise*

Cream of tomato with a garnish of 12 g ($\frac{1}{2}$ oz) plain boiled well-washed rice.

Cream of Tomato and Potato Soup *Crème Solférino*

Half cream of tomato and half potato soup mixed together and garnished with small balls of carrots and potatoes, cooked separately in a little salted water, refreshed and added to the soup just before serving.

32 Mushroom Soup *4 portions* *Crème de Champignons*

50 g	margarine or butter	2 oz
1 litre	white stock (preferably chicken)	2 pt
100 g	onion, leek and celery	4 oz
125 ml or 60 ml	milk or $\frac{1}{8}$ pt cream	$\frac{1}{4}$ pt
50 g	flour	2 oz
100 g	white mushrooms	4 oz
	bouquet garni	
	salt, pepper	

1 Gently cook the sliced onions, leek and celery in the margarine in a thick-bottomed pan without colouring.
2 Mix in the flour, cook over a gentle heat to a sandy texture without colouring.
3 Remove from the heat, cool slightly.
4 Gradually mix in the hot stock.
5 Stir to the boil.
6 Add the well-washed, chopped mushrooms, bouquet garni and season.
7 Simmer 30–45 min. Skim when necessary.
8 Remove the bouquet garni.
9 Pass through a sieve.
10 Pass through a medium strainer.
11 Return to a clean saucepan.
12 Re-boil, correct the seasoning and consistency, add the milk or cream.

33 Chicken Soup *4 portions* — *Crème de Volaille* or *Crème Reine*

1 litre	chicken stock	2 pt	
50 g	flour	2 oz	
100 g	onion, leek and celery	4 oz	
250 ml or			
125 ml	milk or ¼ pt cream	½ pt	
	garnish		
50 g	butter or margarine	2 oz	
	bouquet garni		
	salt, pepper		
25 g	cooked dice of chicken	1 oz	

1 Gently cook the sliced onions, leek and celery in a thick-bottomed pan, in the margarine without colouring.
2 Mix in the flour, cook over a gentle heat to a sandy texture without colouring.
3 Cool slightly, gradually mix in the hot stock.
4 Stir to the boil.
5 Add the bouquet garni and season.
6 Simmer 30–45 min, skim when necessary.
7 Remove the bouquet garni.
8 Pass firmly through a fine strainer.
9 Return to a clean pan, re-boil and finish with milk or cream.
10 Place the garnish in a warm soup tureen and pour on the soup.

34 Vegetable Soup *4 portions* — *Purée de Légumes*

300 g	mixed vegetables (onion, carrot, turnip, leek, celery)	12 oz	84 oz
50 g	butter or margarine	2 oz	14 oz
100 g	potatoes	4 oz	28 oz
	bouquet garni		
25 g	flour	1 oz	7 oz
1 litre	white stock	2 pt	14 pt
	salt, pepper		
	Croûtons		7
	1 slice of stale bread		
50 g	butter	2 oz	14 oz

1 Peel, wash and slice all the vegetables.
2 Cook gently in the margarine, in a pan with the lid on, without colouring.
3 Mix in the flour, cook slowly for a few minutes without colouring, cool slightly.
4 Mix in the hot stock.
5 Stir to the boil.
6 Add the sliced potatoes, bouquet garni and season. Simmer for 30–45 min, skim when necessary.
7 Remove the bouquet garni.
8 Pass through a sieve and then through a medium strainer.

9   Return to a clean pan, re-boil, correct the seasoning and the consistency.
10   Serve with croûtons separately.

35   Cream of Vegetable Soup   *Crème de Légumes*

Ingredients and method as for Vegetable Soup (Recipe 34), but *a*) in place of ½ litre (1 pt) stock use ½ litre (1 pt) thin béchamel; or *b*) finish with milk or ⅛ litre (¼ pt) cream, simmer for 5 min and serve as for Vegetable Soup.

36   Carrot Soup   *4 portions*   *Purée de Carottes*

1 litre	white stock	2 pt
50 g	onion	2 oz
50 g	celery	2 oz
25 g	flour	1 oz
	½ tspn tomato purée	
400 g	sliced carrots	1 lb
50 g	leek	2 oz
50 g	butter or margarine	2 oz
	bouquet garni	
	salt, pepper	
	Croûtons	
	1 slice stale bread	
50 g	butter	2 oz

1   Gently cook the sliced vegetables in the butter, with a lid on the pan, without colour, until soft. Mix in the flour.
2   Cook over a gentle heat for a few minutes without colouring.
3   Mix in the tomato purée.
4   Gradually add the hot stock.
5   Stir to the boil.
6   Add the bouquet garni and season.
7   Simmer 45–60 min.
8   Skim when necessary.
9   Remove the bouquet garni and pass firmly through a sieve, then through a medium strainer.
10   Return to a clean pan, re-boil, correct the seasoning and consistency.
11   Serve croûtons separately.

37   Cream of Carrot Soup   *Crème de Carottes*

Method A—Make as for Carrot Soup (Recipe 36), using ⅛–¼ litre (¼–½ pt) less stock and finish with ¼ litre (½ pt) milk or ⅛ litre (¼ pt) of cream.

Method B—As for Carrot Soup, but use only ½ litre (1 pt) stock and ½ litre (1 pt) béchamel.

38   Cream of Carrot Soup with Rice   *Crème Crécy*

Cream of Carrot Soup garnished with 12 g (½ oz) plain boiled and
well-washed rice.

39   Basic Soup Recipe

200 g	named soup vegetable sliced	8 oz
50 g	flour	2 oz
100 g	sliced onions, leek and celery	4 oz
1 litre	white stock	2 pt
50 g	butter or margarine	2 oz
	bouquet garni	
	salt, pepper	

1   Gently cook all the sliced vegetables, in the butter under a lid,
    without colour.
2   Mix in the flour and cook slowly for a few minutes without
    colour. Cool slightly.
3   Gradually mix in the hot stock.
4   Stir to the boil.
5   Add the bouquet garni and season.
6   Simmer for 45 min approx., skim when necessary.
7   Remove the bouquet garni, pass firmly through the sieve and
    through a medium strainer.
8   Return to a clean pan, re-boil and correct the seasoning and
    consistency.

40   Cauliflower Soup   *Purée de Chou-fleur*

As Basic Recipe 39 garnished with small sprigs of cauliflower
cooked in salted water.

41   Cream of Cauliflower Soup   *Crème Dubarry*

As Basic Recipe 39 but in place of ½ litre (1 pt) stock use ½ litre (1 pt)
thin béchamel or use ⅛–¼ litre (¼–½ pt) less stock and finish with
¼ litre (½ pt) milk or ⅛ litre (¼ pt) of cream and garnish as for
Cauliflower Soup (Recipe 40).

42   Celery Soup   *Purée de Céleri*

X4

As Basic Recipe 39 garnished with 2 cm (1 in) lengths of fine
julienne of celery cooked in salted water.

43   Cream of Celery Soup   *Crème de Céleri*

As Recipe 41 garnished as for Celery Soup (Recipe 42).

44   Leek Soup   *Purée de Poireaux*

As Basic Recipe 39 garnished with 2 cm (1 in) lengths of fine
julienne of leek cooked in salted water.

45   Cream of Leek Soup   *Crème de Poireaux*
As Recipe 41 garnished as for Leek Soup (Recipe 44).

46   Onion Soup (white)   *Purée d'Oignons*
As Basic Recipe 39.

47   Cream of Onion Soup   *Crème d'Oignons*
As Recipe 41.

48   Turnip Soup   *Purée de Navets*
As Basic Recipe 39.

49   Cream of Turnip Soup   *Crème de Navets*
As Recipe 41.

50   Artichoke Soup   *Purée d'Artichauts*
As Basic Recipe 39.

51   Cream of Artichoke Soup   *Crème d'Artichauts ou*
As Recipe 41.   *Palestine ou Topinambours*

52   Potato and Turnip Soup   *Purée de Pomme de Terre et*
As Basic Recipe 39.   *Navets ou Freneuse*

53   Cream of Potato and Turnip Soup   *Crème Freneuse*
As Recipe 41.

54   Asparagus Soup   *4 portions*   *Crème d'Asperges*

400 g	asparagus stalk trimmings or	½ lb
150 g	tin of asparagus	6 oz
1 litre	white stock	2 pt
50 g	butter or margarine	2 oz
50 g	flour	2 oz
50 g	onion	2 oz
50 g	celery	2 oz
	bouquet garni	
250 ml or		½ pt or
125 ml	milk or cream	¼ pt
	salt, pepper	

1   Gently sweat the sliced onions and celery, without colouring, in
     the butter.
2   Remove from the heat, mix in the flour, return to a low heat
     and cook out, without colouring, for a few minutes. Cool.

3   Gradually add the hot stock.
4   Stir to the boil.
5   Add the well-washed asparagus trimmings or the tin of asparagus, bouquet garni and season with salt.
6   Simmer 30–40 min.
7   Remove the bouquet garni.
8   Pass through a sieve, then a fine chinois, but do not push the asparagus fibres through the mesh.
9   Return to a clean pan, re-boil, correct the seasoning and consistency.
10   Add the milk or cream and serve.

55   Mulligatawny   *4 portions*

50 g	butter or margarine	2 oz
100 g	chopped onion	4 oz
	1 dsspn tomato purée	
25 g	chopped apple	1 oz
1 litre	brown stock	2 pt
10 g	cooked rice (for garnish)	$\frac{1}{2}$ oz
50 g	flour	2 oz
	$\frac{1}{2}$ clove of garlic (chopped)	
	1 dsspn curry powder	
	1 dsspn chopped chutney	
	salt	

1   Lightly brown the onion and garlic in the fat.
2   Mix in the flour and curry powder, cook out for a few minutes, browning slightly.
3   Mix in the tomato purée. Cool slightly.
4   Gradually mix in the brown stock.
5   Stir to the boil.
6   Add the remainder of the ingredients and season with salt.
7   Simmer 30–45 min.
8   Pass firmly through a medium strainer.
9   Return to a clean pan, re-boil.
10   Correct the seasoning and consistency.
11   Place the rice in a warm soup tureen and pour in the soup.

56   Brown Onion Soup   *4 portions*   *Soupe à l'Oignon*

600 g	onions	1$\frac{1}{2}$ lb
10 g	flour	$\frac{1}{2}$ oz
	salt, mill pepper	
50 g	grated cheese	2 oz
25 g	butter or margarine	1 oz
1 litre	brown stock	2 pt
	$\frac{1}{4}$ of flute	

1   Peel the onions, halve and slice finely.
2   Melt the butter in a thick-bottomed pan, add the onion and cook steadily over a good heat until cooked and well browned.
3   Mix in the flour and cook over a gentle heat, browning slightly.
4   Gradually mix in the stock, bring to the boil, skim and season.
5   Simmer approx. 10 min until the onion is soft. Correct the seasoning.
6   Pour into an earthenware tureen or casserole or individual dishes.
7   Cut the flute (French loaf, 2 cm (1 in) diameter) into slices and toast on both sides.
8   Sprinkle the toasted slices of bread liberally over the soup.
9   Sprinkle with more grated cheese and brown under the salamander.
10   Place on a silver dish and serve.

57 Kidney Soup   *4 portions*   *Soupe aux Rognons*

50 g	good dripping	2 oz
100 g	onion	4 oz
200 g	kidney (usually ox)	8 oz
1½ litres	brown stock	3 pt
	salt, pepper	
50 g	flour	2 oz
100 g	carrot	4 oz
10 g	tomato purée	½ oz
	bouquet garni	

1   Melt the fat in a thick-bottomed pan, mix in the flour.
2   Cook slowly to a brown roux. Cool slightly.
3   Mix in the tomato purée.
4   Gradually mix in the hot stock.
5   Stir to the boil.
6   Remove the skin and gristle from the kidney and cut into ½ cm (¼ in) dice.
7   Dice the carrots and onions.
8   Quickly fry the kidney in a little hot fat in a frying-pan for a minute, then add the carrot and onion and lightly brown together. Drain off all fat and add to the soup.
9   Add the bouquet garni and seasoning.
10   Simmer 1½–2 hr, skim when necessary.
11   Remove bouquet garni, pass the soup through a fine strainer.
12   Return to a clean pan, re-boil.
13   Correct the seasoning and consistency and serve.
14   This soup may be garnished with a little of the diced kidney.

58   Thick Mock Turtle Soup   *4 portions*   *Potage Fausse Tortue*

	¼ of calf's head	
50 g	good dripping	2 oz
100 g	onion	4 oz
10 g	tomato purée	½ oz
	2 tbspn sherry	
	salt, cayenne pepper	
1½ litres	brown stock	3 pt
50 g	flour	2 oz
100 g	carrot	4 oz
	1 bag turtle herbs	

1   Proceed as for Kidney Soup, 1–5 (previous recipe).
2   Add the calf's head and the fried diced carrot and onion.
3   Simmer for 1½–2 hr. Skim.
4   Place the turtle herbs, which should not be removed from the muslin bag, in the soup 5–10 min, then remove.
5   Pass the soup through a fine strainer.
6   Return to a clean pan, re-boil, correct the seasoning and consistency.
7   Cut a little of the best of the calf's head into 2 mm (⅛ in) dice for garnish.
8   Pour the boiling soup into the warm tureen.
9   Add the sherry at the last moment and immediately place the lid on the tureen.

59   Thick Oxtail Soup   *4 portions*   *Queue de Bœuf Lié*

	½ oxtail	
50 g	flour	2 oz
100 g	carrot and turnip	4 oz
	bouquet garni	
50 g	good dripping	2 oz
100 g	onion	4 oz
10 g	tomato purée	½ oz
1½ litres	brown stock	3 pt

1   Cut the oxtail into pieces through the natural joints.
2   Quickly fry in the hot fat till lightly brown.
3   Add the diced onion and carrot and brown well together.
4   Mix in the flour and cook to a brown roux over gentle heat or in the oven.
5   Cool slightly.
6   Mix in the tomato purée.
7   Gradually mix in the hot stock.
8   Stir to the boil and skim.
9   Add the bouquet garni and seasoning.
10   Simmer 3–4 hr.
11   Remove the bouquet garni and pieces of oxtail.
12   Pass the soup through a fine strainer.

13   Return to a clean pan, re-boil, correct the seasoning and
      consistency.
14   Garnish with the extreme tip of the tail cut into rounds, and a
      little carrot and turnip turned in small balls with a solferino
      spoon, or cut into 2 mm ($\frac{1}{16}$ in) dice and cooked in salted water.
15   Pour the boiling soup and garnish into a warm tureen.
16   This soup may be finished with 2 tbspn sherry.

60   Clear Oxtail Soup   *4 portions*   *Queue de Bœuf Clair*
      1   As above without using any flour.
      2   Drain off all the fat before adding to the stock.
      3   Before adding the garnish add 25 g (1 oz) diluted arrowroot to
           the soup, re-boil until clear, and strain.
      4   Finish and serve as for thick oxtail soup.

61   Cock-A-Leekie

$\frac{1}{2}$ litre (1 pt) good chicken stock and $\frac{1}{2}$ litre (1 pt) good veal stock
garnished with a julienne of prunes and white of chicken and leek.

62   Leek and Potato Soup   *4 portions*   *Potage de Poireaux et Pommes*

400 g	leeks (trimmed and washed)	1 lb
25 g	butter	1 oz
200 g	potato	8 oz
750 ml	white stock	1$\frac{1}{2}$ pt
	salt, pepper	

1   Cut the white and light green of leek into $\frac{1}{2}$ cm ($\frac{1}{4}$ in) squares.
2   Slowly cook in the butter in a pan with a lid on until soft, but
     without colouring.
3   Add the stock, the potatoes cut into $\frac{1}{2}$ cm ($\frac{1}{4}$ in) squares, 2 mm
     ($\frac{1}{8}$ in) thick, season with salt and pepper.
4   Simmer until the leeks and potatoes are cooked, approx. 15 min.

63 —   *Potage Bonne Femme*

1   Prepare as for Leek and Potato Soup.
2   Just before serving add 25–50 g (1–2 oz) of butter and $\frac{1}{16}$ litre
     ($\frac{1}{8}$ pt) of cream and stir in.

64 —   *4 portions*   *Potage Paysanne*

300 g	mixed vegetables (onion, leek, carrots, turnips, cabbage, celery)	12 oz
50 g	butter or margarine	2 oz
25 g	French beans (cut into diamonds) bouquet garni	1 oz
25 g	peas	1 oz
750 ml	good white beef stock	1$\frac{1}{2}$ pt
	salt, pepper	

1   Cut the peeled, washed vegetables into paysanne. Thinly cut
(a) 1-cm-sided (½-in) triangles, or
(b) 1-cm-sided (½-in) squares, or
(c) approx. round small pieces.
2   Cook slowly in the butter in a pan with a lid on until tender.
Do not colour.
3   Add the hot stock, bouquet garni, season and simmer for
approx. 20 min.
4   Add the peas and beans, simmer until all the vegetables are
cooked.
5   Skim off all fat and correct the seasoning.
6   Serve in a warm soup tureen.

65   Minestroni   *4 portions*   *Minestrone*

300 g	mixed vegetables (onion, leek, celery, carrot, turnip, cabbage)	12 oz
50 g	butter or margarine	2 oz
25 g	French beans	1 oz
50 g	potatoes	2 oz
¾ litre	white stock	1½ pt
	1 clove garlic	
	salt, pepper	
	bouquet garni	
25 g	peas	1 oz
100 g	tomatoes	4 oz
25 g	spaghetti	1 oz
50 g	fat bacon	2 oz
	chopped parsley	
	1 tspn tomato purée	

1   Cut the peeled and washed vegetables into paysanne.
2   Cook slowly without colour in the butter in the pan with a lid on.
3   Add the stock, bouquet garni and seasoning, simmer for approx.
20 min.
4   Add the peas, beans cut in diamonds and simmer for 10 min.
5   Add the spaghetti in 2 cm (1 in) lengths, the potatoes cut in
paysanne, the tomato purée and the tomatoes concassé and
simmer gently until all the vegetables are cooked.
6   Meanwhile finely chop the fat bacon, parsley and garlic and
form into a paste.
7   Mould the paste into pellets the size of a pea and drop into the
boiling soup.
8   Remove the bouquet garni, correct the seasoning.
9   Serve grated cheese (parmesan) and thin toasted flutes
separately.

66   Lobster bisque   *4 portions*   *Bisque de Homard*
A bisque is a thickened shellfish soup, e.g. lobster bisque, shrimp
bisque, etc.

500 g	live lobster	1 lb
50 g	onion	2 oz
50 g	carrot	2 oz
	bouquet garni	
100 g	butter	4 oz
75 g	flour	3 oz
60 ml	brandy	$\frac{1}{8}$ pt
120 ml	white wine (dry)	$\frac{1}{4}$ pt
50 g	tomato purée	2 oz
1$\frac{1}{4}$ litres	white stock (beef or veal or chicken or a combination of any 2 or 3)	2$\frac{1}{2}$ pt
120 ml	cream	$\frac{1}{4}$ pt
	salt, cayenne	

1   Wash the live lobster well.
2   Cut in half lengthwise tail first, then the carapace.
3   Discard the sac from the carapace, clean the trail from the tail and wash all the pieces.
4   Crack the claws and the four claw joints.
5   Melt the butter in a thick bottomed pan.
6   Add the lobster and the roughly cut onion and carrot.
7   Allow to cook steadily without colouring the butter for a few minutes stirring with a wooden spoon.
8   Add the brandy and allow it to ignite.
9   Remove from heat and mix in the flour and tomato purée.
10   Return to gentle heat and cook out the roux.
11   Cool slightly and gradually add the white stock and white wine.
12   Stir until smooth and until the bisque comes to the boil.
13   Add the bouquet garni and season lightly with salt.
14   Simmer for 15–20 min.
15   Remove lobster pieces.
16   Remove lobster meat, crush the lobster shells, return them to the bisque and allow to continue simmering for further 15–20 min.
17   Cut lobster neat into large brunoise.
18   Remove bouquet garni and as much bulk from the bisque as possible.
19   Pass the bisque through a coarse and then fine strainer.
20   Return the bisque to a clean pan.
21   Reboil, correct seasoning with a little cayenne, and add the cream.
22   Place the brunoise of lobster meat into a warm soup tureen, pour on the finished bisque and serve. At this stage 25 g (1 oz) butter may be stirred into the bisque as a final enriching finish.

In order to produce a less expensive soup cooked lobster shell (not shell from the claws) may be crushed and used in place of live lobster.

An alternate method of thickening is to delete the flour and ten minutes before the final cooked stage is reached to thicken by stirring in 75 g (3 oz) rice flour diluted in a little cold water.

6
Egg Dishes

EGG DISHES   *LES ŒUFS*

1 Scrambled Eggs (Basic Recipe)   *4 portions*   *Œufs Brouillés*

	6–8 eggs	
50 g	butter	2 oz
	salt, pepper	

1 Break the eggs in a basin, season with salt and pepper and thoroughly mix with a whisk.
2 Melt 25 g (1 oz) butter in a thick-bottomed pan, add the eggs and cook over a gentle heat stirring continuously until the eggs are lightly cooked.
3 Remove from the heat, correct the seasoning and mix in the remaining 25 g (1 oz) butter.
4 Serve in individual egg dishes.

If scrambled eggs are cooked too quickly or for too long the protein will toughen, the eggs will discolour because of the iron and sulphur compounds being released and syneresis or separation of water from the eggs will occur.

2 Scrambled Eggs on Toast

As above, serving each portion on a slice of freshly-buttered toast with the crust removed.

3 Scrambled Eggs with Tomatoes   *Œufs Brouillés aux Tomates*

400 g	tomatoes	1 lb
25 g	chopped onion	1 oz

1 Prepare, cook and serve the eggs as for the basic method.
2 Prepare a cooked tomato concassée (see page 271).
3 To serve place a spoonful of tomato in the centre of each dish of egg and a little chopped parsley on the top of the tomato.

4 Scrambled Eggs with Mushrooms   *Œufs Brouillés aux Champignons*

200 g	button mushrooms	8 oz
25 g	butter	1 oz
	chopped parsley	

1   Prepare, cook and serve the eggs as for the basic method.
2   Peel, wash and slice the mushrooms.
3   Toss in the butter in a frying-pan until cooked.
4   Dress neatly on top of the eggs.

5   Scrambled Eggs with Croûtons   *Œufs Brouillés aux Croûtons*

	2 slices stale bread	
50 g	butter	2 oz

1   Prepare, cook and serve as for the basic method.
2   Remove the crusts from the bread and cut into neat $\frac{1}{2}$ cm ($\frac{1}{4}$ in) dice.
3   Melt the butter in a frying-pan, add the croûtons and fry to a golden brown.
4   Place a spoonful in the centre of each dish of eggs.

6   Scrambled Eggs with Chopped Herbs   *Œufs Brouillés aux Fines Herbes*

1 tspn chopped parsley
chervil, tarragon and chives

1   Prepare, cook and serve as for the basic recipe.
2   Add the herbs with the last ounce of butter.

7   Scrambled Eggs with Ham   *Œufs Brouillés au Jambon*

100 g	thick sliced ham	4 oz

1   Prepare, cook and serve the eggs for as the basic recipe.
2   Trim off all fat from the ham and cut into $\frac{1}{2}$ cm ($\frac{1}{4}$ in) dice.
3   Add to the eggs with the last ounce of butter.

There are many other foods served with scrambled eggs, e.g. shrimps, cheese, asparagus tips, kidneys, etc.

8   Egg in Cocotte (Basic Recipe)   *Œuf en Cocotte*

	4 eggs	
25 g	butter	1 oz
	salt, pepper	

1   Butter and season four egg cocottes.
2   Break an egg carefully into each.
3   Place the cocottes in a sauté pan containing 1 cm ($\frac{1}{2}$ in) water.
4   Cover with a tight-fitting lid, place on a fierce heat so that the water boils rapidly.
5   Cook for 2–3 min until the eggs are lightly set.
6   Serve on a dish paper on a flat silver dish.

9   Egg in Cocotte with Cream   *Œuf en Cocotte à la Crème*

1   Proceed as for the basic recipe.
2   Half a minute before the cooking is completed add 1 dsspn of cream to each egg and complete the cooking.

10 Egg in Cocotte with Thickened Gravy   *Œuf en Cocotte au Jus*

1 Proceed as for the basic recipe.
2 When cooked add 1 dsspn jus-lié to each egg.

11 Egg in Cocotte with Creamed Chicken   *Œuf en Cocotte à la Reine*

50 g	diced cooked chicken	2 oz
125 ml	supreme sauce	¼ pt

1 Combine the chicken with half of the sauce and place in the bottom of the egg cocottes.
2 Break the eggs on top of the chicken and cook as for the basic recipe.
3 When serving pour over the eggs 1 dsspn of the remaining sauce or fresh cream.

12 Egg in Cocotte with Tomato   *Œuf en Cocotte aux Tomates*

200 g	tomatoes (cooked concassée)	8 oz
125 ml	tomato sauce	¼ pt

1 Add the tomato to the egg cocotte.
2 Break the eggs on top and cook as for the basic method.
3 Add 1 dsspn tomato sauce to the eggs before serving.

13 Hard-boiled Eggs   *Œufs Durs*

1 Plunge the eggs into a pan of boiling water.
2 Re-boil and simmer for 8–10 min.
3 Refresh until cold under running water.

If high temperatures or a long cooking time are used to cook eggs, iron in the yolk and sulphur compounds in the white are released to form a blackish ring around the yolk.

14 Eggs Chimay   *Œufs Chimay*

	4 hard-boiled eggs	
	chopped parsley	
250 ml	mornay sauce	½ pt
	Duxelle	
10 g	butter	½ oz
10 g	chopped shallots	½ oz
100 g	mushrooms	4 oz
	salt, pepper	

1 Cut the eggs in halves lengthwise.
2 Remove the yolks and pass through a sieve.
3 Place the whites in an earthenware serving dish.
4 Prepare the duxelle by cooking the chopped shallot in the butter without colouring, add the well-washed and finely chopped mushroom or mushroom trimmings, cook for 3–4 min.

5 Mix the yolks with the duxelle and correct the seasoning.
6 Spoon or pipe the mixture into the egg white halves.
7 Cover the eggs with mornay sauce, sprinkle with grated parmesan cheese and brown slowly under a salamander or in the top of a moderate oven.
8 Place the dish on a silver flat and serve.

15 Eggs Aurore   *Œufs Aurore*

1 Proceed as for Eggs Chimay using béchamel in place of mornay.
2 Add a little tomato sauce or tomato purée to the béchamel to give it a pinkish colour.
3 Mask the eggs, sprinkle with grated cheese.
4 Gratinate under the salamander.

16 Hard Boiled Eggs with Parsley and Onion Sauce   *Œufs à la Tripe*

	4 sliced hard-boiled eggs	
	chopped parsley	
250 ml	soubise sauce	½ pt

1 Place the sliced eggs in a buttered, earthenware dish.
2 Coat with boiling soubise sauce (page 21).
3 Sprinkle with chopped parsley.
4 Place the dish on a silver flat and serve.

17 Egg Croquette   *Croquette d'Œuf*

	4 hard-boiled eggs	
50 g	white breadcrumbs	2 oz
	1 beaten egg	
250 ml	thick béchamel	½ pt
	1 egg yolk	
25 g	flour	1 oz
	salt, pepper	

1 Boil the béchamel in a thick-bottomed pan.
2 Add the eggs cut into ½ cm (¼ in) dice.
3 Re-boil, season, mix in the egg yolk, and remove from the heat.
4 Pour on to a greased tray and leave until cold.
5 Mould into 4 or 8 even croquette shapes.
6 Pass through flour, beaten egg, and crumbs.
7 Shake off surplus crumbs and reshape with a palette knife.
8 Deep fry to a golden brown in hot fat.
9 Drain well.
10 Serve on a dish paper on a silver dish.
11 Garnish with fried or sprig parsley.
12 Serve with a sauceboat of tomato sauce.

18   Curried Eggs

	4 hard-boiled eggs	
250 ml	curry sauce	½ pt
50 g	rice	2 oz

1   Pick and wash the rice, preferably Patna (long grain).
2   Add to plenty of boiling, salt water.
3   Stir to the boil and allow to simmer gently till tender, approx. 12–15 min.
4   Wash well under running water, drain and place on a sieve and cover with a cloth.
5   Place on a tray in a moderate oven or on a hot plate until hot.
6   Place the rice in an earthenware dish.
7   Reheat the eggs in hot salt water, cut in halves and dress neatly on the rice.
8   Coat the eggs with sauce.
9   Place the dish on a silver flat and serve.

19   Scotch Eggs

	4 hard-boiled eggs	
50 g	breadcrumbs	2 oz
25 g	flour	1 oz
300 g	sausage meat	12 oz
	1 beaten egg	

1   Completely cover each egg with sausage meat.
2   Pass through flour, egg and breadcrumbs.
3   Shake off surplus crumbs.
4   Deep fry to a golden brown in a moderately hot fat.
5   Drain well, cut in halves and serve hot or cold.
6   *Hot:*   serve on a dish paper, garnish with fried or sprig parsley, and a sauceboat of suitable sauce, e.g. tomato.
     Cold: garnish with salad in season and a sauceboat of salad dressing.

20   Fried Eggs   *Œufs Frits*

1   Allow 1 or 2 per portion.
2   Melt a little fat in a frying pan.
3   Add the eggs, season lightly.
4   Cook gently until lightly set.
5   Serve on a plate or flat dish.

   To prepare an excellent fried egg it is essential to use a high quality egg and to maintain a controlled low heat.

21   Fried Eggs and Bacon   *Œufs au Lard*

1   Allow 2–3 rashers per portion.
2   Remove the rind and bone.

3   Fry in a little fat or grill on a flat tray under the salamander on both sides.
4   Dress neatly around the egg.

Fried eggs, may also be served with grilled or fried tomatoes, mushrooms, sauté potatoes, etc., as ordered by the customer.

22   French Fried Eggs   *Œufs Frits à la Française*

1   Fry in a frying-pan in a fairly deep hot oil.
2   Shape the egg with a spoon so as to enclose the yolk in crisply fried white.

23   Boiled Eggs   *Œufs à la Coque*

Allow 1 or 2 eggs per portion.
Method I—Place the eggs in cold water, bring to the boil, simmer 2–2½ min, remove from the water and serve at once in an egg cup.
Method II—Plunge the eggs in boiling water, re-boil, simmer 3–5 min.
Boiled eggs are always served in the shell.

24   Soft-Boiled Eggs   *Œufs Mollets*

Plunge the eggs into boiling water, re-boil, simmer for 5½ min. Refresh immediately. Remove the shells carefully, Reheat when required for ½ min in hot salt water.

All the recipes given for poached eggs can be applied to soft-boiled eggs.

25   Poached Eggs   *Œufs Pochés*

High quality eggs should be used for poaching because they have a large amount of thick white and consequently have little tendency to spread in the simmering water. Low quality eggs are difficult to manage because the large quantity of thin white spreads in the simmering water.

A well-prepared poached egg has a firm tender white surrounding the slightly thickened unbroken yolk. The use of a little vinegar (an acid) helps to set the egg white so preventing it from spreading it also makes the white more tender and whiter.

1   Carefully break the eggs one by one into a shallow pan containing at least 6 cm (3 in) gently boiling water to which a little vinegar has been added (1 litre (1 qt) water to 1 tbspn vinegar).
2   Simmer until lightly set, approx. 2½–3 min.
3   Remove carefully with a perforated spoon into a bowl of cold water.
4   Trim the white of egg if necessary.
5   Reheat, when required, by placing into hot salted water for approx. ½–1 min.
6   Drain on a cloth.
7   Use as required.

26 Poached Eggs with Cheese Sauce   *Œufs Pochés Mornay*

	4 eggs	
250 ml	mornay sauce	½ pt
	4 short paste tartlets	
	or	
	4 half slices of buttered toast	

1 Cook eggs as for poached eggs.
2 Place tartlets or toast in an earthenware dish (the slices of toast may be halved, cut round with a cutter, crust removed).
3 Add the hot well-drained eggs.
4 Completely cover with sauce, sprinkle with grated parmesan cheese and brown under the salamander.
5 Place the dish on a silver flat and serve.

27 Poached Eggs with Cheese Sauce and Spinach   *Œufs Pochés Florentine*

	4 eggs	
250 ml	mornay sauce	½ pt
¾ kg	spinach	1 lb 8 oz

1 Remove the stems from the spinach.
2 Wash very carefully in plenty of water several times if necessary.
3 Cook in boiling salted water until tender, approx. 5 min.
4 Refresh under cold water, squeeze dry into a ball.
5 When required for service, place into a pan containing 25–50 g (1–2 oz) butter, loosen with a fork and reheat quickly without colouring, season with salt and mill pepper.
6 Place in an earthenware dish.
7 Place the eggs on top and finish as for eggs mornay.

28 Poached Eggs with Curry Sauce   *Œufs Pochés Bombay*

	4 eggs	
50 g	plain boiled rice	2 oz
250 ml	curry sauce	½ pt

Poached eggs are placed on a bed of rice, coated with strained curry sauce.

29 Poached Eggs with Minced Chicken   *Œufs Pochés à la Reine*

	4 poached eggs	
100 g	minced chicken	4 oz
	4 short pastry tartlets	
250 ml	sauce suprême	½ pt

1 Mix the chicken with half the sauce suprême, correct the seasoning.

2 Place the tartlets in an earthenware dish.
3 Add a spoonful of chicken in each tartlet.
4 Place a hot poached egg on top.
5 Coat with sauce suprême, place the dish on a silver flat and
   serve.

30 Poached Eggs with Sweet Corn   *Œufs Pochés Washington*

	4 poached eggs	
250 ml	sauce suprême	½ pt
100 g	prepared sweet corn	4 oz

1 Boil half the sauce suprême with the sweet corn, correct the
   seasoning.
2 Place in an earthenware dish with the poached eggs on top.
3 Coat with sauce suprême.

31 Omelet (Basic Recipe)   *Omelette*

1 Allow 2–3 eggs per portion.
2 Break the eggs into a basin, season with salt and pepper.
3 Beat well with a fork or whisk until the yolks and whites are
   thoroughly combined and no streaks of white can be seen.
4 Heat the omelet pan.
5 Wipe thoroughly clean with a dry cloth.
6 Add 10 g (½ oz) butter.
7 Heat until foaming but not brown.
8 Add the eggs and cook quickly, moving the mixture
   continuously with a fork until lightly set.
9 Remove from the heat.
10 Half fold the mixture over at right-angles to the handle.
11 Tap the bottom of the pan to bring up the edge of the omelet.
12 Tilt the pan completely over on oval silver flat dish so as to
    allow the omelet to fall carefully into the centre of the dish.
13 Neaten the shape if necessary, and serve immediately.

32 Plain Omelet   *Omelette Nature*
As above.

33 Savoury Omelet   *Omelette Fines herbes*
Add a pinch of chopped parsley, chervil and chives to the mixture
and proceed as for Basic Omelet (No. 31).

34 Mushroom Omelet   *Omelette aux Champignons*
1 25–50 g (1–2 oz) button mushrooms per portion.
2 Wash and slice the mushrooms.
3 Cook in a frying-pan in a little butter, season with salt and
   pepper.

4   Add to the butter in the hot pan and proceed as for Basic
    Omelet (No. 31).

35   Cheese Omelet   *Omelette au Fromage*

1   Allow 25 g (1 oz) grated cheese (parmesan) per portion.
2   Proceed as for Basic Omelet (No. 31).
3   Before folding, add the cheese.
4   Fold and serve as for Basic Omelet.

36   Tomato Omelet   *Omelette aux Tomates ou Portugaise*

400 g	tomatoes	1 lb
25 g	butter	1 oz
	chopped parsley	
25 g	chopped shallots or onion	1 oz
125 ml	tomato sauce	¼ pt

1   Prepare a plain omelet.
2   Make an incision down the centre.
3   Fill with hot tomato concassée.
4   Sprinkle the tomato with a little chopped parsley.
5   Serve tomato sauce separately.

37   Omelet with Chicken Livers   *Omelette aux Foies de Volaille*

100 g	chicken liver	4 oz
125 ml	jus-lié or demi-glace	¼ pt
25 g	butter	1 oz
	chopped parsley	

1   Prepare as for Basic Omelet (No. 31).
2   Make an incision down the centre.
3   Cut the livers into neat scallops.
4   Season with salt and pepper.
5   Fry quickly in the hot butter.
6   Drain and place in the hot jus-lié or demi-glace, correct for
    seasoning.
7   Place a spoonful of the mixture in the incision of each omelet,
    sprinkle a little chopped parlsey on the liver.

38   Kidney Omelet   *Omelette aux Rognons*

	2 sheep's kidneys	
125 ml	jus-lié or demi-glace	¼ pt
25 g	butter	1 oz
	chopped parsley	

1   Skin the kidneys, remove the gristle and cut into 1 cm (½ in) dice.
2   Season with salt and pepper.
3   Quickly fry in the hot butter for 2–3 min.
4   Add to the hot jus-lié or demi-glace, correct the seasoning.

5   Prepare the basic omelet.
6   Make an incision down the centre and fill with kidneys.
7   Sprinkle with chopped parsley on the kidney.

39 Shrimp Omelet   *Omelette aux Crevettes*

250 ml	picked shrimps	½ pt
	salt and pepper	
125 ml	béchamel	¼ pt

1   Prepare a plain omelet.
2   Make an incision down the centre.
3   Place a spoonful of the shrimps, bound with béchamel in the
     centre.

40 Ham Omelet   *Omelette au Jambon*

1   Allow 25–50 g (1–2 oz) lean diced cooked ham per portion.
2   Add to the beaten eggs.
3   Proceed as for Basic Omelet (No. 31).

41 Bacon Omelet   *Omelette au Lard*

1   Allow 1–2 rashers of bacon per portion.
2   Cut the bacon into ½ cm (¼ in) thick strips.
3   Fry in a little dripping or butter in a frying-pan.
4   Add to the beaten eggs.
5   Proceed as for Basic Omelet (No. 31).

42 Onion Omelet   *Omelette Lyonnaise*

1   Allow 50 g (2 oz) onion per portion.
2   Peel, then thinly slice the onion and cook in a little butter,
     colouring slightly.
3   Mix with the beaten eggs. Proceed as for Basic Omelet (No. 31).

43 Potato Omelet   *Omelette Parmentier*

1   Allow 50 g (2 oz) peeled potatoes per portion.
2   Cut the potatoes in neat 3 mm (⅛ in) dice.
3   Wash well and drain.
4   Quickly fry in a little fat in a frying-pan until golden brown,
     drain in a colander.
5   When making omelets place potatoes in the pan with the butter
     before adding the eggs.
6   Proceed as for Basic Omelet (No. 31).

44 Flat Omelets   See the following three recipes

45   Potato, Onion and Bacon Omelet   *Omelette Paysanne*

For 4 omelets allow 50 g (2 oz) peeled potatoes, 50 g (2 oz) onion
and 2 rashers of bacon. Prepare as in the three previous recipes.

1   Proceed as for Basic Omelet (No. 31) to instruction No. 9.
2   Sharply tap the pan on the stove to loosen the omelet.
3   Toss as for a pancake.
4   Turn out on to a flat round silver dish.

46   Fermière Omelet   *Omelette Fermière*

As for ham omelet with chopped parsley. Prepared and served flat.

47   Spanish Omelet   *Omelette Espagnole*

For 4 portions allow 200 g (8 oz) tomatoes (concassé), 100 g (4 oz)
onions (cooked as for Onion Omelet) and 50 g (2 oz) diced pimento.
   Cook and serve flat.

48   Jam Omelet   *Omelette à la Confiture*

1   Allow 25 g (1 oz) sugar and 1 tbspn jam per portion.
2   Proceed as for Basic Omelet (No. 31), without pepper or salt.
3   Add the previously warmed jam before folding.
4   Turn out on to the dish.
5   Sprinkle liberally with icing sugar.
6   Brand criss-cross pattern with a red-hot poker.

49   Eggs on the Dish   *Œuf sur le Plat (Basic Recipe)*

1   Butter and season an egg dish.
2   Add 1–2 eggs.
3   Season with salt and pepper.
4   Allow to cook gently on the side of the stove and finish under
    the salamander or in a hot oven. The yolk should be soft.
5   Place on a dish paper on a silver dish.

50   Eggs on the Dish with Bacon   *Œuf sur le Plat au Lard*

1   Allow 1–2 rashers of bacon per portion.
2   Grill or fry the bacon.
3   Cut each rasher in half.
4   Place in the bottom of a buttered, seasoned egg dish.
5   Break the eggs on top of the bacon.
6   Cook and serve as for the previous recipe.

51   Eggs on the Dish with Black Butter   *Œuf sur le Plat au Beurre Noir*

1   Proceed as for basic recipe (No. 49).
2   Coat with 25 g (1 oz) black butter to which a few drops of
    vinegar have been added.

52   Eggs on the Dish with Chipolata and Tomato Sauce   *Œuf sur le Plat Bercy*

   1   As for the basic recipe (No. 49).
   2   Serve a grilled chipolata on each portion and a thread of hot
      tomato sauce.

53   Eggs on the Dish with Cream   *Œuf sur le Plat à la Crème*

   1   As for the basic recipe (No. 49).
   2   When almost cooked add a tablespoon of cream over each egg.

54   Egg Mayonnaise   *Œuf Mayonnaise*

See page 44, Hors d'Œuvre.

7
Farinaceous Dishes

FARINACEOUS DISHES   *LES FARINEUSES*

These are the Italian pastes (spaghetti, macaroni, etc.), noodles and
gnocchi. They are usually served for luncheon as a separate course,
and they are also used as garnishes. Certain rice dishes, e.g. pilaff and
risotto, are also included in this section.

1 **General Points**

   1   Always cook in plenty of gently boiling salted water.
   2   Stir to the boil. Do not over cook.
   3   If not to be used immediately, refresh and reheat carefully in hot
      salted water when required.
   4   Drain well in a colander.
   5   With most pastes, grated cheese (preferably parmesan) should
      be served separately.
      Allow 10 g ($\frac{1}{2}$ oz) paste per portion as a garnish.
      Allow 25–50 g (1–2 oz) paste per portion for a main course

2 Spaghetti with Cheese *Spaghetti Italienne*

100 g	spaghetti	4 oz
25–50 g	grated cheese (preferably parmesan)	1–2 oz
25 g	butter	1 oz
	salt, mill pepper	

1 Plunge spaghetti into a saucepan containing plenty of boiling salted water.
2 Allow to boil gently.
3 Stir occasionally with a wooden spoon.
4 Cook 12–15 min approx.
5 Drain well in a colander.
6 Return to a clean, dry pan.
7 Mix in the butter and cheese.
8 Correct the seasoning.
9 Serve in an earthenware dish on a silver flat with a dish of grated parmesan cheese separately.

3 Spaghetti with Cheese Sauce *Spaghetti au Gratin*

100 g	spaghetti	4 oz
100 g	grated cheese	4 oz
25 g	butter	1 oz
500 ml	thin béchamel	1 pt
	salt, mill pepper	

1 Plunge spaghetti into a saucepan containing plenty of boiling salted water.
2 Allow to boil gently.
3 Stir occasionally with a wooden spoon.
4 Cook 12–15 min approx.
5 Drain well in a colander.
6 Return to a clean, dry pan containing the butter.
7 Mix in half the cheese and the béchamel.
8 Correct the seasoning.
9 Place in an earthenware dish.
10 Sprinkle with the remainder of the cheese.
11 Brown lightly under the salamander.
12 Place on a silver flat and serve.

4 Spaghetti with Tomato Sauce *Spaghetti Napolitaine*

100 g	spaghetti	4 oz
25 g	grated cheese	1 oz
25 g	butter	1 oz
250 ml	tomato sauce (p. 29)	½ pt
100 g	tomate concassée	4 oz
	salt, mill pepper	
10 g	chopped onion	½ oz
10 g	butter	½ oz
100 g	tomatoes	4 oz

1   Plunge spaghetti into a saucepan containing plenty of boiling salted water.
2   Allow to boil gently.
3   Stir occasionally with a wooden spoon.
4   Cook 12–15 min approx.
5   Drain well in a colander.
6   Return to a clean, dry pan.
7   Mix in the butter and add the tomato sauce.
8   Correct the seasoning.
9   Add the tomato concassée.
10 Serve in an earthenware dish on a silver flat. Grated cheese separately.

Cooked tomate concassée:
Cook the finely chopped onion in the butter without colour, add the chopped tomatoes and cook for a few minutes. Season with salt and mill pepper.

5 Spaghetti Milanaise Style   *Spaghetti Milanaise*

100 g	spaghetti	4 oz
25 g	grated cheese	1 oz
125 ml	tomato sauce	1 gill
25 g	butter	1 oz
25 g	ham, tongue and cooked mushroom in julienne	1 oz
	salt, mill pepper	

1   Plunge the spaghetti into plenty of boiling salted water.
2   Allow to boil gently.
3   Stir occasionally with a wooden spoon.
4   Cook for approximately 12–15 min.
5   Drain well in a colander.
6   Return to a clean pan containing the butter.
7   Add tomato sauce.
8   Correct the seasoning.
9   Add the julienne of ham, tongue, and mushroom and mix in carefully.
10 Serve in an earthenware dish on a silver flat with grated cheese separately.

6 Spaghetti Bolognaise Style   *Spaghetti Bolognaise*

100 g	spaghetti	4 oz
25–50 g	grated cheese	1–2 oz
100 g	lean minced beef or tail end of fillet cut in $\frac{1}{8}$ in dice	4 oz
25 g	butter	1 oz
50 g	chopped onion	2 oz
125 ml	jus-lié or demi-glace	1 gill
	salt, mill pepper	

Prepare the sauce as follows:

1 Place 10 g (½ oz) butter in a sauteuse.
2 Add the chopped onion and cook for 4–5 min without colour.
3 Add the beef and cook, colouring lightly.
4 Add the jus-lié or demi-glace.
5 Simmer till tender.
6 Correct the seasoning.
7 Meanwhile cook the spaghetti in plenty of boiling salted water.
8 Allow to boil gently.
9 Stir occasionally with a wooden spoon.
10 Cook for approximately 12–15 min.
11 Drain well in a colander.
12 Return to a clean pan containing 10 g (½ oz) butter.
13 Correct the seasoning.
14 Serve in an earthenware dish on a silver flat with the sauce in centre of the spaghetti.
15 Serve grated cheese separately.

7 Macaroni Cheese   *Macaroni au Gratin*

100 g	macaroni	4 oz
100 g	grated cheese	4 oz
500 ml	thin béchamel	1 pt
	½ tspn diluted English mustard	
	salt, mill pepper	
25 g	butter	1 oz

1 Plunge the macaroni into a saucepan containing plenty of boiling salted water.
2 Allow to boil gently.
3 Stir occasionally with a wooden spoon.
4 Cook for approximately 15 min.
5 Drain well in a colander.
6 Return to a clean pan containing the butter.
7 Mix with half the cheese add the béchamel and mustard.
8 Place in an earthenware dish.
9 Sprinkle with the remainder of the cheese.
10 Brown lightly under the salamander.
11 Place on a silver flat and serve.

Macaroni may also be prepared and served as for any of the spaghetti dishes.

8 Noodles   *Nouilles*

100 g	flour	4 oz
	1 egg yolk	
	salt	
	1 tbspn olive oil	
	1 egg	

Noodles are usually bought ready prepared but may be made as follows:

1 Sieve the flour and salt.
2 Make a well.
3 Add oil and eggs.
4 Mix to a dough.
5 Knead well till smooth.
6 Leave to rest.
7 Roll out to a thin rectangle 36 cm × 12 cm (18 in × 6 in).
8 Cut into ½ cm (¼ in) strips.
9 Leave to dry.

Semolina is a good dusting agent to use when handling this paste.

The noodles are cooked in the same way as spaghetti and may be served as for any of the spaghetti recipes. The most popular method of serving them is Nouilles au Beurre (Recipe 9).

9 Noodles with Butter   *Nouilles au Beurre*

100 g	noodles	4 oz
50 g	butter	2 oz
	salt, mill pepper	
	a little grated nutmeg	

1 Cook noodles in plenty of gently boiling salted water.
2 Drain well in a colander.
3 Return to the pan.
4 Add the seasoning and butter.
5 Toss carefully until mixed.
6 Correct the seasoning.
7 Serve in an earthenware dish on a silver flat.

Noodles may also be used as a garnish, e.g. with braised beef.

10 Ravioli   *Ravioli*

Ravioli are small envelopes of a noodle-type paste filled with a variety of stuffings, e.g. beef, chicken, veal, spinach, etc.

11 Ravioli Paste   *8 portions approx.*

200 g	flour	8 oz
	salt	
30 g	olive oil	1¼ oz
90 g	water	3¾ oz

1 Sieve flour and salt.
2 Make a well.
3 Add the liquid.
4 Knead to a smooth dough.
5 Rest for at least ½ hr in a cool place.
6 Roll out to a very thin oblong 24 cm × 36 cm (12 in × 18 in).

7   Cut in half and egg wash.
8   Place the stuffing in a piping bag with a large plain tube.
9   Pipe out the filling in small pieces about the size of a cherry approx. 3 cm (1½ in) apart on to one-half of the paste.
10   Carefully cover with the other half of the paste, seal, taking care to avoid air pockets.
11   Mark each with the back of a plain cutter.
12   Cut in between each line of filling, down and across with a serrated pastry wheel.
13   Separate on a well-floured tray.
14   Poach in gently boiling salted water approx. 10 min.
15   Drain well.
16   Place in an earthenware serving dish.
17   Cover with 250 ml (½ pt) jus-lié, demi-glace or tomato sauce.
18   Sprinkle with 50 g (2 oz) grated cheese.
19   Brown under the salamander.
20   Place on a silver flat and serve.

12   Filling for Ravioli

200 g	braised or boiled beef or veal	8 oz
50 g	chopped onion or shallot	2 oz
	1 clove garlic	
400 g	spinach	1 lb
10 g	fat	½ oz
	little demi-glace to bind	
	salt, mill pepper	

1   Mince the beef or veal.
2   Cook and mince the spinach.
3   Cook the onion in the fat without colouring.
4   Mix the meat, spinach and onion.
5   Season and add a little demi-glace to bind the mixture if necessary, but keep the mixture firm.

13   Canneloni   *Canneloni*

These are poached rolls of ravioli paste filled with a variety of stuffings as for Ravioli.
    Paste and fillings as for Ravioli.
1   Roll out the paste as for Ravioli.
2   Cut into squares approx. 5 cm × 5 cm (2½ in × 2½ in).
3   Cook in gently boiling water approx. 10 min. Refresh in cold water.
4   Drain well and lay out singly on the table.
5   Pipe out the filling across each.
6   Roll up like a sausage-roll.
7   Place in an earthenware dish.
8   Add 250 ml (½ pt) demi-glace, jus-lié or tomato sauce.

9   Sprinkle with 25–50 g (1–2 oz) grated cheese.
10   Brown slowly under the salamander or in the oven.
11   Serve on a silver flat dish.

14   Gnocchi—means a small dumpling

15   Gnocchi Parisienne   *4 portions*   *Gnocchi Parisienne*

125 ml	water	⎫	1 gill
50 g	margarine	⎟	2 oz
60 g	flour	⎬ Choux paste	2½ oz
	2 eggs	⎟	
	salt	⎭	
50 g	grated cheese		2 oz
250 ml	béchamel (thin)		½ pt

1   Boil water, margarine, and salt in a saucepan.
2   Remove from the heat.
3   Mix in flour with a wooden spoon.
4   Return to a gentle heat.
5   Stir continuously until mixture leaves sides of pan.
6   Cool slightly.
7   Gradually add the eggs, beating well.
8   Add half the cheese.
9   Place in a piping bag with ½ cm (¼ in) plain tube.
10   Pipe out in 1 cm (½ in) lengths into a shallow pan of gently
     simmering salted water. Do not allow to boil.
11   Cook approx. 10 min.
12   Drain well in a colander.
13   Combine carefully with bechamel.
14   Correct the seasoning.
15   Pour into an earthenware dish.
16   Sprinkle with the remainder of the cheese.
17   Brown lightly under salamander.
18   Serve on a flat silver dish.

16   Gnocchi Romaine   *4 portions*   *Gnocchi Romaine*

500 ml	milk	1 pt
25 g	butter	1 oz
25 g	grated cheese	1 oz
	grated nutmeg	
100 g	semolina	4 oz
	1 egg yolk	
	salt, pepper	

1   Boil milk in a thick-bottomed pan.
2   Sprinkle in the semolina, stirring continuously.
3   Stir to the boil.
4   Season, simmer till cooked 5–10 min.
5   Remove from heat.

6   Mix in egg yolk, cheese and butter.
7   Pour into a buttered tray 1 cm ($\frac{1}{2}$ in) deep.
8   When cold cut into rounds with 4 cm (2 in) round cutter.
9   Place the debris in a buttered earthenware dish.
10   Neatly arrange the rounds on top.
11   Sprinkle with melted butter and the cheese.
12   Lightly brown in the oven or under the salamander.
13   Serve with a thread of tomato sauce round the gnocchi.

17   Gnocchi Piemontaise   *4 portions*   *Gnocchi Piemontaise*

300 g	mashed potato	12 oz
	1 egg	
25 g	butter	1 oz
	grated nutmeg	
100 g	flour	4 oz
	1 egg yolk	
	salt, pepper	
250 ml	tomato sauce	$\frac{1}{2}$ pt

1   Bake or boil potatoes in jackets.
2   Remove from skins and mash with a fork or pass through a sieve.
3   Mix with flour, egg, butter and seasoning while hot.
4   Mould into balls the size of a walnut.
5   Dust well with flour and flatten slightly with a fork.
6   Poach in gently boiling water approx. 5 min.
7   Drain carefully.
8   Dress in a buttered earthenware dish, cover with tomato sauce.
9   Sprinkle with grated cheese and brown lightly under the salamander.
10   Serve on a silver flat dish.

18   Braised Rice   *4 portions*   *Riz Pilaff*

100 g	rice (long grain)	4 oz
185 ml	white stock (preferably chicken)	approx. 1$\frac{1}{2}$ gills
25 g	chopped onion	1 oz
50 g	butter	2 oz
	salt, mill pepper	

1   Place 25 g (1 oz) butter in a small sauteuse.
2   Add the onion.
3   Cook gently without colouring 2–3 min.
4   Add the rice.
5   Cook gently without colouring 2–3 min.
6   Add twice the amount of stock to rice.
7   Season, cover with a buttered paper, bring to the boil.
8   Place a in hot oven 230°–250°C approx. 15 min until cooked.
9   Remove immediately into a cool sauteuse.
10   Carefully mix in the remaining butter.

11   Correct the seasoning.
12   Serve in an earthenware dish on a silver flat.

It is usual to use long-grain rice for pilaff because the grains are firm, and there is less likelihood of them breaking up and becoming mushy. During cooking the long-grain rice absorbs more liquid, loses less starch and retains its shape well as it swells, the short or medium grains may split at the ends and become less distinct in outline.

19   Braised Rice with Cheese   *Riz Pilaff au Fromage*

As above with 50–100 g (2–4 oz) grated cheese added with the butter, before serving.

20   Braised Rice with Mushrooms   *Riz Pilaff aux Champignons*

As for braised rice with the addition of 50–110 g (2–4 oz) button mushrooms.
1   Place 25 g (1 oz) butter in a small sauteuse.
2   Add the onion.
3   Cook gently without colour 2–3 min.
4   Add the rice and well-washed sliced mushrooms.
5   Complete as for braised rice from point 6 (Recipe 18).

21   Braised Rice with Peas and Pimento   *Riz à l'Orientale*

As for braised rice (Recipe 18) plus 25 g (1 oz) cooked peas and 25 g (1 oz) 1 cm ($\frac{1}{2}$ in) diced pimento carefully mixed in when finishing with butter.
Many other variations of pilaff may be made with the addition of such ingredients as tomate concassée, diced ham, etc.

22   —   *Risotto*

100 g	rice (short grain)	4 oz
185 ml	white stock (preferably chicken)	approx. 1$\frac{1}{2}$ gills
25 g	chopped onions	1 oz
50 g	butter	2 oz
	salt, mill pepper	
25 g	grated parmesan cheese	1 oz

1   Melt the butter in a small sauteuse.
2   Add the chopped onion.
3   Cook gently without colour for 2–3 min.
4   Add the rice.
5   Cook without colour 2–3 min.
6   Add the stock, season lightly.
7   Cover with a lid.
8   Allow to simmer on the side of the stove.
9   Stir frequently and if necessary add more stock until the rice is cooked.

10   When cooked all the stock should have been absorbed into the rice and evaporated.

11   A risotto should be more moist than a pilaff.

12   Finally mix in the cheese with a fork and serve.

Any variations given for riz pilaff may be prepared as a risotto.

8
Fish

FISH   *POISSON*

Fish may be divided into two main groups:

A *White*—which may be flat or round, e.g. sole, turbot, whiting, cod, etc.

B *Oily*—these are round, e.g. salmon, herring, mackerel, etc.

1 Indications of Quality

1 The eyes are bright and full, not sunken.
2 The gills are bright red in colour.
3 The flesh should be firm.
4 Scales, if any, should be plentiful.
5 There should be no unpleasant smell.

Certain fish are cured by either salting or smoking, e.g. haddock, herring, salmon, etc.

2 Shellfish

These are also divided into two main groups:

A *Crustacea*—e.g. lobster, crab, crawfish, crayfish, prawns and shrimps.
B *Mollusca*—e.g. oysters, mussels, scallops.

3 Methods of Cookery

Boiling, poaching, grilling, shallow frying and *deep frying.*

Boiling
This method is suitable for whole fish, e.g. salmon, turbot, trout and certain cuts of fish, e.g. salmon, cod, turbot, halibut, brill, etc. In either case the fish should be completely immersed in the cooking liquid which can be water, water and milk, milk, fish stock (for white fish) or a court bouillon (water, vinegar, thyme, bay leaf, parsley stalks, onion, carrot, peppercorns) for oily fish.
Whole fish are covered with a cold liquid and brought to the boil, cut fish are usually placed in a simmering liquid.

Poaching
This is suitable for small whole fish, cuts or fillets. Barely cover the fish with fish stock, cover with a buttered paper, bring to the boil and cook in the oven without allowing the liquid to boil. The cooking liquor is usually used for the sauce which masks the fish.

Grilling
This method is suitable for small whole fish, cuts and fillets. With the exception of fish cooked Saint-Germain (Recipe 27), it is passed through seasoned flour, brushed with oil and grilled on both sides. When grilling fish under the salamander, grill bar marks are made with a red-hot poker before cooking.

Shallow Frying
Shallow fried fish is termed meunière and is suitable for small whole

fish, cuts and fillets. The fish is passed through seasoned flour, shallow fried on both sides, presentation side first, in clarified fat in a frying-pan. It is placed on a serving dish and masked with nut-brown butter, lemon juice, slice of lemon and chopped parsley.

Deep Frying

This is suitable for small whole fish cuts and fillets. The fish must be coated by one of the following:

(a) flour, egg and crumb (pané)   à l'anglaise
(b) milk and flour   à la française
(c) batter

The coating is to form a surface to prevent penetration of the fat into the fish. The fish should always be served on a dish paper with a quarter of lemon and fried parsley.

Unless otherwise stated, as a guide, allow 100 g (4 oz) fish off the bone and 150 g (6 oz) on the bone for a portion.

4   The Cuts of Fish

La Darne	a slice of round fish cut on the bone, e.g.
	Darne de Saumon (Salmon)
	Darne de Cabillaud (Cod)
Le Tronçon	a slice of flat fish cut on the bone, e.g.
	Tronçon de Turbot (Turbot)
	Tronçon de Barbue (Brill)
Le Filet	a cut of fish free from bone. A round fish yields two fillets and a flat fish four fillets.
Le Suprême	usually applied to fillets of large fish cut on the slant, e.g. Suprême de Turbot
Le Délice	a term usually applied to a trimmed and neatly folded fillet of fish, e.g. Délice de Sole
La Goujon	this term is applied to fillet of fish cut into strips approx. 6 cm × $\frac{1}{2}$ cm (3 in × $\frac{1}{4}$ in).
La Paupiette	this is a fillet of fish, usually sole, spread with stuffing and rolled.

FISH RECIPES

5   **Fish Stock**   *5 litres (1 gallon)*   *Fond or Fumet de Poisson*

5 litres	water	1 gal
200 g	onions	8 oz
50 g	margarine	2 oz
	juice of $\frac{1}{2}$ lemon	
	6 peppercorns	
2 kg	white fish bones (preferably sole, whiting, or turbot)	4 lb
	1 bay leaf	
	parsley stalks	

1   Melt the margarine in a thick-bottomed pan.
2   Add the sliced onions, the well-washed fish bones and remainder of the ingredients except the water.
3   Cover with greaseproof paper and a lid and sweat (cook gently without colouring) for 5 min.
4   Add the water, bring to the boil, skim and simmer for 20 min then strain.

6   Fish Glaze   *Glace de Poisson*

This is fish stock reduced by boiling to a gelatinous consistency. It is used for increasing the flavour of fish sauces. When cold it may be kept in jars and stored in a refrigerator.

7   Fish Velouté   *1 litre (1 quart)*   *Velouté de Poisson*

100 g	margarine	4 oz
100 g	flour	4 oz
1 litre	fish stock	1 qt

This is the basic fish sauce made from fish stock and a blond roux.
1   Prepare a blond roux using the margarine and flour.
2   Gradually add the stock, stirring continuously until boiling point is reached.
3   Simmer for 1 hr approx.
4   Pass through a fine conical strainer.

This will give a thick sauce which can be thinned down with the cooking liquor from the fish for which the sauce is intended.

8   Sabayon

This is a mixture of egg yolks and a little water whisked to the ribbon stage over gentle heat. The mixture should be the consistency of thick cream. It is added to finish sauces to assist the sauce to glaze.

9   White Wine Sauce $\frac{1}{4}$ *litre ($\frac{1}{2}$ pint)*   *Sauce Vin Blanc*

250 ml	fish velouté	$\frac{1}{2}$ pt
50 g	butter	2 oz
	salt, cayenne	
	2 tbspn dry white wine	
	2 tbspn cream	
	few drops of lemon juice	

1   Boil the fish velouté.
2   Whisk in the wine.
3   Remove from the heat.
4   Gradually add the butter.
5   Stir in the cream.
6   Correct the seasoning and consistency, add the lemon juice.
7   Pass through a tammy cloth or fine strainer.

10   White Wine Sauce (to be glazed)   *Sauce Vin Blanc Glacé*

If the sauce is to be used for a glazed fish dish then 1 egg yolk or
1 tbspn sabayon should be added as soon as the sauce is removed
from the heat. (Trade practice would be to add 1 tbspn hollandaise
to the sauce.)

11   Mushroom Sauce   ¼ *litre* (½ *pint*)   *Sauce aux Champignons*

250 ml	fish velouté	½ pt
	lemon juice	
10 g	butter	½ oz
100 g	white button mushrooms	4 oz
	salt, cayenne	

1   Boil the fish velouté.
2   Adjust the consistency with fish stock or cream.
3   Correct the seasoning.
4   Peel, wash and slice the mushrooms.
5   Cook the mushrooms in the butter and lemon juice in a covered
     pan.
6   Drain well and add to the sauce.

May be served with boiled halibut, e.g. Flétan Poché Sauce aux
Champignons.

12   Shrimp Sauce   ¼ *litre* (½ *pint*)   *Sauce aux Crevettes*

250 ml	fish velouté or béchamel	½ pt
60 ml	picked shrimps	⅛ pt
	salt, cayenne	

1   Boil the fish velouté or béchamel.
2   Correct the seasoning and consistency using fish stock or cream.
3   Pass through a tammy or fine strainer.
4   Mix in the shrimps.

13   Lobster Sauce   1 *litre* (2 *pints*)   *Sauce Homard*

¾–1 kg	live hen lobster	1½–2 lb
100 g	onion ⎫	4 oz
100 g	carrot ⎬ roughly cut	4 oz
50 g	celery ⎭	2 oz
	½ crushed clove garlic	
	bouquet garni	
100 g	tomato purée	4 oz
75 g	butter	3 oz
75 g	flour	3 oz
60 ml	brandy	⅛ pt
1¼ litres	fish stock	2½ pt
120 ml	dry white wine	¼ pt
	salt	

1   Well wash the lobster.
2   Cut in half lengthwise tail first, then the carapace.

3   Discard the sac from the carapace, clean the trail from the tail, remove any spawn into a basin.
4   Wash the lobster pieces.
5   Crack the claws and the four claw joints.
6   Melt the butter in a thick bottomed pan.
7   Add the lobster pieces and the onion, carrot and celery.
8   Allow to cook steadily without colouring the butter for a few minutes stirring continuously with a wooden spoon.
9   Add the brandy and allow it to ignite.
10 Remove from the heat, mix in the flour and tomato purée.
11 Return to a gentle heat and cook out the roux.
12 Cool slightly, gradually add the fish stock and white wine.
13 Stir to the boil.
14 Add bouquet garni, garlic and season lightly with salt.
15 Simmer for 15–20 min.
16 Remove the lobster pieces.
17 Remove the lobster meat from the pieces.
18 Crush the lobster shells, return them to the sauce and continue simmering for $\frac{1}{4}$–$\frac{3}{4}$ hour.
19 Crush the lobster spawn, stir in to the sauce, reboil and pass through a coarse strainer.

This sauce may be made in a less expensive way by substituting cooked lobster shell (not shell from the claws) which should be well crushed in place of the live lobster.

SHALLOW FRIED FISH

14 Fish Meunière   *Poisson Meunière*

Many fish, whole or filleted, may be cooked by this method, e.g. sole, fillets of plaice, trout, brill, cod, turbot, herring, scampi, etc.
1   Prepare and clean the fish, wash and drain.
2   Pass through seasoned flour, shake off all surplus flour.
3   Shallow fry on both sides, presentation side first in hot clarified butter, margarine or oil.
4   Dress neatly on an oval silver flat dish.
5   Peel a lemon, removing the yellow and white skin.
6   Cut the lemon into slices and place one slice on each portion.
7   Squeeze some lemon juice on the fish.
8   Allow 10–25 g ($\frac{1}{2}$–1 oz) butter per portion and colour in a clean frying-pan to the nut-brown stage (beurre noisette).
9   Pour over the fish.
10 Sprinkle with chopped parsley and serve, e.g. Filets de Plie Meunière.

15 Shallow Fried Fish with Almonds

As for Fish Meunière (Recipe 14) adding 10 g ($\frac{1}{2}$ oz) of almonds cut in short julienne or coarsely chopped to the meunière butter just before it begins to turn brown. This method is usually applied to trout, e.g. Truites meunière aux amandes.

16   Fish Belle Meunière   *Poisson Belle Meunière*

As for Recipe 14 with the addition of a grilled mushroom, a slice of peeled tomato and a soft herring roe (passed through flour and shallow fried), all neatly dressed on each portion of fish, e.g. Sole Belle Meunière.

17   Fish Doria

As for Fish Meunière (Recipe 14) with a sprinkling of small turned pieces of cucumber carefully cooked in 25 g (1 oz) of butter in a small covered pan, e.g. Filet d'Aigrefin Doria.

18   Grenobloise

As for Fish Meunière (Recipe 14), the peeled lemon being cut into segments, neatly dressed on the fish with a few capers sprinkled over, e.g. Truite Grenobloise.

19   Bretonne

As for Fish Meunière (Recipe 14), with a few picked shrimps and cooked sliced mushrooms sprinkled over the fish, e.g. Suprême de Turbot Bretonne.

GRILLED FISH

20   Grilled Cod Steaks   *Darne de Cabillaud Grillé*

1   Wash the steaks well and drain.
2   Pass through seasoned flour.
3   Brush with melted butter, margarine or oil.
4   Place on a greased baking tray.
5   Cook on both sides under the salamander, brushing occasionally with fat.
6   To test if cooked, carefully remove the centre bone.
7   Dress on a silver flat.
8   Garnish with a slice of lemon, picked parsley and serve a suitable sauce or butter separately (e.g. parsley butter), e.g. Darne de Cabillaud Grillée Maître d'Hôtel.

21   Grilled Herring   *Hareng Grillé*

1   Remove the scales from the fish with the back of a knife.
2   Remove the head, clean out the intestines, trim off all fins, take care not to damage the roe, and trim the tail.

3   Wash and drain well.
4   Make three light incisions 2 mm ($\frac{1}{16}$ in) deep on either side of the fish.
5   Pass through seasoned flour.
6   Brush with melted fat, place on a greased baking tray.
7   Grill on both sides taking care not to burn the tails.
8   Neatly dress on a silver flat.
9   Garnish with a slice of lemon and picked parsley.
10   Serve with a sauceboat of mustard sauce, e.g. Hareng Grillé, Sauce Moutarde.

22   Grilled Mackerel   *Maquereau Grillé*

1   Remove the head and intestines and clean the fish.
2   Cut down both sides of the backbone and remove the bone carefully.
3   Trim off all fins and excess rib bones, trim the tail.
4   Wash well and drain.
5   Pass through seasoned flour, shake off all surplus flour.
6   Place on a greased baking tray, cut side down.
7   Brush with melted butter, margarine or oil.
8   Grill on both sides under salamander.
9   Serve on a silver flat dish garnished with slice of lemon and picked parsley. Serve with a suitable sauce separately, e.g. Maquereau Grillé, Beurre d'Anchois.

23   Fillets of Grilled Plaice   *Filets de Plie Grillés*

1   Fillet the plaice, remove the black skin.
2   Wash well and drain.
3   Pass through seasoned flour, shake off all surplus flour.
4   Place on a greased baking tray, skinned side down.
5   Brush with melted butter, margarine or oil.
6   Grill on both sides under the salamander.
7   Serve with a slice of lemon and picked parsley and suitable sauce or butter, e.g. Filet de Plie Grillé, Beurre Maître d'Hôtel.

24   Grilled Whiting   *Merlan Grillé*

Prepare, grill and serve as for mackerel (Recipe 22).

25   Grilled Sole   *Sole Grillé*

1   Remove the black skin.
2   Remove scales from the white skin.
3   Remove the head and side bones, clean well.
4   Wash well and drain.
5   Pass through seasoned flour and shake off surplus flour.
6   Place on a greased baking tray white skin down.

7 Brush with melted butter, margarine or oil.
8 Grill on both sides under salamander.
9 Serve with a slice of lemon and picked parsley, and a suitable sauce or butter, e.g. Sole Grillé, Sauce Anchois.

26 Grilled Fillets of Sole — *Filets de Sole Grillés*

Proceed as for Fillets of Plaice (Recipe 23), e.g. Filets de Sole Grillés, Sauce Diable.

27 Grilled Fish St Germain — *Poisson Grillé St Germain*

1 Clean and prepare the fish (usually fllleted).
2 Pass through seasoned flour, melted butter or margarine and white breadcrumbs.
3 Neaten with a palette knife.
4 Place on a greased baking tray, brush with melted fat.
5 Grill on both sides under salamander.
6 Serve with a sauceboat of Sauce Béarnaise (page 31), e.g. Filet de Sole St Germain.

28 Fish Caprice — *Poisson Caprice*

1 As for Recipe 27, points 1–5.
2 Peel and halve a banana, pass though flour and shallow fry in butter.
3 Place half a banana on each portion of fish and serve a sauceboat of Sauce Robert (page 26) separately.

29 Grilled Salmon — *Darne de Saumon Grillé*

1 Pass darnes of salmon through seasoned flour, shake off all surplus.
2 Place on a greased baking sheet or grill bars.
3 Brush with oil.
4 Grill on both sides, brushing frequently with oil, for approx. 10 min.
5 Remove the centre bone, dress neatly on a silver flat dish. Garnish with picked parsley.
6 Accompany with sliced cucumber and a suitable sauce, e.g. Sauce Verte (page 32). E.g. Darne de Saumon Grillée Sauce Verte.

FRIED FISH

30 Frying Batters *approx. 6–8 portions*

I

200 g	flour	8 oz
10 g	yeast	$\frac{1}{2}$ oz
250 ml	water or milk	$\frac{1}{2}$ pt
	salt	

1   Sift the flour and salt into a basin.
2   Dissolve the yeast in a little of the water.
3   Make a well in the flour.
4   Add the yeast and the liquid.
5   Gradually incorporate the flour and beat to a smooth mixture.
6   Allow to rest for at least 1 hr before using.

II

200 g	flour	8 oz
	1 egg	
	salt	
250 ml	water or milk	½ pt
	2 tbspn oil	

1   Sift the flour and salt into a basin.
2   Make a well.
3   Add the egg and the liquid.
4   Gradually incorporate the flour, beat to a smooth mixture.
5   Mix in the oil.
6   Allow to rest before using.

III

200 g	flour	8 oz
	2 tbspn oil	
	2 stiffly-beaten egg whites	
250 ml	water or milk	½ pt
	salt	

1   As for previous method.
2   Fold in the whites just before using.

IV

200 g	flour	8 oz
	1 tspn baking-powder	
250 ml	water or milk	½ pt
	salt	

1   Sift the flour, salt and baking-powder into a basin.
2   Make a well in the centre.
3   Incorporate the liquid to a smooth paste.

POINTS ON DEEP FRYING

1   Use a suitable recommended fat or oil (see *Theory of Catering*, page 212).
2   When fat or oil smokes at about 177°C (350°F), foams or tastes bad it should be discarded.
3   Refer to page 6 on Deep frying.

31   Fried Whiting   *Merlan Frit*

  1   Skin the fish and remove intestines, clean out the head by removing the gills and the eyes.

  2   Wash well and drain.

  3   Pass through seasoned flour, beaten egg and white bread-crumbs (pané).

  4   Shake off all surplus crumbs.

  5   Deep fry to a golden brown in moderately hot fat 175°C approx. 5–6 min.

  6   Drain well.

  7   Serve on a dish paper on a silver flat garnished with fried or picked parsley, quarter of lemon and serve with a suitable sauce, e.g. Merlan Frit, Sauce Tartare.

32   Fried Fillets of Whiting   *Filets de Merlan Frits*

  1   Fillet, wash well and drain.

  2   Pané, or pass through batter. Cook at 185°C and serve as above and serve with a suitable sauce.

33   Curled Whiting or Whiting with Tail in the Mouth   *Merlan en Colère*

  1   Skin the whiting.

  2   Clean out the head, remove the gills and eyes.

  3   Wash well.

  4   Place tail firmly in the mouth.

  5   Pané, deep fry at 175°C and serve as for fried whiting.

34   Fried Fillets of Plaice   *Filets de Plie Frits*

  1   Fillet the fish, remove the black skin.

  2   Wash well and drain.

  3   Pass through flour and batter or flour, egg and crumb.

  4   Deep fry at 185°C and serve as for fried whiting, e.g. Fried Fillets of Plaice and Lemon.

35   Plaited Fillets of Sole

  1   Remove the black and white skin.

  2   Cut each fillet into three pieces lengthwise to within 1 cm ($\frac{1}{2}$ in) of the top by making two incisions.

  3   Plait neatly.

  4   Pané, deep fry at 185°C.

  5   Serve on a dish paper on a silver flat garnished with fried or picked parsley and a quarter of lemon, sauceboat of suitable sauce, e.g. tartare.

36   Goujon of Sole   *Filets de Sole en Goujon*

   1   Fillet the sole.
   2   Cut each fillet into strips approx. 6 cm × ½ cm (3 in × ¼ in).
   3   Pané, deep fry at 185°C and serve as above, e.g. Filets de Sole en
       Goujon, Sauce Tartare.

   Any filleted white fish may be prepared, cooked and served by this
method.

37   Fried Sole   *Sole Frite*

For fish courses use 200–250 g (8–10 oz) sole per portion, for main
course 300 g (12 oz) sole per portion.
   1   Remove the black and white skin.
   2   Remove the side fins.
   3   Remove the head.
   4   Clean well.
   5   Wash well and drain.
   6   Pané and deep fry at 175°C.
   7   Serve on a dish paper with picked or fried parsley and quarter
       of lemon on a silver flat dish, with a suitable sauce, e.g. Sole
       Frite, Sauce Anchois.

38   Fried Curled Sole   *Sole Colbert*

   1   Remove the black and white skins.
   2   Remove the head and side fins.
   3   Clean well and wash.
   4   Make an incision down the backbone on one side and proceed
       as though filleting, to within an inch of the sides.
   5   Break the backbone in two or three places.
   6   Curl the opened fillets back.
   7   Pané, deep fry at 175°C and drain.
   8   Carefully remove the backbone.
   9   Serve as for fried fish with one or two slices of parsley butter in
       the opened part of the fish.

39   Fried Fish à l'Orly   *Poisson Frit à l'Orly*

This is usually applied to fillets of white fish, e.g. plaice, sole,
haddock, etc.
   1   Marinade the fillets in a little oil, lemon juice and chopped
       parsley for a few minutes.
   2   Pass through seasoned flour and batter.
   3   Deep fry at 175°C and serve on a dish paper with fried or picked
       parsley.
   4   Serve with a sauceboat of tomato sauce (page 29).

40   Whitebait (*100 g (4 oz) per portion*)   *Blanchailles*

1   Pick over the whitebait.
2   Wash carefully and drain well.
3   Pass through milk and seasoned flour.
4   Shake off all surplus flour in a wide mesh sieve and place the
     fish into a frying-basket.
5   Plunge into very hot fat, just smoking (195°C).
6   Cook till brown and crisp, approx. 1 min.
7   Drain well.
8   Season with salt and cayenne pepper.
9   Serve on a dish paper on a silver flat dish.
10   Garnish with fried or picked parsley and quarters of lemon.

41   Fried Scampi   *4 portions*   *Scampi Frits*

375–500 g	shelled scampi	¾–1 lb
50 g	flour	2 oz
	1 egg	
	salt and pepper	
50 g	fresh white breadcrumbs	2 oz
	1 lemon	
	parsley	

1   Pass the scampi through flour, egg-wash and roll in fresh white
     breadcrumbs.
2   Shake off all surplus crumbs and lightly roll each piece of
     scampi to firm the surface.
3   Deep fry at 185°C.
4   Drain well and serve on a dish paper on a silver flat.
5   Garnish with segments of lemon and sprigs of fried or fresh
     parsley.
6   Accompany with a suitable sauce, e.g. tartare.

BOILED FISH

42   Turbot   *Turbot*
Young or Chicken Turbot   *Turbotin*

Allow approximately 300 g (12 oz) per portion on the bone.
Preparation for cutting on the bone, i.e. into tronçons.

1   Remove the head with a large chopping knife.
2   Cut off the side bones.
3   Commencing at the tail end, chop down the centre of the
     backbone dividing the fish into two halves.
4   Divide each half into portions as required.

NOTE: a 3½ kg (7 lb) fish will yield approx. 10 portions.

43 Boiled Turbot   *Tronçon de Turbot Poché*

1   Place the prepared turbot into the simmering salted water,
     containing lemon juice. Use a shallow pan.
2   Allow to simmer gently until cooked, the time depending very
     much on the thickness of the fish.
3   Remove with a fish slice from the pan.
4   Remove the black skin.
5   Place in an earthenware dish with a little of the cooking liquor.
     The fish may also be served on a serviette on a silver flat dish.
6   Garnish with picked parsley and a plain boiled potato.
7   Serve with a suitable sauce separately, e.g. Turbot Poché, Sauce
     Hollandaise.

44 Boiled Brill   *Tronçon de Barbue Poché*
Proceed as for Turbot, Recipe 43.

45 Boiled Halibut   *Tronçon de Flétan Poché*
Proceed as for Turbot, Recipe 43.

46 Boiled Cod   *Cabillaud Poché*

1   If using whole cod cut into 1–2 cm ($\frac{1}{2}$–1 in) slices on the bone
     (darne). Where required, tie with string if using cod fillet cut
     into suitable sized portions.
2   Cook as for turbot (Recipe 43) and serve in the same way.
3   Remove the centre bone before serving.
4   A suitable sauce should be served separately, e.g. parsley, egg,
     anchovy.

47 Boiled Salmon   *Saumon Poché*
$\frac{1}{2}$ kg (1 lb) uncleaned salmon yields 2–3 portions

Salmon may be obtained in varying weights from $3\frac{1}{2}$–15 kg (7–30 lb).
Size is an important consideration, depending on whether the salmon
is to be cooked whole or cut into darnes. A salmon of any size may
be cooked whole. When required for darnes, a medium-sized salmon
will be more suitable.

48 Court Bouillon

1 litre	water	1 qt
10 g	salt	$\frac{1}{2}$ oz
50 g	carrots (sliced)	2 oz
	1 bay leaf	
	2–3 parsley stalks	
60 ml	vinegar	$\frac{1}{8}$ pt
	6 peppercorns	
50 g	onions (sliced)	2 oz
	sprig of thyme	

Simmer all the ingredients for 30–40 min. Pass through a strainer, use as required.

49   Cooking of a Whole Salmon

1   Scrape off all scales with the back of a knife.
2   Remove gills and clean out the head.
3   Remove the intestines and clear the blood from the backbone.
4   Trim off all fins.
5   Wash well.
6   Place in a salmon kettle, cover with cold court bouillon.
7   Bring slowly to the boil, skim, then simmer gently.
8   Allow the following approx. simmering times:

3½ kg (7 lb)	15 min
7 kg (14 lb)	20 min
10½ kg (21 lb)	25 min
14 kg (28 lb)	30 min

Always allow the salmon to remain in the court bouillon until cold.

50   Boiled Cut Salmon   *Darne de Saumon Pochée*

Cooking salmon in darnes.

Place in a simmering court bouillon and simmer gently for approx. 5 min. Drain well, remove the centre bone.

Serve in an earthenware or silver dish with a little of the cooking liquor. Garnish with picked parsley, and a plain boiled potato. Accompany with a sliced cucumber and a suitable sauce, e.g. sauce hollandaise, beurre fondu.

51   Cold Salmon   *8 portions*   *Saumon Froid*

1¼ kg	cleaned salmon	2 lb 8 oz
	1 large lettuce	
	½ cucumber	
1 litre	court bouillon	1 qt
200 g	tomatoes	8 oz
250 ml	mayonnaise or green sauce	½ pt

1   Cook the salmon in the court bouillon, *a)* whole; *b)* cut into 8 darnes; *c)* cut into 4 darnes.
2   Allow to thoroughly cool, then for *a)* divide into eight even portions; *c)* remove centre bone and cut each darne in half.
3   Except when whole, remove the centre bone, also the skin and brown surface and dress neatly on a flat silver dish.
4   Peel and slice the cucumber and neatly arrange a few slices on each portion.

5   Garnish with quarters of lettuce and quarters of tomatoes.
6   Serve the sauce in a sauceboat separately.

52   Blue Trout   *4 portions*   *Truite au bleu*

	4 live trout	
100 g	small carrot ⎱ peeled	4 oz
100 g	button onion ⎰	4 oz
1 litre	water	1 qt
125 ml	vinegar	¼ pt
	8 peppercorns, small bay leaf	
	parsley	
	salt	

1   Groove the carrots with a cannele cutter and cut into thin slices.
2   Cut the onions into thin neat rings.
3   Simmer the water, half of the vinegar, onion and carrot rings,
     bayleaf, and a little salt for 10 min.
4   Hold the live trout firmly, stun with a heavy piece of wood.
5   Make an incision from the vent to the under fins and remove
     gut also the membrane and blood along the back-bone.
6   Remove the gills.
7   Wash the trout and place on a dish with the remainder of the
     vinegar.
8   Pass the trout on both sides through the vinegar, leave for 5
     min.
9   Place the trout into the gently simmering cooking liquid (Court-
     Bouillon) and allow to poach for 5–10 min.
10   Serve the trout in an earthenware dish together with a little of
     the court-bouillon, the slices of onion and carrot and garnish
     with fresh small sprigs of parsley.
11   Accompaniments are plain boiled potatoes and either melted
     butter or hollandaise sauce.

  If this dish is to be prepared authentically then only live freshly
killed trout must be used. This authenticity can be seen at a glance
by the expert as the trout should be mis-shapen not whole when
cooked and also the outer skin should have a delicate pale blue
colour.

POACHED FISH

Although Recipes 53–63 are given for fillets of sole, any white fish
may be prepared and served in the following manner. Always place a
little sauce under the fish before masking; this is to keep the fish
moist, to prevent it overcooking and sticking to the dish, thus
facilitating the service.

53 Fillets of Sole Dugléré   *4 portions*   *Filets de Sole Dugléré*

500–600 g	2 soles, each	1–1¼ lb
200 g	tomatoes concassée	8 oz
60 ml	fish stock	⅛ pt
250 ml	fish velouté	½ pt
	juice of ¼ lemon	
10 g	chopped shallot	½ oz
60 ml	dry white wine	⅛ pt
	pinch chopped parsley	
	salt, pepper	
50 g	butter	2 oz

1   Remove the black and white skins and fillet the soles.
2   Wash and drain well.
3   Butter and season an earthenware dish or sauté pan.
4   Sprinkle in the chopped shallots.
5   Add the fillets which may be folded in two, add the tomatoes and chopped parsley.
6   Season with salt and pepper.
7   Add the fish stock, wine and the lemon juice.
8   Cover with a buttered greaseproof paper.
9   Poach gently in a moderate oven (150°–200°C) for 5–10 min.
10   Remove the fillets and the garnish, place on a silver flat dish, or in a clean earthenware dish, keep warm.
11   Pass and reduce the cooking liquor in a small sauteuse, add the fish velouté, then incorporate the butter.
12   Correct the seasoning and consistency.
13   Coat the fillets with the sauce and serve.

54   Whole Soles may be prepared and served as for any recipe for fillets of sole. A sole weighing 200–300 g (8–12 oz) is usually served, allowing one sole per portion.

Preparation of Whole Soles
Remove the black and white skin, cut off the head, remove the side bones. Clean and wash thoroughly.

Preparation of Soles after Cooking and before coating with sauce.
Place the fish on a flat surface and using a palette knife, remove all the side bones. Carefully fold back two of the fillets and remove approx. 2–4 cm (1–2 in) of backbone.

55   Fillets of Sole with White Wine Sauce   *Filets de Sole Vin Blanc*

4 portions

500–600 g	2 soles, each	1–1¼ lb
60 ml	dry white wine	⅛ pt
	juice of ¼ lemon	
50 g	butter	2 oz
10 g	chopped shallot	½ oz
60 ml	fish stock	⅛ pt
250 ml	fish velouté	½ pt
	2 tbspn cream	

1   Skin and fillet soles, trim and wash.
2   Butter and season an earthenware dish.
3   Sprinkle with the chopped shallot.
4   Add the fillets of sole.
5   Season, add the fish stock, wine and lemon juice.
6   Cover with a buttered greaseproof paper.
7   Poach gently in a moderate oven (150°–200°C) for 5–10 min.
8   Drain the fish well, dress neatly on a silver flat dish or earthenware dish.
9   Bring the cooking liquor to the boil with the velouté.
10   Correct the seasoning and consistency and pass through a tammy cloth or a fine strainer.
11   Mix in the butter, finally add the cream.
12   Coat the fillets with the sauce. Garnish with fleurons (puff paste crescents).

6   Fillets of Sole Véronique   *4 portions*   *Filets de Sole Véronique*

500–600 g	2 soles, each	1–1¼ lb
60 ml	dry white wine	⅛ pt
	juice ¼ lemon	
	2 tbspn cream	
50 g	white grapes (blanched, skinned and pipped)	2 oz
60 ml	fish stock	⅛ pt
50 g	butter	2 oz
250 ml	fish velouté	½ pt
	salt, pepper	

1   Prepare and cook as for Filet de Sole Vin Blanc (Recipe 55), adding an egg yolk or spoonful of sabayon to the sauce.
2   Glaze under the salamander.
3   Arrange the grapes neatly on the dish.

7   Fillets of Sole Bercy   *4 portions*   *Filets de Sole Bercy*

500–600 g	2 soles, each	1–1¼ lb
	chopped parsley	
60 ml	white wine	⅛ pt
50 g	butter	2 oz
25 g	chopped shallot	1 oz
60 ml	fish stock	⅛ pt
250 ml	fish velouté	¼ pt
	2 tbspn cream	
	juice of ¼ lemon	
	yolk or sabayon	

1   Skin, fillet, trim and wash the fish.
2   Season and butter an earthenware dish.
3   Sprinkle with chopped shallots and chopped parsley.
4   Add the fillets of sole, season.
5   Add the stock, wine and lemon juice.

6   Cover with a buttered paper.
7   Poach gently in a moderate oven (150°–200°C) approx. 5–10 min.
8   Remove the fillets, place in a clean earthenware dish or silver flat. Keep warm.
9   Place the cooking liquor and velouté in a small sauteuse.
10 Correct the consistency and seasoning.
11 Finish with the butter and then the cream and sabayon.
12 Mask the fish and glaze under the salamander.

58   Fillets of Sole Bonne Femme   *Filets de Sole Bonne Femme*

As for Fillets of Sole Bercy with the addition of 100 g (4 oz) sliced button mushrooms which are placed in the earthenware dish with raw fish. Finish as for Bercy (Recipe 57).

59   Fillets of Sole Bréval or d'Antin   *Filets de Sole Bréval*
                                                     Filets de Sole d'Antin

As for Bonne Femme (Recipe 58) with the addition of 100 g (4 oz) tomatoes which are added with the mushrooms. The tomatoes are cut concassée. Finish as for Bercy.

60   Fillets of Sole Marguery   *4 portions*   *Filets de Sole Marguery*

As for Fillets of Sole Bercy (Recipe 57). Garnish the fillets of sole with 75 g (3 oz) cooked prawns and twelve cooked mussels before coating with the sauce. Finish the dish by glazing under the salamander and garnish with fleurons.

61   Fillets of Sole Mornay   *4 portions*   *Filets de Sole Mornay*

500–600 g	2 soles, each	1–1¼ lb
250 ml	béchamel sauce	½ pt
	2 tbspn cream	
	salt, cayenne	
125 ml	fish stock	¼ pt
	(p. 18)	
50 g	grated cheese	2 oz
25 g	butter	1 oz
	yolk or sabayon	

1   Prepare fillets, place in a buttered, seasoned earthenware dish or shallow pan, such as a sauté pan.
2   Add the fish stock, cover with a buttered paper.
3   Cook in a moderate oven (150°–200°C) approx. 5–10 min.
4   Drain the fish well, place in a clean earthenware or on a silver flat dish.
5   Bring the béchamel to the boil, add the cooking liquor and the cheese and the yolk; the consistency is actually corrected by the cooking liquor.
6   Correct the seasoning and pass through a fine strainer.
7   Mix in the butter and cream.

8   Mask the fish, sprinkle with grated cheese and gratinate under
    the salamander.

62   Fillets of Sole Florentine   *Filets de Sole Florentine*

As for Fillet Sole Mornay $\frac{1}{2}$ kg (1 lb) leaf spinach

1   Remove the stems from the spinach.
2   Wash very carefully in plenty of water several times if necessary.
3   Cook in boiling salted water until tender, approx. 5 min.
4   Refresh under cold water, squeeze dry into a ball.
5   When required for service, place into a pan containing 25–50 g
    (1–2 oz) butter, loosen with a fork and reheat quickly without
    colouring, season with salt and mill pepper.
6   Place in the serving dish.
7   Proceed as for Fillet of Sole Mornay.
8   Dress the fillets on the spinach. Coat with mornay sauce,
    sprinkle with grated cheese and gratinate under the salamander.

63   Fillets of Sole Walewska   *Filets de Sole Walewska*

Prepare as for Fillet Sole Mornay (Recipe 61, page 118) placing a slice
of cooked lobster on each fish fillet before coating with the sauce.
After the dish is browned decorate each fillet with a slice of truffle.

64   Fish in the Shell with Cheese Sauce   *Coquille de Poisson Mornay*

The fish to be used should be named, e.g. Coquille de Cabillaud
Mornay.

1   Prepare $\frac{1}{2}$ kg (1 lb) duchess potato mixture (page 275).
2   Using a piping bag and a large star tube pipe a neat border
    around 4 scallop shells.
3   Dry in the oven or under the salamander for two or three min.
4   Brush with eggwash.
5   Prepare and cook the fish and sauce as for Filet de Sole
    Mornay (Recipe 61).
6   Place a little sauce in the bottom of each shell.
7   Add the well-drained fish, which is usually flaked.
8   Coat with sauce, taking care not to splash the potato.
9   Sprinkle with grated cheese and brown under the salamander.
10 Dress on a dish paper on a silver flat dish, garnish with picked
    parsley.

65   Fish Kedgeree   *4 portions*   *Cadgery de Poisson*

400 g	fish (usually smoked haddock or fresh salmon)	1 lb
	2 hard-boiled eggs	
250 ml	curry sauce (p. 27)	$\frac{1}{2}$ pt
200 g	rice pilaff (p. 96)	8 oz
50 g	butter	2 oz

The fish to be used should be named, e.g. Cadgery de Saumon.

1 Poach the fish.
2 Remove all skin and bone. Flake
3 Cook the rice pilaff.
4 Cut the eggs in dice.
5 Combine the eggs, fish, rice and heat in the butter. Correct the seasoning.
6 Serve hot in an earthenware dish on a silver flat with a sauceboat of curry sauce separate.

66 Poached Smoked Haddock   *4 portions*   *Haddock Fumé Poché*

400–600 g	smoked haddock	1–1½ lb
250 ml	milk	½ pt
250 ml	water	½ pt

1 Trim off all fins from the fish.
2 Cut into four even pieces.
3 Simmer gently in the milk and water.
4 When cooked, the backbone should be removed easily.
5 Remove the backbone, dress the fish neatly on a silver flat or earthenware dish with a little of the cooking liquor.

67 Skate with Black Butter   *4 portions*   *Raie au Beurre Noir*

400–600 g	skate wings	1–1½ lb
	1 tspn vinegar	
10 g	capers	½ oz
50 g	butter	2 oz
	chopped parsley	

1 Cut the skate into four even pieces.
2 Simmer gently in a court bouillon (page 113) till cooked, approx. 10 min.
3 Drain well, place on a silver flat dish.
4 Heat the butter in a frying-pan until well browned, almost black, add the vinegar, pour over the fish, sprinkle with chopped parsley and a few capers.

68 Fish Cakes *4 portions*

200 g	cooked fish (free from skin and bone)	8 oz
	1 egg	
200 g	mashed potatoes	8 oz
	salt, pepper	
	for coating	
	1 egg	
50 g	breadcrumbs	2 oz
25 g	flour	1 oz

1 Combine the fish, potatoes and egg and season.
2 Divide into four or eight pieces.
3 Mould into balls.
4 Pass through flour, egg and breadcrumbs.

5   Flatten slightly, neaten with a palette knife.
6   Deep fry in hot fat (185°C) for 2–3 min.
7   Serve on a dish paper on a flat silver dish garnished with fried
     or picked parsley.
8   Serve with a sauceboat of suitable sauce, e.g. tomato sauce
     (page 29).

69   Salmon Cutlets

Method A. Prepare a fish-cake mixture using cooked salmon. Shape
into cutlets, insert a piece of macaroni, deep fry and serve as for fish
cakes.

Method B. Boil $\frac{1}{4}$ litre ($\frac{1}{2}$ pt) very thick béchamel (page 20), add
300 g (12 oz) cooked flaked salmon free from skin and bone.
Season, add 1–2 egg yolks, mix in and remove from the heat. Place
on a greased tray.
   When cold mould into four even-sized cutlet-shaped pieces. Flour
egg and crumb and insert a piece of macaroni into each.
   Deep fry (185°C) and serve on a dish paper on a silver flat with fried
or picked parsley. Serve a suitable sauce separate, e.g. anchovy sauce
(page 20).

70   Fish Pie   *4 portions*

200 g	fish cooked free from skin and bone	8 oz
	1 chopped hard-boiled egg	
250 ml	béchamel (thin) (p. 20)	$\frac{1}{2}$ pt
50 g	cooked diced mushrooms	2 oz
	chopped parsley	
	salt, pepper	
200 g	mashed or duchess potatoes	8 oz

1   Bring the béchamel to the boil.
2   Add the fish, mushroom, egg and parsley. Correct the seasoning.
3   Place in a buttered pie-dish.
4   Place or pipe the potato on top.
5   Brush with eggwash or milk.
6   Brown in a hot oven or under the salamander.
7   Serve on a dish paper on a flat dish.

71   Salmon Mayonnaise   *4 portions*   *Mayonnaise de Saumon*

300 g	cooked salmon	12 oz
200 g	tomatoes	8 oz
	$\frac{1}{4}$ cucumber	
5 g	anchovies	$\frac{1}{4}$ oz
	4 olives	
	1 lettuce	
125 ml	mayonnaise (p. 31)	$\frac{1}{4}$ pt
	1 hard-boiled egg	
5 g	capers	$\frac{1}{4}$ oz
	chopped parsley	

1   Shred the washed and drained lettuce, place in a salad bowl.
2   Add the flaked salmon, free from skin and bone.
3   Coat with mayonnaise sauce.
4   Decorate with quarters of tomato, egg, slices of cucumber, thin fillets of anchovies, capers and chopped parsley.
5   Serve on a doily on a flat dish.

72   Salmon Salad   *Salade de Saumon*

Ingredients as for Salmon Mayonnaise (Recipe 71).
   Dress and serve in the same way without coating the fish. Mayonnaise sauce should be served separately.

73   Cold Salmon, Mayonnaise Sauce   *Saumon Froid, Sauce Mayonnaise*

Portions of cold salmon garnished with quarters of lettuce, quarters of tomato, slices of cucumber, quarters of egg.
   Mayonnaise sauce separate.

74   Lobster Mayonnaise   *Mayonnaise de Homard*

As for Salmon Mayonnaise, using one 1 kg (2 lb) lobster, and cut in escalopes, in place of salmon.
   Decorate in addition with the lobster's head, tail, legs and chopped coral.

75   Lobster Salad   *Salade de Homard*

As for Salmon Salad using one 1 kg (2 lb) cooked lobster, cut in escalopes in place of the salmon.
   Decorate in addition as for Lobster Mayonnaise (Recipe 74).

76   Cold Lobster, Mayonnaise Sauce   *Homard Froid, Sauce Mayonnaise*

Half a $\frac{1}{2}$ kg (1 lb) cooked lobster per portion.
   Clean the halves, remove the trail and sac, remove the meat from the claws and place in the sac aperture. Serve on a silver flat dish, garnish with quarters of lettuce, quarters of tomato accompanied by a sauceboat of sauce mayonnaise.

77   Cooking a Lobster

Lobsters are usually bought in sizes from $\frac{1}{4}$–1 kg ($\frac{1}{2}$–2 lb). They should be bought alive in order to ensure freshness. They should be washed, then plunged into a pan of boiling salted water containing 30 ml (1 pt) vinegar to 1 litre (1 qt) water. Cover with a lid, bring to the boil and allow to simmer 15–25 min according to size. When possible allow to cool in the cooking liquor.

78   Cleaning of Cooked Lobster

1   Remove the claws.
2   Remove the pincers.

3   Crack the claws and joints and remove the meat in one piece if possible.
4   Cut the lobster in half with a large knife, by inserting the point of the knife 2 cm (1 in) above the tail on the natural centre line.
5   Cut through the centre of the tail firmly.
6   Turn the lobster round the other way and cut through the carapace.
7   Remove the halves of the sac from each half (this is situated at the top of the head).
8   With a small knife remove the trail.
9   Wash if necessary.

79 Lobster Patty   *4 portions*

¼–½ kg	cooked lobster	½–1 lb
	salt, pepper	
125 ml	béchamel (p. 20)	¼ pt
100 g	puff pastry (flour) (p. 290)	4 oz

1   Remove the meat from the cooked lobster, cut into ½ cm (¼ in) dice.
2   Mix with the cold sauce, season.
3   Roll out half the pastry 2 mm ($\frac{1}{16}$ in) thick.
4   Cut four rounds 8 cm (4 in) diameter.
5   Place on a greased baking sheet. Moisten the edge of the rounds, place the lobster in the centre of each.
6   Roll out the rest of the paste 3 mm (⅛ in) thick.
7   Cut out rounds 9 cm (4½ in) diameter. Place neatly on top.
8   Seal the edges firmly.
9   Brush with eggwash.
10 Bake in a hot oven (230°–250°C) for 15–20 min.
11 Serve on a doily on a flat silver dish; garnish with picked parsley.

A number of variations and additions can be made for variety, e.g. mushroom, shrimp, salmon, etc.

80 Seafood in Puff Pastry   *Bouchées de Fruits de Mer*

	4 bouchée cases (p. 319)	
200 g	cooked lobster, prawns, shrimps, mussels, scallops	½ lb
50 g	button mushrooms	2 oz
25 g	butter	1 oz
	juice ¼ lemon	
125 ml	white wine sauce (p. 103) chopped parsley	¼ pt

1   Peel and wash the mushrooms, cut in neat dice.
2   Cook in butter with the lemon juice.
3   Add the shellfish (mussels, prawns, shrimps left whole, the scallops and lobster cut in dice).

4   Cover the pan with a lid and heat through slowly 3–4 min.
5   Add the white wine sauce, chopped parsley and season.
6   Meanwhile warm the bouchées in the oven or hot plate.
7   Fill the bouchées with the mixture and place the lids on top.
8   Serve on a dish paper on a silver flat, garnish with picked parsley.

81 —   *Vol au Vent de Fruits de Mer*

1   Prepare and cook the puff pastry case (p. 319).
2   Prepare the filling as for Recipe 80.
3   Dress and serve as for Recipe 80.

82   Lobster Mornay   *4 portions*   *Homard Mornay*

350–450 g	2 cooked lobsters, each	¾–1 lb
25 g	butter	1 oz
250 ml	mornay sauce (p. 20)	½ pt
	salt, cayenne	

1   Remove lobster claws and legs.
2   Cut lobster carefully in half lengthwise.
3   Remove all meat. Discard the sac and trail.
4   Wash, shell and drain on a baking sheet upside down.
5   Cut the lobster meat into escalopes.
6   Heat the butter in a thick-bottomed pan, add the lobster and season.
7   Turn two or three times but do not overheat or the meat will toughen.
8   Meanwhile, finish the mornay sauce.
9   Place a little sauce in the bottom of each shell.
10   Add the lobster, press down to make a flat surface.
11   Mask completely with sauce, sprinkle with grated cheese, and brown under the salamander.
12   Dress the lobster on a dish paper on a flat silver dish. Sprig of parsley at the heads of the lobsters.

83   Lobster Thermidor   *4 portions*   *Homard Thermidor*

350–450 g	2 cooked lobsters, each	¾–1 lb
¼ litre	mornay sauce (p. 20)	½ pt
12 g	finely chopped shallot	½ oz
60 ml	dry white wine	⅛ pt
	½ tspn diluted English mustard	
25 g	grated parmesan cheese	1 oz
	chopped parsley	
25 g	butter	1 oz

1   Remove lobsters claws and legs.
2   Cut lobsters carefully in halves lengthwise.
3   Remove all the meat.

4   Discard the sac and remove the trail from the tail.
5   Wash the halves of shell and drain on a baking sheet.
6   Cut the lobster meat into thick escalopes.
7   Melt the butter in a sauteuse, add the chopped shallots and cook until tender without colour.
8   Add the white wine to the shallots and allow to reduce to a quarter of its original volume.
9   Mix in the mustard and chopped parsley.
10 Add the lobster slices, season slightly with salt, mix carefully and allow to heat slowly for 2–3 min. If this part of the process is overdone the lobster will become tough and chewy.
11 Meanwhile spoon a little of the warm mornay sauce into the bottom of each lobster half shell.
12 Neatly add the warmed lobster pieces and the juice in which they were re-heated. If there should be an excess of liquid it should be reduced and incorporated into the mornay sauce.
13 Coat the half lobsters with the remaining mornay sauce, sprinkle with parmesan cheese and place under a salamander until a golden brown.
14 Serve on an oval flat with the dish paper the heads facing the same way and garnish the heads with fresh sprigs of parsley.

84 Lobster Cardinal   *4 portions*   *Homard Cardinal*

350–450 g	2 cooked lobsters, each	¾–1 lb
¼ litre	lobster sauce (p. 104)	½ pt
	2 egg yolks	
60 ml	cream	⅛ pt
50 g	cooked diced mushroom	2 oz
25 g	grated parmesan cheese	1 oz
25 g	butter	1 oz
	4 slices of truffle	
	parsley	
	salt, cayenne pepper	

1   Remove the lobsters' claws and legs.
2   Cut lobsters carefully in halves lengthwise.
3   Remove all the meat.
4   Discard the sac and remove the trail from the tail.
5   Wash the halves of shell and drain on a baking sheet.
6   Cut the lobster meat into thick escalopes.
7   Melt the butter in a sauteuse, add the mushrooms and escalopes of lobster, season with salt and cayenne and allow to heat through slowly.
8   Make a sabayon (Recipe 8, page 103) with the egg yolks.
9   Boil the lobster sauce, remove from the heat and whisk in the sabayon.
10 Mix in the lightly beaten cream.
11 Correct the sauce for seasoning and pass through a fine strainer.

12   Place a little of the sauce into the bottom of each half shell of lobster.
13   Add the lobster meat and mushrooms.
14   Coat with the remainder of the sauce.
15   Sprinkle with the cheese.
16   Place under salamander until golden brown.
17   Garnish each half lobster with a slice of truffle.
18   Serve on a dish paper on an oval flat, garnish with fresh sprigs of parsley.

85   Lobster Americaine   *4 portions*   *Homard Americaine*

1 kg	live hen lobster	2 lb
60 ml	oil	⅛ pt
100 g	butter	4 oz
50 g	chopped shallot	2 oz
	1 chopped clove garlic	
60 ml	brandy	⅛ pt
125 ml	dry white wine	¼ pt
250 ml	fish stock	½ pt
200 g	tomate concassée	½ lb
25 g	tomato purée	1 oz
	coarsely chopped parsley	
	salt, cayenne pepper	

1   Wash the lobster.
2   Remove the legs and claws.
3   Crack the claws.
4   Cut the lobster in halves crosswise between the tail and carapace.
5   Cut the carapace in two lengthwise.
6   Discard the sac but retain the coral and place in a basin.
7   Cut the tail across in thick slices through the shell.
8   Remove the trail.
9   Wash the lobster pieces.
10   Heat 50 g (2 oz) of the butter with the oil, in a sauté-pan.
11   Add the pieces of lobster, season with salt and fry off rapidly until a red colour on all sides.
12   Pour off all the grease.
13   Add the shallots and garlic, cover the pan with a lid and allow to sweat for a few seconds.
14   Add the brandy and allow it to ignite.
15   Add the white wine, fish stock, concasséed tomatoes, tomato purée and a little of the chopped parsley.
16   Allow to simmer 20 min.
17   Remove the lobster, pick the meat from the shells and place in a covered serving dish and keep warm.
18   Reduce the cooking liquor by a half.

19 Pound the lobster coral mixing in the other 50 g (2 oz) butter until smooth.
20 Add this lobster butter to the sauce, mix in well until the sauce thickens then remove it from the heat.
21 Add a little cayenne and correct the seasoning.
22 Pass the sauce through a coarse strainer, mix in a little fresh coarsely chopped parsley and pour over the lobster.
23 Decorate with the head and tail of the lobster and serve.
24 Serve accompanied with a pilaf of rice (recipe page 96).

86 Mussels   *Moules*

When mussels are fresh the shells should be tightly closed. If the shells are open there is the possibility of danger from food poisoning therefore the mussels should be discarded.

Preparation for Cooking
Scrape the shells to remove any barnacles, etc.
    Wash well and drain in a colander.

To Cook
1 Take a thick-bottomed pan with a tight-fitting lid.
2 For 1 litre (1 qt) mussels place in the pan 25 g (1 oz) chopped shallot or onion.
3 Add the mussels, cover with a lid and cook on a fierce fire 4–5 min until the shells open completely.

Preparation for Use
1 Remove the mussels from the shells.
2 Check carefully in each for sand, weed, etc.
3 Remove the tongue and beard.

87 Mussels with White Wine Sauce *4 portions*   *Moules Marinière*

1 litre	mussels	1 qt
	chopped parsley	
	salt, pepper	
	fish stock if necessary	
25 g	chopped shallot	1 oz
60 ml	dry white wine	$\frac{1}{8}$ pt
	juice $\frac{1}{4}$ lemon	
25 g	Beurre Manié (butter/flour)	1 oz

1 Take a thick-bottomed pan.
2 Add chopped shallot, parsley, wine and the well-cleaned and washed mussels.
3 Cover with a tight-fitting lid.
4 Cook over fierce heat till shells open, approx. 4–5 min.

5   Drain off all cooking liquor into a basin, allow to stand in order
     to allow any sand to sink to the bottom.
6   Pick the mussels from the shells, remove the tongue, check for
     sand, etc. If in doubt, discard it. Remove beards if tough.
7   Replace mussels in half a shell, place in an earthenware
     casserole, cover with a lid and keep warm.
8   Carefully pour the cooking liquor into a small sauteuse.
9   If necessary make up to $\frac{1}{4}$ litre ($\frac{1}{2}$ pt) with fish stock.
10   Bring to the boil, whisk in the beurre manié.
11   Correct the seasoning, add a little chopped parsley.
12   Pour over the mussels and serve.
13   Place the casserole on a dish paper on a silver flat dish.

88 Scallops   *Coquille St Jacques*

To remove from shells
If fresh, the shells should be tightly closed. Place the shells on top
of the stove or in the oven for a few seconds, they will then open, the
scallop may be cut away with a small knife.

Wash well, clean and remove the trail leaving only the white
scallop and the orange curved roe. All other parts should be
discarded. Place in cold water, bring to the boil, skim and simmer
5–10 min, refresh. Remove any gristle.

They may be cut into escalopes and deep fried (coated with batter
or egg and crumb) and served with grilled bacon or cooked in a
little butter and fish stock and prepared as for Coquille de Poisson,
e.g. Coquille St Jacques Mornay, Coquille St Jacques Bercy, Coquille
St Jacques Bonne Femme (Pages 117–119).

89 Scallops with Cheese Sauce   *Coquille St Jacques Mornay*

	4 scallops	
$\frac{1}{2}$ kg	duchess potato	1 lb
250 ml	mornay sauce	$\frac{1}{2}$ pt
50 g	parmesan cheese	2 oz

1   Prepare $\frac{1}{2}$ kg (1 lb) duchess potato mixture (page 275).
2   Using a piping bag and a large star tube pipe a neat border
     around 4 scallop shells.
3   Dry in the oven or under the salamander for two or three min.
4   Brush with eggwash.
5   Prepare and cook as above.
6   Place a little sauce in the bottom of each shell.
7   Add the sliced scallop cooked as in recipe 88.
8   Coat with sauce, taking care not to splash the potato.
9   Sprinkle with grated cheese and brown under the salamander.
10   Dress on a dish paper on a silver flat dish, garnish with picked
     parsley.

90 — *4 portions*   *Scampi Provençale*

375–500 g	shelled scampi	$\frac{3}{4}$–1	lb
60 ml	oil	$\frac{1}{8}$	pt
	1 small clove of garlic		
200 g	tomatoes	$\frac{1}{2}$	lb
125 ml	tomato sauce	$\frac{1}{4}$	pt
	coarsely chopped parsley		
30 ml	dry white wine	$\frac{1}{16}$	pt

1   Lightly pass the scampi through seasoned flour and shake off
    all the surplus.
2   Heat $\frac{3}{4}$ of the oil in a frying pan until smoking.
3   Add the scampi and fry to a light golden brown, tossing
    frequently.
4   Drain the scampi in a colander.
5   Place the remaining quarter of the oil in a sauteuse, add the
    garlic and allow to sweat without colour for a few seconds.
6   Pour off the surplus oil, add the tomatoes concasséed and cook
    for 5–10 min.
7   Add the white wine, reduce by a half.
8   Add the tomato sauce and bring to the boil.
9   Correct the seasoning add the chopped parsley.
10 Mix the scampi with the sauce and serve accompanied by a
    dish of pilaff rice (recipe p. 96).

9
Lamb and Mutton

Introduction. As a guide when ordering, allow approximately 100 g (4 oz) meat off the bone per portion, and 150 g (6 oz) on the bone per portion.

It must be clearly understood that the weights given can only be approximate. They must vary according to the quality of the meat and also for the purpose for which the meat is being butchered. For example, a chef will often cut differently from a shop butcher, i.e. a chef frequently needs to consider the presentation of the particular joint whilst the butcher is more often concerned with economical cutting. We have given simple orders of dissection for each carcass. In general, bones need be removed only when preparing joints, so as to facilitate carving.

1 Clarification of Fat

All fat trimmings should be chopped or minced and placed in a pan with a little water, then allowed to cook until there is no movement, and the fat is golden in colour. When cool, pass through clean sacking, then use as required.

2 Lamb and Mutton   *Agneau et Mouton*

				Approx. Weights 16 *kg* (32 *lb*)	25 *kg* (50 *lb*)
3	**Joint**	**French**	**Uses**	*Lamb*	*Mutton*
	1 Shoulders (two)	l'Epaule (f.)	Roasting Stewing	3 (6)	4½ (9)
	2 Legs (two)	le Gigot	Roasting (Mutton Boiled)	3½ (7)	5½ (11)

			Approx. Weights	
3 Breasts (two)	la Poitrine	Roasting	$1\frac{1}{2}$ (3)	$2\frac{1}{2}$ (5)
		Stewing		
4 Middle Neck		Stewing	2 (4)	3 (6)
5 Scrag End	le Cou	Stewing, Broth	$\frac{1}{2}$ (1)	1 (2)
6 Best-End	le Carré	Roasting, Grilling, Frying	2 (4)	3 (6)
7 Saddle	la Selle	Roasting, Grilling, Frying	$3\frac{1}{2}$ (7)	$5\frac{1}{2}$ (11)
Kidneys	le Rognon	Grilling, Sauté		
Heart	le Cœur	Braising		
Liver	le Foie	Frying		
Sweetbreads	le Ris	Braising, Frying		
Tongue	la Langue	Braising, Boiling		

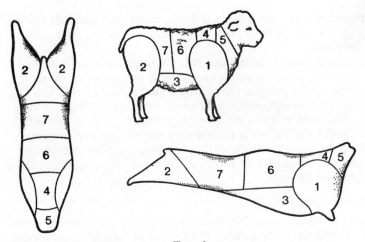

FIG. 1

The bones are used for stock and the excess fat is rendered down for second-class dripping.

4 Quality of Lamb and Mutton
(Lamb is under 1 year old.)

1 A good quality animal should be compact and evenly fleshed.

2 The lean flesh should be firm, of a pleasing dull red colour and of a fine texture or grain.

3 There should be an even distribution of surface fat which should be hard, brittle and flaky in structure and a clear white colour.

4   In a young animal the bones should be pink and porous, so that, when cut, a degree of blood is shown in their structure. As age progresses the bones become hard, dense, white and inclined to splinter when chopped.

5   Order of Dissection of a Carcass

1   Remove the shoulders.
2   Remove the breasts.
3   Remove the middle neck and scrag.
4   Remove the legs.
5   Divide the saddle from the best-end.

6   Preparation of the Joints and Cuts

SHOULDER

Roasting   Clean and trim knucklebone so as to leave approximately 3 cm (1½ in) of clean bone.
Boning   Remove the blade bone and upper arm bone (see Fig. 2), tie with string. The shoulder may be stuffed (page 138) before tying.
Cutting for Stews   Bone out, cut into even 25–50 g (1–2 oz) pieces.

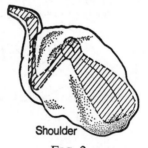

Shoulder

FIG. 2

LEGS

Roasting   Remove the pelvic or aitchbone. Trim the knuckle cleaning 3 cm (1½ in) bone. Trim off excess fat and tie with string if necessary.

BREASTS

Remove excess fat and skin.
Roasting   Bone, stuff and roll, tie with string.
Stewing   Cut into even 25–50 g (1–2 oz) pieces.

MIDDLE NECK

Middle Neck—Stewing Remove excess fat, excess bone and the gristle. Cut into even 50 g (2 oz) pieces. This joint, when correctly butchered, can give good uncovered second-class cutlets.

SCRAG-END

Scrag-End—Stewing This can be chopped down the centre, the excess bone, fat and the gristle removed and cut into even 50 g (2 oz) pieces, or boned out and cut into pieces.

BEST-END

Best-Ends

1   Cut either side of the backbone and divide from the inside, removing the complete chine bone.
2   Skin from head to tail and from breast to back.
3   Remove the sinew and the tip of the blade bone.
4   Complete the preparation of the rib bones as indicated in the diagram.
5   Clean the sinew from between the rib bones and trim the bones.
6   Score the fat neatly to approx. 2 mm ($\frac{1}{16}$ in) deep as shown.

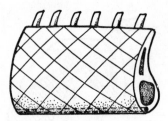

FIG. 3

The overall length of the rib bones to be trimmed to two and a half times the length of the nut of meat.

Roasting—prepare as above.

Cutlets—prepare as for roasting, excluding the scoring and divide evenly between the bones, or the cutlets can be cut from the best-end and prepared separately. A double cutlet consists of two bones; therefore a six bones best-end yields six single or three double cutlets.

French: Côtelette   *Côtelette Double*

7 **Saddle**

A full saddle is illustrated in Fig. 4 (*a*) including the chumps and the tail. For large banquets it is sometimes found better to remove the chumps and use short saddles, Fig 4 (*b*).

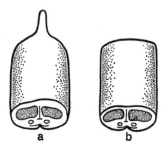

FIG. 4

Saddle	la Selle	Roasting, Pot Roasting (Poêlé)
Loins	la Longe	Roasting
Fillet	le Filet Mignon	Grilling, Frying
Loin Chops	Chop	Grilling, Frying, Stewing
Chump Chops	Chump Chop	Grilling, Frying, Stewing
Kidneys	le Rognon	Grilling, Sauté

The saddle may be divided as follows:

Skin from head to tail and from breast to back, split down the centre of the backbone to produce two loins. Each loin can be roasted whole, boned and stuffed, or cut into loin and chump chops.

Saddle for Roasting

1   Skin and remove the kidney.
2   Trim the excess fat and sinew.
3   Cut off the flaps leaving about 12 cm (6 in) each side so as to meet in the middle.
4   Remove the aitch or pelvic bone.
5   Score neatly and tie with string.
6   For first-class presentation the tail is left on and protected with paper and tied back.

Loin for Roasting

Skin, remove excess fat and sinew, remove the pelvic bone and tie with string.

Loin Boned and Stuffed

Remove the skin, excess fat and sinew. Bone out, the fillet may be then replaced, and tied up. When stuffed, bone out, season, stuff and tie with string.

CHOPS

Loin Chops

Skin the loin, remove the excess fat and sinew, then cut into chops approx. 100–150 g (4–6 oz) in weight. A first-class loin chop should have a piece of kidney skewered in the centre.

Chump Chops

These are cut from the chump end of the loin. Cut into approx. 150 g (6 oz) chops, trim where necessary.

Noisette

This is a cut from a boned-out loin. Cut slantwise into approx. 2 cm (1 in) thick slices, bat out slightly, trim cutlet shape.

8 Preparation of Offal

Kidney, *Grilling*

Skin and split three-quarters the way through lengthwise and skewer.

Sauté

Skin and remove the gristle. Cut slantways into 6–8 pieces.

Hearts, *Braising*

Remove the tubes and excess fat.

Liver

Skin, remove gristle and cut into thin slices on the slant.

Sweetbreads

Wash well, blanch and trim.

Tongue

Remove bone and gristle from the throat end.

9 Roasting of Lamb and Mutton

Allow approx. 150 g (6 oz) meat on the bone per portion. (Legs, shoulders, saddle or loin, best-end and breast.)

1 The joints are seasoned with salt and placed on a trivet, or bones, in a roasting tray.
2 Place a little dripping on top and cook in a hot oven (230°–250°C).
3 Baste frequently and reduce the heat gradually when necessary, as for example in the case of large joints.
4 Roasting time approx. 20 min per ½ kilo (1 lb) and 20 min over.

5　To test if cooked, place on a tray and press firmly in order to see if the juices released contain any blood.

6　In general, all joints should be cooked through, that is to say, not left underdone.

7　Allow to stand for approx. 15–20 min before carving; if this is not done the meat will tend to shrink and curl.

Roast Gravy　　　　　　　　　　　　　　　　・　　　　　*Jus Rôti*

1　Place the roasting tray on the stove over a gentle heat to allow the sediment to settle.

2　Carefully strain off the fat, leaving the sediment in the tray.

3　Return to the stove and brown carefully, swill (déglacé) with good brown stock.

4　Allow to simmer for a few minutes.

5　Correct the seasoning and colour, then strain and skim.

In some establishments the gravy served with stuffed joints and also pork and veal is slightly thickened with diluted cornflour, fêcule or arrowroot.

CARVING

Leg　　　　　　　　　　　　　　　　*Gigot d'Agneau Rôti* or
Gigot de Mouton Rôti

Holding the bone, carve with a sharp knife at an angle of 45° and take off each slice as it is cut. Continue in this manner along the joint, turning it from side to side as the slices get wider.

Shoulder　　　　　　　　　　　　　　*Épaule d'Agneau Rôtie*

Carve in slices starting from the flesh side.

Saddle　　　　　　　　　　　　　　　*Selle d'Agneau Rôtie*

Carving on the bone. There are two usual ways of carving the saddle, one is by carving lengthways either side of the backbone, the other by making a deep cut lengthwise either side of the backbone and then slicing across each loin. It is usual to cut these slices rather on the thick side.

Carving off the bone. For economical kitchen carving it is often found best to bone the loins out whole, carve into slices, then reform on the saddle bone.

The filet mignon may be left on the saddle or removed; in either case it is carved and served with the rest of the meat.

Loin　　　　　　　　　　　　　　　*Longe d'Agneau Rôtie*

On the bone. Proceed as for the saddle.

Boned-out, cut in slices across the joint. When stuffed cut slightly thicker.

Best-End   *Carré d'Agneau Rôti*

Divide into cutlets by cutting between each bone.

SERVICE

All roast joints are served on a silver flat, garnished with watercress and a sauceboat of roast gravy separately.

When carved, serve a little gravy over the slices as well as a sauceboat of gravy. Mint sauce should be served with roast lamb and red-currant jelly should be available. For roast mutton, red-currant jelly and/or onion sauce should be served.

10 Stuffing for Lamb

This is used for stuffing joints, e.g. Loin, Shoulder, Breast.

50 g	chopped suet	2 oz
50 g	chopped onions cooked in a little fat without colour	2 oz
	1 egg yolk or small egg	
100 g	white breadcrumbs pinch powdered thyme pinch chopped parsley salt, pepper	4 oz

Combine all the ingredients together.
Mint Sauce—See Sauce section, page 33.

BEST-END RECIPES

11 Best-End with Crumbs and Parsley   *Carré d'Agneau Persillé*

Roast the best-end and 10 min before the cooking is completed cover the fat surface of the meat with a mixture of 25–50 g (1–2 oz) of fresh white breadcrumbs mixed with plenty of chopped parsley and 25–50 g (1–2 oz) melted butter. Return to the oven to complete the cooking, browning carefully.

12 Best-End Boulangère   *Carré d'Agneau Boulangère*

Any roast lamb joint may be served in this manner.
1 Prepare a dish of pommes boulangère (savoury potatoes) (page 280).
2 Roast the joint.
3 Remove from the tray 15 min before completion of cooking.
4 Place on top of the cooked potatoes.
5 Return to the oven to complete the cooking.
6 Serve the joint whole or carved as required on the potatoes.
7 Garnish with watercress and serve with a sauceboat of gravy separately.

CUTLETS

13   Grilled Cutlet   *Côtelette d'Agneau Grillée*

 1 Season the cutlets with salt and pepper (preferably from the pepper mill).
 2 Brush with oil or fat.
 3 When cooked on the bars of the grill, place the prepared cutlet on the heated bars which have been greased.
 4 Cook for approx. 5 min, turn and complete the cooking.
 5 When cooked under the salamander place on a greased tray, cook for approx. 5 min, turn and complete the cooking.
 6 Serve dressed neatly on an oval silver flat garnished with pommes pailles (straw potatoes) and watercress. Parsley butter may also be served.
 7 Each bone should be covered with a cutlet frill.

14   Mixed Grill

4 sausages	4 rashers streaky bacon
4 cutlets	watercress
4 kidneys	straw potatoes
4 tomatoes	parsley butter (page 31)
4 mushrooms	

These are the usually accepted items for a mixed grill, but it will be found that there are many variations to this list, e.g. steaks, liver.

In economical catering a Welsh Rarebit and fried egg may be used in place of more expensive items.

Grill in the order given and dress neatly on an oval silver flat dish. Garnish with straw potatoes and watercress and a slice of parsley butter on each kidney.

15   Fried Cutlet

Season and carefully cook in a sauté pan (plat à sauter). Garnish as required. For some typical garnishes see page 143.

16   Breadcrumbed Cutlet   *Côtelette d'Agneau Panée*

 1 Pass prepared cutlets through seasoned flour, eggwash and fresh white breadcrumbs.
 2 Shallow fry in hot clarified fat for the first few minutes; then allow to cook gently.
 3 Turn, and continue cooking until a golden brown.
 4 To test if cooked, press firmly, no signs of blood should appear. Approx. time 5 min each side.

In the following recipes prepare cutlets as Recipe 16 and garnish with prepared spaghetti. Finish with a cordon of jus-lié around the dish. Beurre noisette may be served over the cutlets.

17   Breadcrumbed Cutlet with Spaghetti

18   **Côtelette d'Agneau Italienne**
Garnish with Recipe 2 Page 90.

19   **Côtelette d'Agneau Napolitaine**
Garnish with Recipe 4 Page 90.

20   **Côtelette d'Agneau Milanaise**
Garnish with Recipe 5 Page 91.

21   Lamb Cutlet Reform   *Côtelette d'Agneau Réforme*
   1   Pass the prepared cutlets through seasoned flour, eggwash and
       breadcrumbs containing chopped ham and chopped parsley.
   2   Cook as for crumbed cutlet.
   3   Serve on an oval silver flat dish, garnish with reform sauce
       (page 26) and a sauceboat of reform sauce separately.

22   Boiled Leg of Mutton, Caper Sauce
   1   Place the prepared leg into boiling salted water.
   2   Re-boil, skim and simmer.
   3   Add 2–3 whole carrots and onions and a bouquet garni.
   4   Allow to cook 20 min $\frac{1}{2}$ kg (1 lb) and 20 min over.
   5   Serve whole or carved as required on a silver flat dish with a
       little of the cooking liquor, accompanied with a sauceboat of
       caper sauce.

Caper Sauce   *Sauce aux Câpres*

$\frac{1}{2}$ litre	cooking liquor in which the leg has been cooked	1 pt
50 g	margarine	2 oz
50 g	flour	2 oz
	1 tbspn capers	

    Make a velouté and cook out. Correct the seasoning and
consistency, strain and add the capers.

23   Brochette of Lamb   *Kebab à la Turque*
Prime meat must be used, the ideal cuts being the nut of the lean
meat of the loin and best-end.
   1   Cut into thin slices, season and place on a skewer with peeled
       washed mushrooms and two halves of bay leaf per skewer.
   2   Season, brush with melted fat and grill gently, turning and

brushing with fat. Brochettes are usually served on a riz-pilaff (page 96).

24   Grilled Loin Chops   *Chop d'Agneau Grillée*

1   Season with salt and pepper mill.
2   Brush with fat and place on hot greased grill bars or place on a greased baking tray.
3   Cook quickly for the first 2–3 min on each side, in order to seal the pores of the meat.
4   Continue cooking steadily allowing approx. 12–15 min in all.
5   Serve on an oval flat silver dish, remove the skewer.
6   Garnish with picked watercress, and straw potatoes (pommes pailles).

Parsley butter may also be served.

In certain establishments the straw potato is frequently replaced by another type of fried potato such as pommes frites, pommes allumettes or pommes mignonettes.

25   Loin Chop, Toad in the Hole   *4 portions*

Other foods used in this way include cutlets, chump chops, steak and sausages.

	Yorkshire Pudding mixture	
100 g	flour	$\frac{1}{4}$ lb
	4 loin chops	
50 g	dripping	2 oz

1   Neatly arrange the seasoned chops in a suitable-sized roasting tray or shallow earthenware dish with the dripping.
2   Place in a hot oven (230°–250°C) approx. 5 min or until the meat has set.
3   Pour the Yorkshire Pudding mixture over the meat.
4   Return to the hot oven.
5   Allow to cook to a golden brown and the meat is cooked approx. 30 min.
6   When cooked in an earthenware dish, clean the edges and serve in the dish or on an oval silver flat dish.
7   When cooked in a roasting tray, cut into portions and arrange neatly on the oval silver flat.

In both cases serve with a sauceboat of jus-lié (page 28) or demi-glace (page 23).

NOTE. Any thick slices of cooked meat such as corned beef, luncheon meat, etc., may be prepared Toad in the Hole. Place the dripping in the tray, heat and add the meat and pour over the mixture and cook in a hot oven approx. 20 min.

26 Braised Loin Chops or   *Chop d'Agneau Braisée*
Braised Chump Chops   4 portions

	4 chops	
25 g	dripping	1 oz
100 g	onion	4 oz
500 ml	brown stock (p. 16)	1 pt
	seasoning	
25 g	flour	1 oz
100 g	carrot	4 oz
	level tbspn tomato purée	
	bouquet garni	
	chopped parsley	

1 Fry the seasoned chops in a sauté pan quickly on both sides in very hot fat.
2 When turning the chops add the mirepoix.
3 Draw aside, drain off the surplus fat.
4 Add the flour and mix in, singe in the oven or on top of the stove.
5 Add the tomato purée and the hot stock.
6 Stir with a wooden spoon till thoroughly mixed.
7 Add the bouquet garni, season, skim and allow to simmer and cover with a lid.
8 Cook preferably in the oven, skimming off all fat and scum.
9 When cooked transfer chops to a clean pan.
10 Correct the seasoning and consistency of the sauce.
11 Skim off any fat and pass through a fine chinois on to the chops. Serve in an entrée dish, sprinkle with chopped parsley.

27 Chop Champvallon   4 portions   *Chop d'Agneau Champvallon*

	4 chops	
100 g	onion	4 oz
250 ml	brown stock	½ pt
25 g	flour	1 oz
400 g	potatoes	1 lb
	seasoning	
25 g	dripping	1 oz

1 Pass chops through seasoned flour.
2 Fry quickly on both sides in hot fat.
3 Shred onions finely and toss lightly in butter and place in a shallow earthenware dish.
4 Place the chops on top, cover with brown stock.
5 Add ¼ cm (⅛ in) sliced potatoes neatly arranged with a knob or two of good dripping on top.
6 Cook in a hot oven (230°–250°C) till the potatoes are cooked and a golden brown, approx. 1½–2 hrs.
7 Serve sprinkled with chopped parsley, in the earthenware dish on an oval silver flat dish.

28 Grilled Chump Chop
As for Loin Chop, Recipe 24.

29 Noisette of Lamb Grilled   *Noisette d'Agneau Grillée*
This may be grilled as for Lamb Chop, Recipe 24.

30 Noisette of Lamb Sauté   *Noisette d'Agneau Sautée*
Season and shallow fry on both sides in a sauté pan and serve with
the appropriate garnish and sauce. Unless specifically stated a jus-lié
or demi-glace sauce should be served.

Suitable garnishes

Fleuriste	tomatoes filled with jardinière of vegetables and château potatoes.
Dubarry	balls of cauliflower mornay and château potatoes.
Montmorency	artichoke bottoms filled with carrot balls and noisette potatoes.
Princesse	artichoke bottoms filled with asparagus heads and noisette potatoes.
Parisienne	braised lettuce and parisienne potatoes.
Clamart	artichoke bottoms filled with peas and cocotte potatoes.

31 Fillet of Lamb   *Filet Mignon*
As for Noisette d'Agneau, Recipe 30.

32 Irish Stew   *4 portions*

500 g	stewing lamb	1 lb 4 oz
400 g	potatoes	1 lb
100 g	celery	4 oz
	bouquet garni	
100 g	button onions	4 oz
100 g	onions	4 oz
100 g	leeks	4 oz
100 g	savoy cabbage	4 oz
	parsley	

1 Trim the meat and cut into even pieces.
2 Blanch and refresh.
3 Place in a sauteuse or shallow saucepan, cover with water, bring
  to the boil, season and skim.

4   Add the bouquet garni. Meanwhile turn the potatoes into barrel shapes.
5   Cut the potato trimmings, onion, celery, cabbage and leek into small neat pieces and add to the meat, simmer for 30 min.
6   Add the button onions and simmer for a further 30 min.
7   Add the turned potatoes and simmer gently, with a lid on the pan till cooked.

If tough meat is being used allow $\frac{1}{2}$–1 hr stewing before adding any vegetables.

8   Correct the seasoning and skim off all fat.
9   Serve in an entrée dish, sprinkle with chopped parsley.

33 Brown Lamb or Mutton Stew   *4 portions*

500 g	stewing lamb	1 lb 4 oz
25 g	flour	1 oz
500 ml	brown stock (approx.)	1 pt
	(mutton stock or water)	
100 g	onion	4 oz
	salt	
	clove of garlic (if desired)	
25 g	fat	1 oz
	level tbspn tomato purée	
	bouquet garni	
100 g	carrot	4 oz
	pepper	

1   Trim the meat and cut into even pieces.
2   Partly fry off the seasoned meat, then add the mirepoix and continue frying.
3   Drain off the surplus fat, add the flour and mix.
4   Singe in the oven or brown on top of the stove for a few minutes.
5   Add the tomato purée and stir in with a wooden spoon.
6   Add the stock and season.
7   Add the bouquet garni, bring to the boil, skim, cover with a lid.
8   Simmer gently till cooked, preferably in the oven, approx. 1–2 hr.
9   When cooked, place the meat in a clean pan.
10   Correct the sauce and pass the sauce on to the meat.
11   Serve in an entrée dish with chopped parsley.

34 Brown Stew of Lamb or Mutton   *Navarin Printanier*
Garnished with Vegetables

As above, with a garnish of vegetables, i.e. turned glacé carrots and turnips, glacé button onions; potatoes, peas and diamonds of French beans, which may be cooked separately or in the stew (Glacé Vegetables, page 165).

35 Curried Lamb *4 portions* — *Kari d'Agneau* or *Currie d'Agneau*

Metric	Ingredient	Imperial
500 g	stewing lamb	1 lb 4 oz
	1 clove garlic	
10 g	curry powder	½ oz
10 g	tomato purée	½ oz
½ litre	stock or water	1 pt
25 g	chopped chutney	1 oz
	salt	
25 g	dripping	1 oz
200 g	onions	8 oz
10 g	flour	½ oz
5 g	desiccated coconut	¼ oz
10 g	sultanas	½ oz
50 g	chopped apple	2 oz
100 g	rice (long-grain)	4 oz
1½ litres	water	at least 3 pt

1 Trim the meat and cut into even pieces.
2 Season and quickly colour in hot fat.
3 Add the chopped onion and chopped garlic, cover with a lid and sweat for a few minutes.
4 Drain off the surplus fat.
5 Add the curry powder and flour, mix in and cook out.
6 Mix in the tomato purée, gradually add the hot stock, thoroughly stir, bring to the boil, season and skim.
7 Allow to simmer and add the rest of the ingredients.
8 Cover with a lid and simmer in the oven or on top of the stove till cooked.
9 Correct the seasoning and consistency, skim off all fat. At this stage a little cream may be added for first-class service.
10 Serve in an entrée dish accompanied with rice which may be plain boiled, pilaff or pilaff with saffron.

Plain Boiled Rice *4 portions*

100 g	rice (long-grain)	4 oz
1½ litres	water (at least)	3 pt
	salt	

1 Pick and wash the long-grain rice.
2 Add to plenty of boiling, salt water.
3 Stir to the boil and allow to simmer gently till tender, approx. 12–15 min.
4 Wash well under running water, drain and place on a sieve and cover with a cloth.
5 Place on a tray in a moderate oven or on the hot plate until hot.
6 Serve in a vegetable dish separately.

Other Accompaniments to Curry

There are many other accompaniments to curry which may be served, for example grilled Bombay Duck and Popadums which are grilled or deep fried, and served separately on a silver dish with a dish paper. Also:

chopped chutney
sultanas
desiccated coconut
slices of lemon
chopped apple
chow-chow
quarters of orange
sliced banana
chopped onions

36   White Lamb Stew   *4 portions*   *Blanquette d'Agneau*

500 g	stewing lamb	1 lb 4 oz
50 g	carrot	2 oz
	bouquet garni	
	2–3 tbspn cream	
	chopped parsley	
750 ml	(approx.) white stock	1½ pts
50 g	onion piqué	2 oz
25 g	margarine ⎱ Blond Roux	1 oz
25 g	flour ⎰	1 oz

1 Trim the meat and cut into even pieces.
2 Blanch and refresh.
3 Place in a saucepan and cover with cold water.
4 Bring to the boil then place under running cold water until all the scum has been washed away.
5 Drain and place in a clean saucepan and cover with stock, bring to the boil and skim.
6 Add whole onion and carrot, bouquet garni, season slightly and simmer until tender, approx. 1–1½ hr.
7 Meanwhile prepare the roux and make into a velouté with the cooking liquor.
8 Cook out for approx. 20 min.
9 Correct the seasoning and consistency and pass through a fine strainer on to the meat, which has been placed in a clean pan.
10 Reheat and mix in the cream and serve in an entrée dish, finish with chopped parsley.
11 To enrich this dish a liaison of yolks and cream is sometimes added at the last moment to the boiling sauce which must not be allowed to re-boil.

37   Hot Pot of Lamb or Mutton   *4 portions*

500 g	stewing lamb	1 lb 4 oz
400 g	potatoes	1 lb
25 g	dripping	1 oz
100 g	onions	4 oz
1 litre	brown stock	2 pt
	chopped parsley	

1 Trim the meat and cut into even pieces.
2 Place in a deep earthenware dish.
3 Season with salt and pepper.
4 Mix the shredded onion and thinly sliced potatoes together.
5 Season and place on top of the meat.
6 Three parts cover with stock.
7 Neatly arrange an overlapping layer of 2 mm thick ($\frac{1}{16}$ in) sliced potatoes on top.
8 Add the dripping in small pieces.
9 Thoroughly clean the edges of the dish and place to cook in a hot oven (230°–250°C) till lightly coloured.
10 Reduce the heat and allow to simmer gently till cooked, approx. $1\frac{1}{2}$–2 hr.
11 Press the potatoes down occasionally during cooking.
12 Serve with the potatoes brushed with margarine and sprinkle with chopped parsley.

This is a dish to which there are many accepted regional variations.

8 Haricot Mutton *4 portions*

500 g	stewing lamb	1 lb 4 oz
25 g	lard	1 oz
	small clove of garlic	
750 ml	brown stock or water	$1\frac{1}{2}$ pt
50 g	lean bacon	2 oz
	8 button onions	
25 g	flour	1 oz
200 g	haricot beans	8 oz
	chopped parsley	
	bouquet garni	

1 Trim the meat and cut into even pieces.
2 Heat the lard in a sauté pan.
3 Add the bacon cut into dice, and the button onions, colour lightly and remove from the pan.
4 In the same fat fry the meat and colour on all sides.
5 Drain off half of the fat.
6 Add the crushed garlic and flour.
7 Singe in the oven or cook out on top of the stove.
8 Add the hot water or stock.
9 Bring to the boil, season, skim, add the bouquet garni.
10 Cover with a lid and simmer for 30 min.
11 Transfer the meat to clean pan, add the bacon and onions and the previously three-quarter cooked haricot beans.
12 Strain the sauce over and cover with a lid.
13 Complete the cooking, allowing a further 1–2 hr.
14 Correct the seasoning and consistency and skim off all fat.
15 Serve in an entrée dish and sprinkle with chopped parsley.

39 Shepherd's Pie or Cottage Pie   *4 portions*

400 g	cooked lamb or mutton	1 lb
35 g	fat	1½ oz
	salt	
400 g	cooked potato	1 lb
25–50 g	margarine	1–2 oz
100 g	chopped onion	4 oz
125–250 ml	jus-lié or demi-glace	¼–½ pt
	pepper	
	milk	

1   Cook the onion in the fat without colouring.
2   Add the minced cooked meat from which all fat and gristle has been removed.
3   Season and add sufficient sauce to bind.
4   Bring to the boil, simmer 10–15mins.
5   Place in a pie or earthenware dish.
6   Prepare the mashed potatoes and arrange neatly on top.
7   Brush with milk or eggwash.
8   Colour lightly under the salamander or in a hot oven.
9   Serve on an oval silver flat dish (if in a pie dish use a pie frill), accompanied with a sauceboat of jus-lié.

NOTE. This dish may be prepared with cooked beef. When using reheated meats care must be taken to heat thoroughly.

40 Minced Lamb or Mutton   *Hachis d'Agneau* or *de Mouton*

Prepare the meat as for Shepherd's Pie (Recipe 39). This is placed on a dish which has been previously piped with a border of duchess potatoes which have been dried for a few minutes in the oven, egg-washed and lightly browned.

41 Moussaka   *4 portions*

50 g	onions	2 oz
	1 small clove garlic	
25 g	butter	1 oz
25 g	tomato purée	1 oz
400–600 g	cooked mutton	1–1½ lb
125 ml	demi-glace	¼ pt
200 g	tomatoes	½ lb
200 g	aubergine	½ lb
60 ml	oil	⅛ pt
	flour	
25 g	breadcrumbs	1 oz
	chopped parsley	
25 g	grated parmesan cheese	1 oz

1   Finely chop the onions and garlic.
2   Cook the onions and garlic in the butter without colour.
3   Mix in the tomato purée and the cooked mutton, cut in small dice or minced.

4 Add the demi-glace and bring to the boil.
5 Correct the seasoning and allow to simmer 10–15 min. The mixture should be fairly dry.
6 Peel the aubergines and cut into ½ cm (¼ in) slices.
7 Pass the slices of aubergine through the flour.
8 Fry the slices of aubergine in hot oil on both sides and drain.
9 Peel the tomatoes and cut into ½ cm (¼ in) slices.
10 Place the mixture of mutton into an earthenware dish.
11 Cover the mixture with the slices of tomato, and then neatly with the slices of aubergine.
12 Season with salt and pepper.
13 Sprinkle with breadcrumbs and cheese.
14 Lightly coat with melted butter.
15 Gratinate in a hot oven.
16 Sprinkle with chopped parsley and serve.

This is a dish of Greek origin. It may also be seasoned with a little grated cinnamon and oregano. Moussaka may also be finished by masking the dish when all the ingredients have been added with 250 ml (½ pt) of béchamel sauce to which 2 beaten eggs have been added. If this method is being adopted then the breadcrumbs, cheese and melted butter should be added after the béchamel.

2 Cornish Pasties *4 portions*

200 g	short paste	½ lb
100 g	finely diced potato (raw)	4 oz
100 g	raw meat (cut small)	4 oz
50 g	chopped onion	2 oz
	salt, pepper	

1 Roll out the short paste 3 mm (⅛ in) thick and cut into rounds 10 cm (5 in) diameter.
2 Mix the filling together, moisten with a little water and place in the rounds in piles. Eggwash the edges.
3 Fold in half and seal, flute the edge and brush with eggwash.
4 Cook in a moderate oven (150°–200°C) for ¾–1 hr.
5 Serve on a dish paper with a suitable sauce separately, e.g. demi-glace.

3 Braised Lambs' Tongue *4 portions*   *Langue d'Agneau Braisée*

	8–12 tongues (depending on size)	
100 g	carrot	4 oz
10 g	tomato purée	½ oz
500 ml	brown stock	1 pt
	salt	
25 g	dripping	1 oz
100 g	onion	4 oz
	bouquet garni	
250 ml	espagnole	½ pt
	pepper	

1   Fry off the roughly cut carrot and onion, place in a braising pan.
2   Add the washed, trimmed, blanched, refreshed tongues and the remainder of the ingredients.
3   Bring to the boil, skim.
4   Cover with a tight-fitting lid and simmer in a moderate oven, approx. 1½ hr.
5   Remove the tongues, skin them and serve whole in an entrée dish.
6   Correct the sauce and strain over the tongues.

44   Braised Lambs' Hearts   *One per portion*   *Cœur d'Agneau Braisé*

100 g	carrots	4 oz
	bouquet garni	
10 g	tomato purée	½ oz
25 g	dripping	1 oz
100 g	onions	4 oz
500 ml	brown stock (approx.)	1 pt
250 ml	espagnole	½ pt

1   Remove tubes and excess fat.
2   Season and colour quickly on all sides in hot fat to seal the pores.
3   Place into a small braising pan (any pan with a tight-fitting lid which may be placed in the oven) or in a casserole.
4   Place the hearts on the lightly fried, sliced vegetables.
5   Add the stock, which should be two-thirds of the way up the meat, season lightly.
6   Add the bouquet garni and tomato purée and if available add a few mushroom trimmings.
7   Bring to the boil, skim and cover with a lid and cook in a moderate oven (150°–200°C).
8   After approx. 1½ hr cooking add the espagnole, re-boil, skim and strain.
9   Continue cooking till tender.
10   Remove hearts and correct the seasoning, colour and consistency of the sauce.
11   Pass the sauce on to the sliced hearts in an entrée dish.

45   Stuffed Braised Lambs' Hearts   *Cœur d'Agneau Braisé Farci*

50 g	chopped suet	2 oz
50 g	chopped onions cooked in a little fat without colour	2 oz
	1 egg yolk or small egg	
100 g	white breadcrumbs	4 oz
	pinch powdered thyme	
	pinch chopped parsley	
	salt, pepper	

Combine all the ingredients together.

Prepare as for Braised Hearts, then after removing the tubes fill with the stuffing. Place on a lightly fried bed of roots and continue as for Braised Hearts.

Serve in halves in an entrée dish with the corrected sauce.

46 Fried Lambs' Liver and Bacon   *Foie d'Agneau au Lard*

300 g	liver	12 oz
125 ml	jus-lié	1 gill
50 g	streaky bacon	2 oz
50 g	fat for frying	2 oz

1 Skin the liver and remove the gristle.
2 Cut in thin slices on the slant.
3 Pass the slices of liver through seasoned flour.
4 Shake off the excess flour.
5 Quickly fry on both sides in hot fat.
6 Remove the rind and bone from the bacon and grill on both sides.
7 Serve the liver and bacon in an entree dish or silver oval flat with a cordon of jus-lié and a sauceboat of jus-lié separately.

47 Kidney Sauté *4 portions*   *Rognons Sautés*

	8 sheep's kidneys	
250ml	demi-glace	$\frac{1}{2}$p
50g	butter or fat	2oz

1 Skin and halve the kidneys.
2 Remove the sinews.
3 Cut each half into three or five pieces.
4 Season.
5 Fry quickly in a frying-pan using the butter for approx. 4–5 min.
6 Place in a colander to drain.
7 Add to the finished sauce.
8 Do not re-boil.
9 Serve in an entree dish.

48 Kidney Sauté Turbigo   *Rognons Sautés Turbigo*

As for Kidney Sauté, then add 100 g (4 oz) small button mushrooms cooked in a little fat and 8 small 2 cm (1 in) long grilled or fried chipolatas. Serve with the kidneys in an entrée dish.

49 Grilled Kidneys   *Rognons Grillés*

1 Season the prepared skewered kidneys.
2 Brush with melted fat or oil.
3 Place on pre-heated greased grill bars or on a greased baking tray.

4   Grill fairly quickly on both sides, approx. 5–10 min depending
     on size.
5   Serve on an oval flat dish with parsley butter, picked watercress
     and straw potatoes.

50 Braised Lambs' Sweetbreads (White)   *Ris d'Agneau Braisé (à blanc)*

	8 sweetbreads	
100 g	carrot	4 oz
250 ml	veal stock	½ pt
100 g	onion	4 oz
	bouquet garni	
	salt, pepper	

1   Wash, blanch, refresh and trim the sweetbreads.
2   Season and place in a casserole or plat à sauté on a bed of
     roots.
3   Add the bouquet garni and stock.
4   Cover with buttered greaseproof paper and a lid.
5   Cook gently in a moderate oven (150°–200°C) for approx. 1 hr.
6   Serve dressed in an entrée dish with some of the cooking
     liquor thickened with diluted arrowroot, and passed on to the
     sweet-breads.

51 Braised Lambs' Sweetbreads (Brown)   *Ris d'Agneau Braisé (à brun)*

1   Prepare as in previous recipe.
2   Place on a bed of roots which has been lightly coloured.
3   Barely cover with brown veal stock, or half brown veal stock and
     half jus-lié.
4   Cook in a moderate oven (150°–200°C) without a lid, basting
     frequently (approx. 1 hr).
5   Dress neatly in an entrée dish, cover with the corrected, strained
     sauce.
6   If veal stock is used thicken with arrowroot.

52 Sautéd Sweetbread   *Ris d'Agneau Sauté*

53 Grilled Sweetbread   *Ris d'Agneau Grillé*

Proceed as for recipes 39 and 40, page 206.

10
Beef

BUTCHERY

1 Beef (Fig. 5) Side of Beef, approx. weight 180 kg (360 lb)   *Bœuf*

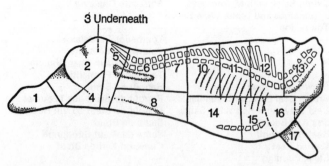

FIG. 5 SIDE

2 Hindquarter of Beef (Fig. 6)

3	Joint	Uses	Approx. Weight	
			(kilo)	(lb)
1	Shin	Consommé, Beef Tea, Stewing	7	14
2	Topside	Braising, Stewing, second-class Roasting	10	20
3	Silverside	Pickled in brine then Boiled	14	28
4	Thick flank	Braising and Stewing	12	24
5	Rump	Grilling and Frying as Steaks Braised in the piece	10	20
6	Sirloin	Roasting, Grilling and Frying Steaks	9	18
7	Wing Ribs	Roasting, Grilling and Frying Steaks	5	10
8	Thin Flank	Stewing, Boiling, Sausages	10	20
9	Fillet	Roasting, Grilling and Frying	3	6
	Fat and Kidney		10	20
		Total weight	90	180

4 Forequarter of Beef (Fig. 7)

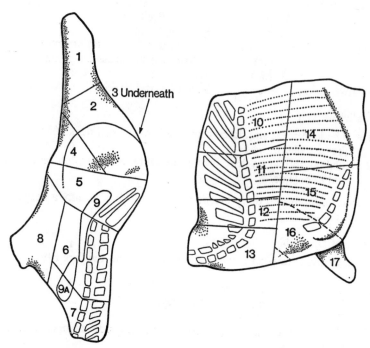

FIG. 6 HINDQUARTER   FIG. 7 FOREQUARTER

5

Joint	Uses	Approx. Weight	
		(kilo)	(lb)
10 Fore Rib	Roasting and Braising	8	16
11 Middle Rib	Roasting and Braising	10	20
12 Chuck Rib	Stewing and Braising	15	30
13 Sticking Piece	Stewing and Sausages	9	18
14 Plate	Stewing and Sausages	10	20
15 Brisket	Pickled in brine and Boiled, Pressed Beef	19	38
16 Leg of Mutton Cut	Braising and Stewing	11	22
17 Shank	Consomme, Beef Tea	6	12
	Total weight	88	176

6 Beef Offal

Offal	French	Uses
Tongue	la Langue	Pickled in brine, Boiling, Braising
Heart	le Cœur	Braising
Liver	le Foie	Braising, Frying
Kidney	le Rognon	Stewing, Soup
Sweetbread	le Ris	Braising, Frying
Tripe	la Tripe	Boiling, Braising
Tail	la Queue	Braising, Soup
Suet	la Graisse de Rognon	Suet Paste and Stuffing or rendered down for first-class Dripping
Bones	les Os (m.)	Beef Stocks
Marrow	la Moêlle	Savouries and Sauces

7 Quality of Beef

1 The lean meat should be bright red, with small flecks of white fat (marbled).
2 The fat should be firm, brittle in texture, creamy white in colour and odourless.

Older animals and dairy breeds have fat which is usually a deeper yellow colour.

8 Order of Dissection

A whole side is divided between the wing ribs and the fore ribs.

Dissection of the Hindquarter

1 Remove the rump suet and kidney.
2 Remove the thin flank.
3 Divide the loin and rump from the leg (topside, silverside, thick flank and shin).
4 Remove the fillet.

5   Divide rump from the sirloin.
6   Remove the wing ribs.
7   Remove the shin.
8   Bone-out the aitchbone.
9   Divide the leg into the three remaining joints (silverside, topside and thick flank).

Dissection of the Forequarter
1   Remove the shank.
2   Divide in half down the centre.
3   Take off the fore ribs.
4   Divide into joints.

9   Brine

2½ litres	cold water	4 qt
15 g	saltpetre	¾ oz
½–1 kg	salt	1–2 lb

Boil the ingredients together for 10 minutes, skimming frequently. Strain into a china, wooden or earthenware container. When the brine is cold, add the meat. Immerse the meat for up to 10 days.

10   Preparation of Joints and Cuts

Shin
Bone-out, remove excess sinew. Cut or chop as required.

Topside
Roasting—remove excess fat, cut into joints and tie with string.
Braising—as for roasting.
Stewing—cut into dice or steaks as required.

Silverside
Remove the thigh bone. This joint is usually kept whole and pickled in brine.

Thick Flank
As for Topside.

Rump
Bone-out. Cut off the first outside slice for pies and puddings. Cut into approx. 1½ cm (¾ in) slices for steaks. The point steak is cut from the pointed end of the slice.
   A triangular joint can be taken from the rump (culotte) and braised.

11 Sirloin

ROASTING

Method I. Whole on the bone   *Aloyau de Bœuf*
Saw through the chine bone, lift back the covering fat in one piece
for approx. 8 cm (4 in). Trim off the sinew and replace the covering
fat. String if necessary. Note the fillet has been removed.

Method II. Boned-out   *Contrefilet de Bœuf*
The fillet is removed and the sirloin boned-out and the sinew is
removed as above. Remove the excess fat and sinew from the boned
side. This joint may be roasted open, or rolled and tied with string.

GRILLING AND FRYING

Prepare as for Method II above and cut into steaks according to
requirements.

Minute Steaks   *Entrecôte Minute*
Cut into 1 cm ($\frac{1}{2}$ in) slices, flatten with a cutlet bat dipped in
water, making as thin as possible, then trim.

Sirloin Steaks   *Entrecôte*
Cut into 1 cm ($\frac{1}{2}$ in) slices and trim. Approx. weight 150 g (6 oz).

Double Sirloin Steaks   *Entrecôte Double*
Cut into 2 cm (1 in) thick slices and trim. Approx. weight 250–300 g
(10–12 oz).

Porterhouse and T-bone Steak
These are complete slices through the sirloin including the bone and
fillet.

12 Fillet   *Filet de Bœuf*

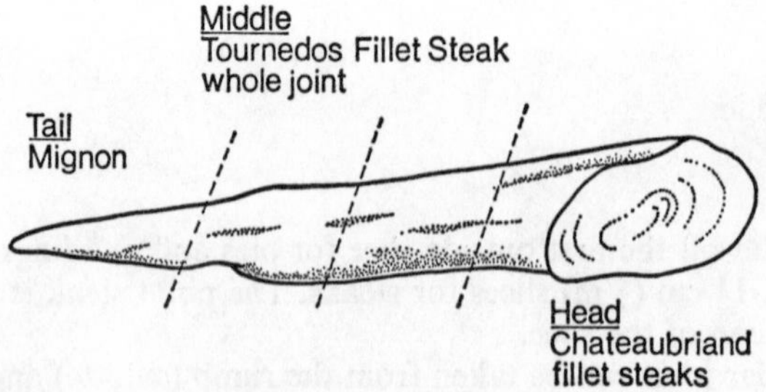

FIG. 8

As a fillet of beef can vary from 2½–4½ kg (5–9 lb) it follows that there must be considerable variation in the number of steaks obtained from it. A typical breakdown of a 3 kg (6 lb) fillet would be as shown in the diagram.

Châteaubriand   Double Fillet Steak 3–8 cm (1¼–4 in) thick
   2–4 portions.   Average weight 300 g–1 kilo (¾–2 lb).
   This is cut from the head of the fillet, trim off all nerve and leave a little fat on the steak.

Fillet Steaks   Approx. 4 steaks of 100–150 g (4–6 oz) each
              1½–2 cm (¾–1 in) thick
   These are cut as shown in the diagram and trimmed as for châteaubriand.

Tournedos   Approx. 6–8 at 100 g (4 oz) each
           2–3 cm (1–1½ in) thick
   Continue cutting down the fillet. Remove all the nerve and all the fat and tie each tournedo with string.

Tail of the Fillet (Mignon)   Approx. ½ kg (1 lb)
Remove all fat and sinew and slice or mince as required.

Whole Fillet
Preparation for roasting and pot roasting (poêlé).
   Remove the head and tail of the fillet leaving an even centre piece from which all nerve and fat is removed. This is then frequently larded by inserting pieces of fat bacon cut into long strips, with a larding needle.

13   Wing Rib   *Côte de Bœuf*
This joint usually consists of the last three rib bones which, because of their curved shape act as a natural trivet and because of its prime quality make it a first-class roasting joint, for hot or cold, particularly when it is to be carved in front of the customer.
   To prepare, cut seven-eighths of the way through the spine or chine bone, remove the nerve, saw through the rib bones on the underside 4–8 cm (2–4 in) from the end. Tie firmly with string.

Thin Flank   *Bavette*
Trim off excessive fat and cut or roll as required.

14   Forequarter

Fore ribs and middle ribs—prepare as for wing ribs.

Chuck Ribs
Sticking Piece
Brisket   } bone-out, remove excess sinew, use as
Plate   required.
Leg of Mutton Cut
Shank

15   Beef Offal

Tongue	Remove bone and gristle from the throat end.
Hearts	Remove tubes and excess fat.
Liver	Skin, remove the gristle and cut in thin slices on the slant.
Kidney	Skin, remove the gristle and cut as required.
Sweetbreads	Wash well, trim, blanch and refresh.
Tripe	Wash well and soak in cold water, then cut into even pieces.
Tail	Cut between the natural joints, trim off excess fat. The large pieces may be split in two.

RECIPES

16	**Roasting of Beef**	*Bœuf Rôti*
17	**Roast Sirloin of Beef (on the bone)**	*Aloyau de Bœuf Rôti*
18	**Roast Boned Sirloin of Beef**	*Contrefilet de Bœuf Rôti*
19	**Roast Ribs of Beef**	*Côte de Bœuf Rôtie*
20	**Roast Fillet of Beef**	*Filet de Bœuf Rôti*

Suitable Joints
First class—Sirloin, wing ribs, fore ribs, fillet.
Second class—Topside, middle ribs.

1   Season the joints with salt and place on a trivet, or bones, in a roasting tray.
2   Place a little dripping on top and cook in a hot oven (230°–250°C).
3   Baste frequently and reduce the heat gradually when necessary, as for example in the case of large joints.
4   Roasting time approx. 15 min per ½ kilo (1 lb) and 15 min over.
5   To test if cooked, place on a tray and press firmly in order to see if the juices released contain any blood.

6   Beef should be underdone and a little blood should show in the juice which issues when the meat is pressed.
7   On removing the joint from the oven rest for 15 min, then carve in thin slices against the grain.

Serve the slices neatly on an oval silver flat dish with a little gravy. Garnish with Yorkshire Pudding (Recipe 22) (allowing 25 g (1 oz) flour per portion) and watercress. Serve separately sauceboats of gravy and horseradish sauce.

Roast Gravy   *Jus Rôti*
1   Place the roasting tray on the stove over a gentle heat to allow the sediment to settle.
2   Carefully strain off the fat, leaving the sediment in the tray.
3   Return to the stove and brown carefully, swill (déglacé) with good brown stock.
4   Allow to simmer for a few minutes.
5   Correct the seasoning and colour, then strain and skim.

21   Horseradish Sauce   *8 portions*

25–30 g	grated horseradish	1–1½ oz
⅛ litre	lightly whipped cream	1 gill
	1 tbspn vinegar	
	pepper	
	salt	

Wash, peel and re-wash the horseradish and grate finely then mix all the ingredients together.

22   Yorkshire Pudding   *4–6 portions*

100 g	flour	4 oz
250 ml	milk or milk and water	½ pt
	1 egg	
25 g	dripping	1 oz
	salt	

Sieve flour and salt into a basin, make a well in the centre. Break in the egg, add half the liquid and whisk to a smooth mixture, gradually adding the rest of the liquid and allow to rest.

Select a shallow pan 12 cm (6 in) in diameter, preferably a plat à sauté. Add 25 g (1 oz) dripping from the joint and heat in the oven, pour in the mixture and cook in a hot oven (230°–250°C) for approx. 15 min.

23   Boiled Silverside, Carrots and Dumplings   *4 portions*

400 g	silverside	1 lb
200 g	carrots	8 oz
200 g	onions	8 oz
100 g	suet paste (p. 292)	4 oz

1   Soak the meat in cold water to remove excess brine for 1–2 hr.
2   Place in a saucepan and cover with cold water, bring to the boil and skim.
3   Add whole prepared onions and carrots and simmer gently for approx. 1¼ hr.
4   Divide the suet paste into 8 even pieces, lightly mould into balls.
5   Add the dumplings and simmer for a further 15–20 min.
6   Serve by carving the meat across the grain and dress on to a silver oval flat or in an entrée dish, garnish with carrots, onions and dumplings and moisten with a little of the cooking liquor.

NOTE. It is usual to cook a large joint of silverside (approx. 6 kg (12 lb)), in which case it is necessary to soak it overnight and to allow 25 min per ½ kg (1 lb) plus 25 min.

24   Boiled Beef—French Style   *4 portions*   *Bœuf Bouilli à la Française*

600 g	thin flank or brisket	1 lb 8 oz
200 g	onion	8 oz
100 g	turnip	4 oz
	small cabbage	
	1 head celery	
200 g	carrot	8 oz
200 g	leek	8 oz
	salt, pepper	

1   Blanch and refresh the meat.
2   Place in a clean pan and cover with cold water.
3   Bring to the boil and skim, season and allow to simmer.
4   Prepare all the vegetables by tying the celery and leek into bundles and by tying the cabbage to keep it in one piece, and leaving the rest of the vegetables whole.
5   After the meat has simmered for 30 min, add the celery, onions and carrots and continue cooking for 30 min.
6   Add the leek, cabbage and turnips and continue cooking till all is tender, approx. 2–2½ hr in all.
7   Serve by carving the meat in slices against the grain and dress on a silver oval flat, garnish with the vegetables and a little liquor over the meat.

This dish may be accompanied by pickled gherkins and coarse salt.

25   Beef Grills

Approximate weight per portion 100–150 g (4–6 oz); in many establishments these weights will be exceeded.

Rump Steak	—
Point Steak	—
Double Fillet Steak	Châteaubriand
Fillet Steak	Filet Grillé

Tournedos	Tournedos Grillé
Porterhouse or T-bone Steak	—
Sirloin Steak	Entrecôte Grillée
Double Sirloin Steak	Entrecôte Double
Minute Steak	Entrecôte Minute

All steaks are seasoned with salt and mill pepper and brushed on both sides with oil. Place on hot pre-heated greased grill bars. Turn half-way through by cooking and brush occasionally with oil and cook to the degree ordered by the customer.

Degrees of Cooking Grilled Meats

Rare	au bleu
Underdone	saignant
Just done	à point
Well done	bien cuit

Test with finger pressure and the springiness or resilience of the meat together with the amount of blood issuing from the meat indicates the degree to which the steak is cooked. This calls for experience, but if the meat is placed on a plate and tested, then the more underdone the steak the greater the springiness and the more blood will be shown on the plate.

Serve on an oval silver flat and garnish with watercress, deep-fried potato, usually straw potatoes (pommes pailles) and offer a suitable sauce, e.g. parsley butter or sauce béarnaise.

Garnishes for Grills

Henry IV	Watercress and Pommes Pont Neuf
Vert Pré	Watercress and Pommes Pailles

26 Sirloin Steak with Red Wine Sauce *4 portions* *Entrecôte Bordelaise*

150–200 g	4 sirloin steaks, each	6–8 oz
50 g	butter	2 oz
60 ml	red wine	$\frac{1}{8}$ pt
$\frac{1}{4}$ litre	bordelaise sauce (p. 23)	$\frac{1}{2}$ pt
100 g	bone marrow	4 oz
	chopped parsley	

1 Heat the butter in a sauté pan.
2 Season the steaks on both sides with salt and pepper.
3 Fry the steaks quickly on both sides, keep them underdone.
4 Dress the steaks on a serving dish.
5 Pour off the fat from the pan.
6 Déglacé with the red wine.
7 Reduce by a half.
8 Add the bordelaise sauce, reboil and correct seasoning.

9   Cut the marrow into ½ cm (¼ in) slices.
10   Poach the marrow in a little stock for 1–2 min.
11   Dress two slices of marrow on each steak.
12   Coat the steaks with the sauce.
13   Sprinkle with chopped parsley and serve.

27   **Sirloin Steak with Mushroom, Tomato**   *4 portions*   *Entrecôte Chasseur*
      and White Wine Sauce

150–200 g	4 sirloin steaks, each	6–8 oz
50 g	butter	2 oz
60 ml	dry white wine	⅛ pt
¼ litre	chasseur sauce (p. 23)	½ pt
	chopped parsley	

1   Heat the butter in a sauté pan.
2   Season the steaks on both sides with salt and pepper.
3   Fry the steaks quickly on both sides, keep them underdone.
4   Drain the steaks on a serving dish.
5   Pour off the fat from the pan.
6   Déglacé with the white wine.
7   Reduce by half.
8   Add the chasseur sauce, reboil, correct seasoning.
9   Coat the steaks with the sauce.
10   Sprinkle with chopped parsley and serve.

28   **Tournedos**

Season and shallow fry on both sides in a sauté pan and serve with
the appropriate garnish or sauce. It is usual to serve the tournedos
cooked underdone on a round croûte of fried bread.

29   —   *Tournedos Bordelaise*

Cook as above and serve Bordelaise Sauce (page 23).

30   —   *Tournedos Chasseur*

Cook as above and sauce over with Chasseur Sauce (page 23).

31   —   *Tournedos aux Champignons*

Cook as above and sauce over with a mushroom sauce made from
¼ litre (½ pt) demi-glace sauce to which has been added 100 g (4 oz)
of sliced button mushrooms cooked in butter.

32   —   *Tournedos Parmentier*

Cook as above and garnish with parmentier potatoes (page 283) and
noisette butter.

33   Brown Beef Stew   *Ragoût de Bœuf*

400 g	prepared stewing beef	1 lb
75 g	carrots	3 oz
25 g	flour	1 oz
750 ml	brown stock	1½ pt
	seasoning	
25 g	dripping	1 oz
75 g	onions	3 oz
	1 tbspn tomato purée	
	bouquet garni	
	clove of garlic (if desired)	

1   Remove excess sinew and fat from the beef.
2   Cut into 2 cm (1 in) pieces.
3   Fry quickly in hot fat till lightly browned.
4   Add the mirepoix (roughly cut onion and carrot) and continue frying to a golden colour.
5   Add the flour and mix in and singe in the oven or brown on top of the stove for a few minutes.
6   Add the tomato purée and stir in with a wooden spoon.
7   Add the stock, bring to the boil and skim.
8   Add the bouquet garni, season and cover with a lid and simmer gently till cooked, preferably in the oven, approx. 1½–2 hr.
9   When cooked place the meat into a clean pan.
10 Correct the sauce and pass on to the meat.
11 Serve in an entrée dish with chopped parsley sprinkled on top of the meat.

34   Brown Beef Stew with Vegetables   *Ragoût de Bœuf aux Légumes*

As above with a garnish of vegetables, that is, turned glazed carrots, turnips and button onions; peas and diamonds of French beans. Mushrooms may also be used. The vegetables are cooked separately and they may be mixed in, arranged in groups or sprinkled on top of the stew.

To cook carrots and turnips glacé (glazed), turn or cut into even shapes, barely cover with water in separate thick-bottomed pans and add 25–50 g (1–2 oz) margarine per ½ kg (1 lb) of vegetables. Season very lightly and allow to cook fairly quickly so as to evaporate the water. Check that the vegetables are cooked, if not add a little more water, then toss over a quick fire to give a glossy appearance and a little colour. Care should be taken with turnips as they may break up easily. This also applies to button onions which may be cooked as above or they may be coloured first in the margarine and then allowed to cook slowly with a little stock or water, in a saucepan with a lid.

Button mushrooms should be used for this purpose, and if of good quality, need not be peeled, but a slice should be removed from the base of the stalk. Wash well, then use whole, halved, quartered or turned depending on size. Cook in a little stock and butter and season lightly, cover with a lid and cook for a few minutes only.

35   Beef Stew with Red Wine Sauce   *Ragoût de Bœuf au Vin Rouge*

As for brown stew using 125–250 ml ($\frac{1}{4}$–$\frac{1}{2}$ pt) of red wine in place of the same amount of stock. It is usually found necessary to add a few drops of cochineal to give a typical red wine appearance. A suitable wine for this purpose is a Beaujolais.

36   Sauté of Beef   *Sauté de Bœuf*

This term is often applied to a brown beef stew, and it will be found that the word 'sauté' in this case is used instead of the word 'ragoût'. Alternatively, a sauté may be made using first-quality meat, e.g. fillet. The meat is then sautéd quickly and served in a finished sauce, this would be a typical à la carte dish.

See Method of Cookery, pages 5 and 6.

37   Beef Strogonoff   *4 portions*   *Sauté de Bœuf Strogonoff*

400 g	fillet of beef (tail end)	1 lb
50 g	butter	2 oz
25 g	finely chopped shallots	1 oz
125 ml	cream	$\frac{1}{4}$ pt
	juice of $\frac{1}{4}$ lemon	
	chopped parsley	

1   Cut the meat into strips approx 1 cm × 5 cm.
2   Place the butter in a sauteuse over a fierce heat.
3   Add the beef strips, season with salt and pepper and allow to cook rapidly for a few seconds. The beef should be brown but underdone.
4   Drain the beef into a colander.
5   Pour the butter back into the pan.
6   Add the shallots, cover with a lid and allow to cook gently until tender.
7   Drain off the fat.
8   Add the cream and reduce by a quarter.
9   Add the lemon juice and the beef strips—do not re-boil.
10   Correct the seasoning.
11   Place in serving dish and sprinkle with chopped parsley.

38 Curried Beef

Currie de Bœuf

500 g	stewing beef	1 lb 4 oz
	1 clove garlic	
10 g	curry powder	½ oz
10 g	tomato purée	½ oz
½ litre	stock or water	1 pt
25 g	chopped chutney	1 oz
	salt	
25 g	dripping	1 oz
200 g	onions	8 oz
10 g	flour	½ oz
5 g	desiccated coconut	¼ oz
10 g	sultanas	½ oz
50 g	chopped apple	2 oz
100 g	rice (long-grain)	4 oz
1½ litres	water	at least 3 pt

1 Trim the meat and cut into even pieces.
2 Season and quickly colour in hot fat.
3 Add the chopped onion and chopped garlic, cover with a lid and sweat for a few minutes.
4 Drain off the surplus fat.
5 Add the curry powder and flour, mix in and cook out.
6 Mix in the tomato purée, gradually add the hot stock, thoroughly stir, bring to the boil, season and skim.
7 Allow to simmer and add the rest of the ingredients.
8 Cover with a lid and simmer in the oven or on top of the stove till cooked.
9 Correct the seasoning and consistency, skim off all fat. At this stage a little cream may be added for first-class service.
10 Serve in an entrée dish accompanied with rice which may be plain boiled, pilaff or pilaff with saffron.

Plain Boiled Rice 4 portions

100 g	rice (long grain)	4 oz
1½ litres	water (at least)	3 pt
	salt	

1 Pick and wash the long-grain rice.
2 Add to plenty of boiling, salt water.
3 Stir to the boil and allow to simmer gently till tender, approx. 12–15 min.
4 Wash well under running water, drain and place on a sieve and cover with a cloth.
5 Place on a tray in a moderate oven or on the hot plate until hot.
6 Serve in a vegetable dish separately.

Other Accompaniments to Curry

There are many other accompaniments to curry which may be served, for example grilled Bombay Duck and Popadums which are grilled or deep fried, and served separately on a silver dish with a dish paper. Also:

chopped chutney
sultanas
desiccated coconut
slices of lemon
chopped apple
chow-chow
quarters of orange
sliced banana
chopped onions

39   Steak Pudding   *4 portions*

400 g	prepared stewing beef, few drops Worcester Sauce	1 lb
	tspn chopped parsley	
	salt	
	1 dspn flour	
50–100 g	onion (if required)	2–4 oz
125 ml	water (approx)	1 gill
	pepper	
200 g	suet paste (p. 292)	8 oz

1   Line a greased ¾ litre (1½ pt) basin with three-quarters of the suet paste and retain one-quarter for the top.
2   Mix all the other ingredients together.
3   Place in the basin with the water to within 1 cm (½ in) of top.
4   Moisten the edge of the suet paste, cover with the top and seal firmly.
5   Cover with greased greaseproof paper and also, if possible, a pudding cloth securely tied with string, or foil.
6   Cook in a steamer for at least 3½ hr.
7   Serve with the paper and cloth removed, clean the basin and place on a silver round flat dish and fasten a serviette round the basin.

Extra gravy may be served separately.

Suet Paste   4 portions

200 g	flour	8 oz
	¼ tspn salt	
125 ml	water (approx.)	1 gill
	½ tspn baking-powder	
75–100 g	prepared beef suet	3–4 oz

1   Sieve the flour and salt and baking powder into a basin.
2   Remove all the skin from the suet and chop finely, using a little of the flour to prevent stickiness.
3   Mix in with the flour and make a well in the centre.
4   Add the water and mix to a soft dough.

40   Steak and Kidney Pudding

As for Steak pudding with the addition of 50–100 g (2–4 oz) ox
kidney, or 1 or 2 sheep's kidneys with the skin and gristle removed
and then cut into neat pieces.

41   Steak, Kidney and Mushroom Pudding

As steak and kidney pudding with the addition of 50–100 g (2–4 oz)
washed, sliced or quartered button mushrooms.

42   Steak Pie   *4 portions*

400 g	prepared stewing beef	1 lb
	salt	
	few drops Worcester Sauce	
	1 tspn chopped parsley	
50–100 g	chopped onion (if desired)	2–4 oz
	pepper	
125 ml	water or stock	1 gill
100 g	puff paste or rough puff (p. 290)	4 oz

1   Cut the meat into 2 cm square (1 in) strips.
2   Cut into thin slices or into small squares.
3   Mix with the remainder of the ingredients.
4   Place in a ½ litre (1 pt) pie dish with a pie funnel in the centre if
  the level of the meat is below that of the rim of the dish. The
  amount of water should barely cover the meat.
5   Roll out the pastry, eggwash the rim of the pie dish and line
  with a 1 cm (½ in) strip of pastry, press down firmly and
  eggwash.
6   Without stretching the pastry, cover the pie and seal firmly.
7   Trim off the excess paste with a sharp knife, knotch the edge
  neatly, eggwash and decorate.
8   Allow to rest in a cool place for a long as possible.
9   Place in a hot oven (approx. Reg. 7 with a 1–9 Regulo) for
  10–15 min till the paste is set and lightly coloured.
10   Cover with greaseproof paper and reduce Regulo to 5 for 15
  min, then to 3 for a further 15 min, then to 1 for 15 min.
11   Complete the cooking on Regulo 1 or 2 ensuring that the liquid
  is simmering in the pie.
12   Allow 2–2½ hr cooking in all.
13   Serve with the pie dish thoroughly cleaned, place on an oval
  silver flat dish and surround the pie dish with a pie collar.

43   Steak and Kidney Pie

As for steak pie with the addition of 50–100 g (2–4 oz) kidney or 1 or
2 sheep's kidneys with skin and gristle removed and cut into neat
pieces.

44   Steak, Kidney and Mushroom Pie

As for steak and kidney pie with the addition of 50–100 g (2–4 oz) washed sliced or quartered button mushrooms.

45   Carbonnade of Beef   *4 portions*   *Carbonnade de Bœuf*

400 g	lean beef (e.g. Topside)	1 lb
500 ml	brown stock (approx.)	1 pt
25 g	dripping	1 oz
100 g	castor sugar	$\frac{1}{2}$ oz
200 g	sliced onions	8 oz
250 ml	beer	$\frac{1}{2}$ pt
25 g	flour	1 oz

1   Cut meat into thin slices.
2   Season with salt and pepper and pass through flour.
3   Quickly colour on both sides in hot fat and place in a casserole.
4   Fry the onions to a light brown colour.
5   Add to the meat.
6   Add the beer and sugar and sufficient brown stock to cover the meat.
7   Cover with a tight-fitting lid and simmer gently in a moderate oven (150°–200°C) till the meat is tender. Approx. 2 hr.
8   Skim and correct the seasoning.
9   Serve in the casserole or in an entrée dish.

46   Goulash of Beef   *4 portions*   *Goulash de Bœuf*

400 g	prepared stewing beef	1 lb
10–25 g	paprika	$\frac{1}{2}$–1 oz
25 g	tomato purée	1 oz
35 g	lard	$1\frac{1}{2}$ oz
125 ml	choux paste (p. 293)	1 gill
100 g	onions	4 oz
25 g	flour	1 oz
750 ml	stock or water (approx.)	$1\frac{1}{2}$ pt
	8 turned potatoes or small new potatoes	

1   Remove excess fat from the beef.
2   Cut into 2 cm (1 in) square pieces.
3   Season and fry in the hot fat till slightly coloured.
4   Add the chopped onion.
5   Cover with a lid and sweat gently for 3 or 4 min.
6   Add the flour and paprika and mix in with a wooden spoon.
7   Cook out in the oven or on top of the stove.
8   Add the tomato purée, mix in.
9   Gradually add the stock, stir to the boil, skim, season and cover with a lid.

10. Allow to simmer preferably in the oven approx. $1\frac{1}{2}$–2 hr, till the meat is tender.
11 Add the potatoes and check that they are covered with the sauce. (Add more stock if required.)
12 Re-cover with the lid and cook gently till the potatoes are cooked.
13 Skim and correct the seasoning and consistency. For first-class service a little cream may be added at the last moment.
14 Serve in an entrée dish sprinkled with a few gnocchis.

Choux paste for Gnocchi (as a garnish, sufficient for 8 portions)

125 ml	water	$\frac{1}{4}$ pt
60 g	flour	$2\frac{1}{2}$ oz
	salt	
50 g	margarine	2 oz
	2 eggs	

1 Bring the water, margarine and salt to the boil in a small saucepan and draw aside.
2 Add the sifted flour and mix in with a wooden spoon.
3 Return to the stove and cook out for a few minutes till the mixtures leaves the side of the pan, stirring continuously.
4 Remove from the heat and allow to cool, add the eggs one by one, beating well.
5 Place the mixture into a piping bag with a $\frac{1}{2}$ cm ($\frac{1}{4}$ in) or 1 cm ($\frac{1}{2}$ in) plain tube.
6 Pipe into a shallow pan of gently simmering salted water, cutting the mixture into 2 cm (1 in) lengths with a small knife, dipping the knife into the water frequently to prevent sticking.
7 Poach very gently for approx. 10 min. If not required at once lift out carefully into cold water and when required reheat in hot salt water.

47 Beef Olives   *4 portions*   *Paupiettes de Bœuf*

400 g	lean beef	1 lb
100 g	carrot	4 oz
35 g	dripping	$1\frac{1}{2}$ oz
500–750 ml	brown stock	1–$1\frac{1}{2}$ pt
	bouquet garni	
50 g	stuffing	2 oz
100 g	onion	4 oz
25 g	flour	1 oz
10 g	tomato purée	$\frac{1}{2}$ oz

1 Prepare the stuffing.
2 Cut the meat into thin slices across the grain and bat out.
3 Trim to approx. 8 × 6 cm (4 × 3 in), chop the trimmings finely and add to the stuffing.

4   Season the slices of meat with salt and pepper and spread a quarter of the stuffing down the centre of each slice.
5   Roll up neatly and secure with string.
6   Fry off the meat to a light brown colour add the mirepoix and continue cooking to a golden colour.
7   Drain off the fat into a clean pan and make up to 25 g (1 oz) fat if there is not enough.
8   Add the flour and cook to a brown roux.
9   Mix in the tomato purée, cool, and add the boiling stock.
10   Bring to the boil, skim, season and pour on to the meat and vegetables.
11   Add the bouquet garni.
12   Cover with a lid and allow to simmer gently, preferably in the oven, approx. 1½–2 hr.
13   Remove the string from the meat and place in an entrée dish.
14   Skim and correct the sauce and pass on to the meat.

Stuffing   4 portions

50 g	white crumbs	2 oz
	1 tspn chopped parsley	
	pinch of thyme	
	approx ½ egg to bind	
5 g	prepared chopped suet	¼ oz
25 g	finely chopped sweated onion	1 oz
	salt, pepper	

Mix all the ingredients together with the chopped meat trimmings. Other stuffings may be used, for example, sausage meat.

48   Braised Steaks

400 g	stewing beef	1 lb
75 g	carrots	3 oz
25 g	flour	1 oz
750 ml	brown stock	1½ pt
	seasoning	
25 g	dripping	1 oz
75 g	onions	3 oz
	1 tbspn tomato purée	
	bouquet garni	
	clove of garlic (if desired)	

1   Remove excess sinew and fat from the beef.
2   Cut into ½–1 cm (¼–½ in) thick steaks.
3   Fry quickly in hot fat till lightly browned.
4   Add the mirepoix (roughly cut onion and carrot) and continue frying to a golden colour.
5   Add the flour and mix in and singe in the oven or brown on top of the stove for a few minutes.
6   Add the tomato purée and stir in with a wooden spoon.

7   Add the stock, bring to the boil and skim.
8   Add the bouquet garni, season and cover with a lid and simmer
     gently till cooked, preferably in the oven, approx. 1½–2 hr.
9   When cooked place the meat into a clean pan.
10   Correct the sauce and pass on to the meat.
11   Serve in an entrée dish with chopped parsley sprinkled on top of
     the meat.
12   Braised steaks may be garnished with vegetables cut in
     macédoine or jardinière or turned.

49 Braised Beef *4 portions*   *Bœuf Braisé*

400 g	lean beef (topside or thick flank)	1 lb
100 g	carrots	4 oz
	bouquet garni	
10 g	tomato purée	½ oz
25 g	dripping	1 oz
100 g	onions	4 oz
500 ml	brown stock (approx.)	1 pt
250 ml	espagnole	½ pt

Method I
1   Trim and tie the joint securely.
2   Season and colour quickly on all sides in hot fat to seal the
     pores.
3   Place into a small braising pan (any pan with a tight-fitting lid
     which may be placed in the oven) or in a casserole.
4   Place the joint on the lightly fried, sliced vegetables.
5   Add the stock, which should be two-thirds of the way up the
     meat, season lightly.
6   Add the bouquet garni and tomato purée and if available add a
     few mushroom trimmings.
7   Bring to the boil, skim and cover with a lid and cook in a
     moderate oven (150°–200°C).
8   After approx. 1½ hr cooking remove the meat.
9   Add the espagnole, re-boil, skim and strain.
10   Replace the meat, do not cover, but baste frequently and con-
     tinue cooking approx. 2–2½ hr in all. Braised beef should be
     well cooked and approx. 35 min per ½ kg (1 lb) plus 35 min
     may be allowed for cooking.
     To test if cooked, pierce with a trussing needle, which should
     penetrate the meat easily and there should be no signs of
     blood.
11   Remove the joint and correct the colour, seasoning and
     consistency of the sauce.
12   To serve: remove the string and carve two or three 2 mm thick
     (⅛ in) slices across the grain. Neatly dress in front of the joint.

Pour some of the sauce over the joint and the slices and serve the remainder of the sauce in a sauceboat.

Suitable garnishes, spring vegetables (see page 165, recipe 34), or noodles (page 92).

Method II
As for Method I, but use for cooking liquor either (*a*) jus-lié or (*b*) half brown stock and half demi-glace or espagnole.

Method III
As for Method I, but when the joint and vegetables are browned sprinkle with 25 g (1 oz) flour and singe in the oven, add the tomato purée and stock, bouquet garni, season and complete the recipe.

50   Braised Steak and Dumplings

1   Cut the beef into ½–1 cm (¼–½ in) thick steaks and proceed as for brown beef stew, page 165.
2   Prepare 100 g (4 oz) suet paste (page 292) and make 8 dumplings.
3   After the meat has cooked for 1½ hr pick out the meat and place into a clean pan.
4   Strain the sauce on to the meat.
5   Re-boil and correct the consistency, which should be fairly thin and sufficient to cover the dumplings.
6   When boiling add the dumplings, cover with a lid.
7   Complete the cooking preferably in the oven ¾–1 hr (150°–200°C).
8   Serve in an entrée dish.

51   Minced Beef   *4 portions*   *Hachis de Bœuf*

300 g	lean minced beef	12 oz
25 g	dripping	1 oz
	jus-lié or stock	
50–100 g	chopped onion	2–4 oz
250 ml	demi-glace	½ pt
	seasoning	

Method I: Using raw minced beef
1   Sweat the onion in the dripping.
2   Add the beef and cook to a light colour.
3   Add the liquid, season.
4   Bring to the boil, skim and simmer gently till cooked, approx. ½ hr.

If using stock, thickening may be added by either adding (*a*) 10 g (½ oz) flour after cooking the meat and before adding the stock or (*b*) by finishing with approx. 5 g (¼ oz) of diluted cornflour or fécule.

Method II: Using cooked beef
Sweat the onion in the dripping and add the minced cooked beef,

add the demi-glace or jus-lié, bring to the boil and skim, season and boil for 10 min.

To aid presentation it is usually served with a border of piped duchess potatoes previously dried, eggwashed and browned. Any suitable dish may be used, e.g. flat or entrée.

52 Rissoles *4 portions*

200 g	cooked minced beef or any cooked meat	8 oz
10 g	chopped onion seasoning	½ oz
10 g	dripping	½ oz
125 ml	demi-glace	¼ pt
200 g	short, puff or rough puff pastry (p. 290)	8 oz

1 Sweat the onion in the dripping.
2 Add the demi-glace and reduce by half.
3 Add the meat, boil well.
4 Season and allow to cool.
5 Roll out the paste thinly into eight 6 cm (3 in) diameter rounds.
6 Place the meat into the centre of each of four of the rounds and eggwash the edges.
7 Place on the four tops and seal well.
8 Deep fry in hot fat (180°C).
9 Serve on a dish paper with fried parsley and a suitable sauce separately, e.g. tomato or demi-glace.

In place of pastry, rissoles may be egg and crumbed.

53 Croquettes of Beef *4 portions*   *Croquettes de Bœuf*

200 g	minced cooked meat	8 oz
50 g	margarine	2 oz
50 g	flour	2 oz
250 ml	stock	½ pt
	1 yolk	
	eggwash	
	crumbs	

1 Make a thick sauce with the margarine, flour and stock or use the demi-glace.
2 Add the meat and bring to the boil.
3 Season, add the yolk and bring back to boiling point, stirring continuously.
4 Spread on a greased tray and cover with greased paper and allow to cool.
5 Divide into even pieces (four or eight).
6 Roll into approx. 4 cm (2 in) lengths.
7 Flour, egg and crumb and reshape and deep fry (180°C).
8 Serve as for Rissoles.

54   Durham Cutlets   *4 portions*

100 g	cooked minced beef	4 oz
10 g	chopped onion	½ oz
	tspn chopped parsley	
	crumbs	
	1 yolk	
100 g	mashed potato	4 oz
10 g	dripping	½ oz
	eggwash	

1   Sweat the onions in the dripping.
2   Add to the meat, potatoes, parsley and yolk.
3   Season and mix well.
4   Shape into cutlets.
5   Flour, egg crumb.
6   Deep fry (180°C).
7   Serve as for Rissoles.

55   Hamburg or Vienna Steak   *4 portions*   *Bitok*

200 g	lean minced beef	½ lb
10 g	dripping	½ oz
	1 small egg	
	salt	
25 g	chopped onion	1 oz
100 g	breadcrumbs	4 oz
	2 tbspn cold water (approx.)	
	pepper	

1   Cook the onions in the dripping without colour.
2   Add to the rest of the ingredients and mix in well.
3   Divide into four even pieces and using a little flour make into balls, flatten and shape round.
4   Shallow fry in hot fat on both sides, reducing the heat after the first few minutes, making certain they are cooked right through.
5   Serve with a demi-glace based sauce, e.g. sauce piquante (page 26). The steaks may be garnished with French fried onions (page 267) and sometimes with a fried egg.

56   Hamburger American Style

The hamburger is a popular dish at all levels of catering in the United States. In its simplest form it is 200 g (8 oz) of minced beef per portion, moulded into a round flat shape and cooked on both sides on a lightly greased hot griddle grill or pan. The hamburger should not be pricked whilst cooking as the juices would seep out leaving a dry product. In its simplest form when cooked it is placed between two halves of a freshly toasted round flat bun.

    There are many variations to the seasonings and ingredients which may be add to the minced beef, and many garnishes and sauces may accompany the hamburger. The bun may be plain or seeded (sesame seed).

57   Miroton of Beef *4 portions*   *Emincé de Bœuf en Miroton*

200 g	piece of cooked beef	8 oz
250 ml	demi-glace	½ pt
	2 tbspn white wine	
50 g	onion	2 oz
	dsspn vinegar	
25 g	margarine	1 oz

1   Cut the beef into thin slices.
2   Place in a shallow earthenware dish.
3   Fry the shredded onion in the margarine till cooked and a golden colour.
4   Drain off the fat.
5   Add the vinegar and wine and reduce by half.
6   Add the demi-glace, bring to the boil.
7   Skim and season.
8   Correct the consistency and pour over the meat.
9   Allow to heat through for a few minutes on top of the stove or in the oven.
10   Sprinkle with chopped parsley.
11   Serve on an underdish.

Sweet white wines are not generally suitable for meat cookery therefore a medium type should be selected, for example a Graves or Entre deux Mers.

58   Kromeski *4 portions*

100 g	cooked beef (or other meat)	¼ lb
10 g	margarine	½ oz
125 ml	stock and milk	¼ pt
	4 rashers streaky bacon	
	coating batter	
10 g	flour	½ oz
	1 yolk	

1   Make a panada by melting the margarine, mix in the flour and cook out for two or three minutes with no colour, gradually mix in the liquid till smooth, simmer for a few minutes.
2   Add the minced beef, season and mix in the yolk and allow to cool.
3   Roll into four even croquette-shaped pieces.
4   Cover each with a batted out rasher of bacon (or pig's caul).
5   Pass through flour and batter.
6   Deep fry in a hot fat (180°C).
7   Serve on a dish paper on an oval silver flat. Garnish with fried parsley.
8   Serve a tomato sauce (page 29) or demi-glace (page 23) sauce.

59   Corned Beef Hash   *4 portions*

400 g	corned beef	1 lb	
50 g	onion	2 oz	
400 g	potatoes (cooked)	1 lb	
100 g	butter	4 oz	

1   Finely chop the onions.
2   Melt the butter in a frying-pan.
3   Add the chopped onion and cook without colour.
4   Cut the corned beef and cooked potato into brunoise.
5   Mix the corned beef and potato and add to the pan.
6   Flatten the mixture out and cook until a golden brown.
7   Half fold the mixture and cook until crisp and brown all over.
8   Turn out on to a silver dish and serve sprinkled with chopped parsley. This is a dish of American origin which has several regional variations, e.g. fried dice of bacon, diced cooked beetroot may also be added.

60   Ox Tongue   *Langue de Bœuf*

Ox tongues are usually pickled in brine. Wash and place in cold water, bring to the boil, skim and simmer 3–4 hr. Cool slightly and peel off the skin and trim off the root. Secure into a neat shape either on a board or in a wooden frame. Unsalted ox tongues may also be braised whole.

61   Braised Ox Tongue with Madeira Sauce   *Langue de Bœuf Braisée au Madère*

Cut the cooked tongue in 3 mm ($\frac{1}{8}$ in) thick slices and arrange neatly in an entrée dish. Sauce over with madeira sauce and allow to heat through slowly and thoroughly.

62   Ox Hearts Braised   *Cœur de Bœuf Braisé*

Method I
1   Remove tubes and excess fat.
2   Season and colour quickly on all sides in hot fat to seal the pores.
3   Place into a braising pan (any pan with a tight-fitting lid which may be placed in the oven) or in a casserole.
4   Place the heart on the lightly fried, sliced vegetables.
5   Add the stock, which should be two-thirds of the way up the meat, season lightly.
6   Add the bouquet garni and tomato purée and if available add a few mushroom trimmings.
7   Bring to the boil, skim and cover with a lid and cook in a moderate oven (150°–200°C).
8   After approx. 4 hr. cooking remove the meat.

9　Add the espagnole, re-boil, skim and strain.

10　Replace the meat, do not cover, but baste frequently and continue cooking approx. 4–6 hr in all. Heart should be well cooked and approx. 35 min per ½ kg (1 lb) plus 35 min may be allowed for cooking.

To test if cooked, pierce with a trussing needle, which should penetrate the meat easily and there should be no signs of blood.

11　Remove the heart and correct the colour, seasoning and consistency of the sauce.

12　To serve: carve two or three 3 mm thick (⅛ in) slices. Neatly dress in front of the heart. Pour some of the sauce over the joint and the slices and serve the remainder of the sauce in a sauceboat.

Suitable garnishes, spring vegetables (see page 165, recipe 34), or noodles (page 92).

Method II

As for Method I, but use for cooking liquor either (a) jus-lié or (b) half brown stock and half demi-glace or espagnole.

Method III

As for Method I, but when the heart and vegetables are browned sprinkle with 25 g (1 oz) flour and singe in the oven, add the tomato purée and stock, bouquet garni, season and complete the recipe.

63　Braised Ox Liver and Onions　*4 portions*　　　*Foie de Bœuf Lyonnaise*

300 g	liver	12 oz
200 g	onions	½ lb
25 g	flour	1 oz
50 g	dripping	2 oz
500 ml	brown stock (approx.)	1 pt

1　Prepare the liver by removing the skin and tubes then cut into slices.

2　Pass the sliced liver through seasoned flour.

3　Fry on both sides in hot fat.

4　Place in a braising pan or casserole.

5　Fry the sliced onion to a light golden brown, drain and add to the liver.

6　Just cover with the stock.

7　Season and cover with a lid.

8　Simmer gently in the oven till tender approx. 1½–2 hr.

9　Correct the sauce.

10　Serve in an entrée dish.

64   Stewed Ox Kidney

400 g	ox kidney	1 lb
75 g	carrots	3 oz
25 g	flour	1 oz
750 ml	brown stock	1½ pt
	seasoning	
25 g	dripping	1 oz
75 g	onions	3 oz
	1 tbspn tomato purée	
	bouquet garni	
	clove of garlic (if desired)	

1   Remove excess sinew and fat from the kidney.
2   Cut into 2 cm (1 in) pieces.
3   Fry quickly in hot fat till lightly browned.
4   Add the mirepoix (roughly cut onion and carrot) and continue frying to a golden colour.
5   Add the flour and mix in and singe in the oven or brown on top of the stove for a few minutes.
6   Add the tomato purée and stir in with a wooden spoon.
7   Add the stock, bring to the boil and skim.
8   Add the bouquet garni, season and cover with a lid and simmer gently till cooked, preferably in the oven, approx. 1½–2 hr.
9   When cooked place the kidney into a clean pan.
10   Correct the sauce and pass on to the kidney.
11   Serve in an entrée dish with chopped parsley sprinkled on top of the kidney.

65   Ox Sweetbreads

First quality sweetbreads may be prepared as follows.

White Method

1   Wash, blanch, refresh and trim the sweetbreads.
2   Season and place in a casserole or plat à sauté on a bed of root vegetables.
3   Add the bouquet garni and stock.
4   Cover with buttered greaseproof paper and a lid.
5   Cook gently in a moderate oven (150°–200°C) for approx. 1 hr.
6   Serve dressed in an entrée dish with some of the cooking liquor thickened with diluted arrowroot, and passed on to the sweetbreads.

Brown Method

Prepare as in previous recipe and place on a bed of roots which has been lightly coloured. Barely cover with brown stock, or half brown stock and half jus-lié. Cook in a moderate oven (150°–200°C) without a lid, basting frequently (approx. 1 hr). Dress neatly in an

entrée dish, cover with the corrected, strained sauce. (If veal
stock is used thicken with arrowroot.)

66 Fried Ox Liver   *Foie de Bœuf Sauté*

First quality ox liver may be fried but it is usually braised.

300 g	liver	12 oz
125 ml	jus-lié	1 gill
50 g	streaky bacon	2 oz
50 g	fat for frying	2 oz

1 Skin the liver and remove the gristle.
2 Cut in thin slices on the slant.
3 Pass the slices of liver through seasoned flour.
4 Shake off the excess flour.
5 Quickly fry on both sides in hot fat.
6 Remove the rind and bone from the bacon and grill on both
   sides.
7 Serve the liver and bacon in an entrée dish or silver oval flat
   with a cordon of jus-lié and a sauceboat of jus-lié separately.

67 Tripe and Onions *4 portions*

400 g	tripe	1 lb
500 ml	milk and water	1 pt
	salt, pepper	
200 g	onion	$\frac{1}{2}$ lb
25 g	flour or cornflour	1 oz

1 Wash the tripe well.
2 Cut into neat 4 cm (2 in) squares.
3 Blanch and refresh.
4 Cook the tripe in the milk and water with the sliced onions.
5 Season and simmer $1\frac{1}{2}$–2 hr.
6 Gradually add the diluted flour or cornflour, stir with a
   wooden spoon to the boil.
7 Simmer for 5–10 min.
8 Serve in an entrée dish.

An alternative thickening is $\frac{1}{8}$ litre (1 gill) of béchamel in place of
the cornflour.

68 Stewed Oxtail *4 portions*   *Ragoût de Queue de Bœuf*

1 kg	oxtail	2 lb
100 g	onion	4 oz
35 g	flour	$1\frac{1}{2}$ oz
1 litre	approx. brown stock	2 pt
100 g	carrot	4 oz
50 g	dripping	2 oz
25 g	tomato purée	1 oz
	bouquet garni	

1 Cut the oxtail into sections.
2 Remove excess fat.

3   Fry on all sides in hot fat.
4   Place in a braising pan or casserole.
5   Add the fried mirepoix.
6   Sprinkle with flour, mix in and singe.
7   Add the tomato purée, brown stock, bouquet garni and season.
8   Bring to the boil, skim.
9   Cover with a lid and simmer in the oven till tender, approx. 3 hr.
10   Remove the meat from the sauce, place in a clean pan.
11   Correct the sauce and pass on to the meat and re-boil.
12   Serve in an entrée dish, sprinkle with chopped parsley.

This dish is usually garnished with glazed turned carrots and turnips, button onions, peas and diamonds of beans.

69 Haricot Oxtail   *Ragoût de Queue de Bœuf aux Haricots Blancs*

As for the previous recipe with the addition of 100 g (1 lb) cooked haricot beans. Add approx. $\frac{1}{2}$ hr before the oxtail has completed cooking.

11
Pork

1 Pork   BUTCHERY   *Porc*

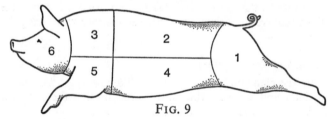

F<small>IG</small>. 9

2

	English	French	Uses	Approx. (kilo)	Weight (lb)
1	Leg	le Cuissot	Roasting and Boiling	5	10
2	Loin	la Longe	Roasting, Frying, Grilling	6	12
3	Spare rib	la Basse Côte	Roasting, Pies	1½	3
4	Belly	la Poitrine	Pickling, Boiling	2	4
5	Shoulder	l'Épaule (f.)	Roasting, Sausages, Pies	3	6
6	Head (whole)	la Tête	Brawn	4	8
7	Trotters	le Pied	Grilling, Boiling		
	Kidneys	le Rognons (m).	Sauté, Grilling		
	Liver	le Foie	Frying, Pâté		

Fresh pork is at its best from September to April. When 5–6 weeks old it is known as a sucking pig.

3   Signs of Quality

1   Lean flesh should be pale pink, firm and of a fine texture.
2   The fat should be white, firm, smooth and not excessive.
3   Bones should be small, fine and pinkish.
4   The skin or rind should be smooth.

4   Order of Dissection

1   Remove the head.
2   Remove the trotters.
3   Remove the leg.
4   Remove shoulder.
5   Remove spare ribs.
6   Divide loin from the belly.

5   Preparation of Joints and Cuts

Leg *Roasting* Remove the pelvic or aitch bone, trim and score the rind neatly. That is to say with a sharp-pointed knife, make a series of 3 mm ($\frac{1}{8}$ in) deep incisions approx. 2 cm (1 in) apart all over the skin of the joint. Trim and clean the knuckle bone.

Boiling It is usual to pickle the joint either by rubbing dry salt and saltpetre into the meat or by soaking in a brine solution (page 157). Then remove the pelvic bone, trim and secure with string if necessary.

Loin *Roasting* (on the bone)
Saw down the chine bone in order to facilitate carving; trim excess fat and sinew and score the rind in the direction that the joint will be carved. Season and secure with string.

Loin *Roasting* (boned-out)
Remove the filet mignon and bone-out carefully. Trim off excess fat and sinew, score the rind and neaten the flap, season, replace the filet, mignon, roll up and secure with string.
    This joint is sometimes stuffed.

Grilling or Frying Chops
Remove the skin, excess fat and sinew, then cut and saw through the loin in approx. 1 cm ($\frac{1}{2}$ in) slices, remove excess bone and trim neatly.

Spare Rib *Roasting*
Remove excess fat, bone and sinew and trim neatly.

Pies

Remove excess fat and sinew, bone-out and cut as required.

Belly

Remove all the small rib bones, season with salt, pepper and chopped sage, roll and secure with string. This joint may be stuffed.

Shoulder   *Roasting*

This is usually boned-out, excess fat and sinew removed, seasoned, scored and rolled and secured with string. This may be stuffed, or may be divided into two smaller joints.

Sausages and Pies

Skin, bone-out, remove the excess fat and sinew and cut into even pieces or mince.

Head—*Brawn*

(*a*) Bone-out as for calf's head (page 194) and keep in acidulated water till required
(*b*) Split down the centre and remove the brain and tongue.

Trotters

Boil in water for a few minutes, scrape with the back of a knife to remove the hairs, wash off in cold water and split in half.

Kidneys

Remove the fat and skin, cut down the middle lengthwise. Remove the sinew and cut into slices or neat dice.

Liver

Skin if possible, remove the gristle and cut into thin slices on the slant.

RECIPES

6 Roast Leg of Pork   *Cuissot de Porc Rôti*

1   Season the prepared leg of pork.
2   Place on a trivet in a roasting tin with a little dripping on top.
3   Start to cook in a hot oven (230°–250°C) basting frequently.
4   Gradually reduce the heat, allowing approx. 25 min per ½ kg (1 lb) and 25 min over. Pork must always be well cooked.
5   When cooked remove from the pan and prepare a roast gravy from the sediment in the usual way.

6   Serve the joint on a flat dish, garnished with picked watercress and accompanied by roast gravy, apple sauce and sage and onion stuffing. If to be carved, proceed as for Roast Lamb, page 137.

7   Roast Loin of Pork   *Longe de Porc Rôtie*
As for Roast Leg of Pork.

8   Roast Shoulder of Pork   *Épaule de Porc Rôtie*
As for Roast Leg of Pork.

9   Roast Spare Rib of Pork   *Basse de Côte Porc Rôtie*
As for Roast Leg of Pork.

10   Sage and Onion Stuffing for Pork   *4 portions*

100 g	white breadcrumbs	4 oz
50 g	pork dripping (from the joint)	2 oz
	pinch chopped parsley	
50 g	chopped onion	2 oz
	good pinch powdered sage	
	salt, pepper	

1   Cook the onion in the dripping without colour.
2   Combine all the ingredients.
3   This is usually served separately.

11   Boiled Leg of Pork   *Cuissot de Porc Bouilli*
1   Place the leg in cold water.
2   Bring to the boil and skim.
3   Add bouquet garni and a garnish of vegetables as for boiled beef (page 161), onions, carrots, leeks and celery.
4   Allow to simmer gently for approx. 25 min per $\frac{1}{2}$ kg (1 lb) and 25 min over.
5   Serve on a flat dish, garnish with the vegetables.
6   A sauceboat of cooking liquor and a dish of pease pudding (purée of peas) is served separately (page 271).

12   Pork Chop Charcutière   *Côte de Porc à la Charcutière*
1   Season the chop on both sides with salt and mill pepper.
2   Brush with melted fat and either grill on both sides with moderate heat for approx. 10 min or cook on both sides in a little fat in a plat à sauté.
3   Serve on an oval flat dish accompanied by a sauceboat of charcutière sauce (page 26).

13   Pork Chop Flamande   *Côte de Porc à la Flamande*

300 g	dessert apples	12 oz
	4 pork chops	

1   Season the chops with salt and mill pepper.
2   Half cook (approx. 5 min), on both sides in a little fat in a plat à sauté.
3   Meanwhile peel, core and slice the apples and place in an earthenware dish.
4   Put the chops on the apples.
5   Sprinkle with a little fat.
6   Complete the cooking in a moderate oven (200°–230°C) approx. 10–15 min.
7   Clean the dish and place on an oval flat and serve.

14   Grilled Pork Chop   *Côte de Porc Grillée*

Season and grill in the usual way and serve on an oval flat with picked watercress and straw potatoes and offer a suitable sauce separately, e.g. apple sauce (page 29).

15   Barbecued Spare Ribs of Pork   *4 portions*

2 kg	spare ribs of pork	4 lb
125 ml	oil	$\frac{1}{8}$ pt
	1 clove of garlic (chopped)	
100 g	onion finely chopped	4 oz
150 g	tomato purée	6 oz
125 ml	vinegar	$\frac{1}{8}$ pt
125 ml	honey	$\frac{1}{8}$ pt
	pinch thyme	
	1 tspn dry mustard	
60 ml	Worcester sauce	$\frac{1}{16}$ pt
250 ml	brown stock	$\frac{1}{4}$ pt

1   Sweat the onions and garlic in the oil without colour.
2   Mix in the vinegar, tomato purée, honey, stock, Worcester sauce, mustard, thyme and season with salt.
3   Allow to simmer 10–15 min—this is the barbecue sauce.
4   Place the prepared spare ribs fat side up on a trivet in a roasting tin.
5   Brush the spare ribs liberally with the barbecue sauce.
6   Place in a moderately hot oven (200°–230°C).
7   Cook for $\frac{3}{4}$–1 hour.
8   Baste generously with the barbecue sauce every 10–15 min.
9   The cooked spare ribs should be brown and crisp.
10   Cut the spare ribs into individual portions and serve.

16   Brawn   *12 portions*

	$\frac{1}{2}$ pig's head	
100 g	carrots	4 oz
	6 peppercorns	
100 g	onions	4 oz
	bouquet garni	

1   Blanch the head and tongue, refresh and clean well.
2   Place with the remainder of the ingredients and cover with water.
3   Simmer until tender, approx. 2 hr.
4   Remove from the liquor and cut the flesh from the bones, return the bones to the liquid and reduce by half.
5   Skin the tongue and with the meat, cut into 1 cm ($\frac{1}{2}$ in) dice. Correct the seasoning.
6   Place in a mould or basin and cover with stock and leave until cold.

RAISED PIES

17 Pork Pie

200 g	hot-water paste (p. 293)	8 oz
	$\frac{1}{2}$ tspn mixed sage, thyme and parsley	
	2 tbspn stock or water	
300 g	shoulder of pork (without bone)	12 oz
	salt, pepper	

1   Cut the pork into small even pieces and combine with the rest of the ingredients.
2   Keep one-quarter of the paste warm and covered.
3   Roll out the remaining three-quarters and carefully line a well-greased raised pie mould.
4   Add the filling and press down firmly.
5   Roll out the remaining pastry for the lid.
6   Eggwash the edges of the pie.
7   Add the lid, seal firmly and neaten the edges, cutting off any surplus paste.
8   Decorate if desired.
9   Make a hole 1 cm ($\frac{1}{2}$ in) in diameter in the centre of the pie.
10   Brush all over with eggwash.
11   Bake in a hot oven (230°–250°C) approx. 20 min.
12   Reduce the heat to moderate (150°–200°C) and cook for $1\frac{1}{2}$–2 hr in all.
13   If the pie colours too quickly, cover with greaseproof paper. Remove from the oven and carefully remove tin, eggwash the pie all over and return to oven for a few minutes.
14   Remove from the oven and fill with approx. 60 ml ($\frac{1}{4}$ pt) of good hot stock in which 5 g ($\frac{1}{4}$ oz) of gelatine has been dissolved
15   Serve when cold, on a flat dish garnished with picked watercress and offer a suitable salad.

18   Veal and Ham Pie

200 g	hot-water paste	8 oz
100 g	fat ham or bacon	4 oz
	salt, pepper	
	1 hard-boiled egg	
200 g	lean veal	8 oz
	½ tspn parsley and thyme	
	grated zest of 1 lemon	
	2 tbspn stock or water	

Proceed as for Pork Pie (page 188). Place the shelled egg in the centre of the mixture.

19   Forcemeat

Forcemeat—is a term given to numerous mixtures of meats (usually veal and pork); meat and poultry; poultry; game; fish; vegetables and bread.

Forcemeats range from a simple sausagemeat to the finer mixtures used in the making of hot mousses (e.g. ham, chicken, fish) and soufflés. Also included are mixtures of bread, vegetables and herbs which alternatively are referred to as stuffings.

Forcemeats are used for galantines, raised pies, terrines, meat balls and a wide variety of other dishes.

Full and detailed explanation of the complete range is obtainable by reference to *The Larder Chef* by Leto and Bode.

12
Veal

BUTCHERY

1 Veal   *Veau*

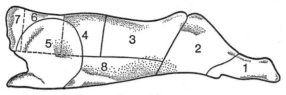

FIG. 10

2 1

Joint	French	Uses	Approx. Weight (kilo)	Weight (lb)
1 Knuckle	le Jarret	Osso Buco, Sauté, Stock	2	4
2 Leg	le Cuissot	Roasting, Braising, Escalopes, Sauté	5	10
3 Loin	la Longe	Roasting, Frying, Grilling	3½	7
4 Best-end	le Carré	Roasting, Frying, Grilling	3	6
5 Shoulder	l'Épaule (f.)	Braising, Stewing	5	10
6 Neck-end	—	Stewing, Sauté	2½	5
7 Scrag	le Cou	Stewing Stock	1½	3
8 Breast	la Poitrine	Stewing, Roasting	2½	5
Kidneys	les Rognons (m.)	Stewing (pies and puddings)	—	—
Liver	Le Foie	Frying	—	—
Sweetbreads	le Ris	Braising, Frying	—	—
Head	la Tête	Boiling, Soup	4	8
Brains	la Cervelle	Boiling, Frying	—	—
Bones	les Os (m.)	are used for stock	—	—

3 Leg of Veal
Average weight of English or Dutch Milk fed—18 kg (36 lb).

Cuts—English	French	Weight	Proportion of leg	Uses
Cushion or Nut	Noix	2·75 kg (5½ lb)	15%	Escalopes, Roasting, Braising, Sauté
Under Cushion or Under Nut	Soux-Noix	3 kg (6 lb)	17%	Escalopes, Roasting, Braising, Sauté
Thick Flank	Gîte à la Noix	2·5 kg (5 lb)	14%	Escalopes, Roasting, Braising, Sauté
Knuckle (whole)	Jarret	2·5 kg (5 lb)	14%	Osso Buco, Sauté
Bones (Thigh and Aitch)		2·5 kg (5 lb)	14%	Stock, Jus-Lié
Usable Trimmings		2 kg (4 lb)	11%	Pies, Stewing, Pojarski
Skin and Fat		2·75 kg (5½ lb)	15%	

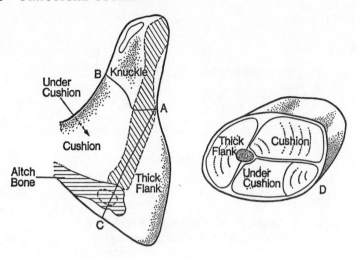

Corresponding Joints in Beef
Cushion=Topside
Under Cushion=Silverside
Thick Flank=Thick Flank

Dissection

1 Remove knuckle by dividing knee joint (A) and cut through the meat away from the cushion-line A–B.
2 Remove aitch bone (C) at thick end of leg separating it at the ball and socket joint.
3 Remove all outside skin and fat thus exposing the natural seams. It will now be seen that the thigh bone divides the meat into 2/3 and 1/3 (thick flank).
4 Stand the leg on the thick flank with point D uppermost. Divide the cushion from the under-cushion, following the natural seam, using the hand and the point of a knife. Having reached the thigh bone, remove it completely.
5 Allowing the boned leg to fall open the 3 joints can easily be seen joined only by membrane. Separate and trim the cushion removing the loose flap of meat.
6 Trim the undercushion removing the layer of thick gristle. Separate into 3 small joints through the natural seams. It will be seen that one of these will correspond with the round in silverside of beef.
7 Trim the thick flank by laying it on its round side and making a cut along the length about 1 in deep. A seam is reached and the two trimmings can be removed.

The anticipated yield of escalopes from this size leg would be 220 ounces. i.e. 55 × 4 oz.

73 × 3 oz.

4   Quality of Veal

1   It is available all the year round, but is best from May to September.
2   The flesh should be pale pink in colour.
3   The flesh should be firm in structure, not soft or flabby.
4   Cut surfaces should be slightly moist, not dry.
5   Bones, in young animals, should be pinkish white, porous and with a degree of blood in their structure.
6   The fat should be firm and pinkish white.
7   The kidney should be hard and well covered with fat.

5   Order of Dissection

1   Remove the shoulders.
2   Remove the breast.
3   Take off the leg.
4   Divide the loin and best-end from the scrag and neck-end.
5   Divide the loin from the best-end.

6   Preparation of the Joints and Cuts of Veal

Shin   *Stewing (on the bone)—Osso Buco*

Cut and saw into 2–3 cm (1–1½ in) thick slices through the knuckle.
   Sauté   Bone-out and trim and cut into even 25 g (1 oz) pieces.

Leg   *Braising or Roasting Whole*

Remove the aitch bone, clean and trim 3 cm (1½ in) off the knuckle bone.
   Trim off excess sinew.

Braising or Roasting the Noix, Sous-noix or Quasi
Remove the sinew and if there is insufficient fat on the joint then bard thinly and secure with string.

Escalopes
Remove all sinew and cut into large 50–75 g (2–3 oz) slices against the grain and bat out thinly.
   Sauté   Remove all sinew and cut into 25 g (1 oz) pieces.

Loin *and* Best-end

Roasting Bone-out and trim the flap, roll out and secure with string. This joint may be stuffed before rolling.
Frying Trim and cut into cutlets (Côte de Veau).

Shoulder

Braising Boned-out as for lamb and usually stuffed.
Stewing Bone-out, remove all sinew and cut into approx. 25 g (1 oz) pieces.

Neck-end *and* Scrag

Stewing and Sauté Bone-out and remove all sinew and cut into approx. 25 g (1 oz) pieces.

Breast

Stewing As for neck-end.
Roasting Bone-out, season, stuff and roll up then tie with string.

Kidneys

Remove the fat and skin and cut down the middle lengthwise.
Remove sinew and cut into thin slices or neat dice.

Liver

Skin if possible, remove gristle and cut into thin slices on the slant.

Sweetbreads

Wash well, blanch and trim.

Head

1 Bone-out by making a deep incision down the middle of the head to the nostrils.
2 Follow the bone carefully and remove all the flesh in one piece.
3 Lastly remove the tongue.
4 Wash the flesh well and keep covered in acidulated water.
5 Wash off, blanch and refresh.
6 Cut into 2–4 cm (1–2 in) squares.
7 Cut off the ears and trim the inside of the cheek.

Brains

Using a chopper or saw, remove the top of the skull, making certain that the opening is large enough to remove the brain undamaged.
Soak the brains in running cold water, then remove the membrane, or skin and wash well to remove all blood. Keep in cold salted water till required.

RECIPES

7 Brown Veal Stew   *Ragoût de Veau*
                                                          Sauté de Veau

400 g	prepared stewing veal	1 lb
75 g	carrots	3 oz
25 g	flour	1 oz
750 ml	brown veal stock	1½ pt
	seasoning	
	1 tbspn tomato purée	
	bouquet garni	
25 g	dripping	1 oz
75 g	onions	3 oz

1   Remove excess sinew from the veal.
2   Cut into 2 cm (1 in) pieces.
3   Fry quickly in hot fat till lightly browned.
4   Add the mirepoix and continue frying to a golden colour.
5   Add the flour, mix in and singe in the oven or brown on top
    of the stove for a few minutes.
6   Add the tomato purée and stir in with a wooden spoon.
7   Add the stock, bring to the boil and skim.
8   Add the bouquet garni, season, cover with a lid and simmer
    gently till cooked, preferably in the oven, approx. 1–1½ hr.
9   When cooked place the meat in a clean pan.
10 Correct the sauce and pass onto the meat:
11 Serve in an entrée dish with chopped parsley sprinkled on the
    meat.

8 White Stew of Veal   *Blanquette de Veau*

400 g	prepared stewing veal	1 lb
50 g	carrots	2 oz
50 g	onion piqué	2 oz
25 g	margarine ⎫ Blond Roux	1 oz
25 g	flour ⎭	1 oz
750 ml	white veal stock	1½ pt
	bouquet garni	
	2–3 tbspn cream	
	chopped parsley	

1   Trim the meat and cut into even pieces.
2   Blanch and refresh as follows.
3   Place in a saucepan, cover with cold water, bring to the boil
    then place under running cold water until all the scum has
    been washed away.
4   Drain and place in a clean pan, cover with stock, bring to the
    boil and skim.
5   Add whole carrot and onion, bouquet garni, season slightly
    and simmer till tender approx. 1–1½ hr.

6 Meanwhile prepare the roux and make into a velouté with the cooking liquor.
7 Cook out for about 20 min.
8 Correct the seasoning and consistency and pass through a fine strainer on to the meat, which has been placed in a clean pan.
9 Reheat, mix in the cream, serve in an entrée dish, finish with chopped parsley.
10 To enrich this dish a liaison of yolks and cream is sometimes added at the last moment to the boiling sauce which must not be allowed to re-boil.

9   Fricassée of Veal   *Fricassée de Veau*

400 g	boned stewing veal (shoulder or breast)	1 lb
25 g	flour	1 oz
	1 egg yolk	
	few drops of lemon juice	
35 g	margarine or butter	1½ oz
500 ml	white veal stock	1 pt
	2–3 tbspn cream	
	salt, pepper	

1 Trim the meat.
2 Cut into even 25 g (1 oz) pieces.
3 Set the meat gently in the butter without colour.
4 Mix in the flour with a wooden spoon and cook out without colour.
5 Allow to cool.
6 Gradually add boiling stock just to cover the meat.
7 Season, bring to the boil, skim.
8 Cover with a lid and allow to simmer gently on the stove till tender, 1½–2 hr.
9 Pick out the meat into a clean pan.
10 Correct the sauce.
11 Pass on to the meat and re-boil.
12 Mix the yolk and cream in a basin.
13 Add a little of the boiling sauce, mix in and pour back on to the meat, shaking the pan till thoroughly mixed; do not re-boil.
14 Add the lemon juice.
15 Serve in an entrée dish and finish with chopped parsley.

10   White Veal Stew with Button Onion and Mushrooms
Fricassée de Veau a l'Ancienne

Proceed as in Recipe 9, after one hour's cooking pick out the meat, strain the sauce back on to the meat, add 8 small button onions, simmer for 15 min, add 8 small button mushrooms, washed and peeled if necessary, and then complete the cooking. Finish and serve as in Recipe 9.

11 Braised Veal *4 portions* *Noix de Veau Braisé*

400 g	cushion or nut of veal	1 lb	
100 g	onion	4 oz	
25 g	tomato purée	1 oz	
250 ml	brown veal stock	$\frac{1}{2}$ pt	
25 g	dripping	1 oz	
100 g	carrot	4 oz	
	bouquet garni		
250 ml	jus-lié or demi-glace	$\frac{1}{2}$ pt	

1 Slice carrots and onions thickly.
2 Fry lightly and place in a braising pan.
3 Trim and tie the joint with string and fry quickly on all sides.
4 Place on the bed of roots.
5 Add the tomato purée, bouquet garni, stock, jus-lié, mushroom trimmings if available.
6 Season lightly.
7 Bring to the boil, skim, cover with a lid and cook gently in a moderate oven (150°–200°C) for 1 hr.
8 Remove the lid and continue cooking with the lid off for a further 30 min basting frequently.
9 Remove the joint from the sauce, take off the strings.
10 Correct the colour, consistency and seasoning of the sauce.
11 Pass through a fine chinois.
12 Serve two or three slices carved against the grain, dressed neatly on a silver flat or entrée dish, together with the joint.
13 Pour some of the sauce over the slices and the joint and serve a sauceboat of sauce separately.

For larger joints allow 30–35 min per $\frac{1}{2}$ kg (1 lb) plus 35 min (approx.) cooking time.

12 Hot Veal and Ham Pie *4 portions*

400 g	stewing veal without bone	1 lb	
100 g	bacon	4 oz	
	1 tspn chopped parsley		
	salt, pepper		
100 g	rough puff or puff paste (p. 290)	4 oz	
50 g	chopped onion	2 oz	
	1 chopped or quartered hard-boiled egg		
250 ml	stock (white)	$\frac{1}{2}$ pt	

1 Cut the bacon thinly and line the bottom and sides of a $\frac{1}{2}$ litre (1 pt) pie dish, leaving two or three pieces for the top.
2 Trim the veal, cut into small pieces and mix with the egg, parsley and onion.

3   Season and place in the pie dish.
4   Just cover with stock.
5   Add the rest of the bacon.
6   Cover and cook as for Steak Pie (page 169) allowing approx.
     1½ hr cooking.

13   Veal Olives   *Paupiettes de Veau*

400 g	lean veal	1 lb
100 g	carrot	4 oz
35 g	dripping	1½ oz
500–750 ml	brown veal stock	1–1½ pt
	bouquet garni	
50 g	stuffing	2 oz
100 g	onion	4 oz
25 g	flour	1 oz
10 g	tomato purée	½ oz

1   Prepare the stuffing.
2   Cut the meat into thin slices across the grain and bat out.
3   Trim to approx. 8 × 6 cm (4 × 3 in), chop the trimmings
     finely and add to the stuffing.
4   Season the slices of meat with salt and pepper and spread a
     quarter of the stuffing down the centre of each slice.
5   Roll up neatly and secure with string.
6   Fry off the meat to a light brown colour, add the mirepoix
     and continue cooking to a golden colour.
7   Drain off the fat into a clean pan and make up to 25 g (1 oz)
     fat if there is not enough.
8   Add the flour and cook to a brown roux.
9   Mix in the tomato purée, cool, and add the boiling stock.
10   Bring to the boil, skim, season and pour on to the meat and
     vegetables.
11   Add the bouquet garni.
12   Cover with a lid and allow to simmer gently, preferably in the
     oven, approx. 1½–2 hr.
13   Remove the string from the meat and place in an entrée dish.
14   Skim and correct the sauce and pass on to the meat.

Stuffing   4 portions

50 g	white crumbs	2 oz
	1 tspn chopped parsley	
	pinch of thyme	
	approx. ½ egg to bind	
5 g	prepared chopped suet	¼ oz
25 g	finely chopped sweated onion	1 oz
	salt, pepper	

Mix all the ingredients together with the chopped meat trimmings. Other stuffings may be used, for example, sausage meat.

14 Escalope of Veal *4 portions* *Escalope de Veau*

400 g	nut or cushion of veal	1 lb
50 g	breadcrumbs	2 oz
	1 egg	
25 g	seasoned flour	1 oz
	for frying	
50 g	oil	2 oz
50 g	butter	2 oz
50 g	beurre noisette	2 oz

1 Trim and remove all sinew from the veal.
2 Cut into four even slices and bat out thinly using a little water.
3 Flour, egg and crumb.
4 Mark with a palette knife.
5 Place the escalopes into shallow hot fat and cook quickly for a few minutes on each side.
6 Serve on an oval silver flat.
7 Pour over 50 g (2 oz) beurre noisette (nut-brown butter).
8 Finish with a cordon of jus-lié (page 28).

15 Escalope of Veal Viennoise *Escalope de Veau Viennoise*
As above.

Garnish the dish with chopped yolk, white of egg and chopped parsley. On top of each escalope place a slice of peeled lemon decorated with chopped egg yolk, egg white and parsley, an anchovy fillet and a stoned olive. Finish with a little lemon juice and beurre noisette.

16 Escalope of Veal with Spaghetti
**   and Tomato Sauce** *Escalope de Veau Napolitaine*
Cook and serve the escalopes as for Recipe 14, and garnish with spaghetti napolitaine (page 90) allowing 10 g (½ oz) spaghetti per portion.
    NOTE. Veal escalopes may be cooked plain (not crumbed) in which case they are only slightly battened.

17 Veal Escalope Holstein *Escalope de Veau Holstein*
1 Prepare and cook the escalopes as for Recipe 14.
2 Each escalope should then have added an egg fried in butter.
3 Place two neat fillets of anchovy criss-crossed on each egg and serve.

18   Veal Escalope Cordon Bleu   *4 portions*   *Escalope de Veau Cordon Bleu*

400 g	nut or cushion of veal	1 lb
	4 slices of cooked ham	
	4 slices of gruyere cheese	
50 g	breadcrumbs	2 oz
	1 egg	
25 g	seasoned flour	1 oz
50 g	oil ⎫ for frying	2 oz
50 g	butter ⎭	2 oz
50 g	butter ⎫ for	2 oz
60 ml	jus-lié (p. 28) ⎭ finishing	⅛ pt

1   Trim and remove all sinew from the veal.
2   Cut into eight even slices and bat out thinly using a little water.
3   Place a slice of ham and a slice of cheese on to four of the veal slices, cover with the remaining four slices and press firmly together.
4   Flour, egg and crumb.
5   Shake off all surplus crumbs.
6   Mark on one side with a palette knife.
7   Place the escalopes marked side down into shallow hot fat and cook quickly for a few minutes on each side, until golden brown.
8   Serve on an oval silver flat.
9   Coat with nut-brown butter (beurre noisette) and a cordon of jus-lié (p. 28).

19   Veal Escalope with Cream   *4 portions*   *Escalope de Veau à la Crème*

	4 veal escalopes (slightly battened)	
25 g	seasoned flour	1 oz
50 g	butter	2 oz
30 ml	sherry	1/16 pt
125 ml	double cream	¼ pt
	salt, cayenne	

1   Heat the butter in a sauté pan.
2   Lightly flour the escalopes.
3   Cook the escalopes gently on both sides with the minimum of colour. They should be a delicate light brown.
4   Place the escalopes in an earthenware serving dish cover and keep warm.
5   Drain off all the fat from the pan.
6   Deglaze the pan with the sherry.
7   Add the cream, bring to the boil and season.
8   Allow to reduce to a lightly thickened consistency.
9   Pass through a fine chinois over the escalopes and serve.

An alternate method of preparing the sauce is to use half the amount of cream and and equal amount of chicken velouté (p. 21).

20 **Veal Escalope with Cream and Mushrooms** *4 portions* *Escalope de Veau à la Crème et Champignons*

	4 veal escalopes (slightly battened)	
25 g	seasoned flour	1 oz
50 g	butter	2 oz
100 g	button mushrooms	4 oz
30 ml	sherry	$\frac{1}{16}$ pt
125 ml	double cream	$\frac{1}{4}$ pt
	salt, cayenne	

1 Heat the butter in a sauté pan.
2 Lightly flour the escalopes.
3 Cook the escalopes on both sides with the minimum of colour. They should be a delicate light brown.
4 Place the escalopes in an earthenware serving dish, cover and keep warm.
5 Peel, wash and slice the mushrooms.
6 Gently sauté the mushrooms in the same butter and pan as the escalopes and add them to the escalopes.
7 Drain off all the fat from the pan.
8 Deglaze the pan with the sherry.
9 Add the cream bring to the boil and season.
10 Allow to reduce to a lightly thickened consistency.
11 Pass through a fine chinois over the escalopes and mushrooms and serve.

An alternative method of preparing the sauce is to use half the amount of cream and an equal amount of chicken velouté (p. 21).

21 **Veal Escalope with Madeira** *4 portions* *Escalope de Veau au Madère*

	4 veal escalopes (slightly battened)	
25 g	seasoned flour	1 oz
50 g	butter	2 oz
30 ml	madeira	$\frac{1}{16}$ pt
125 ml	demi-glace	$\frac{1}{4}$ pt

1 Heat the butter in a sauté pan.
2 Lightly flour the escalopes.
3 Fry to a light brown on both sides.
4 Drain off the fat from the pan.
5 Deglaze with the madeira.
6 Add the demi-glace and bring to the boil.
7 Correct seasoning and consistency.
8 Pass through a fine chinois on to the escalopes and serve.

Veal Escalope with Sherry

Proceed as Recipe 21 using a medium-dry sherry in place of madeira.

Veal Escalope with Marsala

Proceed as Recipe 21 using marsala instead of madeira.

22 Grenadin of Veal   *Grenadin de Veau*

1 Prepare slices of veal, cutting a little thicker than for escalopes.
2 Lard with fat bacon strips.
3 Sauté in oil and butter.
4 Serve with a suitable garnish, e.g. bouquetière, clamart, florentine.

23 Grilled Veal Cutlet   *Côte de Veau Grillée*

1 Season the prepared chop with salt and mill pepper.
2 Brush with oil.
3 Place on previously heated grill bars.
4 Cook on both sides for 8–10 min in all.
5 Brush occasionally to prevent the meat from drying up.
6 Serve with watercress, straw potatoes and a suitable sauce or butter, e.g. béarnaise or parsley butter.

24 Fried Veal Cutlet   *Côte de Veau Sautée*

Season and cook in a plat à sauté, in clarified butter or oil and butter, on both sides for 8–10 min in all. Chops must be started in hot fat, the heat reduced to allow the meat to cook through.

Serve with a suitable garnish, e.g. jardinière or braised celery and finish with a cordon of jus-lié.

25 Crumbed Veal Cutlet   *Côte de Veau Panée*

Cook as for previous recipe and finish with beurre noisette, a cordon of jus-lié and a suitable garnish, e.g. napolitaine, fleuriste.

26 Braised Stuffed Shoulder of Veal *4 portions*   *Épaule de Veau Farcie*

400 g	*shoulder of veal	1 lb
100 g	onion	4 oz
25 g	tomato purée	1 oz
250 ml	brown veal stock	½ pt
25 g	dripping	1 oz
100 g	carrot	4 oz
	bouquet garni	
250 ml	jus-lié or demi-glace	½ pt

1 Slice carrots and onions thickly.
2 Fry lightly and place in a braising pan.
3 Stuff and tie the joint with string and fry quickly on all sides.
4 Place on the bed of roots.

* A whole shoulder will serve from 8 portions depending on size.

5 Add the tomato purée, bouquet garni, stock, jus-lié, mushroom
   trimmings if available.
6 Season lightly.
7 Bring to the boil, skim, cover with a lid and cook gently in a
   moderate oven (150°–200°C) for 1 hr.
8 Remove the lid and continue cooking with the lid off for a
   further 30 min basting frequently.
9 Remove the joint from the sauce, take off the strings.
10 Correct the colour, consistency and seasoning of the sauce.
11 Pass through a fine chinois.
12 Serve two or three slices carved against the grain, dressed neatly
   on a silver or entrée dish, together with the joint.
13 Pour some of the sauce over the slices and the joint and serve a
   sauceboat of sauce separately.

Bone-out the shoulder, season, stuff (Recipe 29) and secure with
string. Cook and serve as for Braised Veal (Recipe 11).

For larger joints allow 30–35 min per ½ kg (1 lb) plus 35 min
(approx.) cooking time.

27 Braised Stuffed Breast of Veal   *Portrine de Veau Farcie*
Prepare and cook as for Stuffed Shoulder.

28 Roast Leg of Veal   *Cuissot de Veau Rôti*
Whole or in joints.

In order to increase the flavour it is usual to roast on a bed of root
vegetables with a sprig of thyme. Baste frequently and allow approx.
25 min per ½ kilo (1 lb) plus 25 min over. There should be no sign of
blood when cooked. Prepare the roast gravy from the sediment and
thicken slightly with a little arrowroot or cornflour diluted with water.

Serve the slices, carved against the grain, dress neatly with thin
slices of ham and veal stuffing (Recipe 29). Lightly cover with gravy
and garnish with watercress and a sauceboat of gravy separately.

29 Veal Stuffing   *4 portions*

100 g	white breadcrumbs	4 oz
50 g	onion cooked in a little fat without colour	2 oz
	pinch of parsley	
50 g	chopped suet	2 oz
	good pinch of powdered thyme	
	juice of ½ lemon	
	salt, pepper	

Combine all the ingredients.

This may be used for stuffing joints or may be cooked separately in
buttered paper or in a basin in the steamer for approx. 1 hr.

30   Roast Stuffed Breast of Veal

Bone, trim, season and stuff. Tie with string and cook and serve as for Roast Leg of Veal.

31   Braised Shin of Veal   *4 portions*   *Osso Buco*

1½ kg	meaty knuckle of veal	3 lb
50 g	butter	2 oz
50 g	onion	2 oz
50 g	carrot	2 oz
25 g	celery	1 oz
	1 small clove garlic	
200 g	tomatoes	½ lb
60 ml	dry white wine	⅛ pt
60 ml	white stock	⅛ pt
	bouquet garni	
25 g	flour	1 oz
60 ml	oil	⅛ pt
	juice of ¼ lemon	
	chopped parsley	

1   Prepare the veal knuckle by cutting and sawing through the bone in 4 cm (2 in) thick pieces.
2   Season the veal pieces with salt and pepper and pass through on both sides.
3   Melt the butter and oil in a sauté pan.
4   Add the veal slices and cook on both sides allowing to colour slightly.
5   Add the finely chopped onion and garlic, cover with a lid and allow to sweat gently for 2–3 min.
6   Add the onion, carrot and celery cut in brunoise, cover with a lid and allow to sweat for 3–4 min.
7   Pour off the fat.
8   Deglaze with the white wine and stock.
9   Add the bouquet garni, replace the lid and allow the dish to simmer gently preferably in an oven for 1 hour.
10   Add the concasséed tomatoes, correct the seasoning.
11   Replace the lid, return to the oven and allow to continue simmering until the meat is so tender that it can be pulled away from the bone easily with a fork.
12   Remove bouquet garni, add lemon juice, correct seasoning and serve.

Osso buco is an Italian regional dish which has many variations.

32   Calf's Head, Vinaigrette Sauce   *Tête de Veau Vinaigrette*

1   Prepare a blanc by gradually mixing 50 g (2 oz) flour into 5 litres (4 qt) water.
2   Add salt and the juice of 2–3 lemons.
3   Strain and bring to the boil, stirring frequently.

4   Add the prepared calf's head (page 194) and tongue, studded onion, carrot and bouquet garni.
5   Simmer 1½–2 hr.
6   Poach the brains in a court-bouillon (½ litre (1 pt) water), 1 tbspn vinegar, 25 g (1 oz) carrot, 25 g (1 oz) onion, ½ bay leaf, sprig of thyme, salt and a few peppercorns).
7   Skim and simmer for approx. 20 min.
8   Serve the pieces of calf's head with thick slices of brain and slices of skinned tongue with a little of the cooking liquor in an entrée dish. A sauceboat of sauce vinaigrette is served separately.

Sauce Vinaigrette   4 portions

    2 tbspn vinegar
    2 tbspn cooking liquor
    1 tbspn capers
    6 tbspn oil
    1 chopped onion
    1 tspn chopped parsley

Mix all the ingredients together and season with salt and mill pepper.

33 Calf's Liver and Bacon   *4 portions*   *Foie de Veau au Lard*

300 g	liver	12 oz
125 ml	jus-lié	1 gill
50 g	streaky bacon	2 oz
50 g	fat for frying	2 oz

1   Skin the liver and remove the gristle.
2   Cut in thin slices on the slant.
3   Pass the slices of liver through seasoned flour.
4   Shake off the excess flour.
5   Quickly fry on both sides in hot fat.
6   Remove the rind and bone from the bacon and grill on both sides.
7   Serve the liver and bacon in an entrée dish or silver oval flat with a cordon of jus-lié and a sauceboat of jus-lié separately.

34 Veal Sweetbreads   *Ris de Veau*

Sweetbreads are glands, and two types are used for cooking. The thymus (throat) are usually long in shape and are of inferior quality. The pancreas (stomach) are heart-shaped and of superior quality.

35 Braised Veal Sweetbreads (White)   *4 portions*

	8 heart-shaped sweetbreads	
100 g	carrot	4 oz
250 ml	veal stock	½ pt
100 g	onion	4 oz
	bouquet garni	
	salt, pepper	

Ris de Veau Braisé (à blanc)

1   Wash, blanch, refresh and trim the sweetbreads.
2   Season and place in a casserole or plat à sauté on a bed of roots.
3   Add the bouquet garni and stock.
4   Cover with buttered greaseproof paper and a lid.
5   Cook gently in a moderate oven (150°–200°C) for approx. 1 hr.
6   Serve dressed in an entrée dish with some of the cooking liquor thickened with diluted arrowroot, and passed on to the sweetbreads.

36   Braised Veal Sweetbreads (Brown)   *Ris de Veau Braisé (à brun)*

Prepare as in previous recipe and place on a bed of roots which has been lightly coloured. Barely cover with brown veal stock, or half-brown veal stock and half jus-lié. Cook in a moderate oven (150°–200°C) without a lid, basting frequently (approx. 1 hr). Dress neatly in an entrée dish, cover with the corrected, strained sauce. (If veal stock is used thicken with arrowroot.)

37   Braised Veal Sweetbreads with Vegetables   *Ris de Veau Bonne Maman*

Braise white (Recipe 35) with a julienne of vegetables in place of the bed roots, the julienne served in the sauce.

38   Sweetbread Escalope   *Escalope de Ris de Veau*

Braise the sweetbreads white, press slightly between two trays and allow to cool. Cut into thick slices, $\frac{1}{2}$–1 cm ($\frac{1}{4}$–$\frac{1}{2}$ in) thick and shallow fry.
   Serve in an entrée dish or flat dish with the garnish and sauce as indicated.

39   Sweetbread Escalope (Crumbed)   *Escalope de Ris de Veau*

Braise the sweetbreads white, press slightly and allow to cool. Cut into thick slices. Then flour, egg and crumb and shallow fry. Serve with a suitable garnish, e.g. asparagus tips and a cordon of jus-lié. Finish with nut-brown butter.

40   Grilled Veal Sweetbreads   *Ris de Veau Grillée*

Blanch, braise, cool and press. Cut in halves crosswise, pass through melted butter and grill gently on both sides. Serve with a sauce and garnish as indicated.
   In some recipes they may be passed through butter and crumbs before being grilled.

41   Brains with Black Butter   *Cervelle au Beurre Noir*

1   Poach the brains in a court-bouillon ($\frac{1}{2}$ litre (1 pt) water), 1
    tbspn vinegar, 25 g (1 oz) carrot, 25 g (1 oz) onion, $\frac{1}{2}$ bay leaf,
    sprig of thyme, salt and a few peppercorns).
2   Skim and simmer for approx. 20 min.
3   Allow to cool and cut into thick slices.
4   Fry quickly in a frying-pan in butter on both sides and place
    in an entrée dish.
5   Clean the pan, add 10–25 g ($\frac{1}{2}$–1 oz) of butter per portion and
    blacken slightly; add coarsely chopped parsley and a few drips
    of vinegar and pour over the brains.

13
Bacon

1 Bacon   *Lard*

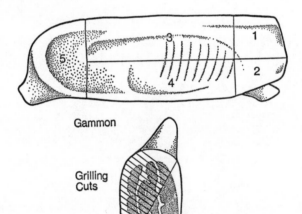

Gammon

Grilling
Cuts

Fig. 11

2 Side of Bacon	**Uses**	**Approx. Weight**	
		(kilo)	(lb)
1 Collar	Boiling, Grilling	4½	9
2 Hock	Boiling, Grilling	4½	9
3 Back	Grilling, Frying	9	18
4 Streaky	Grilling, Frying	4½	9
5 Gammon	Boiling, Grilling, Frying	7½	15

3 Quality

1. There should be no sign of stickiness.
2. There should be a pleasant smell.
3. The rind should be thin, smooth and free from wrinkles.
4. The fat should be white, smooth and not excessive in proportion to the lean.
5. The lean should be a deep pink colour and firm.

4 Preparation of Joints and Cuts

Collar	*Boiling*	Remove bone (if any) and tie with string.
	Grilling	Remove the rind and trim off outside surface and cut into thin slices (rashers), across the joint.
Hock	*Boiling*	Leave whole or bone-out and secure with string.
Back	*Grilling,* *Frying*	Remove all bones and rind and cut into thin rashers.
Streaky		as for Back.
Gammon	*Boiling*	as for Hock.
	Grilling, *Frying*	Fairly thick slices are cut from the middle of the Gammon. They are then trimmed and the rind removed.

RECIPES

5 Boiled Bacon   Hock, Collar or Gammon

1. Soak the bacon in cold water for 24 hr before cooking.
2. Change the water.
3. Bring to the boil, skim and simmer gently, approx. 25 min per $\frac{1}{2}$ kg (1 lb) and 25 min over.
4. Allow to cool in the liquid.
5. Remove the rind and brown skin.
6. Carve in thin slices.
7. Serve in an entrée dish with a little of the cooking liquor.

This may be served with pease pudding and a suitable sauce such as parsley sauce.

6 Grilled Gammon Rashers

Brush the rashers with fat on both sides and cook on greased, pre-heated grill bars on both sides for approx. 5–10 min in all. Serve on a flat dish with watercress and any other food as indicated, e.g. tomatoes, mushrooms, eggs. If a sauce is required, serve any sharp demi-glace sauce, e.g. diable.

7 Grilled Back or Streaky Rashers

Arrange on a baking tray and grill on both sides under the salamander.

8   Fried Bacon

Fry on both sides in a frying-pan in very little fat.

9   Ham   *Jambon*

Ham should not be confused with gammon. A gammon is the hind
leg of a baconer pig, and is cut from a side of bacon. A ham is the
hind leg of a porker pig, and is cut round from the side of pork with
the aitch bone and usually cured by dry salting. It is boiled and can
be served hot or cold. Certain imported hams, e.g. jambon de parme,
may be sliced thinly and eaten raw, generally as an hors d'œuvre. In
order to carve the ham efficiently it is necessary to remove the aitch
bone after cooking.

14
Poultry and Game

POULTRY

1 Poultry   *Volaille*

The term in its general sense is applied to all domestic fowl kept for breeding and means turkeys, geese, ducks, fowls and pigeons.

When the word *volaille* appears on the menu it applies only to fowls (chicken). Originally fowl were classified according to size and feeding by specific names as follows:

Chickens

	Weight			Number of
	(kilo)	(lb)		Portions
Single baby chicken	300 g–$\frac{1}{2}$	12 oz–1	1	Single poussin
Double baby chicken	$\frac{1}{2}$–$\frac{3}{4}$	1–$1\frac{1}{2}$	2	Double poussin
Small roasting chicken	$\frac{3}{4}$–1	$1\frac{1}{2}$–2	3– 4	Poulet de Grain
Medium roasting chicken	1–2	2–4	4– 6	Poulet reine
Large roasting or boiling chicken	2–3	4–6	6– 8	Poularde
Capon	3–$4\frac{1}{2}$	6–9	8–12	Chapon
Old boiling fowl	$2\frac{1}{2}$–4	5–8		Poule

Poussin—4–6 weeks old.
Uses—roasting and grilling.

Poulet de Grain—A young fattened bird 3–4 months old. Sometimes termed a broiler.
Uses—roasting, grilling, en casserole.

Poulet reine—fully-grown, tender, prime bird. Sometimes termed a broiler.
Uses—roasting, grilling, sauté, en casserole, suprêmes, pies.

Poularde—large fully-grown prime bird.
Uses—roasting, boiling, en casserole, galantine.

Chapon—a castrated or caponized cock bird specially fed and fattened.
Uses—roasting.

Poule—an old hen.
Uses—stocks and soups.

2 Signs of Quality
1 Plump breast.
2 Pliable breast bone.
3 Flesh firm.
4 Skin white, unbroken and with a faint bluish tint.

Old birds have coarse scales and large spurs on the legs and long hairs on the skin.

3 Cleaning

1   Pick out any pens or down, using a small knife.
2   Singe in order to remove any hairs, take care not to scorch the skin.
3   Split the neck skin by gripping firmly and making a lengthwise incision on the underside, cut off the neck as close to the body as possible.
4   Cut off the head.
5   Remove the crop and loosen intestines and lungs with forefinger.
6   Cut out vent and wipe clean.
7   Loosen intestines with forefinger.
8   Draw out the innards being careful not to break the gall bladder.
9   Wipe vent end if necessary.
10   Split and clean the gizzard.
11   Cut off the gall bladder from the liver.
12   Keep the neck and heart.

4 Trussing for Roasting

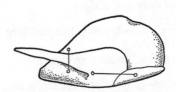

FIG. 12   FIG. 13

1   Clean the legs by dipping in boiling water for a few seconds then remove the scales with a cloth.
2   Cut off the outside claws leaving the centre ones, trim these to half their length.
3   To facilitate carving remove the wish-bone.
4   Place the bird on its back.
5   Hold the legs back firmly.
6   Insert the trussing needle through the bird, midway between the leg joints.
7   Turn on to its side.
8   Pierce the winglet, the skin of the neck, the skin of the carcass and the other winglet.
9   Tie ends of string securely.
10   Secure the legs by inserting the needle through the carcass and over the legs, take care not to pierce the breast.

5   Trussing for Boiling and Entrees

FIG. 14

1   Proceed as for roasting.
2   Cut the leg sinew just below the joint.
3   Either
    (*a*) bend back the legs so that they lie parallel to the breast and
    secure when trussing.
    (*b*) insert the legs through incisions made in the skin at the rear
    end of the bird and secure when trussing.

6   Cuts of Chicken
The pieces of cut chicken are named as follows:

English		French	
Leg { *4 Drumstick* { *3 Thigh*		*Cuisse* { Pilon de Cuisse { Gras de Cuisse	
1 Wing		Aile	
2 Breast		Blanc	
5 Winglet		Aileron	
6 Carcass		Carcasse	

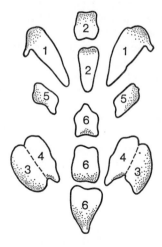

FIG. 15

7 Cutting for Sauté, Fricassée, Pies, etc.

1 Remove the feet at the first joint.
2 Remove the legs from the carcass.
3 Cut each leg in two at the joint.
4 Remove the wish-bone. Remove winglets and trim.
5 Remove the wings carefully, leaving two equal portions on the breast.
6 Remove the breast and cut in two.
7 Trim the carcass and cut into three pieces.

8 Preparation for Grilling

1 Remove the wish-bone.
2 Cut off the claws at the first joint.
3 Place bird on its back.
4 Insert a large knife through the neck-end and out of the vent.
5 Cut through the backbone.
6 Open out.

9 Preparation for Suprêmes

Suprême—this is the wing and half the breast of a chicken with the trimmed wing bone attached, i.e. the white meat of one chicken yields two suprêmes.

1 Use chicken weighing $1\frac{1}{4}$–$1\frac{1}{2}$ kg ($2\frac{1}{2}$–3 lb).
2 Cut off both legs from the chicken.
3 Remove the skin from the breasts.
4 Remove the wishbone.
5 Scrape the wing bone bare adjoining the breasts.
6 Cut off the winglets near the joints leaving $1\frac{1}{2}$–2 cm ($\frac{1}{2}$–$\frac{3}{4}$ in) of bare bone attached to the breasts.
7 Cut the breasts close to the breastbone and follow the bone down to the wing joint.
8 Cut through the joint.
9 Lay the chicken on its side and pull the suprêmes off assisting with the knife.
10 Lift the fillets from the suprêmes and remove the sinew from each.
11 Make an incision lengthways, along the thick side of the suprêmes, open and place the fillets inside.
12 Close, lightly flatten with a bat moistened with water and trim if necessary.

10 Preparation for Ballotines

1 A ballotine is a boned stuffed leg of bird.
2 Using a small sharp knife remove the thigh bone.

3   Scrape the flesh off the bone of the drumstick towards the claw joint.

4   Sever the drumstick bone leaving approx 2–3 cm ($\frac{3}{4}$–1 in) at the claw joint end.

5   Fill the cavities in both the drumstick and thigh with a savoury stuffing.

6   Neaten the shape and secure with string using a trussing needle.

Ballotines of chicken may be cooked and served using any of the recipes for chicken sauté pages 221–3.

11   Cutting of Cooked Chicken (Roasted or Boiled)   *4 portions*

1   Remove the legs and cut in two (drumstick and thigh).

2   Remove the wings.

3   Separate breast from the carcass and divide in two.

4   Serve a drumstick with a wing and the thigh with the breast.

12   Duck   *Canard*

Approx. 2–3 kilo (4–6 lb).

Duckling   *Caneton*
Approx. 1$\frac{1}{2}$–2 kilo (3–4 lb).

Signs of Quality
1   Plump breast.
2   Lower beak bends easily.
3   Webbed feet tear fairly easily.
4   The feet and bill should be yellow.

The preparation of duck for roasting is the same as for Roast Chicken. The gizzard is not split but trimmed off with a knife.

13   Goose   *Oie*

Approx. 6 kilo (12 lb).

Gosling   *Oison*

Signs of Quality—as for duck
Roast Goose is the same as for Roast Duck.

14   Turkey   *Dinde*

Young Turkey   *Dindonneau*
These can vary in weight from 3$\frac{1}{2}$–20 kilo (7–40 lb).

They are cleaned and trussed in the same way as chicken. The wish-bone should always be removed before trussing. The sinews should be drawn out of the legs. Allow 200 g ($\frac{1}{2}$ lb) per portion raw weight.

Roast Turkey   *Dinde Rôti*

5 kilo	turkey	10 lb
600 g	sausage meat ⎱ stuffing for neck cavity	1½ lb
200 g	chestnuts ⎰	½ lb
50 g	chopped onion	2 oz
100 g	dripping	4 oz
100 g	white breadcrumbs	4 oz
	pinch powdered thyme	
	pinch chopped parsley ⎬ stuffing for inside bird	
	chopped turkey liver	
	salt, pepper	
375 ml	brown stock	3 gills
100 g	fat bacon	4 oz
	bread sauce (p. 27)	

1   Slit the chestnuts on both sides using a small knife.
2   Boil chestnuts in water for 5–10 min.
3   Drain and remove outer and inner skins whilst warm.
4   Cook the chestnuts in a little stock for 15 min.
5   When cold mix them into the sausage meat.
6   Cook the onion in dripping without colour.
7   Remove from the heat add the seasoning crumbs and herbs.
8   Mix in the liver.
9   Stuff the crop (neck cavity) with the chestnut stuffing.
10 Stuff the inside of the bird with the other stuffing.
11 Truss the bird firmly.
12 Season with salt and pepper.
13 Cover the breast with fat bacon.
14 Place the bird in a roasting tray on its side and coat with 200 g
    (4 oz) dripping.
15 Roast in a moderate oven (200°–230°C).
16 Allow to cook on both legs and complete the cooking with the
    breast upright for the last 30 min.
17 Baste frequently and allow 15–20 min per lb.
18 When cooked prepare the gravy from the sediment.
19 Remove the string and serve with roast gravy, bread sauce and/
    or hot cranberry sauce.
20 The turkey may be garnished with chipolata sausages and bacon
    rolls.

CHICKEN RECIPES

15   Roast Chicken   *4 portions*   *Poulet Rôti*

1¼–1½ kg	1 chicken	2½–3 lb
125 ml	bread sauce (27)	1 gill
25 g	game chips	1 oz
50 g	dripping	2 oz
125 ml	brown stock	1 gill
	1 bunch watercress	

1   Season the chicken inside and out with salt.
2   Place on its side in a roasting tin.
3   Cover with the dripping.
4   Place in hot oven approx. 20–25 min.
5   Turn on to the other leg.
6   Cook for a further 20–25 min approx.
7   Baste frequently.
8   To test if cooked pierce with a fork between the drumstick
     and thigh and hold over a plate. The juice issuing from the
     chicken should not show any signs of blood.
9   Prepare roast gravy with the stock and the sediment in the
     roasting tray.
10 Serve on a flat silver dish with game chips in front and the
     watercress at the back of the bird.

Roast gravy and bread sauce are served separately.
Always remove the trussing string from the bird before serving.

16   Roast Chicken and Bacon   *Poulet Rôti au Lard*

As for Roast Chicken with four grilled rashers of streaky bacon
which may be rolled.

17   Roast Stuffed Chicken   *Poulet Rôti à l'Anglaise*

As for Roast Chicken, but before trussing stuff with the following:

25 g	chopped onion	1 oz
50 g	white breadcrumbs	2 oz
	pinch powdered thyme	
	the chopped chicken liver	
50 g	good dripping	2 oz
	pinch chopped parsley	
	salt, pepper	

1   Gently cook the onion in the dripping without colour.
2   Add the seasoning, herbs and crumbs.
3   Mix in the liver.
4   Correct seasoning.

18   Roast Stuffed Spring Chicken   *4 portions*   *Poussin Polonaise*

	4 single or 2 double spring chicken		
200 g	chicken livers		½ lb
100 g	fat bacon		¼ lb
25 g	onion (chopped)	stuffing	1 oz
	½ bay leaf		
	small sprig thyme		
50 g	butter		2 oz
25 g	white breadcrumbs		1 oz
	chopped parsley		
	juice of ½ lemon		
100 g	butter		4 oz
¼ l	brown stock		½ pt

1 Prepare the stuffing by cutting the fat bacon in small pieces.
2 Fry off quickly in a frying pan with the 50 g (2 oz) butter, herbs and chopped onion for a few seconds.
3 Add the trimmed chicken livers.
4 Season with salt and pepper.
5 Fry quickly until brown.
6 Pass all the mixture through a fine sieve.
7 Clean, prepare, season and truss the spring chicken as for entrée (p. 215).
8 Fill the chicks with the prepared stuffing.
9 Pot-roast (poêlé) the chicks.
10 Remove the lid half way through cooking to obtain a golden brown colour.
11 When cooked, remove the strings and place the chicks on a flat serving dish and keep warm.
12 Remove the fat from the cooking dish, déglacé with brown stock and lightly thicken with a little diluted arrowroot. Pass through a fine chinois and serve separately.
13 Cook the 100 g (4 oz) butter in a frying pan to a beurre noisette.
14 Mix in the breadcrumbs and the lemon juice and pour over the chicks.
15 Sprinkle with chopped parsley and serve.

19 Grilled Chicken *Poulet Grillé*

1 Season the chicken prepared for grilling (see page 216) with salt and mill pepper.
2 Brush with oil or melted fat and place on pre-heated greased grill bars or on a flat baking tray under a salamander.
3 Brush frequently with melted fat during cooking and allow approx. 15–20 min each side.
4 Test if cooked by piercing the drumstick with a skewer or trussing needle; there should be no sign of blood issuing from the leg.
5 Serve on a silver flat dish, garnish with picked watercress and offer a suitable sauce separately, e.g. Poulet Grillé, Sauce Diablé.

Grilled chicken is frequently served garnished with streaky bacon, tomatoes and mushrooms.

20 Grilled Devilled Chicken *Poulet Grillé Diablé*

Devil Mixture
1 tbspn English mustard
cayenne pepper
1 tspn Worcester sauce
2 tbspn water or vinegar
25 g   white breadcrumbs   1 oz

1   Combine all the ingredients, except the crumbs.
2   Proceed as for Grilled Chicken.
3   Approx. 5 min before each side of chicken is cooked brush
     liberally with the devil mixture, sprinkle with crumbs and complete
     the grilling.
4   Serve as for Grilled Chicken.

21 Chicken Spatchcock *4 portions*   *Poulet Grillé à la Crapaudine*

    1¼–1½ kg   1 chicken   2½–3 lb

1   Prepare the chicken as in recipe 5 (page 215) but do not string.
2   Cut horizontally from below the point of the breast over the
     top of the legs down to the wing joints without removing the
     breasts.
3   Fold back the breasts.
4   Force back and flatten the legs on either side.
5   Flatten slightly with a bat.
6   The shape will resemble a toad.
7   Season with salt and mill pepper.
8   Brush with oil or melted fat.
9   Place on pre-heated grill bars or on a flat tray under a sala-
     mander.
10   Brush frequently with melted fat or oil during cooking and
     allow approx 15–20 min on each side.
11   Test if cooked by piercing the drumstick with a needle or
     skewer—there should be no sign of blood.
12   When serving, two eyes for the 'toad' may be made from slices
     of hard boiled white of egg with a pupil of truffle or gherkin.
13   Serve on a silver flat dish, garnish with picked watercress and
     offer a suitable sauce separately, e.g. Sauce Diablé, Beurre
     Maître d'Hôtel.

22 Grilled Devilled Chicken Spatchcock   *Poulet Grillé à la Crapaudine*
                                                                Diablé

Proceed as for Recipes 21 and 20.

23 Sauté of Chicken *4 portions*   *Poulet Sauté*

1¼–1½ kg	1 chicken	2½–3 lb
250 ml	jus-lié or demi-glace	½ pt
	salt, pepper	
50 g	butter	2 oz
	chopped parsley	

1   To prepare the chicken for sauté remove the feet at the first
     joint.
2   Remove the legs from the carcass.
3   Cut each leg in two at the joint.
4   Remove the wish-bone. Remove winglets and trim.

5   Remove the wings carefully, leaving two equal portions on the breast.
6   Remove the breast and cut in two.
7   Trim the carcass and cut into three pieces.
8   Place the butter in a sauté pan on a fairly hot stove.
9   Season the pieces of chicken and place in the pan in the following order: drumsticks, thighs, carcass, wings, winglets and breast.
10   Cook to a golden brown on both sides.
11   Cover with a lid and cook on the stove or in the oven until tender.
12   Dress neatly in an entrée dish.
13   Drain off all fat from the sauté pan.
14   Return to the heat and add the jus-lié or demi-glace.
15   Simmer for 3–4 min.
16   Correct the seasoning and skim.
17   Pass through a fine strainer on to the chicken.
18   Sprinkle with chopped parsley and serve.

NOTE. The chicken giblets should always be used in the making of the jus-lié or demi-glace.

24   Chicken Sauté Chasseur   *4 portions*   *Poulet Sauté Chasseur*

1¼–1½ kg	1 chicken cut for sauté	2½–3 lb
100 g	button mushrooms	4 oz
250 ml	jus-lié or demi-glace	½ pt
	3 tbspn white wine	
50 g	butter	2 oz
200 g	tomatoes	8 oz
10 g	chopped shallot	½ oz
	chopped parsley and tarragon	

1   Place the butter in a sauté pan on a fairly hot stove.
2   Season the pieces of chicken and place in the pan in the following order: drumsticks, thighs, carcass, wings, winglets and breast.
3   Cook to a golden brown on both sides.
4   Cover with a lid and cook on the stove or in the oven until tender. Dress neatly in an entrée dish.
5   Add the shallots to the sauté pan, cover with a lid, cook on a gentle heat for 1–2 min without colour.
6   Add washed sliced mushrooms, cover with a lid, cook gently 3–4 min without colour.
7   Drain off fat.
8   Add white wine and reduce by half.
9   Add the demi-glace or jus-lié.
10   Add the tomate concassée.
11   Simmer for 5 min.

12   Correct the seasoning.
13   Pour over the chicken.
14   Sprinkle with chopped parsley and tarragon and serve.

25   Chicken Sauté with Mushrooms   *4 portions*

Poulet Sauté aux Champignons

1¼–1½ kg	1 chicken cut for sauté	2½–3 lb
250 ml	demi-glace or jus-lié	½ pt
10 g	chopped shallot	½ oz
	salt	
	pepper	
50 g	butter	2 oz
60 ml	white wine	⅛ pt
100 g	button mushrooms	4 oz
	chopped parsley	

1   Place the butter in a sauté pan on a fairly hot stove.
2   Season the pieces of chicken and place in the pan in the following
order: drumsticks, thighs, carcass, wings, winglets and breast.
3   Cook to a golden brown on both sides.
4   Cover with a lid and cook on the stove or in the oven until
tender. Dress neatly in an entrée dish.
5   Add the shallots to the sauté pan, cover with a lid, cook on a
gentle heat for 1–2 min without colour.
6   Add washed sliced mushrooms, cover with a lid, cook gently
3–4 min without colour.
7   Pour off the fat.
8   Add the white wine.
9   Reduce by half.
10   Add the demi-glace.
11   Simmer for 5 min
12   Correct the seasoning.
13   Pour over the pieces of chicken.
14   Sprinkle with chopped parsley.

26   Chicken Sauté with Potatoes   *4 portions*   *Poulet Sauté Parmentier*

1¼–1½kg	1 chicken cut for sauté	2½–3 lb
250 ml	demi-glace or jus-lié	½ pt
200 g	potatoes	8 oz
	chopped parsley	
50 g	butter	2 oz
	3–4 tbspn white wine	
	salt	
	pepper	

1   Cook and dress chicken as for sauté.
2   Pour off the fat.
3   Add wine and reduce by half.

4   Add the demi-glace or jus-lié.
5   Simmer for 5 min.
6   Pass through fine strainer over the chicken.
7   Meanwhile peel and wash the potatoes.
8   Cut into 1 cm (½ in) dice.
9   Wash well, drain and shallow fry to a golden brown in hot fat
     in a frying-pan.
10   Drain, season and sprinkle over the chicken.
11   Sprinkle with chopped parsley and serve.

27 Wing and Breast of Chicken in   *4 portions*   *Suprême de Volaille à la*
    Cream Sauce   *Crème*

	4 suprêmes of chicken (p. 216)	
50 g	butter	2 oz
25 g	seasoned flour	1 oz
30 ml	sherry	$\frac{1}{16}$ pt
125 ml	double cream	$\frac{1}{4}$ pt
	salt	
	cayenne	

1   Heat the butter in a sauté pan.
2   Lightly flour the suprêmes.
3   Cook the suprêmes gently on both sides (7–9 min) with the
     minimum of colour.
4   Place the suprêmes in an earthenware serving dish, cover
     to keep warm.
5   Drain off the fat from the pan.
6   Déglacé the pan with the sherry.
7   Add the cream, bring to the boil and season.
8   Allow to reduce to a lightly thickened consistency.
9   Pass through a fine chinois on to the suprêmes and serve.

An alternative method of preparing the sauce is to use half the
amount of cream and an equal amount of chicken velouté (p. 21).

28 Wing and Breast of Chicken in   *4 portions*   *Suprême de Volaille aux*
    Cream Sauce with Mushrooms   *Champignons à la Crème*

	4 suprêmes of chicken (p. 216)	
50 g	butter	2 oz
100 g	button mushrooms	4 oz
25 g	seasoned flour	1 oz
30 ml	sherry	$\frac{1}{16}$ pt
125 ml	double cream	$\frac{1}{4}$ pt
	salt	
	cayenne	

1   Heat the butter in a sauté pan.
2   Lightly flour the suprêmes.
3   Cook the suprêmes on both sides (7–9 min) with the minimum
     of colour.

4   Place the suprêmes in an earthenware serving dish, cover to keep warm.
5   Peel, wash and slice the mushrooms.
6   Gently sauté the mushrooms in the same butter and pan as the escalopes and add them to the escalopes.
7   Drain off all the fat from the pan.
8   Déglacé the pan with the sherry.
9   Add the cream, bring to the boil and season.
10 Allow to reduce to a lightly thickened consistency.
11 Pass through a fine chinois on to the suprêmes and serve.

An alternative method of preparing the sauce is to use half the amount of cream and an equal amount of chicken velouté (p. 21).

29 Crumbed Breast of Chicken with   *4 portions*   *Suprême de Volaille aux*
    Asparagus   *Pointes d'Asperges*

	4 suprêmes of chicken (p. 216)	
25 g	seasoned flour	1 oz
	1 egg	
50 g	breadcrumbs	2 oz
	For frying	
50 g	oil	2 oz
50 g	butter	2 oz
200 g	asparagus sprue	½ lb
	For finishing	
50 g	butter	2 oz
60 ml	jus-lié	⅛ pt

1   Pané the chicken suprêmes.
2   Shake off all surplus crumbs.
3   Neaten and mark on one side with a palette knife.
4   Heat the oil and butter in a sauté pan.
5   Gently fry the suprêmes to a golden brown on both sides (6–8 min).
6   Dress the suprêmes on a silver flat and keep warm.
7   Mask the suprêmes with the remaining 50 g (2 oz) butter cooked to the nut-brown stage.
8   Surround the suprêmes with a cordon of jus-lié.
9   Garnish each suprême with a neat bundle of asparagus points (previously cooked, refreshed and reheated with a little butter).
10 Place a cutlet frill on to each wing bone and serve.

30 Breast of Chicken in breadcrumbs   *4 portions*   *Suprême de Volaille*
    with Asparagus and Truffle   *Maréchale*

Proceed as for Recipe 29 adding one or two slices of truffle on to each suprême.

31 Boiled Chicken with Rice *4 portions* and Suprême Sauce

Poulet Poché au Riz, Sauce Suprême

2–2½ kg	1 boiling fowl	4–5 lb
	For the chicken	
50 g	onion	2 oz
	bouquet garni	
50 g	carrot	2 oz
	6 peppercorns	
	For the rice	
50 g	chopped onion	2 oz
50 g	butter	2 oz
200 g	rice (long grain)	8 oz
500 ml	chicken stock	1 pt
	For the sauce	
75 g	margarine	3 oz
1 litre	chicken stock	2 pt
	few drops of lemon juice	
75 g	flour	3 oz
	4 tbspn cream	

1 Place the chicken in cold water.
2 Bring to the boil and skim.
3 Add peeled, whole, washed vegetables, bouquet garni, peppercorns and salt.
4 Simmer till cooked. To test, remove the chicken from the stock and hold over a plate to catch the juices from the inside of the bird. There should be no sign of blood. Also test the drumstick with a trussing needle.
5 Prepare ½ litre (1 pt) of velouté from the cooking liquor, cook out, correct the seasoning and pass through a fine strainer.
6 Finish with cream.
7 Prepare a pilaff of rice (see page 96).

To serve, cut into portions. Dress the rice neatly in an entrée dish, arrange the portions of chicken on top and coat with sauce.

32 Chicken à la King *4 portions*

Emincé de Volaille à la King

400 g	cooked boiled chicken	1 lb
50 g	red pimento (skinned)	2 oz
100 g	button mushrooms	4 oz
30 ml	sherry	$\frac{1}{16}$ pt
125 ml	chicken velouté	$\frac{1}{4}$ pt
30 ml	cream	$\frac{1}{16}$ pt
25 g	butter	1 oz

1 Wash, peel and slice the mushrooms.
2 Cook them without colour in the butter.
3 If using raw pimento, discard the seeds, cut the pimento in dice and cook with the mushrooms.
4 Cut the chicken in escalopes.
5 Add the chicken to the mushrooms and pimento.

6   Drain off the fat.
7   Add the sherry.
8   Add the velouté, bring to the boil.
9   Finish with the cream and correct the seasoning.
10   Place into a serving dish and decorate with small strips of
     cooked pimento.

1 or 2 egg yolks may be used to form a liaison with the cream mixed
into the boiling mixture at the last possible moment and immediately
removed from the heat. Chicken à la king may be served in a border
of golden brown duchesse potato or a pilaff of rice (p. 96) may be
offered as an accompaniment.

33   Chicken Galantine   *approx. 8 portions*   *Galantine de Volaille*

This is a basic recipe which may be garnished with strips of tongue,
truffle, fat pork and pistachio nuts.

2–2½ kg	1 chicken	4–5 lb
¼ litre	cream	½ pt
	nutmeg	
	2 egg whites	
	salt, pepper	

1   Bone-out the chicken whole, taking care to leave the skin unbroken.
2   Remove all the flesh from the bone and pass the flesh two or
     three times through the mincer.
3   Place in a pan in a bowl of ice water and using a wooden
     spoon, beat in the egg white and seasoning.
4   Gradually beat in the ice-cold cream.
5   Spread out the chicken skin.
6   Lay on the prepared mixture (farce).
7   Mould into a neat roll.
8   Roll securely in a cloth.
9   Tie at each end and in the centre.
10   Simmer gently in chicken stock, made from the bones, for
     approx. 1–1½ hr.
11   When thoroughly cold remove cloth.
12   Cut in slices, serve on a silver flat dish and garnish with salad.

Galantines may be coated with a white chaud-froid sauce, decorated
and then masked with aspic jelly.

34   Chicken Vol-au-Vent   *8 portions*   *Vol-au-Vent de Volaille*

2 kg	1 boiling chicken	4 lb
½ litre	chicken velouté	1 pt
400 g	puff paste (p. 290)	1 lb
	4 tbspn cream	

1   Prepare the puff pastry using ½ kg (1 lb) flour and ½ kg (1 lb)
     margarine and ¼ litre (½ pt) water.
2   Roll out sufficient to cut eight rounds 6 cm (3 in) diameter.

3   Turn upside down on a lightly greased, dampened baking sheet.
4   Using a smaller plain cutter, make incisions half-way through
    each leaving approx. $\frac{1}{2}$ cm ($\frac{1}{4}$ in) border.
5   Egg wash and bake in a hot oven (230°–250°C) approx. 15–20 min.
6   When cool remove the lids carefully.
7   Empty out the raw pastry from the centre.
8   Cook the chicken as for Boiled Chicken (recipe 31).
9   Make a velouté and cook out, correct the seasoning and pass
    through a fine strainer, finish with cream.
10 Remove all skin and bone from the chicken.
11 Cut into neat pieces, mix with the sauce.
12 Fill the warm puff pastries to overflowing.
13 Serve on a silver dish.
14 Add the lids and garnish with picked parlsey.

35   Chicken and Mushroom Vol-au-Vent

As for Chicken Vol-au-Vent with the addition of 100 g (4 oz) of
well-washed button mushrooms cut into quarters and cooked in a
little stock with a few drops of lemon juice and 5 g ($\frac{1}{4}$ oz) butter.

36   Chicken Cutlets   *4 portions*   *Côtelettes de Volaille*

200 g	cooked chicken free from bone and skin	$\frac{1}{2}$ lb
	1 egg yolk	
125 ml	thick béchamel or chicken velouté	$\frac{1}{4}$ pt
	salt, pepper	
	For coating	
	1 egg	
25 g	flour	1 oz
50 g	white crumbs	2 oz

1   Cut the chicken into 2 mm ($\frac{1}{8}$ in) dice.
2   Boil béchamel in a thick-bottomed pan.
3   Add the chicken and mix with a wooden spoon.
4   Bring to the boil and season.
5   Add the yolk, mix well.
6   Correct the seasoning, remove from fire.
7   Turn out on to a buttered tray.
8   Cover with a greased paper and allow to set cold.
9   Mould into four even-sized cones.
10 Pass through flour, egg and breadcrumbs.
11 Flatten and shape like cutlets.
12 Insert a small piece of macaroni to resemble a cutlet bone.
13 Deep or shallow fry in hot fat (180°C) until golden brown.
14 Drain and serve on a dish paper on a silver dish.
15 Garnish with fried or picked parsley.

   A suitable sauce should be served separately, e.g. madeira, demi-
glace, mushroom.

37 Chicken and Mushroom Cutlets

As for recipe 36, adding 50–100 g (2–4 oz) well-washed mushrooms, cut the same as the chicken and cooked in a tablespoonful stock and 10 g (½ oz) butter and lemon juice. Add to the sauce with the chicken.

38 Chicken and Ham Cutlets

As for Chicken Cutlets (recipe 36) using 300 g (12 oz) chicken and 100 g (4 oz) lean cooked ham.

39 Chicken Pancakes *4 portions*   *Crêpes de Volaille*

	Pancake mixture	
100 g	flour	4 oz
¼ litre	milk	½ pt
	salt, pepper	
	chopped parsley	
	1 egg	
50 g	lard	2 oz
10 g	melted butter	½ oz
	Filling	
200 g	cooked chicken free from bone and skin	½ lb
125 ml	thick béchamel or chicken velouté	¼ pt
	salt, pepper	

1 Sieve flour into a bowl and make a well in the centre.
2 Add the egg, salt, pepper, parsley and milk.
3 Gradually incorporate the flour from the sides of the bowl and whisk to a smooth batter.
4 Mix in the melted butter.
5 Heat the pancake pan, clean thoroughly.
6 Add 5 g (¼ oz) lard and heat until smoking.
7 Add sufficient mixtures to thinly cover the bottom of the pan.
8 Cook for a few seconds until lightly brown.
9 Turn and cook on the other side.
10 Turn onto a plate.
11 Wipe pan clean if necessary, and make a total of 8 small or 4 large pancakes.
12 Meanwhile prepare the filling by boiling the sauce.
13 Cut the chicken in neat small pieces and add to the sauce.
14 Mix in and correct the seasoning.
15 Divide the mixture between the pancakes, roll up each one and place in an earthenware dish.
16 Reheat in a hot oven and place on a silver flat dish and serve.

40 Chicken Pancakes with Cheese Sauce *4 portions* *Crêpes de Volaille*
                                                                      Mornay

1 Proceed as for recipe 39.
2 Coat the pancakes with ¼ litre (½ pt) mornay sauce.

3   Sprinkle with 10 g ($\frac{1}{2}$ oz) grated cheese.
4   Brown under the salamander and serve.

41   Chicken Pancakes with Tomato, Mushroom and   *4 portions   Crêpes de*
White Wine Sauce   *Volaille Chasseur*

1   Proceed as for Recipe 39.
2   Coat pancake with $\frac{1}{4}$ litre ($\frac{1}{2}$ pt) chasseur sauce (p. 23).

42   Chicken and Mushroom Pancakes   *4 portions   Crêpes de Volaille et*
Champignons

Add 50–100 g (2–4 oz) washed sliced cooked mushrooms to the filling and proceed as for Recipe 39.

43   Chicken and Mushroom Pancakes with   *4 portions   Crêpes de Volaille*
Cheese Sauce   *et Champignons Mornay*

1   Add 50–100 g (2–4 oz) cooked mushrooms to the filling as Recipe 39.
2   Coat with $\frac{1}{4}$ litre ($\frac{1}{2}$ pt) mornay sauce.
3   Sprinkle with grated cheese.
4   Brown under the salamander and serve.

44   Chicken and Ham Pancakes   *4 portions   Crêpes de Volaille et Jambon*

Proceed as for Recipe 39 using 100 g ($\frac{1}{4}$ lb) chicken and 100 g ($\frac{1}{4}$ lb) lean ham cut in neat pieces.

45   Fricassée of Chicken   *4 portions*   *Fricassée de Volaille*

1$\frac{1}{4}$–1$\frac{1}{2}$ kg	1 chicken	2$\frac{1}{2}$–3 lb
35 g	flour	1$\frac{1}{2}$ oz
	1–2 yolks of eggs	
	chopped parsley	
50 g	butter	2 oz
$\frac{1}{2}$ litre	chicken stock	1 pt
	(approx.)	
	4 tbspn cream	

1   Cut the chicken as for sauté and season with salt and pepper.
2   Place the butter in a sauté pan.
3   Heat gently.
4   Add pieces of chicken.
5   Cover with a lid.
6   Cook gently on both sides without colouring.
7   Mix in the flour.

8   Cook out carefully without colouring.
9   Gradually mix in the stock.
10   Bring to the boil and skim.
11   Allow to simmer gently till cooked.
12   Mix yolks and cream in a basin (liaison).
13   Pick out the chicken into a clean pan.
14   Pour a little of the boiling sauce on to the yolks and cream and mix well.
15   Pour all back into the sauce, combine thoroughly but do not re-boil.
16   Correct the seasoning.
17   Pour over the chicken, reheat without boiling.
18   Dress in an entrée dish.
19   Sprinkle with chopped parsley.

46   Fricassée of Chicken with   *Fricassée de Volaille*
    Button Onions and Mushrooms   *à l'Ancienne*

As for Fricassée of Chicken with 50–100 g (2–4 oz) button onions and 50–100 g (2–4 oz) button mushrooms. They are peeled and the mushrooms left whole, turned or quartered depending on size and quality. The onions are added to the chicken as soon as it comes to the boil and the mushrooms 15 min later.

47   Chicken Pie   *4 portions*

1¼–1½ kg	1 chicken	2½–3 lb
100 g	button mushrooms	4 oz
	1 chopped onion	
¼ litre	approx chicken stock	½ pt
	pinch of chopped parsley	
100 g	streaky bacon	¼ lb
	1 hard-boiled egg (chopped)	
	salt	
	pepper	
200 g	puff paste (p. 290)	8 oz

1   Cut the chicken as for sauté or bone-out completely and cut into pieces 3 × 1 cm (1½ × ½ in).
2   Season with salt and pepper.
3   Wrap each piece in thin streaky bacon.
4   Place in a pie dish.
5   Add the washed sliced mushrooms.
6   Add remainder of the ingredients.
7   Add sufficient cold stock to barely cover the chicken.
8   Cover and cook as for Steak Pie (page 169). Allow approx. 1–1½ hr cooking.
9   Serve on an oval silver flat dish with a pie collar.

48   Chicken in Casserole or Cocotte   *Poulet en Casserole ou en Cocotte*

A casserole is made of earthenware, a cocotte of porcelain.

Basic Method

1¼–1½ kg	1 chicken	2½–3 lb
50 g	onion	2 oz
50 g	carrot	2 oz
¼ litre	jus-lié or demi-glace	½ pt
50 g	butter	2 oz
50 g	celery	2 oz
	bouquet garni	
	chopped parsley	

1   Prepare the chicken and truss for entrée.
2   Slice the onion, carrot and celery, place in the bottom of the casserole or cocotte with the bouquet garni.
3   Season the chicken and place on the bed of roots.
4   Spread the butter on the bird.
5   Cover with a lid and place in a hot oven (230°–250°C).
6   Baste occasionally, allow approx. ¼–1 hr.
7   When cooked remove the chicken.
8   Pour off the fat from the casserole, remove the bouquet garni.
9   Déglacé the casserole or cocotte with the demi-glace or jus-lié.
10 Pour the sauce into a sauteuse, boil, skim and correct the seasoning and consistency.
11 Clean the casserole, remove the string from the bird and place in the casserole.
12 Pass the sauce through a fine strainer on to the bird.
13 Sprinkle with chopped parsley.
14 Place the casserole or cocotte with the lid on a silver flat dish and serve.

Chicken casserole is usually served garnished, e.g.:

Bonne Femme	pomme cocotte, glazed button onions, lardons.
Champeaux	as bonne femme with white wine in the sauce.
Grandmère	dice of mushrooms and croûtons.
Parmentier	parmentier potatoes, white wine in the sauce.
Paysanne	paysanne of vegetables.

49   Chicken Salad   *4 portions*   *Salade de Poulet*

400 g	cooked chicken free from skin and bone	1 lb
	2 tomatoes	
10 g	anchovies	½ oz
5 g	capers	¼ oz
	1 lettuce (washed)	
	1 hard-boiled egg	
10 g	olives	½ oz
	4 tbspn vinaigrette	

1   Remove heart from the lettuce.

2   Shred the remainder.
3   Place in a glass salad bowl.
4   Cut the chicken in neat pieces and place on the lettuce.
5   Decorate with quarters of tomato, hard-boiled egg, anchovies, olives, heart of the lettuce and capers.
6   Serve on a doily on a silver flat dish. Vinaigrette separate.

50   Chicken Mayonnaise   *Mayonnaise de Poulet*

As above, using 60 ml (⅛ pt) mayonnaise instead of vinaigrette. The chicken is dressed on the lettuce, then coated with mayonnaise and the garnish neatly dressed on top.

51   Curried Chicken   *4 portions*   *Kari de Poulet* or *Currie de Poulet*

1¼–1½ kg	1 chicken	2½–3 lb
	1 clove garlic	
10 g	curry powder	½ oz
10 g	tomato purée	½ oz
10 g	sultanas	½ oz
25 g	chopped chutney	1 oz
50 g	fat approx.	2 oz
200 g	onion	8 oz
10 g	flour	½ oz
5 g	desiccated coconut	¼ oz
½ litre	chicken stock	1 pt
50 g	chopped apple	2 oz

1   Cut the chicken as for sauté, season with salt.
2   Heat the fat in a sauté pan, add the chicken.
3   Lightly brown on both sides.
4   Add the chopped onion and garlic.
5   Cover with lid, cook gently 3–4 min.
6   Mix in the flour and curry powder.
7   Mix in the tomato purée.
8   Moisten with stock.
9   Bring to the boil, skim.
10 Add remainder of the ingredients.
11 Simmer till cooked.
12 The sauce may be finished with 30 ml (½ gill) cream.
13 Serve in an entrée dish.

Accompany with 100 g (4 oz) plain boiled rice, grilled poppadum and Bombay duck.

52   Braised Rice with Chicken Livers   *4 portions*

Pilaff aux Foies de Volailles

100 g	chicken livers	4 oz
25 g	butter	1 oz
200 g	braised rice (p. 96)	½ lb
60 ml	demiglace or jus-lié	½ gill
	salt, mill pepper	

1   Trim the livers, cut into 1 cm ($\frac{1}{2}$ in) dice.
2   Season with salt and pepper.
3   Fry quickly in the butter in a frying-pan.
4   Drain well.
5   Mix with the demi-glace or the jus-lié, do not re-boil.
6   Correct the seasoning.
7   Make a well with the riz pilaff on a silver dish.
8   Serve the livers in the centre of the rice.

DUCK RECIPES

53   Roast Duck or Duckling   *Canard* or *Caneton Rôti*

	1 duck	
$\frac{1}{4}$ litre	brown stock	$\frac{1}{2}$ pt
	bunch watercress	
50 g	dripping	2 oz
125 ml	apple sauce	$\frac{1}{4}$ pt

1   Season the duck inside and out with salt.
2   Place on its side in a roasting tin.
3   Cover with the dripping.
4   Place in hot oven approx. 20–25 min.
5   Turn on to the other leg.
6   Cook for a further 20–25 min approx.
7   Baste frequently.
8   To test if cooked pierce with a fork between the drumstick and thigh and hold over a plate. The juice issuing from the duck should not show any signs of blood.
9   Prepare roast gravy with the stock and the sediment in the roasting tray.
10   Serve on a flat silver dish, garnish with picked watercress.
11   Accompany with a sauceboat of hot apple sauce and a sauce-boat of gravy and Game chips. Also serve sauceboat of sage and onion stuffing as prepared in the following recipe for Roast Stuffed Duck.

54   Roast Stuffed Duck   *Canard Rôti à l'Anglaise*

	Stuffing	
50 g	good dripping	2 oz
50 g	white breadcrumbs	2 oz
	chopped parsley	
	chopped duck liver	
100 g	chopped onion	4 oz
	$\frac{1}{2}$ tspn powdered sage	
	salt, pepper	

1   Gently cook the onion in the dripping without colour.
2   Add the herbs and seasoning.
3   Mix in the crumbs and liver.
   Cook and serve as for Roast Duck.

55   Roast Duckling and Orange Salad   *Caneton Rôti Salade d'Orange*

Proceed as for Roast Duck and serve separately in a glass bowl 4 hearts of lettuce or good leaves of lettuce and on each heart place 3 segments of orange, free from pips and skin, and a little blanched julienne of orange zest sprinkled over.

Accompany with a sauceboat of cream slightly acidulated with lemon juice.

56   Duckling with Orange Sauce   *4 portions*   *Caneton Bigarade*

2 kg	duckling	4 lb
	Mirepoix	
50 g	carrots ⎫	2 oz
50 g	onions ⎬ roughly cut	2 oz
25 g	celery ⎭	1 oz
	1 bay leaf	
	1 small sprig thyme	
50 g	butter	2 oz
250 ml	brown stock	½ pt
10 g	arrowroot	½ oz
	2 oranges	
	1 lemon	
	2 tbsp vinegar	
25 g	sugar	1 oz

1   Use 10 g (½ oz) butter to grease a deep pan.
2   Add the mirepoix.
3   Season the cleaned and trussed duck.
4   Place the duck on the mirepoix.
5   Coat the duck with the remaining butter.
6   Cover the pan with a tight fitting lid.
7   Place the pan in oven (200°–230°C).
8   Baste occasionally, cook approx. 1 hour.
9   Remove the lid and continue cooking the duck basting frequently until tender (approx. a further ½ hour).
10   Remove the duck, cut out the string and keep the duck in a warm place.
11   Drain off all the fat from the pan.
12   Déglacé with the stock bring to the boil and allow to simmer for a few minutes.
13   Thicken by gradually adding the arrowroot diluted in a little cold water.
14   Reboil, correct seasoning, degrease and pass through a fine chinois.
15   Thinly remove the zest from one orange and the lemon and cut into fine julienne.
16   Blanch the julienne of zest for 3–4 min, refresh.

17   Place the vinegar, sugar and the juice of the lemon and the oranges in a small sauteuse and cook to a light caramel stage.
18   Add the sauce from the duck.
19   Bring to the boil, correct seasoning and pass through a fine chinois.
20   Add the julienne to the sauce, keep warm.
21   Remove the legs from the duck, bone out and cut in thin slices.
22   Carve the duck breasts into thin slices and neatly dress on a serving dish.
23   Coat with the sauce and serve.

NOTE: an alternative method is to cut the duck into eight pieces which may then be either left on the bone or the bones removed.

57   Duckling with Cherries   *4 portions*   *Caneton aux Cerises*

2 kg	duckling	4 lb
	Mirepoix	
50 g	carrots ⎱	2 oz
50 g	onions ⎬ roughly cut	2 oz
25 g	celery ⎰	1 oz
	1 bay leaf	
	1 small sprig thyme	
50 g	butter	2 oz
250 ml	brown stock	$\frac{1}{2}$ pt
10 g	arrowroot	$\frac{1}{2}$ oz
30 ml	sherry or madeira	$\frac{1}{16}$ pt
	24 stoned cherries	

1   Use 10 g (1 oz) butter to grease a deep pan.
2   Add the mirepoix.
3   Season the cleaned and trussed duck.
4   Place the duck on the mirepoix.
5   Coat the duck with the remaining butter.
6   Cover the pan with a tight fitting lid.
7   Place the pan in oven (200°–230°C).
8   Baste occasionally, cook approx. 1 hour.
9   Remove the lid and continue cooking the duck basting frequently until tender (approx. a further $\frac{1}{2}$ hour).
10   Remove the duck, cut out the string and keep the duck in a warm place.
11   Drain off all the fat from the pan.
12   Déglacé the pan with the sherry.
13   Add the stock bring to the boil, simmer 4–5 min.
14   Thicken by gradually adding the arrowroot diluted in a little cold water.
15   Reboil, correct seasoning, degrease and pass through a fine chinois.
16   Add the stoned cherries to the sauce and simmer gently 3–4 min.

17   Remove the legs from the duck, bone out and cut into thin slices.
18   Cut the duck breasts into thin slices and neatly dress on a serving dish.
19   Coat with the sauce and cherries and serve.

NOTE: an alternative method is to cut the duck into eight pieces which may then be either left on the bone or the bones removed.

58 Braised Duck with Peas *4 portions*   *Canard Braisé aux Petits Pois*

2 kg	duck	4 lb
50 g	butter	2 oz
100 g	thick cut streaky bacon	4 oz
200 g	button onions	½ lb
375 ml	brown stock	¾ pt
375 ml	demi glace	¾ pt
200 g	peas	½ lb

1   Place the butter in a braising pan.
2   Cut the bacon into thick lardons.
3   Add the lardons and button onions to the pan.
4   Gently fry to a light brown colour.
5   Remove the lardons and onions taking care not to burn the butter.
6   Add the prepared seasoned and trussed duck to the pan.
7   Carefully brown the duck on all sides without burning the butter.
8   Drain off all the fat.
9   Add the demi-glace and brown stock (the duck should be ½–¾ covered).
10   Bring to the boil and cover with a lid.
11   Place in a moderate oven (150°–200°C) and allow to simmer gently for approx. ¾–1 hour.
12   Add the lardons, button onions and the peas (only add the peas at this stage if raw fresh peas are being used—if frozen peas are being used they should be added 10–15 min. later).
13   Replace the lid, return the dish to the oven.
14   Continue simmering gently until the duck and garnish is tender— approx. a further ½–¾ hour.
15   Remove the duck, cut out the string and keep warm.
16   Degrease the sauce and correct the seasoning and consistency.
17   Cut the duck into portions and neatly place on a serving dish.
18   Mask with the sauce and garnish and serve.

GAME   *GIBIER*

59

Game may be divided into two groups:
(*a*) furred—venison, hare; (*b*) feathered.

FURRED GAME

60   Venison

This name applies to the flesh of deer. It is by nature dry, tough meat. This is overcome by hanging the carcass for 12–21 days according to the temperature, and by well-marinading the joints.

61   *Marinade*

125 ml	oil	¼ pt
200 g	onions	8 oz
200 g	carrots	8 oz
	sprig of thyme	
	2 bay leaves	
100 g	celery	4 oz
	12 peppercorns	
	parsley stalks	
	4 tbspn vinegar	
	salt	

The vegetables are washed, peeled and chopped, combined with the other ingredients and sprinkled over the joint. The joint is turned occasionally and left to marinade for several hours.

The hindquarters only are used for good-class joints. Roast joints are usually accompanied by a piquante or peppery sauce, cold joints by an Oxford or Cumberland sauce. Recipes for these sauces are in the sauce section.

62   Hare   *Lièvre*

Young hare 2½–3 kg (5–6 lb) in weight should be used. To test a young hare it should be possible to take the ear between the fingers and tear it quite easily, also the hare lip which is clearly marked in old animals, should only be faintly defined.

A hare should be hung for about a week before cleaning it out. It may be prepared as a brown stew known as a civet.

63   Jugged Hare   *Civet de Lièvre*

	1 young hare	
50 g	fat	2 oz
½ litre	approx. brown stock	1 pt
	1 clove garlic	
¼ litre	red wine	½ pt
25 g	flour	1 oz
25 g	tomato purée	1 oz
	Garnish	
100 g	button onions	4 oz
100 g	streaky bacon	4 oz
	chopped parsley	
100 g	button mushrooms	4 oz
100 g	stale bread	4 oz

1 Skin hare carefully.
2 Make an incision along the belly.
3 Clear out the intestines.
4 Clean out the forequarter end carefully collecting all the blood into a basin.
5 Cut as follows: each leg into two pieces,
   each foreleg into two pieces,
   the forequarter into two,
   the saddle into three or four pieces.
6 Soak in a marinade as for vension, for 5–6 hr, but substitute the red wine with vinegar.
7 Drain well in a colander.
8 Quickly fry the pieces of hare until brown on all sides.
9 Place into a thick-bottomed pan, mix in the flour, cook out, browning slightly.
10 Mix in the tomato purée.
11 Gradually add the stock.
12 Add all the juice and vegetables and herbs from the marinade.
13 Bring to the boil, skim, add the garlic.
14 Cover with a lid and allow to simmer till tender.
15 Pick out the hare into a clean pan.
16 Re-boil the sauce, correct the seasoning and thicken by gradually pouring in the blood (after which it must not be re-boiled).
17 Pass through a fine strainer on to the hare.
18 Meanwhile prepare the garnish by cooking the button onions glacé, cooking the mushrooms whole, turned or in quarters in a little stock and cutting the bacon into lardons, strips $2 \times \frac{1}{2} \times \frac{1}{2}$ cm ($1 \times \frac{1}{4} \times \frac{1}{4}$ in), and lightly browning them in a little fat in a frying-pan. Cut the bread into heart-shaped croûtons and fry to a golden brown.
19 Mix the garnish with the civet, serve in an entrée dish, dip the point of the croûton into the sauce, then into the chopped parsley and place on the edge of the dish.

Red-currant jelly may be spread on the heart-shaped croûton.

FEATHERED GAME

64

This includes all the edible birds which live in freedom, but only the following are generally used in catering today:

Pheasant	Faisan
Partridge	Perdreau
Woodcock	Bécasse
Snipe	Bécassine
Wild Duck	Canard Sauvage

Teal	Sarcelle
Grouse	—
Plover	Pluvier

The flavour of most game birds is improved by their being hung for a few days in a moderate draught before being plucked. During hanging the flesh begins to decompose and the particular flavour of the flesh is accentuated. Care should be taken with the water-birds, wild duck, teal, etc., not to allow them to get too high.

When game birds are roasted they should always be served on a croûte of fried bread, garnished with thick round pieces of toasted French bread spread with game farce (see below), game chips and picked watercress.

A piece of fat bacon should always be tied over the breast during cooking, and this is also placed on the breast when serving. Roast gravy, bread sauce and browned breadcrumbs (toasted or fried) are served separately.

65   Game Farce   *Farce de Gibier*

100 g	game livers	4 oz
	sprig of thyme	
50 g	butter	2 oz
25 g	chopped onion	1 oz
	1 bay leaf	
	salt, pepper	

1   Heat 25 g (1 oz) butter in a frying-pan.
2   Quickly toss the seasoned livers, onions and herbs, browning well but keeping underdone.
3   Pass through a sieve or mincer.
4   Mix in the remaining 25 g (1 oz) butter.
5   Correct the seasoning.

66   Pheasant   *Faisan*
Approx. 1½–2 kg (3–4 lb)   *4 portions*

Young birds have pliable breast bone, grey legs and the last large feather in the wing is pointed.
They may be roasted or braised or pot roasted.
Season—October 1st to February 1st.
They should be well hung.

67   Partridge   *Perdreau*
Approx. ¼–½ kg (½–1 lb)   *1-2 portions*

Young birds indicated as for pheasant, the legs should also be smooth.
May be roasted, braised, etc.
Season—September 1st to February 1st.
Three to five days' hanging is ample time.

68   Woodcock   *Bécasse*
Approx. 200–300 g (8–12 oz)   *1 per portion*

A good quality bird should have soft supple feet, clean mouth and
throat, fat and firm breast. It has a distinctive flavour which is
accentuated by the entrails being left in during cooking.
Hang for 3–4 days.
Usually roasted.
Season—October to November.

69   Snipe   *Bécassine*
Approx. 100 g (4 oz)   *1 per portion*

Snipe resemble woodcock but are smaller. Points of quality are the
same as for woodcock. They are cooked and served undrawn.
May be roasted and are sometimes cooked in steak pudding or pies.
Hang for 3–4 days.
Season—October to November.
Snipe and Woodcock are prepared with the head left on and the
beak is used for trussing.

70   Wild Duck   *Canard Sauvage*
Approx. 1–1½ kg (2–3 lb)   *2–4 portions*

The most common is the mallard, which is the ancestor of the
domestic duck. The beak and webbed feet should be soft and pliable.
They may be roasted, slightly underdone or braised.
Season—August to February.
It is particularly important that water-birds be eaten only in
season, out of season the flesh becomes coarse and acquires a fishy
flavour.

71   Teal   *Sarcelle*
Approx. ½–¾ kg (1–1½ lb)   *1–2 portions*

This is a smaller species of wild duck. Select as for wild duck.
May be roasted or braised.
Season—October to January.

72   Grouse
Approx. 300 g (12 oz)   *1–2 portions*

This is one of the most popular game birds.
Young birds have soft downy plumes on the breast and under the
wings. They also have pointed wings and a rounded, soft spur knob,
the spur becomes hard and scaly in older birds.
Usually served roasted, left slightly underdone.
Grouse is equally popular hot or cold.
Season—August 12th to December 10th.

73 Plover   *Pluvier*

Approx. ¼ kg (8 oz)   *1 per portion*

Good quality birds are plump and firm, particularly at the vent.
The feet should be soft and pliable. Served undrawn.
    Usually roasted.
    Season—October to December.
    Should be hung for 3–4 days.

74 Salmis of Game   *4 portions*   *Salmis de Gibier*

This is usually prepared from partridge or pheasant.

	1 cooked pheasant or	
	2 cooked partridges	
100 g	mushrooms	4 oz
	bouquet garni	
50 g	onion	2 oz
½ litre	demi-glace	1 pt
25 g	butter	1 oz
	4 tbspn red wine	
50 g	carrot	2 oz
25 g	celery	1 oz

1   Cut the bird into portions.
2   Chop the carcass.
3   Melt the butter in a thick-bottomed pan.
4   Add the carcass, sliced onion, carrot, celery and colour slightly.
5   Pour off the fat.
6   Déglacé with the wine.
7   Add the bouquet garni and mushroom trimmings and demi-
     glace. Simmer for 1 hr.
8   Pass the sauce through a fine strainer on to the bird and heat
     through in a sauté pan, together with the quartered or turned
     cooked mushrooms.

Serve in a casserole or entrée dish, garnish with heart-shaped
croûtons spread with game farce.

RABBIT

75 Preparation of Rabbit
    1   Skin rabbit carefully.
    2   Make an incision along the belly.
    3   Clear out the intestines.
    4   Clean out the forequarter end carefully.
    5   Cut as follows: each leg into two pieces,
                        each foreleg into two pieces if large,
                        the forequarter into two,
                        the saddle into three or four pieces.

Rabbit may be cooked as follows:

76 **Blanquet de Lapin,** see Blanquette d'Agneau, page 146.

77 **Fricassée de Lapin,** see Fricassée de Veau, page 196.

78 **Ragoût de Lapin,** see Ragoût de Bœuf, page 165.

79 **Currie de Lapin,** see Currie d'Agneau, page 145.

80 **Rabbit Pie,** see Chicken Pie, page 231.

In Recipes 76–80 substitute rabbit for the main ingredient and follow the appropriate method.

15
Salads

Salads may be divided into two sections:

(*a*) Simple Salads—using one ingredient.

(*b*) Mixed Salads—using more than one ingredient.

A dressing should always be offered with any salad.

1 Salad Dressings

   1   Vinaigrette.

   2   Mayonnaise.

   3   Acidulated Cream.

These dressings may be varied by the addition of other ingredients.

Vinaigrette

> 3 tbspn olive oil
> 1 tspn French mustard
> 1 tbspn vinegar
> salt, mill pepper

Combine all the ingredients.

Variations to Vinaigrette
(*a*) English mustard in place of French mustard;
(*b*) chopped herbs (chives, parsley, tarragon, etc.);
(*c*) chopped hard-boiled egg;
(*d*) lemon juice in place of vinegar (lemon dressing).

Mayonnaise

250 ml	olive oil	$\frac{1}{2}$ pt
	2 tspn vinegar	
	salt, ground white pepper	
	2 egg yolks	
	$\frac{1}{8}$ tspn English mustard	
	1 tspn boiling water (approx.)	

1 Place yolks, vinegar and seasoning in a bowl and whisk well.
2 Gradually pour on the oil very slowly, whisking continuously.
3 Finally whisk in the boiling water.
4 Correct the seasoning.

Acidulated Cream

4 tbsps cream
juice of $\frac{1}{4}$ lemon

Gently stir the juice into the cream at the last moment before serving.

Roquefort Dressing

50 g	Roquefort cheese	2 oz
125 ml	vinaigrette	1 gill

1 Mash the cheese with a fork.
2 Gradually add the vinaigrette mixing continuously.

Thousand Island Dressing

	2 hard-boiled eggs	
50 g	red pimento	2 oz
50 g	green pimento	2 oz
	chopped parsley	
375 ml	oil	$\frac{3}{4}$ pt
125 ml	vinegar	$\frac{1}{4}$ pt
	salt, pepper	
	3–4 drops tabasco	

1 Place salt, pepper, tabasco and vinegar in a basin.
2 Mix well.
3 Mix in the oil.
4 Add the chopped pimentos and parsley.
5 Mix in the sieved hard-boiled eggs.

SALADS   *SALADES*

2 Beetroot   *Betterave*

200 g	cooked beetroot	8 oz
	chopped parsley	
10 g	chopped onion or chive	½ oz
	4 tbspn vinaigrette	

1 Combine all the ingredients.
2 Dress neatly in a ravier.
3 Sprinkle with chopped parsley.

3 Celery   *Céleri*

Trim off the green part and wash well. Remove any discoloured
outer stalks. Cut into thin strips, serve crisp.

4 Celeriac   *Céleri-Rave*

200 g	celeriac	8 oz
	1 tbspn diluted English mustard	
	salt, pepper	
	½ lemon	
60 ml	mayonnaise or cream	½ gill

1 Wash and peel celeriac.
2 Cut into julienne.
3 Combine with lemon juice and remainder of the ingredients.
4 Dress in a ravier.

5 Curled Chicory   *Endive Frisée*

Thoroughly wash and trim off the stalk. Drain well.

6 Cucumber   *Concombre*

½ cucumber
chopped parsley
4 tbspn vinaigrette

1 Peel and slice the cucumber.
2 Sprinkle with vinaigrette and parsley.

7 Mustard and Cress

Trim off the stalk ends of the cress. Wash well and lift out of the
water so as to leave the seed cases behind. Drain well.

8 Watercress   *Cresson*

Trim off the stalk ends, discard any discoloured leaves, thoroughly
wash and drain.

9   Chicory *Endive Belge*

Trim off the root end. Cut into 1 cm ($\frac{1}{2}$ in) lengths, wash well and drain.

10   Lettuce *Laitue*

Trim off the root end and remove the outside leaves. Wash thoroughly and drain well. The outer leaves can be pulled off and the hearts cut into quarters.

11   Cos Lettuce *Laitue Romaine*

Trim off the root end and remove the outside leaves. Wash thoroughly and drain well. Cut into quarters.

12   Potato Salad *Salade de Pommes de Terre*

200 g	cooked potatoes	8 oz
60 ml	mayonnaise	$\frac{1}{2}$ gill
	1 tbspn vinaigrette, salt, pepper	
10 g	chopped onion or chive	$\frac{1}{2}$ oz
	chopped parsley	

1   Cut the potatoes in $\frac{1}{2}$–1 cm ($\frac{1}{4}$–$\frac{1}{2}$ in) dice, sprinkle with vinaigrette.
2   Mix with the onion or chive, add the mayonnaise and correct the seasoning.
3   Dress neatly in a ravier.
4   Sprinkle with chopped parsley.

13   Vegetable

Arrange neat bouquets of cooked vegetables, carrots, turnips, peas, beans, etc., around a bunch of cooked cauliflower buds. Season with vinaigrette or mayonnaise and finish with chopped parsley.

14   Tomato Salad *Salade de Tomates*

200 g	4 tomatoes	(approx. 8 oz)
10 g	chopped onion or chive	$\frac{1}{2}$ oz
	chopped parsley	
	$\frac{1}{4}$ lettuce	
	4 tbspn vinaigrette	

1   Peel tomatoes if necessary.
2   Slice thinly.
3   Arrange neatly on lettuce leaves.
4   Sprinkle with vinaigrette, onion, and parsley.

15   Mixed Salad *Salade Panachée*

Neatly arrange in a salad bowl. A typical mixed salad would consist of lettuce, tomato, cucumber, watercress, radishes, etc. Almost any kind of salad vegetable can be used.

Offer a vinaigrette separately.

16   Green Salad   *Salade Verte*

Any of the green salads, lettuce, cos lettuce, curled chicory, or any combination of green salads may be used. Neatly arrange in a salad bowl, serve with vinaigrette separately.

17   French Salad   *Salade Francaise*

The usual ingredients are lettuce, tomato and cucumber, but these may be varied with other salad vegetables, in some cases with quarters of egg. A vinaigrette made with French mustard (French dresssing) should be offered.

18   Florida Salad   *Salade Florida*

Allow ¼ lettuce and ½ large orange per portion.

1   Remove the orange zest with a peeler.
2   Cut into fine julienne.
3   Blanch for 2–3 min and refresh.
4   Peel the oranges and remove all the white skin.
5   Cut into segments between the white pith and remove all the pips.
6   Dress the lettuce in a bowl, keeping it in quarters if possible.
7   Arrange 3 or 4 segments in each portion.
8   Sprinkle with a little orange zest.
9   Serve an acidulated cream dressing separately.

19   Orange Salad   *Salade d'Orange*

Segments of orange cut as above with a little of the orange juice, neatly dressed in a salad dish.

20   Potato and Watercress Salad   *4 portions*   *Salade Cressonnière*

400 g	small cooked potatoes	1 lb
	1 hard-boiled egg	
	salt, pepper	
	1 bunch watercress	
	chopped parsley	
	4 tbspn vinaigrette	

1   Cut the potatoes into 3 mm (⅛ in) slices.
2   Mix with the picked watercress.
3   Dress in a salad bowl.
4   Pass the hard-boiled egg through a sieve and sprinkle over the salad with chopped parsley.

21   Japanese Salad   *Salade Japonaise*

Dice of tomato, pineapple, orange and apple bound with acidulated cream dressing and served on leaves of lettuce or with quarters of lettuce.

22 Manon Salad *Salade Manon*

Allow ¼ lettuce and ½ grapefruit per portion.

Peel the grapefruit and cut into segments. Dress neatly on leaves of lettuce or on quarters of lettuce.

Serve a vinaigrette with a little lemon juice and sugar added separately.

23 Mimosa Salad *Salade Mimosa*

Segments of oranges, slices of banana, skinned and pipped grapes mixed with acidulated cream and dressed with leaves or quarters of lettuce.

24 Niçoise Salad *Salade Niçoise*

200 g	cooked French beans	8 oz
10 g	anchovy fillets	½ oz
5 g	capers	¼ oz
	4 tbspns vinaigrette	
100 g	tomatoes	4 oz
10 g	stoned olives	½ oz
100 g	cooked diced potatoes	4 oz
	salt, pepper	

1 Peel tomatoes, remove seeds.
2 Cut into neat segments.
3 Dress the beans, tomato and potato neatly in a ravier.
4 Season with salt and pepper.
5 Add the vinaigrette.
6 Decorate with anchovies, capers and olives.

25 Waldorf Salad *Salade Waldorf*

Dice of celery or celeriac and crisp russet apples mixed with shelled and peeled walnuts bound with a mayonnaise and dressed on quarters or leaves of lettuce.

16
Vegetables

As a general rule all root vegetables are started to cook in cold salted water, with the exception of new potatoes: those vegetables which grow above the ground are started in boiling salted water.

VEGETABLES   *LEGUMES*

1   Cuts of Vegetables

Julienne (strips)
1   Cut the vegetables into 3 cm (1½ in) lengths.
2   Cut the lengths into thin slices.
3   Cut the slices into thin strips.

Brunoise (small dice)
1   Cut the vegetables into convenient-sized lengths.
2   Cut the lengths into 2 mm ($\frac{1}{16}$ in) slices.
3   Cut the slices into 2 mm ($\frac{1}{16}$ in) strips.
4   Cut the strips into 2 mm ($\frac{1}{16}$ in) squares.

Macédoine ($\frac{1}{2}$ cm ($\frac{1}{4}$ in) dice)
1   Cut the vegetables into convenient lengths.
2   Cut the lengths into $\frac{1}{2}$ cm ($\frac{1}{4}$ in) slices.
3   Cut the slices into $\frac{1}{2}$ cm ($\frac{1}{4}$ in) strips.
4   Cut the strips into $\frac{1}{2}$ cm ($\frac{1}{4}$ in) squares.

Jardinière (batons)
1   Cut the vegetables into 1$\frac{1}{2}$ cm ($\frac{3}{4}$ in) lengths.
2   Cut the lengths into 3 mm ($\frac{1}{8}$ in) slices.
3   Cut the slices into batons (2 × 2 × 15 mm ($\frac{1}{8}$ × $\frac{1}{8}$ × $\frac{3}{4}$ in)).

Paysanne
There are at least four accepted methods of cutting paysanne. In order to cut economically, the shape of the vegetables should decide which method to choose. All are cut thinly.
1   1 cm sided ($\frac{1}{2}$ in) triangles.
2   1 cm sided ($\frac{1}{2}$ in) squares.
3   1 cm diameter ($\frac{1}{2}$ in) rounds.
4   1 cm diameter ($\frac{1}{2}$ in) rough-sided rounds.

2   Globe Artichokes   *Artichauts en Branche*
1   Allow 1 artichoke per portion.
2   Cut off the stems close to the leaves.
3   Cut off approx. 2 cm (1 in) across the tops of the leaves.
4   Trim the remainder of the leaves with scissors or a small knife.
5   Place a slice of lemon at the bottom of each artichoke.
6   Secure with string.
7   Simmer in gently boiling salted water until the bottom is tender (approx. 20–30 min).
8   Refresh under running water until cold.
9   Remove the centre of the artichoke carefully.
10 Scrape away all the furry inside and leave clean.
11 Replace the centre, upside down.
12 Reheat by placing in a pan of boiling salted water for about 3–4 min.
13 Drain and serve on a serviette on a flat silver dish accompanied by a suitable sauce, e.g. Artichaut en Branche Sauce Hollandaise.

They may also be served cold, e.g. Artichaut en Branche Sauce Vinaigrette.

3   Artichoke Bottoms *Fonds d'Artichauts*

1   Cut off the stalk and pull out all the underneath leaves.
2   With a large knife cut through the artichoke leaving only 1½ cm (¾ in) at the bottom of the vegetable .
3   With a small sharp knife, whilst holding the artichoke upside down, peel carefully removing all the leaf and any green part, keeping the bottom as smooth as possible. If necessary smooth with a peeler.
4   Rub immediately with lemon and keep in lemon water.
5   Using a spoon or the thumb, remove the centre furry part which is called the choke. The choke is sometimes removed after cooking.
6   Artichoke bottoms should always be cooked in a blanc.

Fonds d'Artichauts are served as a vegetable; they are sometimes filled with another vegetable, e.g. peas, spinach, etc.

When they are served ungarnished they are usually cut into quarters, e.g. Fonds d'Artichauts Sautés au Beurre.

4   Blanc

½ litre	cold water	1 pt
10 g	flour	¼ oz
	juice of ½ lemon	
	salt	

1   Mix the flour and water together.
2   Add the salt and lemon juice.
3   Pass through a strainer.
4   Place in a pan, bring to the boil, stirring continuously.

5   Purée of Jerusalem Artichokes   *4 portions*   *Topinambours en Purée*

600 g	Jerusalem artichokes	1 lb 8 oz
25 g	butter	1 oz
	salt, pepper	

1   Wash, peel and rewash the artichokes.
2   Cut in pieces if necessary.
3   Barely cover with water, add salt,
4   Simmer gently until tender.
5   Drain well.
6   Pass through a sieve.
7   Return to the pan, reheat and mix in the butter and correct the seasoning.
8   Serve dome shape in a hot vegetable dish, decorate with a palette knife.

6   Purée of Jerusalem Artichokes with Cream
                         Topinambours en Purée à la Crème
As above with ¼ litre (⅛ pt) cream mixed in before serving.

7   Jerusalem Artichokes in Cream Sauce   *Topinambours à la Crème*

1   Wash and peel the artichokes and rewash.
2   Cut to an even size.
3   Barely cover with water, add salt and simmer till tender.
4   Drain well and add ¼ litre (½ pt) cream sauce.
5   Serve in a vegetable dish.

8   Asparagus   *Asperges*

Allow 6–8 good-sized pieces per portion.
An average bundle will yield 3–4 portions.

1   Using the back of a small knife, carefully remove the tips of the leaves.
2   Scrape the stem, either with the blade of a small knife or a peeler.
3   Wash well.
4   Tie into bundles of approx. 12 heads.
5   Cut off the excess stem.
6   Cook in boiling salted water approx. 15 min.
7   Test if cooked by gently pressing the green part of the stem, which should be tender.
8   Lift carefully out of the water and dress neatly on a serviette on a silver flat dish. Remove the string.

Serve a suitable sauce separately, e.g. Hollandaise or Melted Butter.
Asparagus are usually served as a separate course. They may also be served cold, in which case they should be immediately refreshed when cooked in order to retain the green colour. Serve with vinaigrette or mayonnaise.

9   Asparagus Points or Tips   *Pointes d'Asperges*

Young thin asparagus, approx. 50 pieces to the bundle, known as sprew or sprue.
They are prepared in the same way as asparagus except that when they are very thin the removing of the leaf tips is dispensed with. They may be served as a vegetable, e.g. Pointes d'Asperges au Beurre.
They are also used in numerous garnishes for soups, egg dishes, fish, entrée, cold dishes, salad, etc.

10   Fried Egg Plant   *Aubergine Frite*

1   Allow ½ aubergine per portion.
2   Remove alternate strips with a peeler.
3   Cut into ½ cm (¼ in) slices on the slant.
4   Pass through seasoned flour.
5   Shake off all surplus flour.

6   Deep fry in hot fat (185°C).
7   Drain well, serve on a dish paper in a vegetable dish.

They may also be shallow fried.

11   Stuffed Aubergine or Egg Plant   *Aubergine Farcie*

	2 aubergines	
10 g	chopped shallot	½ oz
	chopped parsley	
125 ml	demi-glace	¼ pt
100 g	mushrooms	4 oz
100 g	tomate concassée	4 oz
	salt, pepper	

1   Cut the aubergine in two lengthwise.
2   With the point of a small knife make a cut around the halves
     approx. ½ cm (¼ in) from the edge, then make several cuts ½ cm
     (¼ in) deep in the centre.
3   Deep fry in hot fat (185°C) for 2–3 min.
4   Scoop out the centre pulp and finely chop it.
5   Cook the chopped shallot in a little oil or fat without colouring.
6   Add the well-washed chopped mushrooms.
7   Cook gently for a few minutes.
8   Mix in the pulp, parsley, tomato, and season.
9   Replace in the aubergine skins.
10   Sprinkle with breadcrumbs and melted butter.
11   Brown under the salamander.
12   Serve in a vegetable dish with a cordon of demi-glace.

12   Ratatouille   *4 portions*

200 g	baby marrow	½ lb
200 g	aubergines	½ lb
50 g	onion (finely sliced)	2 oz
200 g	tomatoes	½ lb
	1 clove garlic	
	1 tsp chopped parsley	
50 ml	oil	⅛ pt
	salt, pepper	

1   Trim off both ends of the marrow and aubergines.
2   Remove the skin using a peeler.
3   Cut into 5 mm (¼ in) slices.
4   Concassée the tomatoes (peel, remove seeds, roughly chop).
5   Place the oil in a thick bottomed pan and add the onions.
6   Cover with a lid and allow to cook gently 5–7 min without
     colouring.
7   Add the peeled chopped garlic and the marrow and aubergine
     slices.
8   Season with salt and mill pepper.

9   Allow to cook gently 4–5 min, toss occasionally and keep covered with a lid.

10   Add the tomato and allow to continue cooking gently until all is tender (approx. 20–30 min).

11   Mix in the parsley, correct the seasoning and serve in a vegetable dish.

13 Broccoli   *Brocolis*

Cook and serve as for any of the cauliflower recipes (p. 261).

14 Carrots   *Carottes*

15 Buttered Carrots   *4 portions*   *Carottes au Beurre ou Carottes Glacées*

400 g	carrots	1 lb
	salt, sugar	
25 g	butter	1 oz
	chopped parsley	

1   Peel and wash the carrots.
2   Cut into neat even pieces or turn barrel shape.
3   Place in a pan with a little salt, a pinch of sugar and butter. Barely cover with water.
4   Cover with a buttered paper and allow to boil steadily in order to evaporate all the water.
5   When the water has completely evaporated check that the carrots are cooked, if not, add a little more water and continue cooking.
6   Toss the carrots over a fierce heat for 1–2 min in order to give them a glaze.
7   Serve in a vegetable dish, sprinkle with chopped parsley.

16 Purée of Carrots   *Purée de Carottes*

600 g	carrots	1 lb 8 oz
25 g	butter	1 oz
	salt, pepper	

1   Wash, peel and rewash the carrots.
2   Cut in pieces.
3   Barely cover with water, add salt.
4   Simmer gently until tender.
5   Drain well.
6   Pass through a sieve.
7   Return to the pan, reheat and mix in the butter and correct the seasoning.
8   Serve dome shape in a hot vegetable dish, decorate with a palette knife.

17 **Vichy Carrots** *Carottes Vichy*

1 Allow the same ingredients as for Buttered Carrots, substitute Vichy water for the liquid.
2 Peel and wash the carrots (which should not be larger than 2 cm (1 in) in diameter).
3 Cut into 2 mm ($\frac{1}{16}$ in) slices on the mandolin.
4 Cook and serve as for buttered carrots.

18 **Carrots in Cream Sauce** *Carottes à la Crème*

400 g	carrots	1 lb	
$\frac{1}{4}$ litre	thin béchamel	$\frac{1}{2}$ pt	
10 g	butter	$\frac{1}{2}$ oz	
	salt, pepper		

Prepare and cook the carrots as for Buttered Carrots. Mix with the sauce, correct the seasoning, serve in a vegetable dish.

19 **Braised Celery** *4 portions* *Céleri Braisé*

	2 heads of celery		
100 g	carrots, sliced	4 oz	
	bouquet garni		
$\frac{1}{4}$ litre	approx. white stock	$\frac{1}{2}$ pt	
100 g	onion, sliced	4 oz	
50 g	fat bacon or suet	2 oz	
	2 crusts of bread		
	salt, pepper		

1 Trim the celery heads and the root, cutting off any outside discoloured stalks and cutting the heads to approx. 12 cm (6 in) lengths.
2 Wash well under running cold water.
3 Place in a pan of boiling water. Simmer for approx. 10 min until limp.
4 Refresh and rewash.
5 Place the sliced vegetables in a sauté pan, sauteuse or casserole.
6 Add the celery heads whole or cut them in halves lengthwise, fold over and place on the bed of roots.
7 Add the bouquet garni, barely cover with stock, season with salt and pepper.
8 Add the fat bacon or suet, the crust of bread, cover with a buttered greaseproof paper and a tight lid and cook gently in a moderate oven (150°–200°C) for 2–3 hr.
9 Remove the celery from the pan, drain well and dress neatly in a vegetable dish.
10 Add the cooking liquor to an equal amount of jus-lié or demi-glace, reduce and correct the seasoning and consistency.
11 Mask the celery and finish with chopped parsley.

20 Grilled Mushrooms   *4 portions*   *Champignons Grillés*

200 g	grilling mushrooms	8 oz
	salt, pepper	
50 g	butter or fat	2 oz

1 Peel and remove the stalks and wash well.
2 Place on a tray and season with salt and pepper.
3 Brush with melted fat and grill on both sides for approx.
   3–4 min.
4 Serve in a vegetable dish with picked parsley.

21 Stuffed Mushrooms   *Champignons Farcis*

300 g	grilling mushrooms	12 oz
25 g	breadcrumbs	1 oz
	salt, pepper	
10 g	chopped shallot	½ oz
50 g	butter or fat	2 oz

1 Peel, remove the stalk and wash well.
2 Retain 8 or 12 of the best mushrooms. Finely chop the
   remainder with the peelings and stalks.
3 Cook the shallots, without colour, in a little fat.
4 Add the chopped mushrooms and cook for 3 or 4 min (duxelle).
5 Grill as in the previous recipe.
6 Place the duxelle in the centre of each mushroom.
7 Sprinkle with a few breadcrumbs and melted butter.
8 Reheat in the oven or under the salamander.
9 Serve in a vegetable dish.

22 Cabbage   *3–4 portions to ½ kg (1 lb)*   *Chou Vert*

1 Cut cabbage in quarters.
2 Remove the centre stalk and outside leaves.
3 Shred and wash well.
4 Place into plenty of boiling salted water.
5 Boil steadily until cooked.
6 Drain immediately in a colander.
7 Place between two small plates, press firmly to squeeze out any
   water.
8 Cut into four even pieces.
9 Dress neatly in a vegetable dish.
10 Overcooking will lessen the vitamin content and the addition
   of soda will destroy the vitamin content.
   These points are also true when cooking any green vegetables.

23 Spring Greens   *Choux de Printemps*
3–4 portions to ½ kg (1 lb)
Prepare and cook as for cabbage for approx. 15 min.

24 Braised Cabbage *Choux Braisés*

½ kg	cabbage	1 lb
100 g	carrot	4 oz
100 g	onion	4 oz
¼ litre	white stock	½ pt
	bouquet garni	
	salt, pepper	
⅛ litre	jus-lié	¼ pt

1 Quarter the cabbage.
2 Remove the centre stalk and discoloured leaves, wash well.
3 Place in boiling salted water, boil for 10 min.
4 Refresh until cold.
5 Take the four best green leaves and lay out flat on the table.
6 Place the remainder of the cabbage on the centre of each and season.
7 Wrap each in a tea-cloth and shape into a fairly firm ball.
8 Remove from the tea-cloth. Place on a bed of roots.
9 Add the stock half way up cabbage, seasoning and bouquet garni.
10 Bring to the boil, cover with a lid and cook in the oven approx. 1 hr.
11 Dress the cabbage in a vegetable dish.
12 Add the cooking liquor to the jus-lié, correct the seasoning and consistency.
13 Pour over the cabbage.

25 Braised Stuffed Cabbage *Choux Farcis Braisés*

As for braised cabbage with the addition of 25–50 g (1–2 oz) sausage meat placed in the centre before shaping into a ball.

26 Sauerkraut (a pickled white cabbage) *Choucroûte*

400 g	sauerkraut	1 lb
	6 juniper berries	
50 g	carrot	2 oz
¼ litre	approx. white stock	½ pt
50 g	onion piqué	2 oz
	6 peppercorns	
	bouquet garni	

1 Season the sauerkraut and place in a casserole or pan, suitable for placing in the oven.
2 Add the whole onion and carrot, the bouquet garni and the peppercorns and berries.
3 Barely cover with good white stock.
4 Cover with a buttered paper and lid.
5 Cook slowly in a moderate oven 3–4 hr.
6 Remove the bouquet garni and onion. Cut the carrot in slices.
7 Dress the sauerkraut in a vegetable dish and garnish with slices of carrot.

Garnished Sauerkraut   *Choucroûte Garni*

This dish is served as an entrée.

1   Proceed as for Choucroûte.
2   Place a ¼ kg (8 oz) piece of blanched streaky bacon in the centre
     of the cabbage so that it is completely enclosed.
3   Half an hour before the sauerkraut is cooked add 4 or 8
     frankfurter sausages.
4   When serving, remove the rind from the bacon and cut into
     4 or 8 slices. Dress neatly on the sauerkraut with the frankfurters
     and the carrots.

27   Braised Red Cabbage   *4 portions*   *Choux à la Flamande*

300 g	red cabbage	¾ lb
125 ml	vinegar	¼ pt
10 g	castor sugar	½ oz
50 g	butter	2 oz
100 g	cooking apples	4 oz
	salt	
	pepper	

1   Quarter, trim and shred the cabbage.
2   Wash well and drain.
3   Season with salt and pepper.
4   Place in a well-buttered casserole or pan suitable for placing in
     the oven (not aluminium or iron).
5   Add the vinegar, cover with a buttered paper and lid.
6   Cook in a moderate oven (150°–200°C) for approx. 1½ hr.
7   Add the peeled and cored apples cut into 1 cm (½ in) dice.
     Re-cover with the lid and continue cooking until tender, approx.
     2 hr in all. If a little more cooking liquor is needed use stock.
     Serve in a vegetable dish.

28   Brussels Sprouts   *Choux de Bruxelles*
         ½ *kg (1 lb) will yield 3–4 portions*

1   Using a small knife trim the stems and cut a cross 2 mm ($\frac{1}{16}$ in)
     deep and remove any discoloured leaves.
2   Wash well.
3   Cook in plenty of boiling salted water approx. 15–20 min.
4   Drain well in a colander.
5   Serve in a vegetable dish.

29   Brussels Sprouts with Butter   *Choux de Bruxelles au Beurre*

1   Cook and serve as in previous recipe.
2   Brush with 25–50 g (1–2 oz) melted butter.

30 Brussels Sprouts fried in Butter   *Choux de Bruxelles Sautés au Beurre*

1   Cook and drain.
2   Melt 25–50 g (1–2 oz) butter in a frying-pan.
3   When foaming, add the sprouts and toss lightly, browning slightly.

31 Cauliflower   *Chou-fleur Nature*

Allow 1 medium-sized cauliflower for 4 portions.

1   Trim the stem and remove the outer leaves.
2   Hollow out the stem with a peeler.
3   Wash well.
4   Cook in boiling salted water approx. 20 min.
5   Drain well and serve either (*a*) whole on a serviette on a flat silver dish, or (*b*) cut into 4 even portions in a vegetable dish.

32 Buttered Cauliflower   *Chou-fleur au Beurre*

As for Cauliflower, brush with 25–50 g (1–2 oz) melted butter when serving.

33 Buttered Cauliflower with Parsley   *Chou-fleur Persillé*

As for Buttered Cauliflower, sprinkle with chopped parsley.

34 Cauliflower fried in Butter   *Chou-fleur Sautée au Beurre*

1   Cut the cooked cauliflower in 4 portions.
2   Lightly colour on all sides in 25–50 g (1–2 oz) butter.

35 Cauliflower, Cream Sauce   *Chou-fleur, Sauce Crème*

1   Cook and serve as for Cauliflower.
2   Accompany with $\frac{1}{4}$ litre ($\frac{1}{2}$ pt) cream sauce in a sauceboat.

36 Cauliflower, Melted Butter   *Chou-fleur, Beurre Fondu*

As for Cauliflower, with a sauceboat of 100 g (4 oz) melted butter (see page 30).

37 Cauliflower, Hollandaise Sauce   *Chou-fleur, Sauce Hollandaise*

As for Cauliflower, accompany with a sauceboat of $\frac{1}{8}$ litre ($\frac{1}{4}$ pt) Hollandaise sauce (see page 30).

38 Cauliflower au Gratin   *Chou-fleur au Gratin*

or   *ou*

39 Cauliflower Mornay   *Chou-fleur Mornay*

1   Cut the cooked cauliflower into 4 portions.
2   Reheat in a pan of hot salted water (chauffon), or reheat in butter.

3   Place in a vegetable dish.
4   Coat with ¼ litre (½ pt) Mornay sauce (see page 20).
5   Sprinkle with grated cheese.
6   Brown under the salamander.

40   Cauliflower Polonaise   *Chou-fleur Polonaise*
1   Cut the cooked cauliflower into four, reheat in a chauffon or in butter.
2   Heat 50 g (2 oz) butter, add 10 g (½ oz) white crumbs in a frying-pan and lightly brown. Pour over the cauliflower and sprinkle with sieved hard-boiled egg and chopped parsley.

41   Sea-kale   *Choux de Mer*
½ *kg (1 lb) will yield approx. 3 portions*
1   Trim the roots, remove any discoloured leaves.
2   Wash well and tie into a neat bundle.
3   Cook in boiling salted water until tender, approx. 15–20min.
4   Drain well.
5   Serve on a serviette on a silver dish accompanied with a suitable sauce, e.g. Beurre Fondu, Hollandaise, etc.

42   Sea-kale Mornay   *Choux de Mer Mornay*
   or   *ou*
43   Sea-kale au Gratin   *Chou de Mer au Gratin*
1   Prepare and cook as for Sea-kale (Recipe 41).
2   Reheat and cut into 4 cm (2 in) lengths, place in a vegetable dish.
3   Coat with ¼ litre (½ pt) Mornay sauce and sprinkle with grated cheese.
4   Brown under the salamander.

44   Marrow   *Courge*
All the variations for cauliflower may be used with marrow.

Baby Marrow   *Courgette*
½ *kg (1 lb) will yield 2–3 portions*
1   Peel the marrow with a peeler or small knife.
2   Cut in half lengthwise.
3   Remove the seeds with a spoon.
4   Cut into even pieces approx. 4 cm (2 in) square.
5   Cook in boiling salted water approx. 10–15 min.
6   Drain well and serve in a vegetable dish.

45 Stuffed Marrow
Courge Farcie

Various stuffings may be used. 100 g (4 oz) sausage meat or 100 g (4 oz) rice for 4 portions, e.g. cooked rice with chopped cooked meat, seasoned with salt, pepper and herbs.

Well-seasoned cooked rice with sliced mushrooms, tomatoes, etc.

1. Peel the marrow and cut in half lengthwise.
2. Remove the seeds with a spoon.
3. Season and add the stuffing.
4. Replace the two halves.
5. Cook as for Braised Celery (page 257) allowing approx. 1 hr.
6. To serve, cut into thick slices and dress neatly in a vegetable dish. Baby marrows are ideal for this.

46 Marrow Provençale *4 portions*
Courge Provençale

400 g	marrow	1 lb
50 g	chopped onion	2 oz
	1 clove garlic (chopped)	
	salt, pepper	
50 g	oil or butter	2 oz
400 g	tomatoes	1 lb
	chopped parsley	

1. Peel the marrow, remove the seeds and cut into 2 cm (1 in) square pieces.
2. Cook the onion and garlic in the oil in a sauteuse for 2–3 min. without colouring.
3. Add the marrow, season with salt and pepper.
4. Add the tomate concassée.
5. Cover with a lid, cook gently in the oven or on the side of the stove until tender, approx. 1 hr.
6. Sprinkle with chopped parsley and serve in a vegetable dish.

47 Stuffed Cucumber
Concombre Farci

1. Peel the cucumber with a peeler.
2. Cut into 2 cm (1 in) pieces.
3. Remove two-thirds of the centre with parisienne cutter.
4. Cook in boiling salted water for 10 min. Refresh.
5. Fill centre with a duxelle-base stuffing to which may be added chopped cooked meat, rice, tomato, etc.
6. Cover with a buttered paper and reheat in a moderate oven.
7. Dress neatly in a vegetable dish.

48 Belgian Chicory
Endive Belge à l'Etuvée

½ kg (*1 lb*) *will yield 3 portions*

1. Trim the stem, remove any discoloured leaves, wash.
2. Place in a well-buttered casserole or pan suitable to place in the oven.

3   Season lightly with salt.
4   Add the juice of half a lemon.
5   Add 25–50 g (1–2 oz) butter per ½ kg (1 lb) and a few drops of water.
6   Cover with a buttered paper and lid.
7   Cook gently in a moderate oven (150°–200°C) approx. 1 hr.
8   Dress neatly in a vegetable dish.

49   Shallow Fried Chicory   *Endive Meunière*

Cook the chicory as in previous recipe, drain, shallow fry in a
little butter, colour lightly on both sides. Dress in a vegetable
dish, finish with 10 g (½ oz) per portion nut-brown butter,
lemon juice and chopped parsley.

50   Braised Chicory   *Endive au Jus*

Cook the chicory as à l'Etuvée (Recipe 48), when dressed surround
with a cordon of jus-lié.

51   Leaf Spinach   *Epinards en Branches*
½ kg (1 lb) will yield 2 portions

1   Remove the stems.
2   Wash very carefully in plenty of water several times if necessary.
3   Cook in boiling salted water until tender, approx. 5 min.
4   Refresh under cold water, squeeze dry into a ball.
5   When required for service, place into a pan containing 25–50 g
     (1–2 oz) butter, loosen with a fork and reheat quickly without
     colouring, season with salt and mill pepper.
6   Serve in a vegetable dish.

52   Spinach Purée   *Epinards en Purée*

1   Cook, refresh and drain spinach as above.
2   Pass through a sieve or mincer.
3   Reheat in 25–50 g (1–2) oz) butter, mix with wooden spoon,
     correct the seasoning.
4   Serve dome shaped in a vegetable dish and flute or scroll with a
     palette knife.

53   Creamed Spinach Purée   *Epinards en Purée à la Crème*

1   As for Spinach Purée.
2   Mix in 30 ml (⅛ pt) cream or 60 ml (¼ pt) béchamel, before
     serving.
3   Serve as for Spinach Purée and serve with a border of cream.

54   Spinach with Croûtons   *Epinards aux Croûtons*

As for Creamed Spinach with the cordon of cream and surround
with 1 cm ($\frac{1}{2}$ in) triangle fried croûtons.

55   Broad Beans   *Fèves*

$\frac{1}{2}$ *kg (1 lb) will yield approx. 2 portions*

1   Shell the beans and cook in boiling salted water until tender,
    approx. 20 min.
2   If the inner shells are tough they should also be removed.
3   Serve the beans in a vegetable dish.

56   Broad Beans with Butter   *Fèves au Beurre*

As above, brush liberally with butter.

57   Broad Beans with Parsley   *Fèves Persillées*

As for Broad Beans with Butter, then sprinkle with chopped
parsley.

58   Broad Beans with Cream Sauce   *Fèves à la Crème*

Prepare and cook as above, bind with $\frac{1}{4}$ litre ($\frac{1}{2}$ pt) cream sauce or
fresh cream.

59   Haricot Beans   *Haricot Blancs*

$\frac{1}{2}$ *kg (1 lb) will yield 6–8 portions*

1   Soak in cold water overnight in a cool place.
2   Change the water.
3   Cover with cold water, bring to the boil.
4   Skim when necessary.
5   Add salt, 50 g (2 oz) carrot, 50 g (2 oz) onion piqué, 50 g (2 oz)
    bacon trimmings and a bouquet garni to every $\frac{1}{2}$ kg (1 lb) beans.
6   Continue simmering gently until tender.

60   French Beans   *Haricots Verts*

$\frac{1}{2}$ *kg (1 lb) will yield 3–4 portions*

1   Top and tail the beans, carefully and economically.
2   Using a large sharp knife cut the beans into thin strips approx.
    4 cm × 3 mm (2 × $\frac{1}{8}$ in).
3   Wash.
4   Cook in boiling salted water until tender, approx. 15 min.
5   Drain well and serve in a vegetable dish.

61   French Beans with Butter   *Haricots Verts au Beurre*

As previous recipe, brush the beans liberally with butter.

62   French Beans tossed in Butter   *Haricots Verts Sautés au Beurre*

Gently toss the cooked beans in butter over heat without colouring.

63   Runner Beans

Wash and string the beans, then cut them into thin strips approx.
4–6 cm (2–3 in) long.
    Cook in boiling salt water approx. 15 min.
    Drain well. Serve in a vegetable dish.

64   Braised Lettuce   *Laitue Braisée*

	2 large lettuce	
50 g	carrot (sliced)	2 oz
	bouquet garni	
60 ml	jus-lié or demi-glace	$\frac{1}{8}$ pt
	salt, pepper	
50 g	onion (sliced)	2 oz
50 g	fat bacon	2 oz
	2 slices stale bread	
	chopped parsley	
125 ml	approx. white stock	$\frac{1}{4}$ pt

1   Wash the lettuce.
2   Place in boiling salted water and cook for 5 min, refresh.
3   Squeeze carefully.
4   Arrange the sliced vegetables in a pan or casserole suitable for
placing in the oven.
5   Season lightly, add the bouquet garni and stock to come half-
way up the lettuce, add the bacon.
6   Cover with a buttered greaseproof paper and a lid.
7   Cook in a moderate oven (150°–200°C) approx. 1 hr.
8   Remove the lettuce, cut in halves lengthwise, flatten slightly and
fold each in half.
9   Meanwhile cut 4 neat heart-shaped croûtons and fry in butter
to a golden brown.
10   Reduce the cooking liquor from the lettuce with the jus-lié or
demi-glace, keeping the sauce thin.
11   Dress the lettuce in a vegetable dish, mask with the thin sauce.
12   Dip the points of the croûtons in the sauce and then into
chopped parsley and arrange neatly on the dish.

65   Corn on the Cob   *Mais*

Allow 1 cob per portion

1   Trim the stem.
2   Cook in boiling salted water until the corn is tender (approx.
15–20 mins).
3   Remove the outer leaves and fibres.
4   Serve on a serviette on a flat silver dish with a sauceboat of
melted butter.

66   Buttered Turnips or Swedes   *Navets au Beurre*
                                                       Rutabaga au Beurre

400 g	turnips or swedes	1 lb
	salt, sugar	
25 g	butter	1 oz
	chopped parsley	

1   Peel and wash the vegetables.
2   Cut into neat even pieces or turn barrel shape.
3   Place in a pan with a little salt, a pinch of sugar and butter. Barely cover with water.
4   Cover with a buttered paper and allow to boil steadily in order to evaporate all the water.
5   When the water has completely evaporated check that the vegetables are cooked, if not, add a little more water and continue cooking.
6   Toss the vegetables over a fierce heat for 1–2 min in order to give them a glaze.
7   Drain well, serve in a vegetable dish. Take care not to overcook turnips.

67   Purée of Turnips or Swedes   *Purée de Navets*
                                                       Purée de Rutabaga

600 g	turnips or swedes	1 lb 8 oz
25 g	butter	1 oz
	salt, pepper	

1   Wash, peel and rewash the vegetables.
2   Cut in pieces if necessary.
3   Barely cover with water, add salt.
4   Simmer gently until tender.
5   Drain well.
6   Pass through a sieve.
7   Return to the pan, reheat and mix in the butter and correct the seasoning.
8   Serve dome shape in a hot vegetable dish, decorate with a palette knife.

68   Fried Onions   *Oignons Sautés ou Oignons Lyonnaise*

½ *kg (1 lb) will yield approx. 2 portions*

1   Peel and wash the onions, cut in halves, slice finely.
2   Cook slowly in 25–50 g (1–2 oz) fat in a frying-pan, turning frequently until tender and nicely browned, season with salt and pepper.

69   French Fried Onions   *Oignons Frits à la Française*

1   Peel and wash the onions.
2   Cut into 2 mm (⅛ in) thick slices, against the grain.

3   Separate into rings.
4   Pass through milk and seasoned flour.
5   Shake off the surplus.
6   Deep fry in hot fat (185°C).
7   Drain well and season with salt.
8   Serve on a dish paper in a vegetable dish.

70   Braised Onions   *Oignons Braisés*

1   Select medium even-sized onions, allow 2–3 portions per ½ kg (1 lb).
2   Peel, wash and cook in boiling salted water for ½ hr.
3   Drain and place in a pan or casserole suitable for placing in the oven.
4   Add a bouquet garni, half-cover with stock and a lid and braise gently (150°–200°C) in the oven till tender.
5   Drain well and dress neatly in a vegetable dish.
6   Reduce the cooking liquor with an equal amount of jus-lié or demi-glace. Correct the seasoning and consistency and pass. Mask the onions and sprinkle with chopped parsley.

71   Peas (Fresh)   *Petits Pois*

½ kg (1 lb) will yield approx. 2 portions

1   Shell and wash the peas.
2   Cook in boiling salted water with a sprig of mint until tender, approx. 15–20 min.
3   Drain in a colander.
4   Add 25 g (1 oz) butter and ½ tspn castor sugar, toss gently.
5   Serve in a vegetable dish with blanched, refreshed mint leaves.

Peas (Frozen)

½ kg (1 lb) will yield approx. 8 portions

Cook in boiling salted water until tender approx. 5 min.
  Drain in a colander.
  Add 25 g (1 oz) butter and ½ tspn castor sugar, toss gently.
  Serve in a vegetable dish with blanched refreshed mint leaves.

72   Peas, French Style   *4 portions*   *Petits Pois à la Française*

1 kg	peas (in the pod)	2 lb
	1 small lettuce	
	½ tspn castor sugar	
5 g	flour	¼ oz
	12 spring or button onions	
25 g	butter	1 oz
	salt	

1   Shell and wash the peas and place in a sauteuse.
2   Peel and wash the onions, shred the lettuce and add to the peas
    with 10 g (½ oz) butter, salt and the sugar.
3   Barely cover with water. Cover with a lid and cook steadily,
    preferably in the oven, until tender.
4   Correct the seasoning.
5   Mix the other 10 g (½ oz) butter with 5 g (¼ oz) flour and shake
    into the boiling peas until thoroughly mixed.
6   Serve in a vegetable dish.

NOTE. When using frozen peas allow the onions to almost cook
before adding the peas.

73   Peas, Flemish Style   *4 portions*   *Petits Pois à la Flamande*

400 g	peas	1 lb
200 g	carrots	8 oz
50 g	butter	2 oz

1   Wash and peel the carrots and cut into batons or dice.
2   Cover with water, season and cook until tender.
3   Meanwhile cook the peas.
4   Drain the peas and carrots.
5   Mix together in pan containing the butter.
6   Serve in a vegetable dish.

74   Stuffed Pimento   *4 portions*   *Piment Farci*

4 medium-sized red pimentos

	Pilaff	
200 g	rice(long-grain)	½ lb
½ litre	white stock approx.	1 pt
50 g	carrot (sliced)	2 oz
	salt, pepper	
50 g	chopped onion	2 oz
50 g	butter	2 oz
50 g	onion (sliced)	2 oz
	bouquet garni	

1   Place the pimentos on a tray in the oven or under the
    salamander for a few minutes in order to be able to skin them.
2   Remove the stalk carefully and empty out all the seeds.
3   Stuff with a well-seasoned pilaff of rice which may be varied by
    the additions of mushrooms, tomatoes, ham, etc.
4   Replace the stem.
5   Place the pimentos on the sliced carrot and onion in a pan
    suitable for the oven, add the bouquet garni, stock, seasoning.
    Cover with a buttered paper and lid.
6   Cook gently in a moderate oven (150°–200°C) until tender,
    approx. 1 hr.
7   Dress in a vegetable dish, garnish with picked parsley.

75 Salsify   *Salsifis*

$\frac{1}{2}$ *kg (1 lb) will yield 2–3 portions*

1   Wash, peel and rewash the salsify.
2   Cut into 4 cm (2 in) lengths.
3   Cook in a blanc as for artichokes (Recipe 4, page 253).
4   They may then be served as for any of the cauliflower recipes.
5   Salsify may also be passed through batter and deep fried.

76 Grilled Tomatoes   *Tomates Grillées*

Allow 1 or 2 per portion according to size
$\frac{1}{2}$ *kg (1 lb) will yield approx. 3–4 portions*

1   Wash the tomatoes, and remove the eyes with a small knife.
2   Place on a greased, seasoned baking tray.
3   Make an incision 2 mm ($\frac{1}{16}$ in) cross-shape on the opposite side to the eye and peel back the four corners.
4   Brush with melted fat and season with salt and pepper.
5   Grill under a moderately hot salamander.
6   Dress neatly in a vegetable dish, garnish with picked parsley.

77 Stuffed Tomatoes   *Tomates Farcies*

	8 medium-sized tomatoes	
	chopped parsley	
25 g	white breadcrumbs	1 oz
	salt, pepper	
	Duxelle	
100 g	mushrooms	4 oz
10 g	chopped shallot	$\frac{1}{2}$ oz

1   Wash the tomatoes, remove the eyes.
2   Remove approx. one-quarter of the tomato with a sharp knife.
3   Carefully empty out the seeds without damaging the flesh.
4   Place on a greased baking tray.
5   Cook the shallot in a little oil or fat without colouring.
6   Add the washed chopped mushrooms, season with salt and pepper and cook for 2–3 min.
7   Add a little of the strained tomato juice, the breadcrumbs and the parsley, mix to a piping consistency. Correct the seasoning. At this stage several variations may be made, e.g. chopped ham, cooked rice, etc., can be added.
8   Place the mixture in a piping bag with a large star tube and pipe into the tomato shells.
9   Replace the tops.
10 Brush with melted fat, season with salt and pepper.
11 Cook in a moderate oven (150°–200°C) approx. 4–5 min.
12 Serve in a vegetable dish, garnish with picked parsley.

78 Basic Tomato Preparation *Tomate Concassée*

This is a cooked preparation which is usually included in the normal *mise en place* of a kitchen as it it used in a great number of dishes.

400 g	tomatoes	1 lb
25 g	fat	1 oz
25 g	chopped shallot or onion	1 oz
	salt, pepper	

1 Remove the eyes from the tomatoes.
2 Plunge into *boiling* water 5–6 sec. Refresh *immediately*.
3 Remove the skins, cut in halves across the tomato and remove all the seeds.
4 Roughly chop the flesh of the tomatoes.
5 Meanwhile cook the chopped onion or shallot without colouring in the fat.
6 Add the tomatoes and season.
7 Simmer gently on the side of the stove until the moisture is evaporated.

79 Braised Leeks *Poireaux Braisés*

½ kg (*1 lb*) *of leeks will yield approx. 2 portions*

1 Cut the roots from the leek, remove any discoloured outside leaves and trim the green.
2 Cut through lengthwise and wash well under running water.
3 Tie into a neat bundle.
4 Place in boiling salted water for 10 min approx.
5 Place on a bed of roots.
6 Barely cover with stock add the bouquet garni and season.
7 Cover with a lid and cook until tender, approx. ½–1 hr.
8 Remove leeks from pan and fold neatly, arrange in a vegetable dish.
9 Meanwhile add jus-lié to the cooking liquor and correct the seasoning and consistency.
10 Pour the sauce over the leeks.

80 Parsnips *Panais*

Wash well. Peel the parsnips and again wash well. Cut into quarters lengthwise, remove the centre root if tough. Cut into neat pieces and cook in salt water till tender. Drain and serve with melted butter or in a cream sauce. They may also be cooked in the oven in a little fat.

81 Pease Pudding

200 g	yellow split peas	8 oz
½ litre	approx. water	1 pt
50 g	onion piqué	2 oz
50 g	carrot	2 oz
50 g	bacon trimmings	2 oz
50 g	margarine	2 oz
	salt, pepper	

1 Place all the ingredients, except the margarine, in a saucepan with a tight-fitting lid.
2 Bring to the boil, cook in a moderate oven (150°–200°C) approx. 2 hrs.
3 Remove onion, carrot and bacon and pass the peas through a sieve.
4 Return to a clean pan, mix in the margarine, correct the seasoning and consistency (this should be firm).

82 Mixed Vegetables *4 portions*   *Macédoine de Légumes*
                                                        Jardinière de Légumes

100 g	carrot	4 oz
50 g	turnips	2 oz
	salt	
50 g	peas	2 oz
50 g	French beans	2 oz

1 Peel and wash the carrots and turnips.
2 Cut into ½ cm (¼ in) dice (macédoine) or batons (jardinière).
3 Cook separately in salted water.
4 Refresh.
5 Top and tail the beans.
6 Cut into ½ cm (¼ in) dice, cook and refresh.
7 Cook the peas and refresh.
8 Mix the vegetables together and when required reheat in hot salted water.
9 Drain well, serve in a vegetable dish, brush with melted butter.

17
Potatoes

POTATOES   *POMMES DE TERRES*

½ kg (1 lb) old potatoes will yield approx. 3 portions
½ kg (1 lb) new potatoes will yield approx. 4 portions

1 Plain Boiled Potatoes   *Pommes Nature*
  1   Wash, peel and again wash the potatoes.
  2   Cut or turn into even-sized pieces allowing 2–3 pieces per portion.
  3   Cook carefully in salted water approx. 20 min.
  4   Drain well and serve in a vegetable dish.

2 Parsley Potatoes   *Pommes Persillées*
  1   Prepare and cook potatoes as for Plain Boiled.
  2   Brush liberally with melted butter and sprinkle with chopped parsley.

3 Riced or Snow Potatoes   *Pommes à la Neige*
  1   Wash, peel and rewash the potatoes. Cut to an even size.
  2   Cook in salted water.
  3   Drain off the water, place a lid on the saucepan and return to a low heat so as to dry out the potatoes.
  4   Pass through a medium sieve or a special potato masher directly into the vegetable dish. Serve without further handling.

4 Mashed Potatoes   *Pommes Purée*
  1   Wash, peel and rewash the potatoes. Cut to an even size.
  2   Cook in salted water.
  3   Drain off the water, place a lid on the saucepan and return to a low heat so as to dry out the potatoes.
  4   Pass through a medium sieve or a special potato masher
  5   Return the potatoes to a clean pan.
  6   Add 25 g (1 oz) butter per ½ kg (1 lb) and mix in with a wooden spoon.
  7   Gradually add warm milk 30 ml (⅛ pt) stirring continuously until a soft creamy consistency is reached.
  8   Correct the seasoning.
  9   Serve dome shaped in a vegetable dish, flute or scroll with a palette knife.

5 Mashed Potatoes with Cheese   *Pommes Purée au Gratin*
Proceed as for Pommes Purée, 1–6, then sprinkle with grated cheese and melted butter and gratinate.

6   Mashed Potatoes with Cream   *Pommes Purée à la Crème*

Proceed as for Pommes Purée, 1–6, then surround with a cordon of
fresh cream.

7   Biarritz Potatoes   *Pommes Biarritz*

As for mashed potatoes with the addition, for four portions, of:

50 g	diced cooked lean ham	2 oz
25 g	diced red pimento	1 oz
	chopped parsley	

8   Duchess Potatoes—Basic Recipe   *Pommes Duchesse*

1   Wash, peel and rewash the potatoes. Cut to an even size.
2   Cook in salted water.
3   Drain off the water, place a lid on the saucepan and return to a
    low heat so as to dry out the potatoes.
4   Pass through a medium sieve or a special potato masher.
5   Place the potatoes in a clean pan.
6   Add 1 yolk per $\frac{1}{2}$ kg (1 lb) and stir in vigorously with a
    wooden spoon.
7   Mix in 25 g (1 oz) butter or margarine per $\frac{1}{2}$ kg (1 lb).
8   Correct the seasoning.
9   Place in a piping bag with a large star tube.
10 Pipe out into neat spirals approx. 2 cm (1 in) diameter and
    4 cm (2 in) high on to a lightly greased baking sheet.
11 Place in a hot oven (230°–250°C) for 2–3 min in order to
    slightly harden the edges.
12 Remove from the oven and brush with eggwash.
13 Brown lightly in a hot oven or under the salamander.
14 Serve in a vegetable dish.

9   Brioche Potatoes   *Pommes Brioche*

Duchess mixture in small brioche or cottage loaf shape, i.e. 2 cm
(1 in) diameter ball with a $\frac{1}{2}$ cm ($\frac{1}{4}$ in) diameter ball on top pierced
completely through with a small knife. Place in a hot oven to harden
the surface. Brush with eggwash and brown lightly in a hot oven or
under a salamander. Serve in a vegetable dish.

10 Croquette Potatoes   *Pommes Croquettes*

1   Duchess mixture moulded cylinder shape 4 × 2 cm (2 × 1 in).
2   Pass through flour, eggwash and breadcrumbs.
3   Reshape with a palette knife and deep fry in hot deep fat (185°C)
    in a frying-basket.
4   When a golden colour drain well and serve on a dish paper.

11   Almond Potatoes   *Pommes Amandines*

Prepare cook and serve as for Croquette potatoes, using nibbed almonds in place of bread crumbs.

12   Marquis Potatoes   *Pommes Marquise*

1   Pipe out Duchess mixture in the shape of an oval nest 4 × 2 cm (2 × 1 in).
2   Glaze as for Duchess Potatoes, 8–10.
3   Place a spoonful of cooked tomato concassée (page 271) in the centre and sprinkle with a little chopped parsley.
4   Serve in a vegetable dish.

13   Dauphine Potatoes   *Pommes Dauphine*

1   Combine ½ kg (1 lb) Duchess potato mixture with ⅛ litre (¼ pt) choux paste (no sugar in the choux paste).
2   Mould cylinder shape 4 × 2 cm (2 × 1 in).
3   Deep fry in hot fat (185°C).
4   Serve on a dish paper.

14   Lorette Potatoes   *Pommes Lorette*

1   Prepare a Dauphine potato mixture.
2   Shape like short cigars.
3   Deep fry in hot fat (185°C).
4   Serve on a dish paper.

15   Steamed Potatoes   *Pommes Vapeur*

1   Prepare potatoes as for Plain Boiled, season with salt.
2   Cook in a steamer.
3   Serve in a vegetable dish.

16   Steamed Potatoes in Jacket   *Pommes en Robe de Chambre*

1   Select even-sized potatoes.
2   Scrub well.
3   Cook in a steamer or boil in salted water.
4   Serve unpeeled on a serviette or on a silver dish.

17   Sauté Potatoes   *Pommes Sautées*

1   Select medium even-sized potatoes.
2   Scrub well.
3   Plain boil or cook in the steamer.
4   Cool slightly and peel.
5   Cut into approx. 3 mm (⅛ in) slices.
6   Toss in hot shallow fat in a frying-pan until lightly coloured, season with salt.
7   Serve in a vegetable dish, sprinkle with chopped parsley.

18   Sauté Potatoes with Onions   *Pommes Lyonnaise*

   1   Allow ¼ kg (8 oz) onion to ½ kg (1 lb) potatoes.
   2   Cook the onions as for fried onion.
   3   Prepare sauté potatoes as above.
   4   Combine the two and toss together.
   5   Serve as for Pommes Sautées.

19   Crisps (Game Chips)   *Pommes Chips*

   1   Wash, peel and rewash the potatoes.
   2   Cut in thin slices on the mandolin.
   3   Wash well and dry in a cloth.
   4   Cook in hot deep fat (185°C) until golden brown and crisp.
   5   Drain well and season with salt.

These potatoes are not usually served as a potato by themselves, but
are used as a garnish and are also served in bars and for cocktail
parties.

20   Wafer Potatoes   *Pommes Gaufrettes*

   1   Wash, peel and rewash the potatoes.
   2   Using a corrugated mandolin blade, cut in slices, giving a half
      turn in between each cut in order to obtain a wafer or trellis
      pattern.
   3   Cook and serve as for Crisps.

21   Straw Potatoes   *Pommes Pailles*

   1   Wash, peel and rewash potatoes.
   2   Cut into fine julienne.
   3   Wash well and drain in a cloth.
   4   Cook in hot deep fat (185°C) until golden brown and crisp.
   5   Drain well and season with salt.

This potato is used as a garnish.

22   Matchstick Potatoes   *Pommes Allumettes*

   1   Select medium even-sized potatoes.
   2   Wash, peel and rewash.
   3   Trim on all sides to give straight edges.
   4   Cut into slices 4 cm × 3 mm (2 × ⅛ in).
   5   Cut the slices into 4 cm × 3 mm × 3 mm (2 × ⅛ × ⅛ in) strips.
   6   Wash well and dry in a cloth.
   7   Fry in hot deep fat (185°C) till golden brown and crisp.
   8   Season with salt, serve on a dish paper in a vegetable dish.

These may also be blanched as for Pommes Frites.

23 Mignonette Potatoes   *Pommes Mignonnette*

1   Prepare, wash and trim as in previous recipe.
2   Cut into 2 × 2 cm (1 × ¼ in) slices.
3   Cut into 2 × ½ × ½ cm (1 × ¼ × ¼ in) strips.
4   Cook and serve as for Matchstick Potatoes.

These may also be blanched as for Fried Potatoes (below).

24 Fried or Chipped Potatoes   *Pommes Frites*

1   Prepare, wash and trim as in previous recipe.
2   Cut into slices 1 cm (½ in) thick and 4 cm (2 in) long.
3   Cut the slices into strips 4 × 1 × 1 cm (2 × ½ × ½ in).
4   Wash well and dry in a cloth.
5   Cook in a frying-basket without colour in moderately hot fat (165°).
6   Drain and place on kitchen paper on trays till required.
7   When required place in a frying-basket and cook in hot fat (185°) till crisp and golden.
8   Drain well, season with salt.
9   Serve on a dish paper in a vegetable dish.

25 Pont Neuf Potatoes   *Pommes Pont Neuf*

1   Select large even-sized potatoes.
2   Prepare, wash and trim as in previous recipe.
3   Cut into slices 2 cm (1 in) thick, 4 cm (2 in) long.
4   Cut the slices into strips 4 × 2 × 2 cm (2 × 1 × 1 in).
5   Wash and dry on a cloth.
6   Cook in moderately hot fat (165°C) without colour. Drain.
7   Heat the fat until almost smoking (185°C).
8   Re-cook the potatoes to a golden brown.
9   Drain well, season with salt.
10 Serve on a dish paper in a vegetable dish.

26 Bataille Potatoes   *Pommes Bataille*

1   Select large even-sized potatoes.
2   Wash, peel and rewash.
3   Cut into 1 cm (½ in) slices.
4   Cut the slices into 1 cm (½ in) strips.
5   Cut the strips into 1 cm (½ in) dice.
6   Cook as for Fried Potatoes.

27 Baked Jacket Potatoes   *Pommes au Four*

1   Select good-sized potatoes and allow 1 per portion.
2   Scrub well, make a 2 mm (1/16 in) deep incision round the potato.

3 Place on a bed of salt on a tray in a hot oven (230°–250°C) for approx. 1 hr. Turn the potatoes over after 30 min.
4 Test by holding the potato in a cloth and squeezing gently; if cooked it should feel soft.
5 Serve in between the folds of a serviette on a flat silver dish or on a dish paper.

28 Baked Jacket Potatoes with Cheese   *Pommes Gratinées*

	4 large potatoes	
75 g	butter	3 oz
25 g	grated Parmesan	1 oz

1 Bake the potatoes as for Recipe 27.
2 Cut the potatoes in halves, lengthwise.
3 Remove the potato from the skin using a spoon.
4 Place the potato in a basin.
5 Add 50 g (2 oz) butter, season with salt and pepper.
6 Mix lightly with a fork.
7 Refill the potato skin with the mixture.
8 Place on a baking sheet.
9 Sprinkle with grated cheese and the remaining 25 g (1 oz) melted butter.
10 Place in the oven (200°C) until golden brown.
11 Serve in a vegetable dish.

29 Macaire Potatoes   *Pommes Macaire*

1 ½ kg (1 lb) will yield 2–3 portions.
2 Prepare and cook as for Baked Jacket Potatoes.
3 Cut in halves, remove the centre with a spoon, into a basin.
4 Add 25 g (1 oz) butter per ½ kg (1 lb) salt and mill pepper.
5 Mash and mix as lightly as possible with a fork.
6 Using a little flour, mould into a roll, then divide into pieces, allowing one or two per portion.
7 Mould into 2 cm (1 in) round cakes, flour lightly.
8 Shallow fry on both sides in very hot clarified fat.
9 Serve in a vegetable dish.

30 Byron Potatoes   *Pommes Byron*

1 Prepare and cook as for Macaire Potatoes.
2 Using the back of a dessert spoon make a shallow impression on each potato.
3 Carefully sprinkle the centres with grated cheese. Make sure no cheese is on the edge of potato.
4 Cover the cheese with cream.
5 Brown lightly under the salamander.
6 Serve in a vegetable dish.

31 Savoury Potatoes *4 portions*   *Pommes Boulangère*

400 g	potatoes	1 lb
¼ litre	white stock	½ pt
	salt, pepper	
100 g	onions	4 oz
25–50 g	butter, margarine or dripping	1–2 oz
	chopped parsley	

1 Cut the potatoes into 2 mm ($\frac{1}{16}$ in) slices on a mandolin. Keep the best slices for the top.
2 Peel, halve and finely slice the onions.
3 Mix the onions and potatoes together and season with pepper and salt.
4 Place in a well-buttered shallow earthenware dish or roasting tin.
5 Barely cover with stock.
6 Neatly arrange overlapping slices of potato on top.
7 Add a few knobs of butter.
8 Place in a hot oven (230°–250°C) approx. 20 min until lightly coloured.
9 Reduce the heat and allow to cook steadily, pressing down firmly from time to time with a flat-bottomed pan or fish slice.
10 When ready all the stock should be cooked into the potato. Allow 1½ hr cooking time in all.
11 Serve in a vegetable dish, finish with chopped parsley. If cooked in an earthenware dish, clean the edges with a cloth dipped in salt, place on a silver flat and serve.

32 Fondant Potatoes   *Pommes Fondantes*

1 Select small or even-sized medium potatoes.
2 Wash, peel and rewash.
3 Turn into eight-sided barrel shapes, allowing 2–3 per portion, approx. 4 cm (2 in) long, end diameter 1½ cm (¾ in), centre diameter 2½ cm (1¼ in).
4 Brush with melted butter or margarine.
5 Place in a pan suitable for the oven.
6 Half cover with white stock, season with salt and pepper.
7 Cook in a hot oven (230°–250°C), brushing the potatoes frequently with melted butter or margarine.
8 When cooked the stock should be completely soaked up in the potato.
9 Dress in a vegetable dish, brush with melted butter or margarine.

33 Berrichonne Potatoes   *Pommes Berrichonne*

400 g	peeled potatoes	1 lb
100 g	streaky bacon	4 oz
50 g	chopped onion	2 oz
¼ litre	white stock	½ pt
25 g	butter	1 oz
	chopped parsley	

1   Turn the potatoes barrel shape, 3–4 pieces per portion.
2   Melt the butter in a sauteuse.
3   Add the chopped onion, cover with a lid. Cook for 2–3 min without colour.
4   Add the bacon cut in lardons.
5   Replace the lid and cook gently for 1–2 min without colour.
6   Add the potatoes and sufficient white stock to come half way up the potatoes.
7   Season with salt and pepper, add half the chopped parsley.
8   Replace the lid, cook in the oven (230°–250°C) until tender.
9   Serve in a vegetable dish, sprinkle with chopped parsley.

34   Roast Potatoes   *Pommes Rôties*

1   Wash, peel and rewash the potatoes.
2   Cut into even-sized pieces, allow 3–4 pieces per portion.
3   Heat a good measure of dripping in a roasting tray.
4   Add the well-dried potatoes and lightly brown on all sides.
5   Season with salt and cook in a hot oven (230°–250°C).
6   Turn the potatoes over after approx. 30 min.
7   Cook to a golden brown. Drain.
8   Serve in a vegetable dish.

Cooking time approx. 1 hr.

35   Château Potatoes   *Pommes Château*

1   Select small even-sized potatoes.
2   Wash, and, if they are of a fairly even size, they need not be peeled, but can be turned into barrel-shaped pieces approx. the size of Fondant Potatoes.
3   Place in a saucepan of boiling water for 2–3 min, refresh immediately. Drain in a colander.
4   Finish as for Roast Potatoes (Recipe 34).

36   Rissolées Potatoes   *Pommes Rissolées*

Proceed as for Château Potatoes, with the potatoes half the size. Cooked potatoes may also be used, in which case they are browned in shallow fat in a frying-pan.

37   Cocotte Potatoes   *Pommes Cocotte*

Proceed as for Château Potatoes, but with the potatoes a quarter the size, cooking them in a sauté pan or frying-pan.

38   Noisette Potatoes   *Pommes Noisette*

$\frac{1}{2}$ *kg (1 lb) will yield 2 portions*

1   Wash, peel and rewash the potatoes.
2   Scoop out balls with a noisette spoon.

3   Cook in a little fat in a sauté pan or frying-pan. Colour on top
     of the stove and finish cooking in the oven (230°–250°C).

39 Parisienne Potatoes   *Pommes Parisienne*

1   Prepare and cook as for Noisette Potatoes.
2   Just before serving, for each ½ kg (1 lb) potatoes melt a
     tablespoon of meat glaze in a pan, add the cooked potatoes, roll
     them round so as to give a light overall coating and serve.

40 Potatoes with Bacon and Onions   *Pommes au Lard*

400 g	peeled potatoes	1 lb
100 g	button onions	4 oz
	salt	
	pepper	
100 g	streaky bacon (lardons)	4 oz
¼ litre	white stock (approx.)	½ pt
	chopped parsley	

1   Cut the potatoes in 1 cm (½ in) dice.
2   Cut the bacon into ½ cm thick (¼ in) lardons, lightly fry in a
     little fat together with the onions, brown lightly.
3   Add the potatoes, half cover with stock, season with salt and
     pepper. Cover with a lid and cook steadily in the oven
     (230°–250°C) approx. 30 min.
4   Correct the seasoning, serve in a vegetable dish and sprinkle
     with chopped parsley.

41 —   *Pommes à la Crème*

1   Cook the potatoes in their jackets in water.
2   Peel and cut into slices.
3   Barely cover with milk, season and allow to simmer for approx.
     10 min. Add two tablespoons of cream and toss gently.
4   Serve in a vegetable dish.

42 Maître d'Hôtel Potatoes   *Pommes Maître d'Hôtel*

Proceed as for Pommes à la Crème with chopped parsley.

43 Delmonico Potatoes   *Pommes Delmonico*

1   Wash, peel and rewash the potatoes.
2   Cut into 6 mm (⅜ in) dice.
3   Barely cover with milk, season with salt and pepper and allow
     to cook approx. 30–40 min.
4   Place in an earthenware dish, sprinkle with crumbs and melted
     butter and brown in the oven or under the salamander.
5   Serve on a silver flat dish.

44 New Potatoes *Pommes Nouvelles*

Method I

1 Wash the potatoes and boil or steam in their jackets until cooked.
2 Cool slightly, peel while warm and place in a pan of cold water.
3 When required for service add salt and a bunch of mint to the potatoes and heat through slowly.
4 Drain well, serve in a vegetable dish, brush with melted butter and sprinkle with chopped mint or decorate with blanched refreshed mint leaves.

Method II

1 Scrape the potatoes and wash well.
2 Place in a pan of salted boiling water with a bunch of mint and boil gently until cooked. Approx. 20 min. Serve as above.

45 New Rissolée Potatoes *Pommes Nouvelles Rissolées*

Cooked, drained, new potatoes fried to a golden brown in good fat or preferably butter.

46 Parmentier Potatoes *Pommes Parmentier*

½ kg (*1 lb*) *will yield 2–3 portions*

1 Select medium to large size potatoes.
2 Wash, peel and rewash.
3 Trim on three sides and cut into 1 cm (½ in) slices.
4 Cut the slices into 1 cm (½ in) strips.
5 Cut the strips into 1 cm (½ in) dice.
6 Wash well and dry in a cloth.
7 Cook in hot shallow fat in a frying-pan till golden brown.
8 Drain, season and serve in a vegetable dish with chopped parsley.

47 Anna Potatoes *Pommes Anna*

50 g	butter	2 oz
600 g	peeled potatoes	1½ lb

1 Grease a pomme anna mould using 25 g (1 oz) butter.
2 Trim the potatoes to an even cylindrical shape.
3 Cut into slices 2 mm ($\frac{1}{16}$ in) thick.
4 Place a layer of slices neatly overlapping in the bottom of the mould, season with salt and pepper.
5 Continue arranging the slices of potato in layers, seasoning in between.
6 Add the remaining 25 g (1 oz) butter to the top layer.

7   Cook in a hot oven (230°–250°C) for ¾–1 hr, occasionally pressing the potatoes flat.

8   To serve, turn out of the mould and leave whole or cut into four portions.

48   Dauphin Potatoes   *Pommes Dauphin*

Prepare, cook and serve as for Anna Potatoes, cutting the potatoes in julienne instead of slices.

49   Voisin Potatoes   *Pommes Voisin*

Prepare, cook and serve as for Anna Potatoes, sprinkling a little grated parmesan between each layer of potato.

18
Pastry

PASTES

1 Short Pastry   *Pâte à Foncé*

200 g	flour (soft)	8 oz
50 g	lard	2 oz
	2–3 tbspn water (approx.)	
50 g	margarine	2 oz
	pinch salt	

1 Sieve the flour and salt.
2 Rub in the fat to a sandy texture.
3 Make a well in the centre.
4 Add sufficient water to make a fairly firm paste.
5 Handle as little and as lightly as possible.

The amount of water used varies according to: the type of flour, e.g. a very fine soft flour is more absorbent; the degree of heat, e.g. prolonged contact with hot hands and weather conditions.

Uses: fruit pies, Cornish pasties, etc.

Possible reasons for faults in short pastry:

1	*Hard:*	too much water
		too little fat
		fat rubbed in insufficiently
		too much handling and rolling
		over baking.
2	*Soft-crumbly:*	too little water
		too much fat.
3	*Blistered:*	too little water
		water added unevenly
		fat not rubbed in evenly.
4	*Soggy:*	too much water
		too cool an oven
		baked for insufficient time.
5	*Shrunken:*	too much handling and rolling
		pastry stretched whilst handling.

2 Puff Pastry   *Feuilletage*

200 g	flour (strong)	8 oz
125 ml	ice-cold water	$\frac{1}{4}$ pt
	few drops of lemon juice	
200 g	margarine or butter	8 oz
	salt	

1 Sieve the flour and salt.
2 Rub in 50 g (2 oz) margarine.
3 Make a well in the centre.
4 Add the water, and lemon juice (which is to make the gluten more elastic), and knead well into a smooth dough in the shape of a ball.
5 Relax the dough in a cool place for approx. 30 min.
6 Cut a cross half-way through the dough and pull out the corners to form a star shape.
7 Roll out the points of the star square, leaving the centre thick.
8 Knead the remaining 150 g (6 oz) of margarine to the same texture as the dough. This is most important, if the fat is too soft it will melt and ooze out, if too hard it will break through the paste when being rolled.
9 Place the margarine on the centre square which is four times thicker than the flaps.
10 Fold over the flaps.
11 Roll out approx. 30 × 15 cm (1 × $\frac{1}{2}$ ft), cover with a cloth, rest for 5–10 min in a cool place.
12 Roll out approx. 60 × 20 cm (2 × $\frac{2}{3}$ ft), fold both ends to the centre, fold in half again to form a square. This is one double turn.

13 Allow to rest in a cool place approx. 20 min.
14 Half-turn the paste to the right or the left.
15 Give one more double turn, allow to rest 20 min.
16 Give two more double turns, allowing to rest between each.
17 Allow to rest before using.

Care must be taken when rolling out the paste to keep the ends and sides square.

The lightness of puff pastry is mainly due to the air which is trapped when giving the pastry folds during preparation. The addition of lemon juice (acid) is to strengthen the gluten in the flour thus helping to make a stronger dough so that there is less likelihood of the fat oozing out. The rise is caused by the fat separating layers of paste and air during rolling. When heat is applied by the oven, steam is produced causing the layers to rise and give the characteristic flaky formation.

Uses: meat pies, sausage rolls, jam-puffs, etc.

Possible reasons for faults in puff pastry:

1 *Not flaky:* fat too warm thus preventing layers of fat and paste during rolling
excessively heavy use of rolling pin.

2 *Fat oozes out:* fat too soft
dough too soft
edges not sealed
uneven folding and rolling
oven too cool.

3 *Hard:* too much water
flour not brushed off between rollings
over handling.

4 *Shrunken:* insufficient resting between rolling
overstretching.

5 *Soggy:* under baked
oven too hot

6 *Uneven Rise:* uneven distribution of fat
sides and corners not straight
uneven folding and rolling.

3 Rough Puff Pastry

200 g	flour (strong)	8 oz
125 ml	ice-cold water (approx.)	$\frac{1}{4}$ pt
150 g	margarine	6 oz
	salt	

1 Sieve the flour and salt.
2 Cut the fat into 10 g ($\frac{1}{2}$ oz) pieces and lightly mix them into the flour without rubbing in.

3   Make a well in the centre.
4   Add the water and mix to a fairly stiff dough.
5   Turn on to a floured table and roll into an oblong strip, approx.
     30 × 10 cm (12 × 4 in), keeping the sides square.
6   Give one double turn as for Puff Pastry.
7   Allow to rest in a cool place, covered with a cloth for approx.
     30 min.
8   Give three more double turns, resting between each.
9   Allow to rest before using.

4 Sugar Pastry   *Pâte à Sucre*

200 g	flour (soft)	8 oz
50 g	sugar	2 oz
	pinch salt	
125 g	margarine or butter	5 oz
	1 egg	

Method I
1   Taking care not to over soften, cream the egg and sugar.
2   Add the margarine and mix for a few seconds.
3   Gradually incorporate the sieved flour and salt.
4   Mix lightly until smooth.
5   Allow to rest in a cool place before using.

Method II
1   Sieve the flour and salt.
2   Lightly rub in the margarine to a sandy texture.
3   Make a well in the centre.
4   Add the sugar and beaten egg.
5   Mix the sugar and egg until dissolved.
6   Gradually incorporate the flour and margarine and lightly mix
     to a smooth paste.
Uses: flans, fruit tartlets.

5 Suet Paste

200 g	flour	8 oz
10 g	baking-powder	$\frac{1}{2}$ oz
125 ml	water (approx.)	$\frac{1}{4}$ pt
100 g	finely chopped beef suet	4 oz
	pinch salt	

1   Sieve the flour, baking-powder and salt.
2   Mix in the suet.
3   Make a well.
4   Add the water.
5   Mix lightly to a fairly stiff paste.

To chop the suet, break the suet into pieces with the fingers remove all the sinew, then place on a lightly floured board, sprinkle with flour and finely chop with a large, floured, chopping knife.

Uses: steamed fruit puddings, steamed jam rolls, steamed meat puddings and dumplings.

Possible reasons for faults in suet paste:

1 *Heavy and soggy:* cooking temperature too low.
2 *Tough:* too much handling, over-cooking.
3 *Lumps of suet:* under-cooked, suet insufficiently chopped.

6 Hot Water Paste—Raised Pie Paste

200 g	flour	8 oz
125 ml	water	$\frac{1}{4}$ pt
50 g	lard	2 oz
	salt	

1 Sieve the flour and salt into a warm basin, make a well in the centre.
2 Boil the lard in the water.
3 Pour into the middle of the flour.
4 Mix quickly with a wooden spoon.
5 Knead with hands while warm until smooth.
6 Use while still warm. If this paste is not kept warm during the process of mixing and moulding it will become hard, brittle and difficult to manipulate. If the paste is too warm it will be too soft and will not support its own weight when handled.

Uses: raised pork pies, veal and ham pies.

7 Choux Paste   *Pâte à Choux*

$\frac{1}{4}$ litre	water	$\frac{1}{2}$ pt
125 g	flour	5 oz
	salt	
100 g	margarine	4 oz
	4 eggs (approx.)	
	pinch of sugar	

1 Bring the water, sugar and fat to the boil in a saucepan.
2 Remove from heat.
3 Add the sieved flour and salt and mix in with a wooden spoon.
4 Return to a moderate heat and stir continuously until the mixture leaves the sides of the pan.
5 Remove from the heat and allow to cool.
6 Gradually add the beaten eggs, mixing well.
7 The paste should be of dropping consistency.

Uses: éclairs, cream buns, profiterolles, etc.

Possible reasons for faults in choux paste:

1 *Greasy and heavy:* basic mixture over-cooked.
2 *Soft—not aerated:* flour insufficiently cooked, eggs insufficiently
   beaten in the mixture, oven too cool,
   under-baked.

CAKES

8 Scones *yield: 8 Scones*

200 g	flour	8 oz
50 g	margarine	2 oz
125 ml	milk or water (approx.)	¼ pt
10 g	baking-powder	½ oz
25–50 g	castor sugar	1–2 oz

1   Sieve the flour, baking-powder and salt.
2   Rub in the fat to a sandy texture.
3   Make a well in the centre.
4   Add the sugar and the liquid.
5   Dissolve the sugar in the liquid.
6   Gradually incorporate the flour, mix lightly.
7   Roll out two rounds 1 cm (½ in) thick.
8   Place on a greased baking sheet.
9   Cut a cross half-way through the rounds with a large knife.
10 Milk wash and bake in a moderate oven 15–20 min.

   The comparatively small amount of fat, rapid mixing to a soft
dough, quick and light handling are essentials to produce a light
scone.

   Further information on the use of baking-powder, page 236, *Theory
of Catering*.

9 Fruit Scones

Add 50 g (2 oz) washed and dried sultanas to the Scone mixture.

10 SMALL CAKES—basic mixture *yield: 10 good-sized or 20 small cakes*

200 g	flour	8 oz
125 g	castor sugar	5 oz
	½ tspn baking-powder	
125 g	margarine	5 oz
	2–3 egg	

Method A—Rubbing In
1   Sieve the flour, baking-powder and salt.
2   Rub in margarine to sandy texture.
3   Add the sugar.

4 Gradually add the well-beaten eggs and mix as lightly as possible until combined.

Method B—Creaming
1 Cream the margarine and sugar in a bowl until soft and fluffy.
2 Slowly add the well-beaten eggs, mixing continously and beating really well between each addition.
3 Lightly mix in the sieved flour, baking-powder and salt.
   In both cases the consistency should be a light dropping one, and if necessary it may be adjusted with the addition of a few drops of milk.

Possible reasons for faults in cakes:
1 *Uneven texture:* fat insufficiently rubbed in
   too little liquid
   too much liquid.
2 *Close texture:* too much fat
   hands too hot when rubbing in
   fat to flour ratio.
3 *Dry:* too little liquid
   oven too hot.
4 *Bad shape:* too much liquid
   oven too cool
   too much baking-powder.
5 *Fruit sunk:* fruit wet
   too much liquid
   oven too cool.
6 *Cracked:* too little liquid
   too much baking-powder.
   Refer to *Theory of Catering*, 4th Edition, page 226, for use of baking-powder.

11 Rock Cakes

Add 50 g (2 oz) washed, dried fruit (sultanas, currants) and a little grated nutmeg to the basic mixture. Method A. Keep the mixture slightly firm. Place with a fork into eight rough shapes on a greased baking sheet, milk or egg wash and bake in a fairly hot oven (200°–230°C) approx. 20 min.

12 Cherry Cakes

Add 50 g (2 oz) glacé cherries cut in quarters and $\frac{1}{2}$ tspn vanilla essence to the basic mixture, Method B, and divide into 8–12 lightly greased cake tins. Bake in a hot oven (200°–230°C) approx. 15–20 min.

13 Coconut Cakes

Add 50 g (2 oz) desiccated coconut and ½ tspn vanilla essence to the basic mixture, Method B, and cook as for Cherry Cakes.

14 Raspberry Buns

Divide basic mixture, Method A, into eight pieces. Roll into balls, flatten slightly, dip tops into milk then into castor sugar. Place on a greased baking sheet, make a hold in the centre of each, add a little raspberry jam, Bake in a hot oven (200°–230°C) 15–20 min.

15 Queen Cakes

To the basic mixture, Method B, add 100 g (4 oz) washed and dried mixed fruit.

16 Large Fruit Cake

200 g	flour	8 oz
125 g	margarine	5 oz
50 g	glacé cherries	2 oz
	2–3 eggs	
100 g	chopped peel	4 oz
125 g	castor sugar	5 oz
200 g	fruit—currants, sultanas	8 oz
50 g	almonds	2 oz
	½ tspn mixed spice	
	½ tspn baking powder	

1 Cream fat and sugar till soft and fluffy.
2 Gradually add the beaten eggs, mix well.
3 Fold in the sieved flour, washed and dried fruit, chopped cherries, spice and peel, combine lightly
4 Place in a lightly greased 14 cm (7 in) cake tin lined with greased greaseproof paper.
5 Place the almonds on top, whole, sliced or chopped.
6 Bake Regulo 3 (150°C) for approx. ¾ hr.
7 Reduce the heat to Regulo 1 (120°C). Cover with a sheet of paper. Bake for a further 1¼ hr approx.

Test by inserting a thin needle or skewer in the centre. If the cake is cooked it should come out clean. If not cooked a little raw cake mixture sticks to the needle. The Regulo times are calculated on a ¼–9 scale oven.

When baking avoid slamming the oven door, open and close it gently. An inrush of cold air checks the rising and may cause the mixture to rise unevenly.

Moving or shaking the cake before it has set will cause it to sink in the middle.

Possible reasons for faults in sponges:

1	*Close texture:*	underbeating
		too much flour
		oven too cool or too hot.
2	*Holey texture:*	flour insufficiently folded in
		tin unevenly filled.
3	*Cracked crust:*	oven too hot.
4	*Sunken:*	oven too hot
		tin removed during cooking.
5	*White spots on surface:*	insufficient beating.

17 Victoria Sandwich

100 g	castor sugar	4 oz
100 g	flour	4 oz
	½ tspn baking-powder	
100 g	margarine	4 oz
	2 eggs	

1 Cream the fat and sugar until soft and fluffy.
2 Gradually add the beaten eggs.
3 Lightly mix in the sieved flour, and baking-powder.
4 Divide into two 14 cm (7 in) greased sponge tins.
5 Bake in a hot oven (230°–250°C) approx. 12–15 min.
6 Turn out on to a wire rack to cool.
7 Spread one half with jam, place the other half on top.
8 Dust with icing sugar.
9 Serve on a doily on a silver flat.

18 Genoese Sponge   *Genoise*

	4 eggs	
100 g	castor sugar	4 oz
100 g	flour	4 oz
50 g	butter	2 oz

1 Whisk the eggs and sugar with a balloon whisk in a bowl over a pan of hot water.
2 Continue until the mixture is light, creamy, double in bulk.
3 Remove from the heat and whisk until cold and thick (ribbon stage).
4 Fold in the flour very gently.
5 Fold in the melted butter very gently.
6 Place in a greased, floured Genoese mould.
7 Bake in a moderately hot oven (200°–230°C) approx. 30 min.

19   Chocolate Genoese

	4 eggs	
75 g	flour	3 oz
50 g	butter	2 oz
100 g	castor sugar	4 oz
25 g	cocoa powder	1 oz

Sift the flour and the cocoa together, then proceed as for Genoese Sponge (previous recipe).

Possible reasons for faults in Genoese sponges:
1   *Close texture:* eggs and sugar overheated
eggs and sugar underbeaten
too much flour
flour insufficiently folded in
oven too hot.
2   *Sunken:* too much sugar
oven too hot
tin removed during cooking.
3   *Heavy:* butter too hot
butter insufficiently mixed in
flour overmixed.

20   Chocolate Gâteau   *Gâteau au Chocolat*

	4 egg chocolate Genoese sponge (247)	
100 g	unsalted butter	4 oz
75 g	icing sugar	3 oz
50 g	block chocolate (melted in a basin in a bain-marie)	2 oz
50 g	chocolate vermicelli	2 oz

1   Cut Genoese into three slices crosswise.
2   Prepare butter cream as in Recipe 194, page 351, and mix in melted chocolate.
3   Lightly spread each slice of Genoese with butter cream and sandwich together.
4   Lightly coat the sides with butter cream and coat with chocolate vermicelli.
5   Neatly smooth the top using a little more butter cream if necessary.

Many variations can be used in decorating this gâteau, chocolate fondant may be used on the top and various shapes of chocolate can be used to decorate the top and sides.

21   Coffee Gâteau   *Gâteau Moka*

	4 egg Genoese sponge (p. 297)	
100 g	unsalted butter	4 oz
75 g	icing sugar	3 oz
	coffee essence	
50 g	toasted flaked or ribbed almonds	2 oz

1   Cut Genoese into three slices crosswise.
2   Prepare butter cream as on page 351, and flavour with coffee essence.
3   Lightly spread each slice with butter cream and sandwich together.
4   Lightly coat the sides with butter cream and coat with almonds.
5   Smooth the top using a little more butter cream if necessary.
6   Decorate by piping the word MOKA in butter cream.
7   Coffee-flavoured fondant may be used in place of butter cream for the top.

22   Springtime Gateau   *Gâteau Printanier*

This is a plain Genoese decorated with 3 or 4 different flavoured, coloured butter creams.

23   Swiss Roll

	4 eggs	
100 g	castor sugar	4 oz
100 g	flour	4 oz

1   Whisk the eggs and sugar with a balloon whisk in a bowl over a pan of hot water.
2   Continue until the mixture is light, creamy, double in bulk.
3   Remove from the heat and whisk until cold and thick (ribbon stage).
4   Fold in the flour very gently.
5   Grease a Swiss Roll tin and line with greased greaseproof paper.
6   Pour in Genoese mixture and bake in a hot oven (230°–250°C) approx. 8 min.
7   Turn out on to a sheet of paper sprinkled with castor sugar.
8   Remove the paper from the Swiss Roll.
9   Spread quickly with warm jam.
10 Roll into a fairly tight roll, leaving the paper on the outside for a few minutes.
11 Remove the paper and allow to cool on a wire rack.

24   Sponge Fingers   *yield: approx. 32 Fingers*   *Biscuits à la Cuillère*

	4 eggs	
100 g	flour	4 oz
100 g	castor sugar	4 oz

1   Cream the egg yolks and sugar in a bowl until creamy and almost white.
2   Whip the egg whites stiffly.

3   Add a little of the whites to the mixture and cut in.
4   Gradually add the sieved flour and remainder of the whites alternately, mixing as lightly as possible.
5   Place in a piping bag with 1 cm (½ in) plain tube and pipe in 6 cm (3 in) lengths on to baking sheets lined with greaseproof paper.
6   Sprinkle liberally with icing sugar.
7   Rest for 5 min.
8   Bake in a moderately hot oven (200°–230°C) approx. 10 min.
9   Remove from the oven, lift the paper on which the biscuits are piped and place upside down on the table.
10   Sprinkle liberally with water. This will assist the removal of the biscuits from the paper.

25   Shortbread Biscuits   *yield: 12 Biscuits*

150 g	flour	6 oz
50 g	castor sugar	2 oz
100 g	margarine	4 oz
	pinch of salt	

1   Sift the flour and salt.
2   Mix in the fat and sugar with the flour.
3   Combine all the ingredients to a smooth paste.
4   Roll carefully on a floured table or board to the shape of a rectangle or round, ½ cm (¼ in) thick.
5   Place on a lightly greased baking sheet.
6   Mark into the desired size and shape.
7   Prick with a fork.
8   Bake in a moderate oven (230°–250°C) approx. 15–20 min.

26   Piped Shortbread Biscuits   *yield: 12 Biscuits*

150 g	flour	6 oz
50 g	castor sugar	2 oz
100 g	margarine	4 oz
	1 egg	

1   Cream the margarine and sugar thoroughly.
2   Add the egg and mix in.
3   Lightly mix in the flour.
4   Pipe on to lightly greased and floured baking sheets.
5   Bake in a hot oven (230°–250°C) approx. 15 min.

YEAST GOODS

Before using yeast of any kind please refer to page 226 of *Theory of Catering*, 4th Edition, for essential information.

Possible reasons for faults using yeast doughs:

1	*Close texture:*	insufficiently proved
		insufficiently kneaded
		insufficient yeast
		oven too hot
		too much water
		too little water.
	Uneven texture:	insufficient kneading
		oven too cool
		over-proving.
3	*Coarse texture:*	too much water
		too much salt
		over-proved and uncovered
		unsufficient kneading.
4	*Wrinkled:*	over-proved.
5	*Sour:*	stale yeast
		too much yeast.
6	*Broken crust:*	under-proved at the second stage.
7	*White spots on crust:*	not covered before second proving.

27 Bread Rolls   *yield: 8 Rolls*

200 g	flour (strong)	8 oz
10 g	margarine	½ oz
	salt	
5 g	yeast	¼ oz
125 ml	liquid (half water, half milk)	¼ pt
	¼ tspn castor sugar	

1 Sieve the flour into a bowl and warm in the oven or above the stove.
2 Cream the yeast and sugar in a small basin, add a quarter of the liquid.
3 Make a well in the centre of the flour, add the dissolved yeast.
4 Sprinkle over a little of the flour, cover with a cloth, leave in a warm place until the yeast ferments (bubbles).
5 Add the remainder of the liquid (warm), the fat and the salt.
6 Knead firmly until smooth and free from stickiness.
7 Return to the basin, cover with a cloth and leave in a warm place until double its size. (This is called *proving* the dough.)
8 Knock back.
9 Divide into eight even pieces.
10 Mould into desired shapes.
11 Place on a floured baking sheet.
12 Cover with a cloth.
13 Leave in a warm place to prove (double in size).
14 Brush carefully with eggwash.
15 Bake in a hot oven (230°–250°C) approx. 10 min.

At all times extreme heat must be avoided as the yeast will be killed and the dough spoiled.

28   Bun Dough—Basic Mixture   *yield: 8 Buns*

200 g	flour (strong)	½ lb
25 g	castor sugar	1 oz
	1 egg	
	pinch of salt	
5 g	yeast	¼ oz
50 g	margarine	2 oz
125 ml	approx. milk and water	¼ pt

1   Sieve the flour into a bowl and warm.
2   Dissolve the yeast and sugar in a basin with a little of the liquid.
3   Make a well in the centre of the flour.
4   Add the dissolved yeast, sprinkle with a little flour, cover with a cloth, leave in a warm place until the yeast ferments (bubbles).
5   Add the beaten egg, margarine and remainder of the liquid. Knead well to form a soft, slack dough, knead until smooth and free from stickiness.
6   Keep covered and allow to prove in a warm place.
7   Use as required.

29   Bun Wash

| 100 g | sugar | ¼ lb |
| 125 ml | water | ¼ pt |

Boil together until the consistency of a thick syrup.

30   Fruit Buns

1   Add 50 g (2 oz) washed, dried fruit (currants, sultanas) and a little mixed spice to the basic mixture.
2   Mould into eight round balls.
3   Place on a lightly greased baking sheet.
4   Cover with a cloth, allow to prove.
5   Bake in a hot oven (230°–250°C) approx. 15–20 min.
6   Brush liberally with bun wash as soon as cooked.

31   Hot Cross Buns

1   Proceed as for Fruit Buns using a little more spice.
2   When moulded make a cross with the back of a knife, or make a slack mixture of flour and water and pipe on crosses using a greaseproof paper cornet.
3   Allow to prove and finish as for Fruit Buns.

32   Bath Buns

  1   Add to basic bun dough 50 g (2 oz) washed and dried fruit (currants and sultanas), and 25 g (1 oz) chopped mixed peel and 25 g (1 oz) sugar nibs.

  2   Proceed as for Fruit Buns. Pull off into eight rough-shaped pieces.

  3   Sprinkle with a little broken loaf sugar or sugar nibs.

  4   Cook as for Fruit Buns.

33   Chelsea Buns

  1   Take the basic bun dough and roll out into a large square.

  2   Brush with melted margarine.

  3   Sprinkle liberally with castor sugar.

  4   Sprinkle with 25 g (1 oz) currants, 25 g (1 oz) sultanas and 25 g (1 oz) chopped peel.

  5   Roll up like a Swiss Roll, brush with melted margarine.

  6   Cut into slices across the roll 3 cm (1½ in) wide.

  7   Place on a greased baking tray with sides.

  8   Cover and allow to prove.

  9   Complete as for Fruit Buns.

34   Swiss Buns

  1   Take the basic bun dough and divide into eight pieces.

  2   Mould into balls, then into 8 cm (4 in) lengths.

  3   Place on a greased baking sheet, cover with a cloth.

  4   Allow to prove.

  5   Bake in a hot oven (230°–250°C) approx. 15–20 min.

  6   When cool, glaze with fondant or water icing.

35   Water Icing

200 g	icing sugar	8 oz
	few drops vanilla essence	
	2–3 tbspn warm water	

  1   Pass sugar through a fine sieve into a basin.

  2   Gradually mix in warm water with a wooden spoon until the required consistency.

36   Fondant

200 g	loaf sugar	8 oz
	1 tspn glucose	
125 ml	water	¼ pt

  1   Place the water, sugar and glucose in a pan and boil gently. Keep the sides of the pan clean until a temperature of 115°C (240°F) is reached. This is assessed by using a special thermometer.

2   Pour on to a lightly watered marble slab.
3   Allow to cool.
4   Using a metal spatula, turn frequently.
5   Finally knead with the palm of the hand till smooth.
6   Keep covered with a damp cloth to prevent a hard surface forming.

To glaze Swiss Buns warm sufficient fondant in a saucepan and adjust the consistency with a little syrup (equal quantities of sugar and water boiled together) if necessary. Fondant must not be heated to more than 37°C (98°F) or it will lose its gloss.

37   Doughnuts

1   Take the basic bun dough (R. 28) and divide into eight pieces.
2   Mould into balls.
3   Press a floured thumb into each.
4   Add a little jam in each hole.
5   Mould carefully to seal the hole.
6   Cover and allow to prove on a well-floured tray.
7   Deep fry in moderately hot fat (175°C) approx. 12–15 min.
8   Lift out of the fat, drain and roll in a tray containing castor sugar mixed with a little cinnamon.

38   Savarin Paste—Basic Mixture   *8 portions*

200 g	flour	8 oz
10 g	sugar	$\frac{1}{2}$ oz
	2 eggs	
	pinch salt	
5 g	yeast	$\frac{1}{4}$ oz
125 ml	milk	1 gill
50 g	butter	2 oz

1   Sieve flour in a bowl and warm.
2   Cream the yeast with a little of the warm milk in a basin.
3   Make a well in the centre of the flour and add the dissolved yeast.
4   Sprinkle with a little of the flour from the sides, cover with a cloth and leave in a warm place till it ferments.
5   Add the remainder of the warm milk and the beaten eggs, knead well to a smooth elastic dough.
6   Replace in the bowl, add the butter in small pieces, cover with a cloth and allow to prove in a warm place.
7   Add the sugar and salt, mix well till absorbed in the dough.
8   Half fill a greased savarin mould, and prove.
9   Cook in a hot oven (233°–250°C) approx. 30 min.
10   Turn out when cooked, cool slightly.
11   Soak carefully in hot syrup.
12   Brush over with apricot glaze.

39 Rum Baba *8 portions*

Baba au Rhum

200 g	flour	8 oz
10 g	sugar	½ oz
	2 eggs	
	pinch salt	
5 g	yeast	¼ oz
125 ml	milk	1 gill
50 g	butter	2 oz
50 g	currants	2 oz
	1 small glass of rum	

1 Sieve flour in a bowl and warm.
2 Cream the yeast with a little of the warm milk in a basin.
3 Make a well in the centre of the flour and add the dissolved yeast.
4 Sprinkle with a little of the flour from the sides, cover with a cloth and leave in a warm place till it ferments.
5 Add the remainder of the warm milk and the washed, dried currants and the beaten eggs, knead well to a smooth elastic dough.
6 Replace in the bowl, add the butter in small pieces, cover with a cloth and allow to prove in a warm place.
7 Add the sugar and salt, mix well till absorbed in the dough.
8 Half fill 8 greased dariole moulds, and prove.
9 Cook in a hot oven (233°–250°) approx. 20 min.
10 Turn out when cooked, cool slightly.
11 Soak carefully in hot syrup.
12 Sprinkle liberally with rum.
13 Brush all over with apricot glaze.
14 Dress neatly on a flat dish.

They may be decorated with a rose of whipped cream which should be sweetened with castor sugar and flavoured with a little vanilla essence. This is known as Crème Chantilly.

40 Crème Chantilly

Crème Chantilly

This is whipped cream which is sweetened with castor sugar and flavoured with a little vanilla essence.

41 Syrup for Baba and Savarin and Marignans

100 g	sugar	4 oz
	1 bay leaf	
	rind and juice of 1 lemon	
¼ litre	water	½ pt
	2–3 coriander seeds	
	½ small cinnamon stick	

Boil all the ingredients together.

42 Savarin with Fruit *8 portions* *Savarin aux Fruits*

Prepare the basic Savarin mixture. Prove and cook for approx.
30 min in a large greased Savarin mould. Complete in exactly the
same way as Rum Baba including the cream. The rum is optional
for Savarin. Fill the centre with fruit salad.

43 Marignans *Marignans Chantilly*

1 Marignans are prepared in the same way as a Savarin, cooking
them in barquette moulds.
2 After the marignans have been soaked, carefully make a deep
incision along one side.
3 Decorate generously with whipped sweetened vanilla flavoured
cream.
4 Brush with apricot glaze.

44 Fruit Pies

Apple (tarte aux pommes), *blackberry, blackberry and apple, cherry,
rhubarb, gooseberry, damson, damson and apple, raspberry and
redcurrant,* etc.

400 g	fruit	1 lb
	2 tbspn water	
100 g	sugar	4 oz
150 g	flour	6 oz
35 g	margarine	1½ oz
35 g	lard	1½ oz
	water to mix	

1 Prepare the fruit, wash and place half in a ½ litre (1 pt) pie dish.
2 Add the sugar and water and the remainder of the fruit.
3 Place a clove in the apple pie.
4 Roll out the pastry ½ cm (¼ in) thick to the shape of the pie
dish, allow to relax. Edge the rim of the pie dish with a strip of
the pastry. Damp the rim first.
5 Damp the edge of pastry.
6 Carefully lay the pastry on the dish without stretching it and
firmly seal the rim of the pie.
7 Cut off any surplus pastry.
8 Brush with milk and sprinkle with castor sugar.
9 Place the pie on a baking sheet and bake in a hot oven
(230°–250°C) for approx. 10 min.
10 Reduce the heat or transfer to a cooler part of the oven and
continue cooking for a further 30 min approx. If the pastry
colours too quickly cover with a sheet of paper.
11 To serve, clean the pie dish, place on a dish paper on a silver
dish and serve with a sauceboat of custard ¼ litre (½ pt).

Preparation of Fruit for Pies, etc.

Apples	peeled, quartered, cored, washed, cut in slices.
Cherries	remove the stalks, wash.
Blackberries	stalks removed, washed.
Gooseberries	stalks and tails removed, washed.
Damsons	picked and washed.
Raspberries	stalks removed and washed.
Redcurrants	stalks removed and washed.
Rhubarb	leaves and root removed, tough strings removed, cut into 2 cm (1 in) pieces, washed.

45 Jam Tart   (short or sugar paste may be used)

Short Paste   4 portions

100 g	flour	4 oz
25 g	lard	1 oz
	water to mix	
25 g	margarine	1 oz
	salt	
	2 tbspn jam	

1 Prepare short paste, mould into a ball.
2 Roll out into a 3 mm thick ($\frac{1}{8}$ in) round.
3 Place carefully on a greased plate.
4 Cut off any surplus pastry.
5 Neaten the edges.
6 Prick the bottom several times with a fork.
7 Spread on the jam to within 1 cm ($\frac{1}{4}$ in) of the edge.
8 Roll out any surplus pastry, cut into $\frac{1}{2}$ cm ($\frac{1}{4}$ in) strips and decorate the top.
9 Place on a baking sheet and bake in a hot oven (230°–250°C) approx. 20 min.

A jam tart may also be made in a shallow flan ring.
Serve off the plate on a doily on a silver dish.

46 Lemon Curd Tart

As Recipe 45, using Lemon Curd, page 315.

47 Syrup or Treacle Tart

As for Jam Tart, but spread with:

100 g	syrup or treacle	4 oz
	3–4 drops lemon juice	
15 g	white breadcrumbs	$\frac{3}{4}$ oz
	1 tbspn water	

Warm the syrup or treacle slightly, then mix in the remainder of the ingredients.

48 Baked Jam Roll *4 portions*

> 200 g   short paste (8 oz flour with ¼ oz
>   baking-powder added when
>   sifting flour)
>   2–3 tbspn jam

1   Roll out pastry into a rectangle 3 dm × 12 cm (12 × 6 in)
    approx.
2   Spread with jam leaving 1 cm (½ in) clear on all edges.
3   Fold over the two sides.
4   Roll the pastry from the top.
5   Moisten the bottom edge to seal the roll.
6   Place edge down on a greased baking sheet.
7   Brush with eggwash or milk. Sprinkle with sugar.
8   Bake in a moderate oven (200°–230°C) approx. 40 min.
9   Serve on an oval flat silver dish with a sauceboat of jam sauce
    or custard sauce separately.

49 Baked Apple Dumplings *4 portions*

> 200 g   short paste (8 oz flour)
>   4 cloves
> 100 g   4 small cooking apples (4 oz each)
> 50 g   sugar   2 oz

1   Roll out pastry 3 mm (⅛ in) thick into a square.
2   Cut into four even squares.
3   Damp the edges.
4   Place a whole peeled, cored and washed apple in the centre of
    each square.
5   Pierce the apple with a clove.
6   Fill the centre with sugar.
7   Fold over the pastry to completely seal the apple, without
    breaking the pastry.
8   Roll out any debris of pastry and cut neat 2 cm (1 in) fancy
    rounds and place one on top of each apple.
9   Egg or milk wash and place on a lightly greased baking sheet.
10 Bake in a moderately hot oven (200°–230°C) approx. 30 min.
11 Serve on a silver dish with a sauceboat of custard.

50 Dutch Apple Tart *6–8 portions*

> 200 g   sugar paste (8 oz flour)
> 50 g   sultanas   2 oz
> 400 g   cooking apples   1 lb
> 100 g   sugar   4 oz
>   pinch of cinnamon
>   zest of lemon

1   Roll out half the pastry 3 mm (⅛ in) thick into a neat round
    and place on a greased plate.

2   Prick the bottom several times with a fork.

3   Peel, core and wash and slice the apples.

4   Place them in a saucepan with the sugar and a little water.

5   Partly cook the apples, add the cinnamon and zest of lemon.

6   Add the washed, dried sultanas and allow to cool.

7   Place on the pastry.

8   Moisten the edges.

9   Roll out the other half of the pastry to a neat round and place on top.

10   Seal firmly, trim off excess pastry, mould the edges.

11   Brush with milk and sprinkle with castor sugar.

12   Place on a baking sheet, bake in a moderately hot oven (200°–230°C) approx. 40 min.

13   Remove from the plate carefully. Serve on a doily on a silver dish.

51 Flans

Allow 25 g (1 oz) flour per portion and prepare sugar pastry (page 292).

1   Grease the flan ring and baking sheet.

2   Roll out the pastry 2 cm (1 in) larger than the flan ring.

3   Place the flan ring on the baking sheet.

4   Carefully place the pastry on the flan ring, by rolling it loosely over the rolling-pin, picking up, and unrolling it over the flan ring.

5   Press the pastry into shape without stretching it, being careful to exclude any air.

6   Allow a ½ cm (¼ in) ridge of pastry on top of the flan ring.

7   Cut off the surplus paste by rolling the pin firmly across the top of the flan ring.

8   Mould the edge with thumb and forefinger.

9   Decorate (*a*) with pastry tweezers or (*b*) with thumbs and forefingers, squeezing the pastry neatly to form a corrugated pattern.

52 Apple Flan   *4 portions*   *Flan aux Pommes*

100 g	sugar paste (4 oz flour)	
50 g	sugar	2 oz
400 g	cooking apples	1 lb
	2 tbspn apricot glaze	

1   Line flan ring as above. Pierce the bottom several times with a fork.

2   Keep the best-shaped apple and make the remainder into a purée.

3   When cool place in the flan case.

4   Peel, quarter and wash the remaining apple.

5   Cut in neat thin slices and lay carefully on the apple purée (see

below), overlapping each slice. Ensure that each slice points to the centre of the flan then no difficulty should be encountered in joining the pattern up neatly.

6   Sprinkle a little sugar on the apple slices and bake the flan in a moderately hot oven (200°–230°C) 30–40 min.

7   When the flan is almost cooked, remove the flan ring carefully, return to the oven to complete the cooking. Mask with Apricot Glaze.

53 Apricot Glaze

Prepare by boiling apricot jam with a little water and passing it through a strainer. Glaze should be used hot.

54 Apple Meringue Flan   *Flan aux Pommes Meringuées*

Cook as for Apple Flan, without arranging sliced apples. Pipe with meringue, Recipe 127, page 333, using two egg whites. Return to moderately hot oven to cook and colour meringue, approx. 5 min.

Apple Purée   4 portions   *Marmalade de Pomme*

400 g	cooking apples	1 lb
10 g	margarine	½ oz
50 g	sugar	2 oz

Peel, core and slice the apples. Place the margarine in a thick-bottomed pan, heat until melted, add the apples and sugar, cover with a lid and cook gently until soft. Drain off any excess liquid and pass through a sieve.

55 Cherry Flan—using Fresh Cherries   *4 portions*   *Flan aux Cerises*

100 g	sugar paste (4 oz flour)	
50 g	sugar	2 oz
200–300 g	cherries	8–12 oz
	2 tbspn red glaze	

1   Line the flan ring, pierce the bottom.
2   Stone the cherries.
3   Arrange neatly in the flan case.
4   Sprinkle with sugar.
5   Bake in a moderately hot oven (200°–230°C) approx. 30 min.
6   Remove ring and eggwash sides.
7   Complete the cooking.
8   Brush with hot red glaze (Recipe 56).

56 Red Glaze

(*a*) Boil sugar and water or fruit syrup with a little red colour and thicken with diluted arrowroot or fecule, re-boil till clear, strain.

(*b*) Red jam and a little water boiled and passed through a strainer.

57 Goosberry Flan *4 portions*   *Flan aux Groseilles*

100 g	sugar paste (¼ lb flour)	
100 g	sugar	4 oz
200–300 g	gooseberries	8–12 oz
	2 tbspn apricot glaze	

1 Line flan ring and pierce.
2 Sprinkle with sugar.
3 Add the topped and tailed, washed gooseberries.
4 Arrange neatly in the flan case.
5 Sprinkle with the remainder of the sugar.
6 Bake in a moderately hot oven (200°–230°C).
7 When the flan is almost cooked carefully remove the flan ring and return the flan to the oven to complete the cooking.
8 Mask with apricot glaze.

58 Rhubarb Flan *4 portions*

100 g	sugar paste (4 oz flour)	
100 g	sugar	4 oz
300 g	rhubarb	¾ lb
	2 tbspn apricot or red glaze	

1 Trim the roots and leaves from the rhubarb and remove the tough string. Cut into 2 cm (1 in) pieces and wash.
2 Line flan ring and pierce.
3 Sprinkle with sugar.
4 Arrange the fruit neatly in the flan case.
5 Sprinkle with the remainder of the sugar.
6 Bake in a moderately hot oven (200°–230°C).
7 When the flan is almost cooked, carefully remove the flan ring and return the flan to the oven to complete the cooking.
8 Mask with apricot glaze.

A ½ cm (¼ in) layer of pastry cream or thick custard may be placed in the flan case before adding the rhubarb then complete as above.

59 Plum or Apricot Flan

100 g	sugar paste (¼ lb flour)	
100 g	sugar	4 oz
200–300 g	plums or apricots	8–12 oz
	2 tbspn apricot glaze	

1 Line flan ring and pierce.
2 Sprinkle with sugar.
3 Quarter or halve the fruit.
4 Arrange neatly in the flan case.
5 Sprinkle with the remainder of the sugar.
6 Bake in a moderately hot oven (200°–230°C).

7   When the flan is almost cooked carefully remove the flan ring and return the flan to the oven to complete the cooking.

8   Mask with apricot glaze.

60–63   Soft Fruit and Tinned Fruit Flans

For soft fruits (e.g. strawberry, raspberry, banana), and tinned fruits (e.g. pear, peach, pineapple, cherry), the flan case is lined in the same way, the bottom pierced and then cooked 'blind', i.e. tearing a piece of paper 2 cm (1 in) larger in diameter than the flan ring, place it carefully in the flan case.

Fill the centre with dried peas, beans or small pieces of stale bread. Bake in a moderately hot oven (200°–230°C) approx. 30 min. Remove the flan ring, paper and beans before the flan is cooked through, eggwash and return to the oven to complete the cooking. Add pastry cream and sliced or whole drained fruit. Mask with glaze. The glaze may be made with the fruit juice thickened with arrowroot, approx. 10 g ($\frac{1}{2}$ oz) to $\frac{1}{4}$ litre ($\frac{1}{2}$ pt).

64	**Strawberry Flan** *4 portions*		*Flan aux Fraises*
65	**Raspberry Flan**		*Flan aux Framboises*

100 g	sugar paste (using 4 oz flour)	
	2 tbspn red glaze	
200 g	fruit	8 oz

1   Cook the flan blind, allow to cool.
2   Pick and wash the fruit, drain well.
3   Dress neatly in flan case.
4   Coat with the glaze.

66   Banana Flan   *4 portions*   *Flan aux Bananes*

100 g	sugar paste (using 4 oz flour)	
125 ml	pastry cream or thick custard	$\frac{1}{4}$ pt
	2 bananas	
	2 tbspn apricot glaze	

1   Cook flan blind, allow to cool.
2   Make pastry cream (page 345) or custard and pour while hot into the flan case.
3   Allow to set.
4   Peel and slice the bananas neatly.
5   Arrange overlapping layers on the pastry cream.
6   Coat with glaze.

67   Fruit Tartlets

These are made from the same pastry and the same fruits as the fruit flans. The ingredients are the same. The tartlets are made by rolling out the pastry 3 mm ($\frac{1}{8}$ in) thick and cutting out rounds with a flutter cutter and neatly placing them in greased tartlet moulds. Depending on the fruit used they may sometimes be cooked blind, e.g. strawberries, raspberries.

68   Fruit Barquettes

Certain fruits (e.g. strawberries, raspberries) are sometimes served in boat-shaped moulds. The preparation is the same as for tartlets.

Both tartlets and barquettes should be served on a doily on a silver flat dish allowing one large or two small per portion.

69   Jam Tartlets   *4 portions*

100 g	sugar paste (using 4 oz flour)	
50 g	jam	2 oz

1   Prepare the tartlets as above.
2   Prick the bottom with a fork.
3   Add a little jam in each.
4   Place on a baking sheet.
5   Bake in a moderately hot oven (200°–230°C) 20–30 min.

Lemon Curd Tartlets—prepare as for jam tartlets.
Syrup or Treacle Tartlets

100 g	syrup or treacle	4 oz
	3–4 drops lemon juice	
15 g	white breadcrumbs	$\frac{3}{4}$ oz
	1 tbspn water	

Warm the syrup or treacle slightly, then mix in the remainder of the ingredients. Use in place of jam.

70   Bakewell Tart   *8 portions*

200 g	sugar paste (using 8 oz flour)	
35 g	icing sugar	1$\frac{1}{2}$ oz
50 g	raspberry jam	2 oz
50 g	apricot glaze	2 oz
	Frangipane	
100 g	margarine	4 oz
50 g	ground almonds	2 oz
	2 eggs	
100 g	castor sugar	4 oz
50 g	flour	2 oz
	almond essence	

1   Line a flan ring using three-quarters of the paste 2 mm ($\frac{1}{8}$ in) thick.
2   Pierce the bottom with a fork.
3   Spread with jam and the frangipane.
4   Roll the remaining paste, cut into neat $\frac{1}{2}$ cm ($\frac{1}{4}$ in) strips and arrange neatly criss-cross on the frangipane, trim off surplus paste.

5   Brush with eggwash.
6   Bake in a moderately hot oven (200°–230°C) 30–40 min.
7   Brush with hot apricot glaze.
8   When cooled brush over with very thin water icing.

71   Frangipane for Bakewell Tart (alternative)

100 g	butter	4 oz
	2 eggs	
10 g	flour	$\frac{1}{2}$ oz
100 g	castor sugar	4 oz
100 g	ground almonds	4 oz

Cream the butter and sugar, gradually beat in the eggs. Mix in the almonds and flour, mix lightly.

72   Date and Apple Slice   *4 portions*

100 g	sugar paste (using 4 oz flour)	
50 g	chopped dates	2 oz
200 g	cooking apples	8 oz
50 g	sugar	2 oz

1   Roll out the paste 3 mm ($\frac{1}{8}$ in) thick into a square.
2   Peel, core and wash the apples, cook with the sugar to a dry purée using the minimum of water.
3   Allow to cool.
4   Mix with the dates.
5   Cut the pastry in half and place one half on a greased baking sheet.
6   Spread the apple and date mixture on this half.
7   Moisten the edge and place on top the other half of the pastry.
8   Gently flatten with a rolling-pin.
9   Mark in portions.
10   Brush with milk and sprinkle with castor sugar.
11   Bake in a moderately hot oven (200°–230°C) 20–30 min.
12   Cut into portions, serve on a doily on a silver flat dish.

73   Lemon Meringue Pie   *8 portions*   (Economic Recipe)

200 g	sugar paste (8 oz flour)		
100 g	sugar	4 oz	
25 g	butter	1 oz	
	3 yolks		Economic lemon curd
185 ml	water	1$\frac{1}{2}$ gills	
15 g	cornflour	$\frac{3}{4}$ oz	
	1 lemon		
	4 egg whites		meringue
200 g	castor sugar	8 oz	

1   Line a flan ring and cook blind.
2   Prepare the lemon curd by boiling the water and sugar to a

syrup, thicken with diluted cornflour, remove from the heat, add
the butter and the grated zest and juice of lemon, whisk in yolk.

3   Place in the flan case.
4   When set, pipe in the meringue, Recipe 127 (page 333) and
    colour in a hot oven (230°–250°C).
5   Serve on a doily on a silver flat dish.

Lemon Curd

100 g	butter	4 oz
	2 eggs	
100 g	castor sugar	4 oz
	1 lemon	

Cream the egg yolks and sugar in a bowl with a whisk, add the
butter, zest and juice of lemon. Place in a bain-marie on low heat and
whisk continuously till it thickens (20–30 min).

74 Mincemeat Tart

200 g	sugar paste	8 oz
200 g	mincemeat	8 oz

1   Roll out half pastry 3 mm (⅛ in) thick into a neat round
    and place on a greased plate.
2   Prick the bottom several times with a fork.
3   Add the mincemeat.
4   Moisten the edges.
5   Roll out the other half of the pastry to a neat round and place
    on top.
6   Seal firmly, trim off excess pastry, mould the edges.
7   Brush with milk and sprinkle with castor sugar.
8   Place on a baking sheet, bake in a moderately hot oven
    (200°–230°C) approx. 40 min.
9   Remove from the plate carefully. Serve on a doily on a silver
    dish.

PUFF PASTRY GOODS

75 Eccles Cakes   *yield: 12 Cakes*

200 g	puff or rough	8 oz
	puff pastry	
50 g	margarine	2 oz
50 g	mixed peel	2 oz
50 g	demerara sugar	2 oz
200 g	currants	8 oz
	pinch mixed spice	

1   Roll out the pastry 1 mm ($\frac{1}{16}$ in) thick.
2   Cut into rounds 8–10 cm (4–5 in) diameter.
3   Damp the edges.
4   Place a tablespoon of the mixture in the centre of each.

5   Fold the edges over to the centre and completely seal in the mixture.
6   Brush the top with egg white and dip into castor sugar.
7   Place on a greased baking sheet.
8   Cut two or three incisions with a knife so as to show the filling.
9   Bake in a hot oven (230°–250°C) approx. 15–20 min.

76   Jam Turnovers   *yield: 12 Turnovers*   *Chausson aux Confitures*

| 200 g | puff pastry (8 oz flour) | |
| 200 g | jam | 8 oz |

1   Roll out pastry 2 mm ($\frac{1}{16}$ in) thick.
2   Cut with a fancy cutter into 8 cm diameter (4 in) rounds.
3   Roll out slightly oval 10 × 8 cm (5 × 4 in).
4   Moisten the edges.
5   Place a little jam in the centre of each.
6   Fold over and seal firmly.
7   Brush with egg white and dip in castor sugar.
8   Place sugar side up on a greased baking sheet.
9   Bake in a hot oven (230°–250°C) approx. 15–20 min.

77   Jam Puffs   *yield: 8 Puffs*
Ingredients as for Jam Turnovers.

1   Roll out pastry 2 mm ($\frac{1}{16}$ in) thick.
2   Cut into 12 cm (6 in) rounds.
3   Moisten edges.
4   Place a little jam in the centre of each.
5   Fold over three sides to form a triangle. Finish as for Jam Turnovers.

78   Cream Horns   *yield: 16 Horns*

200 g	puff pastry (8 oz flour)	
½ litre	cream	1 pt
	few drops vanilla essence	
50 g	jam	2 oz
50 g	castor sugar	2 oz

1   Roll out the pastry 2 mm ($\frac{1}{16}$ in) thick, 30 cm (1 ft) long.
2   Cut into 1½ cm wide ($\frac{3}{4}$ in) strips.
3   Moisten one side of the strip.
4   Wind carefully round lightly greased cream horn moulds, starting at the point and carefully overlapping each round slightly.
5   Brush with eggwash on one side and place on a greased baking sheet.
6   Bake in a hot oven (230°C–250°C) approx. 20 min.
7   Sprinkle with icing sugar and return to a hot oven for a few seconds to glaze.

8 Remove carefully from the moulds and allow to cool.
9 Place a little jam in the bottom of each.
10 Add the sugar and essence to the cream and whip stiffly.
11 Place in a piping bag with a star tube and pipe a neat rose into each horn.

79 Cream Slice   *yield: 6–8 Slices*   *Mille-feuilles*

200 g	puff pastry (8 oz flour)	
100 g	apricot jam	4 oz
$\frac{1}{4}$ litre	pastry cream	$\frac{1}{2}$ pt
200 g	fondant or water icing	8 oz

1 Roll out the pastry 2 mm ($\frac{1}{16}$ in) thick into an even-sided square.
2 Roll up carefully on a rolling-pin and unroll into a greased, dampened baking sheet.
3 Using two forks pierce as many holes as possible.
4 Cut in half with a large knife then cut each half in two to form four even sized rectangles.
5 Bake in a hot oven (230°–250°C) approx. 15–20 min, turn the strips over after 10 min.
6 Allow to cool.
7 Keep the best strip for the top.
8 Spread pastry cream on one strip.
9 Place another strip on top and spread with jam.
10 Place the third strip on top and spread with pastry cream.
11 Place the last strip on top, flat side up.
12 Press down firmly with a flat tray.
13 Decorate by feather-icing as follows:
14 Warm the fondant to blood heat and correct the consistency with sugar syrup if necessary.
15 Separate a little of the fondant into two colours and place into paper cornets.
16 Pour the fondant over the mille-feuille in an even coat.
17 Immediately pipe on one of the colours lengthwise in strips 1 cm ($\frac{1}{2}$ in) apart.
18 Then quickly pipe on the second colour between each line of the first.
19 With the back of a small knife, wiping after each stroke, mark down the slice strokes 2 cm (1 in) apart.
20 Quickly turn the slice around and repeat in the same direction with strokes in between the previous ones.
21 Allow to set and trim the edges neatly.
22 Serve on a doily on a silver dish.

80 Jalousie   *8 portions*

200 g	puff pastry (8 oz flour)	
200 g	mincemeat, jam or frangipane	8 oz

1   Roll out one-third of the pastry 3 mm ($\frac{1}{8}$ in) thick into a strip approx. 20 × 8 cm (10 × 4 in) and place on a greased, dampened baking sheet.
2   Pierce with a fork.
3   Moisten the edges.
4   Spread on the filling, leaving 2 cm (1 in) free all the way round.
5   Roll out the remaining two-thirds of the pastry to the same size.
6   Fold in half lengthwise and, with a sharp knife, cut slits across the fold about $\frac{1}{2}$ cm ($\frac{1}{4}$ in) apart and coming to within 2 cm (1 in) of the edge.
7   Carefully open out this strip and neatly place on to the first strip.
8   Neaten and decorate the edge.
9   Brush with eggwash.
10   Bake in a hot oven (230°–250°C) approx. 25–30 min.
11   Sprinkle with icing sugar and return to a very hot oven to glaze.

81   Pithivier   *8 portions*

200 g	puff pastry (8 oz flour)
	1 tbspn apricot jam
	frangipane (Recipe 70)
	using $\frac{1}{2}$ the recipe

1   Roll out one-third of the pastry into a round 20 cm (8 in), 2 mm ($\frac{1}{16}$ in) thick, moisten the edges and place on a greased, dampened baking sheet, spread the centre with jam.
2   Prepare the frangipane by creaming the margarine and sugar in a bowl, gradually adding the beaten eggs and folding in the flour and almonds.
3   Spread on the frangipane, leaving a 2 cm (1 in) border round the edge.
4   Roll out the remaining two-thirds of the pastry and cut into a slightly larger round.
5   Place neatly on top, seal and decorate the edge.
6   Using a sharp pointed knife make approximately twelve curved cuts 2 mm ($\frac{1}{16}$ in) deep radiating from the centre to about 2 cm (1 in) from the edge.
7   Brush with eggwash.
8   Bake in a hot oven (230°–250°C) approx. 25–30 min.
9   Glaze with icing sugar as for Jalousie.

82   Palmiers

Puff pastry trimmings are suitable for these.

1   Roll out the pastry 2 mm ($\frac{1}{16}$ in) thick into a square.
2   Sprinkle liberally with castor sugar on both sides and roll into the pastry.
3   Fold into three from each end so as to meet in the middle, brush with eggwash and fold in two.

4   Cut into strips approx. 2 cm ($\frac{1}{4}$ in) thick, dip one side in castor sugar.
5   Place on a greased baking sheet, sugared side down, leaving a space of at least 2 cm (1 in) between each.
6   Bake in a very hot oven approx. 10 min.
7   Turn with a palette knife, cook on the other side until brown and the sugar caramelised.

They may be made in all sizes.

Two joined together with a little whipped cream may be served as a pastry.

83   Apple Turnover   *yield: 8 Turnovers*   *Chausson aux Pommes*

Proceed as for Jam Turnover (see page 316), using a dry, sweetened apple purée.

84   Mince Pies   *yield: 8–12 Pies*

200 g	puff pastry (8 oz flour)	
200 g	mincemeat	8 oz

1   Roll out the pastry 3 mm ($\frac{1}{8}$ in) thick.
2   Cut half the pastry into fluted rounds approx. 5 cm ($2\frac{1}{2}$ in) diameter.
3   Place on greased, dampened baking sheet.
4   Moisten the edges.
5   Place a little mincemeat in the centre of each.
6   Cut remainder of the pastry into fluted rounds 6 cm (3 in) diameter.
7   Cover the mincemeat, seal the edges.
8   Brush with eggwash.
9   Bake in a hot oven (230°–250°C) approx. 20 min.
10 Sprinkle with icing sugar and serve warm on a doily on a silver dish. Accompany with a suitable sauce, e.g. custard, brandy sauce, brandy cream, etc.

85   Puff Pastry Cases   *yield: 12 Cases*   *Bouchées*

200 g	puff pastry (8 oz flour)

1   Roll out pastry approx. $\frac{1}{2}$ cm ($\frac{1}{4}$ in) thick.
2   Cut out with a round, fluted 4 cm (2 in) cutter.
3   Place on a greased, dampened baking sheet, eggwash.
4   Dip a plain 3 cm ($1\frac{1}{2}$ in) diameter cutter into hot fat or oil and make an incision 3 mm ($\frac{1}{8}$ in) deep in the centre of each.
5   Allow to rest in a cool place.
6   Bake in a hot oven (230°–250°C) approx. 20 min.
7   When cool remove caps or lids carefully and remove all the raw pastry from inside the cases.

Bouchées are filled with a variety of savoury fillings and are served hot or cold.

They may also be filled with cream and jam or lemon curd as a pastry.

Large bouchées are known as Vol au Vent; details of their preparation are on pages 227–228. They may be produced in one, two, four or six portion sizes, and a single sized vol au vent would be approximately twice the size of a bouchée. When preparing one and two portion size vol au vent the method for bouchées may be followed. When preparing larger sized vol au vent it is advisable to have two layers of puff pastry each ½ cm (¼ in) thick sealed together with eggwash. One layer should be a plain round, and the other of the same diameter with a circle cut out of the centre.

86   Sausage Rolls   *yield: 12 Rolls*

200 g	puff pastry (8 oz flour)	
400 g	sausage meat	1 lb

1   Roll out pastry 3 mm (⅛ in) thick into a strip 8 cm (4 in) wide.
2   Make sausage meat into a roll 2 cm (1 in) diameter.
3   Place on the pastry.
4   Moisten the edges of the pastry.
5   Fold over and seal.
6   Cut into 6 cm (3 in) lengths.
7   Mark the edge with the back of a knife.
8   Brush with eggwash.
9   Place on to a greased, dampened baking sheet.
10   Bake in a hot oven (230°–250°C) approx. 20 min.

87   Fruit Slice   *8 portions*   *Bande aux Fruits*, or *Tranche aux Fruits*

These may be prepared from any fruit suitable for flans.

200 g	puff pastry (8 oz flour)	
	sugar to sweeten	
400 g	fruit	1 lb
	2 tbspn appropriate glaze	

1   Roll out the pastry 2 mm (1/16 in) thick in a strip 12 cm (6 in) wide.
2   Place on a greased, dampened baking sheet.
3   Moisten two edges with eggwash, lay two 1½ cm (⅜ in) wide strips along each edge.
4   Seal firmly and mark with the back of a knife.
5   Prick the bottom of the slice.
6   Then depending on the fruit used, either put the fruit on the slice and cook together (e.g. apple), or cook the slice blind and afterwards place the pastry cream and fruit on the pastry. Glaze and serve as for flans.

CHOUX PASTRY GOODS

88 Éclairs—Chocolate *yield: 12 Éclairs* *Éclairs au Chocolat*

125 ml	choux paste (¼ pt water) (Recipe 7)	
100 g	fondant	4 oz
¼ litre	whipped cream	½ pt
25 g	chocolate couverture	1 oz

1 Place the choux paste into a piping bag with 1 cm (½ in) plain tube.
2 Pipe into 6 cm (3 in) lengths on to a lightly greased baking sheet.
3 Bake in a moderate oven (200°–230°C) approx. 30 min.
4 Allow to cool.
5 Slit down one side, with a sharp knife
6 Fill with sweetened, vanilla-flavoured whipped cream, using a piping bag and small tube.
7 Warm the fondant, add the finely cut chocolate, allow to melt slowly, adjust the consistency with a little sugar and water syrup if necessary. *Do not overheat or the fondant will lose its shine.*
8 Glaze the éclairs by dipping them in the fondant, remove the surplus with the finger.
9 Allow to set.
10 Serve on a doily on a silver flat.

89 Coffee Éclairs *Éclairs au Café*

Add a few drips of coffee essence instead of chocolate to the fondant.

90 Cream Buns *yield: 8 Buns* *Choux à la Crème*

	choux paste (¼ pt water) (Recipe 7)	
¼ litre	whipped cream	½ pt
25 g	chopped almonds	1 oz

1 Place the choux paste into a piping bag with a 1 cm (½ in) plain tube.
2 Pipe out on to a lightly greased baking sheet into pieces the size of a walnut.
3 Sprinkle each with chopped almonds.
4 Cook, split and fill as for éclairs.
5 Sprinkle with icing sugar and serve.

91 Profiterolles *Profiterolles*

These are small choux paste buns which can be made in a variety of sizes:

(*a*) pea size—for consommé garnish,
(*b*) double pea size (stuffed) for garnish,

(c) half-cream-bun size—filled with cream and served with chocolate sauce.

92   Profiterolles and Chocolate Sauce   *Profiterolles au Chocolat*

	choux paste (¼ pt water) (Recipe 7)	
¼ litre	chocolate sauce (Recipe 191)	½ pt
¼ litre	whipped, sweetened, vanilla flavoured cream	½ pt

1   Proceed as for Cream Buns (Recipe 90), pipe out half the size and omit the almonds.
2   Fill with cream and dredge with icing sugar.
3   Dress neatly on a doily on a silver flat dish and serve with a sauceboat of cold chocolate sauce.

93   Choux Paste Fritters   *8 portions*   *Beignets Soufflés Sauce Abricot*

125 ml	choux paste	¼ pt
125 ml	apricot sauce (Recipe 181)	¼ pt

1   Using a tablespoon and the finger, break the paste off into pieces the size of a walnut into a moderately hot fat (170°C).
2   Allow to cook gently for approx. 10–15 min.
3   Drain well, sprinkle liberally with icing sugar.
4   Dress on a doily on a silver dish with a sauceboat of hot apricot sauce separately.

PUDDINGS

94   Steamed Fruit Puddings   *6 portions*

Apple, apple and blackberry, rhubarb, rhubarb and apple, etc.

200 g	suet paste (8 oz flour) (recipe 5)	
¾–1 kg	fruit	1½–2 lb
100 g	sugar	4 oz
	2 tbspn water	

1   Grease the basin.
2   Line, using three-quarters of the paste.
3   Add prepared and washed fruit and sugar. Add 1–2 cloves in an apple pudding.
4   Add two tablespoons water.
5   Moisten the edge of the paste.
6   Cover with the remaining quarter of the pastry.
7   Seal firmly.
8   Cover with greased greaseproof paper and a pudding cloth.
9   Steam for 1½ hr approx.
10   Clean the basin and wrap a folded serviette around. Serve in the basin on a silver flat dish. Sauceboat of custard separate.

95 Steamed Jam Roll *6 portions*

200 g	suet paste (8 oz flour) (recipe 5)	
100 g	jam	4 oz

1 Roll out paste into a rectangle 3 dm × 12 cm (12 × 6 in) approx.
2 Spread with jam leaving 1 cm ($\frac{1}{2}$ in) clear on all edges.
3 Fold over the two sides.
4 Roll the pastry from the top.
5 Moisten the bottom edge to seal the roll.
6 Wrap in buttered greaseproof paper and a pudding cloth, tie both ends. Steam for $1\frac{1}{2}$–2 hr.
7 Serve with jam or custard sauce.

96 Steamed Currant Roll *6 portions*

300 g	flour	12 oz
10 g	baking-powder	$\frac{1}{2}$ oz
75 g	sugar	3 oz
185 ml	water or milk, approx.	$1\frac{1}{2}$ gills
150 g	chopped suet	6 oz
100 g	currants	4 oz
	pinch salt	

1 Sieve the flour, salt and baking-powder into a bowl.
2 Mix in the suet.
3 Mix in the sugar and currants.
4 Add sufficient water or milk to make a fairly firm dough.
5 Roll in greased greaseproof paper and a pudding cloth. Tie with string at both ends.
6 Steam $1\frac{1}{2}$–2 hr.
7 Remove the cloth and paper, serve on a silver flat dish with a sauceboat of custard.

97 Steamed Currant or Sultana Pudding *6 portions*

100 g	suet	4 oz
100 g	breadcrumbs	4 oz
	1 tspn baking-powder	
125 ml	milk	1 gill
100 g	flour	4 oz
100 g	fruit	4 oz
	1 egg	
100 g	sugar	4 oz

1 Mix all the dry ingredients together.
2 Add the liquid and mix.
3 Place in a greased pudding basin and steam $1\frac{1}{2}$–2 hr.
4 Serve with custard sauce or vanilla sauce.

98   Golden Syrup or Treacle Pudding   *6 portions*

150 g	flour	6 oz
75 g	chopped suet	3 oz
	1 egg	
125 ml	milk, approx.	¼ pt
	pinch salt	
	1 tspn baking-powder	
50 g	castor sugar	2 oz
125 ml	golden syrup or light treacle	¼ pt
	zest 1 lemon	

1   Sieve the flour, salt and baking-powder into a bowl.
2   Mix the suet, sugar and zest.
3   Mix to a medium dough, with the beaten egg and milk.
4   Pour the syrup in a well-greased basin.
5   Place mixture on top.
6   Cover securely, steam for 1½–2 hr.
7   Turn on to a flat dish. Serve with a sauceboat of warm syrup containing the lemon juice.

99   Steamed Sponge Pudding—Basic Recipe   *6 portions*

100 g	castor sugar	4 oz
	2 eggs	
10 g	baking-powder	½ oz
100 g	margarine	4 oz
150 g	flour	6 oz
	few drops of milk	

1   Cream the margarine and sugar in a bowl until fluffy and almost white.
2   Gradually add the beaten eggs, mixing vigorously.
3   Sieve the flour and baking-powder.
4   Gradually incorporate into the mixture as lightly as possible keeping to a dropping consistency by the addition of the milk.
5   Place in a greased pudding basin.
6   Cover securely with greased greaseproof paper.
7   Steam for 1–1½ hr.
8   Turn out on to a flat silver dish and serve with a suitable sauce.

100   Vanilla Sponge Pudding

Add a few drops of vanilla essence to the Basic Mixture (Recipe 99), and serve with a vanilla-flavoured sauce (Recipe 187).

101   Chocolate Sponge Pudding

Add 25 g (1 oz) chocolate or cocoa powder in place of 25 g (1 oz) flour—that is 125 g (5 oz) flour, 25 g (1 oz) chocolate to Basic Recipe 99.
    Serve with a chocolate sauce (Recipe 191).

102 Lemon Sponge Pudding

Add the grated zest of one of two lemons, and a few drops of lemon essence to Basic Recipe 99.

Serve with a lemon sauce (Recipe 183).

103 Orange Sponge Pudding

Proceed as for Lemon Sponge Pudding, but using oranges in place of lemons.

Serve with an orange sauce (Recipe 182).

104 Cherry Sponge Pudding

Add 100 g (4 oz) chopped or quartered glacé cherries to Recipe 99.
Serve with a custard sauce (Recipe 187) or almond sauce (186).

105 Sultana Sponge Pudding

106 Currant Sponge Pudding

107 Raisin Sponge Pudding

Add 100 g (4 oz) of washed, well-dried fruit to Recipe 99.
Serve with a custard sauce (Recipe 187).

108 Soufflé Pudding   *6 portions*   *Pudding Soufflé*

185 ml	milk	1½ gills
25 g	butter	1 oz
	3 eggs	
25 g	castor sugar	1 oz
25 g	flour	1 oz

1 Boil the milk in a sauteuse.
2 Combine the flour, butter and sugar.
3 Whisk into the milk.
4 Re-boil.
5 Remove from the heat, add the yolks one at a time, whisking continuously.
6 Stiffly beat the whites.
7 Carefully fold into the mixture.
8 Three-quarters fill greased and sugared dariole moulds.
9 Place in a roasting tin, half full of water.
10 Bring to the boil and place in a hot oven (230°–250°C) 12–15 min.
11 Turn out on to a flat silver dish and serve with a suitable hot sauce, e.g. custard sauce.

108a Orange or Lemon Soufflé Pudding

Flavour the Basic Mixture (Recipe 108) with the grated zest of 1 orange or lemon and a little appropriate essence. Use the juice in the accompanying sauce.

109 Vanilla Soufflé *4 portions*   *Soufflé Vanille*

125 ml	milk	$\frac{1}{4}$ pt
10 g	flour	$\frac{1}{2}$ oz
10 g	butter	$\frac{1}{2}$ oz
50 g	castor sugar	2 oz
	4 eggs	
	vanilla	

1   Coat the inside of a soufflé case/dish with fresh butter (as thinly as possible).
2   Coat the butter in the soufflé case with castor sugar.
3   Boil the milk and vanilla in a thick-bottomed pan.
4   Mix 2 egg yolks, 10 g flour, 50 g sugar to a smooth consistency in a basin.
5   Add the boiling milk to the mixture, stir vigorously until completely mixed.
6   Return this mixture to a *clean* thick-bottomed pan and stir continuously with a wooden spoon over gentle heat until the mixture thickens, then remove from heat.
7   Allow to cool slightly.
8   Add 2 egg yolks and 15 g butter, mix thoroughly.
9   Stiffly whip the 4 egg whites and *carefully* fold into the mixture which should be just warm.
10   Place mixture into the prepared mould, level it off with a palette knife, do not allow it to come above the level of the soufflé case.
11   Place on a baking sheet and cook in a moderately hot oven 200°–230°C (400°–450°F) until the soufflé has well risen and is firm to touch—approx. 15–20 min.
12   Remove carefully from oven, dredge with icing sugar.
13   Serve on a doily on a silver flat.
14   A hot soufflé *cannot* stand and must be served immediately.

109a Chocolate Soufflé   *Soufflé Chocolat*

1   Proceed as for vanilla soufflé, dissolving 50 g (2 oz) grated couverture or powdered chocolate in the milk.
2   If the mixture is found to be too stiff an extra beaten egg white may be added.

109b Arlequin Soufflé   *Soufflé Arlequin*

1   This is half vanilla, half chocolate.
2   The mixture should be carefully placed side by side in the mould.

109c Grand Marnier Soufflé   *Soufflé Grand Marnier*

1   Proceed as for vanilla soufflé.
2   Before adding the beaten egg whites to the basic mixture in

15 ml (1 fluid oz) of Grand Marnier and *2–3 drops* of cochineal in order to give a delicate pink colour to the mixture.

109d Cold Lemon Soufflé *6 portions*   *Soufflé Milanaise*

10 g	leaf gelatine	½ oz
	3 eggs	
200 g	castor sugar	½ lb
	2 lemons	
¼ litre	cream	½ pt

1   Prepare a soufflé dish by tying a 6 cm (3 in) wide strip of oiled greaseproof paper around the outside top edge with string, so that it extends 2–3 cm (1–1½ in) above the top of the dish.
2   Soak the gelatine in cold water.
3   *Lightly* grate the zest of the lemons.
4   Squeeze the juice of the lemons into a bowl.
5   Add the lemon zest, 3 yolks, sugar and whisk over a pan of hot water until the mixture thickens and turns a very light colour.
6   Add the well-squeezed gelatine and stir until dissolved, remove from heat.
7   Lightly whisk cream until three-quarters stiff.
8   Stiffly beat the egg whites.
9   Stir the basic mixture frequently until almost on setting point.
10 Gently fold in the cream.
11 Gently fold in the egg whites.
12 Pour into the prepared dish (ref. point 1).
13 Place in refrigerator to set.
14 To serve, remove paper collar and decorate sides with green chopped almonds or pistachio nuts. The top may be similarly decorated or by using rosettes of sweetened vanilla-flavoured whipped cream.

110 Queen of Puddings *4 portions*

½ litre	milk	1 pt
50 g	castor sugar	2 oz
	vanilla essence	
50 g	castor sugar for the meringue	2 oz
25 g	butter	1 oz
75 g	cake or breadcrumbs	3 oz
50 g	jam	2 oz
	3 eggs	

1   Boil the milk.
2   Pour on to 2 yolks, 1 egg and 50 g (2 oz) sugar.
3   Place the crumbs in a buttered pie dish.
4   Strain the custard on to the crumbs.

5   Bake in a moderate oven in a bain-marie, until set, approx. 30 min.
6   Allow to cool.
7   Stiffly beat the egg whites, fold in the 50 g (2 oz) castor sugar.
8   Warm the jam and spread over the baked mixture.
9   With a star tube and piping bag pipe on the meringue.
10   Brown in a hot oven (230–°250°C).
11   Serve on a doily on a silver flat dish.

111 Apple Charlotte   *4 portions*   *Charlotte aux Pommes*

400 g	stale bread	1 lb
50–75 g	sugar	2–3 oz
35 g	breadcrumbs	1½ oz
400 g	cooking apples	1 lb
100 g	margarine or butter	4 oz

1   Use either one charlotte mould or four dariole moulds.
2   Cut the bread into 3 mm (⅛ in) slices and remove the crusts.
3   Cut a round the size of the bottom of the mould, dip into melted margarine on one side and place in the mould fat side down.
4   Cut fingers of bread 2–3 cm (1–1½ in) wide, and fit overlapping well to the sides of the mould after dipping each one in melted fat. Take care not to leave any gaps.
5   Peel, core and wash the apples, cut into thick slices and three parts cook in a little butter and sugar (a little cinnamon or a clove may be added), and add the breadcrumbs.
6   Fill the centre of the mould with the apple.
7   Cut round pieces of bread to seal the apple in.
8   Bake in a hot oven approx. 30–40 min.
9   Turn out very carefully on to a silver dish with a sauceboat of apricot sauce.

NOTE. A few breadcrumbs may be added to the apples. The round base may be cut into the required portions before being placed in the mould.

112 Apple Fritters   *6 portions*   *Beignets de Pommes*

400 g	cooking apples	1 lb
125 ml	apricot sauce (Recipe 181)	¼ pt
150 g	frying batter (6 oz flour) p. (108)	

1   Peel and core the apples and cut into ½ cm thick (¼ in) rings.
2   Pass through flour, shake off the surplus.
3   Dip into frying batter.
4   Lift out with the fingers, into fairly hot deep fat (185°C).
5   Cook approx. 5 min on each side.
6   Drain well, dust with icing sugar and glaze under the salamander.

7   Serve on a doily on a flat silver dish with a sauceboat of hot apricot sauce.

113 Banana Fritters   *4 portions*   *Beignets de Bananes*

	4 bananas	
125 ml	apricot sauce (Recipe 181)	¼ pt
150 g	frying batter (6 oz flour) (p. 108)	

Peel and cut the bananas in half lengthwise then in half across. Cook and serve as for Apple Fritters (Recipe 112).

114 Pineapple Fritters   *Beignets d'Ananas*

4 rings of pineapple

Cut the rings in half, cook and serve as for Apple Fritters (Recipe 112).

115 Pancakes with Lemon   *4 portions*   *Crêpes au Citron*

100 g	flour	4 oz
¼ litre	milk	½ pt
	pinch of salt	
50 g	lard	2 oz
	1 egg	
10 g	melted butter or margarine	½ oz
50 g	sugar	2 oz

1   Sieve the flour into a bowl, make a well in the centre.
2   Add the egg and milk gradually incorporating the flour from the sides, whisk to a smooth batter.
3   Mix in the melted butter.
4   Heat the pancake pan, clean thoroughly.
5   Add 5 g (¼ oz) lard, heat until smoking.
6   Add enough mixture to just cover the bottom of the pan thinly.
7   Cook for a few seconds until brown.
8   Turn and cook on the other side.
9   Turn on to a plate.
10 Sprinkle with sugar.
11 Fold in half then half again.

When making a batch of pancakes it is best to keep them all flat one on top of the other on a plate. Sprinkle sugar between each. Fold them all when ready for service, sprinkle again with sugar and dress neatly overlapping on a flat silver dish. Garnish with quarters of lemon free from pips. Serve very hot, two per portion.

116 Pancakes with Jam   *Crêpes à la Confiture*

50 g	warm jam	2 oz
25 g	sugar	1 oz

Mixture as for Recipe No. 115, page 329.

1   Prepare pancakes as above.
2   Spread each with warm jam.
3   Roll like a Swiss Roll, trim the ends.
4   Dredge with castor sugar.
5   Dress neatly on a silver flat dish.

117 Pancakes with Apple   *Crêpes Normande*

Method I

Cook as for Recipe 115 and spread with a purée of apple, then roll up, sprinkle with castor sugar.

Method II

Sprinkle a dice of cooked apple in the pan, add the pancake mixture and cook on both sides. Turn out, sprinkle with castor sugar and roll up.

118 Pancakes with Orange   *Crêpes à l'Orange*

Proceed as for Lemon Pancakes (page 329), using orange in place of lemon.

119 Baked Apple   *4 portions*   *Pomme Bonne Femme*

	4 medium-sized cooking apples	
50 g	sugar	2 oz
60 ml	water	$\frac{1}{8}$ pt
25 g	butter	1 oz
	4 cloves	

1   Core the apples and make an incision 2 mm ($\frac{1}{16}$ in) deep round the centre of each. Wash well.
2   Place in a roasting tin.
3   Fill the centre with sugar and add a clove.
4   Place 5 g ($\frac{1}{4}$ oz) butter on each.
5   Add the water.
6   Bake in a moderate oven (200°–230°C) 15–20 min approx.
7   Turn the apples over carefully.
8   Return to the oven until cooked, approx. 40 min in all.
9   Serve on a silver flat dish with a little of the cooking liquor and a sauceboat of custard separately.

120 Stuffed Baked Apple

Proceed as for Baked Apples, but fill the centre with washed sultanas.

121 Fresh Fruit Salad   *Salade des Fruits*
                                                        Macédoine des Fruits

All the following fruits may be used: *dessert apples, pears, pineapple, oranges, grapes, melon, strawberries, peaches, raspberries, apricots, bananas.*

Allow approx. 150 g (6 oz) unprepared fruit per portion.

	4 portions	
	1 orange	
	1 banana	
	1 dessert apple	
50 g	cherries	2 oz
	1 dessert pear	
50 g	castor sugar	2 oz
50 g	grapes	2 oz
	juice of ½ lemon	

1   Boil the sugar with ⅛ litre (¼ pt) water to make a syrup, place in a bowl.
2   Allow to cool, add the lemon juice.
3   Peel and cut the orange into segments as for cocktail.
4   Quarter the apple and pear, remove the core, peel and cut each quarter into two or three slices, place in the bowl and mix with the orange.
5   Stone the cherries, leave whole.
6   Cut the grapes in half, remove the pips.
7   Mix carefully and place in a glass bowl in the refrigerator to chill.
8   Just before serving, peel and slice the banana and arrange on top.
9   Place the bowl on a doily on a flat silver dish and serve.

122 Jelly   *8 portions*

1 litre	water	1 qt
	2 egg whites	
	zest and juice of 1 orange and lemon	
	1 cinnamon stick	
200 g	sugar	8 oz
35–50 g	gelatine	1½–2 oz
	¼ bay leaf	
	6–8 coriander seeds	
	2 cloves	

1   Place all the ingredients in a thick-bottomed pan and bring slowly to the boil, whisking well, approx. 15–20 min.
2   Turn off the heat, cover with a lid, leave for 20 min.
3   Strain carefully through a jelly bag.
4   Pour the jelly into a mould, place in the refrigerator to set.
5   When set, plunge into boiling water for one second, wipe mould with a tea cloth and turn the jelly carefully out on to a silver flat dish.

NOTE. When possible use fruit juice in place of water.

123 Fresh Fruit Jelly

1 Prepare jelly as in previous recipe.
2 Prepare ¼ kg (½ lb) fruit as for fruit salad, keep dry and place in the jelly. Allow to set and serve as for jelly.

124 Junket   *4–6 portions*

½ litre	milk	1 pt
10 g	castor sugar	½ oz
	1 tspn rennet	
	grated nutmeg	

1 Warm the milk to blood heat and pour into a glass dish.
2 Add sugar and rennet, stir gently.
3 Leave until set.
4 Sprinkle lightly with nutmeg.
5 Serve on a doily on a silver flat dish.

The addition of rennet causes the clotting or coagulation of milk.

125 Fruit Fool   *4 portions*

Method I
Apple, Gooseberry, Rhubarb, etc.

400 g	fruit	1 lb
60 ml	water	⅛ pt
100 g	sugar	4 oz

Cook to a purée and pass through a sieve.

¼ litre	milk	½ pt
25 g	sugar	1 oz
25 g	cornflour	1 oz

1 Dilute the cornflour in a little of the milk, add the sugar.
2 Boil remainder of the milk.
3 Pour on the diluted cornflour, stir well.
4 Return to the pan on low heat and stir to the boil.
5 Mix with the fruit purée. The quantity of mixture should not be less than ½ litre (1 pt).
6 Pour into four glass coupes and allow to set.
7 Decorate with a rose of whipped sweetened cream.

Method II   4 portions
Raspberries, Strawberries, etc.

400 g	fruit in purée	1 lb
100 g	castor sugar	4 oz
¼ litre	fresh whipped cream	½ pt

Mix together and serve in coupes.

Method III   4 portions

400 g	fruit	1 lb
375 ml	water	3 gills
35 g	cornflour	1½ oz
185 ml	cream	1½ gills
100 g	sugar	4 oz

1 Dilute the cornflour in a little of the water.
2 Boil the remainder of the water with the sugar and prepared fruit until soft.
3 Pass through a fine sieve.
4 Return to a clean pan and re-boil.
5 Stir in the diluted cornflour and reboil. Allow to cool.
6 Lightly whisk the cream and fold into the mixture.
7 Serve as for method I, points 6 and 7.

126 Trifle   *6–8 portions*

	1 sponge (3 eggs)	
	1 tin fruit (pears, peaches, pineapple)	
25 g	glacé cherries	1 oz
25 g	jam	1 oz
¼ litre	whipped sweetened cream	½ pt
25 g	angelica	1 oz
	Custard	
375 ml	milk	3 gills
50 g	castor sugar	2 oz
35 g	custard	1½ oz
125 ml	cream	1 gill

1 Cut the sponge in half, sideways, and spread with jam.
2 Place in a glass bowl and soak with fruit syrup.
3 A few drops of sherry may be added.
4 Cut the fruit into small pieces and add to the sponge.
5 Dilute the custard powder in a basin with some of the milk, add the sugar.
6 Boil the remainder of the milk, pour a little on the custard powder, mix well, return to the saucepan and over a low heat stir to the boil.
7 Pour on to the sponge.
8 Leave to cool.
9 Decorate with whipped cream, angelica and cherries.
10 Serve on a doily on a silver flat dish.

127 Meringue

	4 egg whites	
200 g	castor sugar	8 oz

1 Whip the egg whites stiffly.
2 Sprinkle on the sugar and carefully mix in.

3   Place in a piping bag with a plain tube and pipe on to grease-proof paper on a baking sheet.
4   Bake in the slowest oven possible or in a hot plate (90°–100°C). The aim is to cook the meringues without any colour whatsoever.

To gain maximum efficiency when whipping egg whites, the following points should be observed:

(a) Eggs should be fresh.
(b) When separating yolks from whites *no* speck of egg yolk must be allowed to remain in the white; egg yolk contains fat, the presence of which can prevent the white being correctly whipped.
(c) The bowl and whisk must be scrupulously clean, dry and free from any grease.
(d) When egg whites are half whipped the addition of a little sugar (15 g—4 whites) will assist the efficient beating and lessen the chance of overbeating.

The reason egg whites increase in volume when whipped is because they contain so much protein (11%). The protein forms tiny filaments which stretch on beating, incorporate air in minute bubbles then set to form a fairly stable puffed-up structure expanding to seven times its bulk.

128 Meringue with Whipped Cream   *Meringue Chantilly*

1   Allow two meringues per portion.
2   Join together with a little sweetened, vanilla-flavoured whipped cream.
3   Place on a doily on a silver flat dish.
4   Decorate on top with a good rose of cream.
5   Add a glacé cherry, or crystallised violet or rose and two diamonds of angelica.

129 —   *4 portions*   *Vacherin aux Fraises*

A vacherin is a round case of meringue shell piped into a suitable shape so that the centre may be filled with sufficient strawberries and whipped cream to form a rich sweet.

The vacherin may be prepared in one, two, four or larger portion sizes.

	4 egg whites	
200 g	castor sugar	8 oz
200–300 g	strawberries (picked and washed)	½–¾ lb
125 ml	cream (whipped and sweetened)	¼ pt

1   Stiffly whip the egg whites.
2   Carefully fold in the sugar.
3   Place the mixture into a piping bag with a 1 cm (½ in) plain tube.
4   Pipe on to greaseproof paper on a baking sheet.
5   Start from the centre and pipe round in a circular fashion to

form a base 12 cm (6 in) then pipe around the edge so as to
form approx. 2–3 cm (1–1½ in) high.

6   Bake in a cool oven (90°–100°C) until the meringue case is completely dry. Do not allow to colour.
7   Allow the meringue case to cool then remove from the paper.
8   Spread a thin layer of cream on the base.
9   Add the strawberries.
10 Decorate with the remainder of the cream.

A. Melba sauce (Recipe 185) may be used to coat the strawberries
before decorating with cream.
B. Refer to recipe 127, points *a–d* before whipping the egg whites.

---

130 —   *4 portions*   *Vacherin aux Framboises*

Proceed as in recipe 129 using raspberries in place of strawberries.

---

131 Baked Alaska   *4 portions*   *Omelette Soufflé Surprise*

	4 pieces sponge cake	
60 ml	fruit syrup	⅛ pt
	4 egg whites	
	4 scoops vanilla	
	ice-cream	
200 g	castor sugar	8 oz

1   Neatly arrange the pieces of sponge cake in the centre of a
round or oval flat silver dish.
2   Sprinkle the sponge cake with a little fruit syrup.
3   Place a flattened scoop full of vanilla cream on to each piece of
sponge.
4   Meanwhile stiffly whip the egg whites and fold in the sugar
(meringue).
5   Use half the meringue and completely cover the ice cream and
sponge.
6   Neaten with a palette knife.
7   Place the remainder of the meringue into a piping bag with a
large tube (plain or star) and decorate the omelette.
8   Place the omelette into a hot oven (230°–250°C) and colour a
golden brown.
9   Serve immediately.

---

132 Baked Alaska with Peaches   *Omelette Soufflé Milady*

Proceed as for Recipe 131 adding a little maraschino to the fruit
syrup and using raspberry ice-cream instead of vanilla ice-cream.
Cover the ice-cream with four halves of peaches.

---

133 Baked Alaska with Pears   *Omelette Soufflé Milord*

Proceed as for Recipe 131 adding a little Kirsch to the fruit syrup
and adding halves of poached pears to the ice-cream.

134 Poached Fruits *4 portions*   *Compôte des Fruits*

400 g	fruit	1 lb
	Stock Syrup	
100 g	sugar	4 oz
¼ litre	water	½ pt
	½ lemon	

Apples, Pears
1   Boil the water and sugar.
2   Quarter the fruit, remove the core and peel.
3   Place in a shallow pan in sugar syrup.
4   Add a few drops of lemon juice.
5   Cover with greaseproof paper.
6   Allow to simmer slowly, preferably in the oven.
7   Serve the fruit and juice in a glass bowl on a doily on a flat silver dish.

Soft Fruits—Raspberries, Strawberries
1   Pick and wash the fruit.
2   Place in a glass bowl.
3   Pour on the hot syrup.
4   Allow to cool and serve.

Stone Fruits—Plums, Damsons, Greengages, Cherries
Wash the fruit, barely cover with sugar syrup and cover with greaseproof paper or a lid. Cook gently in a moderate oven until tender.

Rhubarb
Trim off the stalk and leaf and wash. Cut into 4 cm (2 in) lengths and cook as above, adding extra sugar if necessary.

Gooseberries, Blackcurrants, Redcurrants
Top and tail gooseberries, wash and cook as for stone fruit, adding extra sugar if necessary.
    The currants should be carefully removed from the stalks, washed and cooked as for stone fruits.

Dried Fruits—Prunes, Apricots, Apples
Dried fruits should be washed and soaked in cold water overnight. Gently cook in the liquor with sufficient sugar to taste.
    A piece of cinnamon stick and a few slices of lemon may be added to the prunes.

135 Jam Omelet   *Omelette aux Confitures*
1   Allow 2–3 eggs per portion.
2   Break the eggs into a basin.

3 Beat well with a fork or whisk until the yolks and whites are thoroughly combined and no streaks of white can be seen.
4 Heat the omelet pan.
5 Wipe thoroughly clean with a dry cloth.
6 Add 10 g ($\frac{1}{2}$ oz) butter.
7 Heat until foaming but not brown.
8 Add the eggs and cook quickly, moving the mixture continuously with a fork until lightly set.
9 Remove from the heat. Add 1 tablespoon warmed jam.
10 Half fold the mixture over at right-angles to the handle.
11 Tap the bottom of the pan to bring up the edge of the omelet.
12 Tilt the pan completely over an oval silver flat dish so as to allow the omelet to fall carefully into the centre of the dish.
13 Neaten the shape if necessary.
14 Sprinkle liberally with icing sugar.
15 Brand criss-cross pattern with a red-hot poker or branding iron to caramelise the sugar.

MILK PUDDINGS

136 Cornflour Mould, Jam Sauce *4 portions*

$\frac{1}{4}$ litre	milk	1 pt
50 g	castor sugar	2 oz
	3 or 4 drops vanilla essence	
50 g	cornflour	2 oz
10 g	butter	$\frac{1}{2}$ oz

1 Dilute cornflour with a little of the milk.
2 Boil the remainder in a thick-bottomed pan.
3 Add a little boiled milk to the cornflour.
4 Return all to the saucepan, stir to the boil.
5 Simmer for a few minutes whisking all the time.
6 Mix in the butter, sugar and essence.
7 Pour into a damp mould or four dariole moulds.
8 Leave until cold, ease the mixture away from the sides with the fingers.
9 Turn out on to a flat silver dish, surround with a cold jam sauce.

137 Neapolitain Blancmange *4 portions*

$\frac{1}{4}$ litre	milk	1 pt
10 g	butter	$\frac{1}{2}$ oz
	vanilla essence–white	
	strawberry essence–pink colour	
50 g	cornflour	2 oz
50 g	castor sugar	2 oz
	almond essence–green colour	

1   Prepare cornflour mixture as above.
2   Divide into three basins.
3   Colour and flavour as indicated.
4   Pour the pink mixture into a damp mould, leave for 2–3 min.
5   Pour in the white mixture and keep the green mixture warm.
6   When the second layer is almost set pour in the green mixture.
7   Leave to cool thoroughly in the refrigerator.
8   Loosen the mixture away from the sides with the fingers.
9   Carefully shake the blancmange on to a flat silver dish. Serve with a cold jam sauce separately.

138 Rice Mould   *4 portions*

½ litre	milk	1 pt
50 g	sugar	2 oz
	1–2 egg yolks	
75 g	rice (short grain)	3 oz
	2–3 drops vanilla essence	

1   Boil the milk, add the washed rice and simmer, stirring frequently until the rice is tender and thick.
2   Mix in the sugar, essence and yolks.
3   Pour into a damp mould, or four dariole moulds, leave till cold and set.
4   Turn out as for Cornflour Mould.
5   Serve with a jam sauce or with Poached Fruit.

139 Semolina Mould   *4 portions*

½ litre	milk	1 pt
50 g	sugar	2 oz
	1–2 egg yolks	
50 g	semolina	2 oz
	2–3 drops lemon juice	

1   Boil the milk, rain in the semolina, stir to the boil.
2   Simmer for 5–10 min stirring continuously.
3   Mix in the sugar, flavouring and yolks.
4   Pour into a damp mould or four dariole moulds, leave to set and become cold.
5   Turn out as for Cornflour Mould.
6   Serve with jam sauce or Poached Fruit.

140 Baked Rice Pudding   *4 portions*   *Pouding de Riz*

½ litre	milk	1 pt
50 g	sugar	2 oz
	2–3 drops vanilla essence	
50 g	rice (short grain)	2 oz
10 g	butter	½ oz
	grated nutmeg	

1   Wash the rice, place in a pie dish.
2   Add the sugar and milk, mix well.
3   Add the butter, essence and nutmeg.
4   Place on a baking sheet, clean the rim of the pie dish.
5   Bake in a moderate oven (150°–200°C) until the milk starts simmering.
6   Reduce the heat and allow the pudding to cook slowly, allowing approx. $1\frac{1}{2}$–2 hr in all.

141 Rice Pudding

Ingredients as for Baked Rice Pudding.

1   Boil the milk in a thick-bottomed pan.
2   Add the washed rice, stir to the boil.
3   Simmer gently stirring frequently until the rice is cooked.
4   Mix in the sugar, flavouring and butter (at this stage an egg yolk may also be added).
5   Pour into a pie dish, place on a baking sheet and brown lightly under the salamander. Serve on a doily on a silver dish.

142 Semolina Pudding   *4 portions*

$\frac{1}{2}$ litre	milk	1 pt
50 g	sugar	2 oz
10 g	butter	$\frac{1}{2}$ oz
35 g	semolina	$1\frac{1}{2}$ oz
	2–3 drops lemon juice or lemon essence	

1   Boil the milk in a thick-bottomed pan.
2   Sprinkle in the semolina and stir to the boil.
3   Simmer 15–20 min.
4   Add the sugar, butter, flavouring (an egg yolk if desired).
5   Pour into a pie dish.
6   Brown under the salamander.
7   Serve on a doily on a silver flat dish.

143 Sago Pudding

144 Tapioca Pudding

145 Ground Rice Pudding

These are made in the same way as for Semolina Pudding using sago, tapioca or ground rice in place of semolina and vanilla essence instead of lemon essence.

146 — *4 portions*   *Riz à l'Impératrice*

½ litre	milk	1 pt
75 g	sugar	3 oz
125 ml	lightly whipped cream	¼ pt
25 g	angelica	1 oz
	3–4 drops vanilla essence	
50 g	rice (long grain)	2 oz
25 g	gelatine	1 oz
25 g	glacé cherries	1 oz
125 ml	red jelly	¼ pt
	2 whites of egg	

1 Prepare the jelly and pour into the bottom of a charlotte mould, leave to set.
2 Boil the milk, add the washed rice, simmer until tender.
3 Mix in the sugar, essence, gelatine (if leaf gelatine is used soak in cold water) and diced fruit.
4 Allow to cool, stirring occasionally.
5 When setting point is almost reached fold in the whipped cream and stiffly beaten whites and pour into the mould.
6 Leave to set in the refrigerator.
7 Turn out carefully on to a silver flat dish.

147 Pear Condé *4 portions*   *Poire Condé*

½ litre	milk	1 pt
50 g	sugar	2 oz
	2 dessert pears	
	2 glacé cherries	
75 g	rice (short grain)	3 oz
	3–4 drops vanilla essence	
125 ml	apricot glaze	¼ pt
10 g	angelica	½ oz

148 Pineapple Creole *4 portions*   *Ananas Créole*

½ litre	milk	1 pt
60 g	rice (short grain)	2½ oz
50 g	sugar	2 oz
	3–4 drops vanilla essence	
125 ml	apricot glaze	¼ pt
	4 rings pineapple	
	(if fresh poach in syrup)	
25 g	currants	1 oz
50 g	angelica	2 oz

1 Cook the rice in the milk, sweeten and flavour.
2 Allow to cool.
3 Dress the rice in a glass bowl or silver flat dish.
4 Mark the rice with a knife in small diamonds and add a currant in each space.
5 Drain the pineapple and arrange in half slices around the dish.
6 Coat the rice and fruit with warmed apricot glaze.
7 Decorate with the angelica cut in long thin strips.

Many other fruits may be prepared as a Condé, e.g. banana, pineapple, peach.

149 Baked Egg Custard *4 portions*

½ litre	milk	1 pt	
50 g	sugar	2 oz	
	grated nutmeg		
	3 small eggs		
	2–3 drops vanilla essence		

1 Whisk the eggs, sugar and essence in a bowl.
2 Pour on the warmed milk, whisking continuously
3 Pass through a fine strainer into a pie dish.
4 Add a little grated nutmeg. Wipe the edge of the pie dish clean.
5 Stand in a roasting tray half full of water and cook slowly in a moderate oven (120°–150°C) approx. 45 min to 1 hr.
6 Clean the edges of the pie dish, serve on a doily on a silver flat dish.

150 Bread and Butter Pudding *4 portions*

½ litre	milk	1 pt	
50 g	sugar	2 oz	
	2 slices of well-buttered bread		
	3 small eggs		
	2–3 drops vanilla essence		
25 g	sultanas	1 oz	

1 Wash the sultanas and place in a pie dish.
2 Remove the crusts from the bread and cut each slice into four triangles, neatly arrange overlapping in the pie dish.
3 Prepare an egg custard as in the previous recipe.
4 Strain on to the bread, dust lightly with castor sugar.
5 Cook and serve as in the previous recipe

151 Bread Pudding

½ kg	stale bread	1 lb	
125 g	sugar	5 oz	
125 g	currants or sultanas	5 oz	
	½ tsp mixed spice		
75g	margarine	3 oz	
	1 egg		

1 Soak the bread in cold water until soft.
2 Squeeze bread dry and place in a bowl.
3 Mix in 100 g sugar and rest of ingredients.
4 Place in a greased baking tray.
5 Sprinkle with 25 g sugar.
6 Bake in a moderate oven for approx. 1 hr.

152 Cabinet Pudding   *Pouding Cabinet*

½ litre	milk	1 pt
50 g	castor sugar	2 oz
100 g	plain sponge cake	4 oz
25 g	glacé cherries	1 oz
	3–4 eggs	
	2–3 drops vanilla essence	
25 g	currants and sultanas	1 oz

1   Cut the cake into ½ cm (¼ in) dice.
2   Mix with the chopped cherries and fruits.
3   Place in a greased, sugared charlotte mould or four dariole moulds. Do not fill more than half-way.
4   Warm the milk and whisk on to the eggs, sugar and essence.
5   Strain on to the mould.
6   Place in a roasting tin, half full of water, allow to stand for 5–10 min.
7   Cook in a moderate oven (120°–150°C) approx. 30–45 min.
8   Leave to set for a few minutes.
9   Turn out on to a warm silver flat dish.
10   Serve a fresh egg custard or hot apricot sauce separately.

153 Diplomat Pudding   *Pouding Diplomate*

As for Cabinet Pudding, but served cold.

154 Cream Caramel   *6 portions*   *Crème Caramel*

½ litre	milk	1 pt
50 g	sugar	2 oz
	4 eggs	
	3–4 drops vanilla essence	
	Caramel	
100 g	sugar	4 oz
125 ml	water	¼ pt

1   Prepare the caramel by placing three-quarters of the water in a thick-bottomed pan, adding the sugar and allowing to boil gently, without shaking or stirring the pan.
2   When the sugar has cooked to a golden brown caramel colour, add the remaining quarter of the water, re-boil until the sugar and water mix, then pour into the bottom of six dariole moulds.
3   Prepare the cream by warming the milk and whisking on to the beaten eggs, sugar and essence.
4   Strain and pour into the prepared moulds.
5   Place in a roasting tin half full of water.
6   Cook in a moderate oven (120°–150°C) approx. 30 min.
7   When thoroughly cold, loosen the edges of the cream caramels with the fingers, shake firmly to loosen and turn out on to a flat silver dish.
8   Pour any caramel remaining in the mould around the creams.

155 — *6 portions*   *Crème Beau Rivage*

25 g	butter	1 oz
50 g	praline (Recipe 209)	2 oz
½ litre	milk	1 pt
	4 eggs	
50 g	sugar	2 oz
	6 vanilla cornets (Recipe 204)	
¼ litre	cream	½ pt

1   Liberally butter a 6 portion savarin mould.
2   Evenly coat the buttered mould with the praline.
3   Warm the milk.
4   Pour the warm milk on to the beaten eggs, sugar and vanilla and mix well.
5   Pass the mixture through a fine strainer into a basin.
6   Carefully pour the mixture into the savarin mould.
7   Place the mould into a bain-marie in a moderate oven (120°–150°C) to cook and set approx. 30–40 min.
8   When cooked, remove from the oven, allow to cool, then place in the refrigerator.
9   To serve turn the mould out carefully on to a round silver flat.
10   Fill the cornets with the whipped sweetened cream and pipe the remainder into the centre of the ring.
11   Neatly arrange the cornets on top of the cream, points to the centre.
12   Place a crystallised violet or rose in the centre of the cream in cornet.

156 Bavarois (Basic Recipe)   *6–8 portions*

¼ litre	milk	½ pt
50 g	castor sugar	2 oz
125 ml	cream	¼ pt
	2 eggs	
10 g	gelatine	½ oz

1   If using leaf gelatine, soak in cold water.
2   Cream the yolks and sugar in a bowl until almost white.
3   Whisk on the milk which has been brought to the boil, mix well.
4   Clean the milk saucepan which should be a thick-bottomed one, and return the mixture to it.
5   Return to a low heat and stir continuously with a wooden spoon until the mixture coats the back of the spoon. The mixture must not boil.
6   Remove from the heat, add the gelatine, stir until dissolved.
7   Pass through a fine strainer into a clean bowl, leave in a cool place, stirring occasionally until almost setting point.
8   Then fold in the lightly beaten cream.
9   Fold in the stiffly beaten whites.

10   Pour the mixture into a mould (this may be very lightly greased with oil).

11   Allow to set in the refrigerator.

12   Shake and turn out on to a silver flat dish.

All Bavarois may be decorated with sweetened, flavoured whipped cream.

157 Vanilla Bavarois   *Bavarois Vanille*

Add a few drops of vanilla essence to the milk. Decorate with vanilla-flavoured cream.

158 Coffee Bavarois   *Bavarois au Café*

Proceed as for Bavarois with the addition of coffee essence to taste.

159 Orange Bavarois   *Bavarois à l'Orange*

Add a few drops of orange essence and 1 or 2 drops orange colour to the mixture. Decorate with blanched, fine julienne of orange zest, orange segments and whipped cream.

160 Chocolate Bavarois   *Bavarois au Chocolat*

Dissolve 50 g (2 oz) chocolate couverture in the milk. Decorate with whipped cream and chocolate vermicelli.

161 Strawberry Bavarois   *Bavarois aux Fraises*

162 Raspberry Bavarois *4 portions*   *Bavarois aux Framboises*

200 g	fruit (picked, washed and sieved) to	½ lb
60 ml	yield ½ gill of fruit purée	
	2 eggs	
10 g	gelatine	½ oz
180 ml	milk	⅜ pt
50 g	sugar	2 oz
125 ml	cream	¼ pt

Prepare as for the Basic Mixture (Recipe 156).
When the custard is almost cool add the fruit purée.
Decorate with whole fruit and whipped cream.

163 —   *Charlotte Russe*

A charlotte russe is a vanilla bavarois (Recipe 157) set in a charlotte mould which has been lined with finger biscuits (biscuits à la cuillère, Recipe 24, p. 299). The bottom of the charlotte mould should be lined with fan shaped pieces of finger biscuit. If, in place of fan shaped biscuit, 2 cm. (¼ in) of red jelly is used, the charlotte is called Charlotte Moscovite.

1   Prepare and cook the finger biscuits.
2   Remove on to a cooling grid.
3   Prepare the bavarois.
4   While the bavarois is setting line the bottom of the charlotte mould by either method described in 5 below.
5   Trim sufficient biscuits into fan shaped pieces of a length half the diameter of the base of the mould and neatly arrange in the bottom of the mould round side down, OR pour in sufficient red jelly for a thickness of 2 cm ($\frac{1}{4}$ in).
6   Neatly line the sides of the mould with trimmed finger biscuits, round sides facing outwards (if using a red jelly base, allow this to set first).
7   Pour the bavarois mixture into the lined mould at the last possible moment before setting point is reached.
8   Place the charlotte in the refrigerator to set.
9   To serve, trim off any ends of the biscuit which may project above the mould.
10   Carefully turn the charlotte out on to a serving dish (if red jelly base is used dip the bottom of the mould into boiling water for 2–3 seconds, wipe dry and turn out).
11   Decorate the charlotte with whipped sweetened cream (crème chantilly).

164 Pastry Cream   *Crème Patissier*

$\frac{1}{2}$ litre	milk	1 pt
100 g	castor sugar	4 oz
	vanilla	
	4 egg yolks	
50 g	flour	2 oz

1   Whisk the egg yolks and sugar in a bowl until almost white.
2   Mix in the flour.
3   Boil the milk in a thick-bottomed pan.
4   Whisk on to the yolks, sugar and flour and mix well.
5   Return to the cleaned pan, stir to the boil.
6   Add a few drops of vanilla.
7   Remove from the heat and pour into a basin.
8   Sprinkle the top with a little castor sugar to prevent a skin forming.

ICE-CREAM

165 Vanilla Ice-cream   *8 portions*   *Glace Vanille*

375 ml	milk	$\frac{3}{4}$ pt
100 g	castor sugar	4 oz
	vanilla	
	4 egg yolks	
125 ml	cream	$\frac{1}{4}$ pt

1   Whisk the yolks, sugar and essence in a bowl until almost white.
2   Boil the milk in a thick-bottomed pan.
3   Whisk on to the eggs, add sugar, mix well.
4   Return to the cleaned saucepan, place on a low heat.
5   Stir continuously with a wooden spoon until the mixture coats the back of the spoon.
6   Pass through a fine strainer into a bowl.
7   Freeze in an ice-cream machine, gradually adding the cream.

166 Coffee Ice-cream   Glace au Café

Add coffee essence to taste to the custard after it is cooked.

167 Chocolate Ice-cream   Glace au Chocolat

Add 50–100 g (2–4 oz) of chopped couverture to the milk before boiling.

168 Strawberry Ice-cream   Glace aux Fraises

Add ⅛ litre (¼ pt) of strawberry pulp in place of ⅛ litre (¼ pt) of milk. The pulp is added after the custard is cooked.

169 Meringue and Ice-cream   Meringue Glacée Chantilly

1   Allow 2 meringues per portion.
2   Join together with a small ball of vanilla ice-cream.
3   Serve in a coupe or ice-cream dish.
4   Decorate with whipped cream.

170 Mixed Ice-cream   Glace Panachée

Balls or spoonfuls of two or more flavoured ice-creams arranged in a timbale, the lower part of the timbale being filled with crushed ice or in individual coupes.

Rocher de Glace

The ice-cream is scooped out with a dessert or serving spoon which has been dipped into hot water. The spooned-out ice-cream is placed in a timbale containing crushed ice.

The ice-cream may be prepared in this way when served with other sweets. It may be shown on the menu with the name of the ice-cream, e.g. Rocher de Glace Vanille.

WATER ICES

171 Lemon Ice   *8 portions*   Glace Citron

½ litre	water	1 pt
	2 lemons	
200 g	sugar	8 oz
	1 egg white	

1   Bring the sugar, water and peeled zest of lemons to the boil.
2   Remove from the heat and cool.
3   Add the juice of the lemons.
4   Add the whites and mix well.
5   Pass through a fine strainer and freeze.

172 Orange Ice   *Glace Orange*

½ litre	water	1 pt
	2 large oranges	
	1 egg white	
	1 lemon	
200 g	sugar	8 oz

Prepare and freeze as for Lemon Ice.

173 Strawberry Ice   *Glace Fraises*

174 Raspberry Ice   *Glace Framboises*

375 ml	water	¾ pt
	1 lemon	
125 ml	fruit purée	¼ pt
200 g	sugar	8 oz

Prepare and freeze as for Lemon Ice.

175 Tutti Frutti Ice   *Glace Tutti Frutti*

Lemon and Strawberry Ice with candied fruits.

176 Fruit Melba (Peach, Pear, Banana, etc.)
Peach Melba 4 portions   *Pêche Melba*

	2 peaches	
125 ml	vanilla ice-cream	¼ pt
125 ml	melba sauce	¼ pt

If using fresh peaches they should be dipped in boiling water for a
few seconds, cooled by placing into cold water, peeled and halved.

Dress the fruit on a ball of ice-cream in an ice-cream coupe and
coat with melba sauce. May be decorated with whipped cream.

Fresh pears should be peeled, halved and poached.

Bananas should be peeled at the last moment.

177 —   *Poire Belle Hélène*

Serve a cooked pear on a ball of vanilla ice-cream in a coupe.
Decorate with whipped cream. Serve with a sauceboat of hot
chocolate sauce (Recipe 191).

178 Peach Cardinal   *Pêche Cardinal*

Place half a prepared peach on a ball of strawberry ice-cream in a coupe. Coat with melba sauce, may be decorated with whipped cream and sprinkled with almonds cut in slices.

179 Coupe Jacques

Place in a coupe some fruit salad, on top arrange one scoop of lemon ice-cream and one of strawberry ice-cream. May be decorated with whipped cream.

SWEET SAUCES $\frac{1}{4}$ *litre* ($\frac{1}{2}$ *pt*) = *4–8 portions*

180 Jam Sauce

200 g	jam	8 oz
10 g	cornflour	$\frac{1}{2}$ oz
100 ml	water	4 oz

1 Boil jam and water together.
2 Adjust the consistency with a little cornflour or arrowroot diluted with water.
3 Re-boil until clear and pass through a conical strainer.

181 Apricot Sauce   *Sauce Abricot*

200 g	apricot jam	8 oz
10 g	cornflour	$\frac{1}{2}$ oz
100 ml	water	4 oz

Proceed as for Jam Sauce above.

182 Orange Sauce

250 ml	water	$\frac{1}{2}$ pt
	1 orange	
50 g	sugar	2 oz
10 g	cornflour or arrowroot	$\frac{1}{2}$ oz

1 Boil the sugar and water.
2 Add the cornflour diluted with water, stirring continuously.
3 Re-boil till clear, strain.
4 Add blanched julienne of orange zest and the juice of orange.

183 Lemon Sauce

Proceed as for Orange Sauce using a lemon in place of the orange.

184 Syrup Sauce

200 ml	syrup	8 oz
	juice of 1 lemon	
125 ml	water	$\frac{1}{4}$ pt
10 g	cornflour or arrowroot	$\frac{1}{2}$ oz

Bring the syrup, water and lemon juice to the boil and thicken with diluted cornflower. Boil for a few minutes.

185 Melba Sauce

Method I

| 400 g | raspberry jam | 1 lb |
| 125 ml | water | ¼ pt |

Boil together and pass through a conical strainer.

Method II

400 g	raspberries	1 lb
125 ml	water	¼ pt
100 g	sugar	4 oz

Boil together and pass through a strainer.

Method III

| 400 g | raspberries | 1 lb |
| 200 g | icing sugar | 8 oz |

Pass through a fine sieve and add a little lemon juice.

186 Almond Sauce

250 ml	milk	½ pt
25 g	castor sugar	1 oz
10 g	cornflour	½ oz
	few drops almond essence	

1   Dilute the cornflour with a little of the milk.
2   Boil remainder of the milk.
3   Whisk on to the cornflour.
4   Return to the pan, stir to the boil.
5   Simmer 3–4 min.
6   Mix in the sugar and essence.
7   Pass through a strainer.

187 Custard Sauce

250 ml	milk	½ pt
25 g	castor sugar	1 oz
10 g	custard powder	½ oz

1   Dilute the custard powder with a little of the milk.
2   Boil the remainder of the milk.
3   Pour a little of the boiled milk on to the diluted custard powder.
4   Return to the saucepan.
5   Stir to the boil and mix in the sugar.

188 Fresh Egg Custard Sauce

250 ml	milk	½ pt
25 g	castor sugar	1 oz
	2 egg yolks	
	2–3 drops vanilla essence	

1   Mix yolks, sugar and essence in a basin.
2   Whisk on the boiled milk.
3   Return to a thick-bottomed pan.
4   Place on a low heat and stir with a wooden spoon till it coats
     the back of the spoon. Do *not* boil.
5   Pass through a fine strainer.

189 Sabayon Sauce   *8 portions*   *Sabayon Sauce*

	4 egg yolks	
100 g	castor sugar	4 oz
¼ litre	dry white wine	½ pt

1   Whisk egg-yolks and sugar in a 1 litre (2 pt) pan or basin un til
     almost white.
2   Dilute with the wine.
3   Place pan or basin in a bain-marie of warm water.
4   Whisk mixture continuously until it increases to 4 times its
     bulk and is firm and frothy.

Sauce Sabayon may be offered as an accompaniment to any
suitable hot sweet, e.g. pudding soufflé.

NOTE: a Sauce Sabayon may also be made using milk as the liquid
which can be flavoured according to taste, e.g. vanilla, nutmeg,
cinnamon.

190 Sabayon au Marsala   *4 portions*   *Zabaglione alla Marsala*

This recipe is of Italian origin and in Italy it is sold as commonly as
a milk shake would be in England.

	8 egg yolks	
200 g	castor sugar	8 oz
150 ml	marsala	⅛ pt

1   Whisk egg yolks and sugar in a bowl until almost white.
2   Mix in the marsala.
3   Place the bowl and contents in a bain-marie of warm water.
4   Whisk mixture continuously until it increases to 4 times its
     bulk and is firm and frothy.
5   Pour the mixture into glass goblets.
6   Place on a doily on a silver flat and serve.
7   Accompany with a suitable biscuit, e.g. sponge finger, palmier
     or shortbread.

191 Chocolate Sauce   *Sauce Chocolat*

250 ml	milk	½ pt
65 g	sugar	1½ oz
5 g	butter	¼ oz
25 g	chocolate (block) or	1 oz
10 g	cocoa powder	½ oz
10 g	cornflour	½ oz

With Cocoa
1 Dilute the cornflour with a little of the milk, mix in the cocoa.
2 Boil the remainder of the milk.
3 Pour a little of the milk on to the cornflour.
4 Return to the saucepan.
5 Stir to the boil.
6 Mix in the sugar and butter.

With Chocolate
Shred the chocolate, add to the milk and proceed as above, omitting the cocoa.

192 Rum or Brandy Cream

Whipped, sweetened, cream flavoured with rum or brandy.

193 Rum or Brandy Butter

Cream equal quantities of butter and sieved icing sugar together and add rum or brandy to taste.

194 Butter Cream

| 200 g | butter | 8 oz |
| 150 g | icing sugar | 6 oz |

1 Sieve the icing sugar.
2 Cream the butter and icing sugar until light and creamy.
3 Flavour and colour as required.

195 Christmas Pudding   *6–8 portions*

100 g	chopped suet	4 oz
50 g	flour	2 oz
100 g	stoned raisins	4 oz
100 g	sultanas	4 oz
50 g	mixed peel	2 oz
50 g	currants	2 oz
5 g	nutmeg	$\frac{1}{4}$ oz
5 g	mixed spice	$\frac{1}{4}$ oz
100 g	barbados sugar	4 oz
60 ml	milk	$\frac{1}{2}$ gill
100 g	breadcrumbs	4 oz
25 g	ground almonds	1 oz
	pinch salt	
	wineglass of stout	
	$\frac{1}{2}$ wineglass brandy	
	2 eggs	
	$\frac{1}{2}$ lemon grated zest and juice	
	$\frac{1}{2}$ orange grated zest and juice	

Mix all the dry ingredients together, add the liquid and mix well.

Leave in a cool place for 3–4 days. Place into greased basins, cover with greased greaseproof paper and steam for 6–8 hr.

Serve with rum or brandy cream or butter or custard sauce.

196 Mincemeat

100 g	suet (chopped)	4 oz
100 g	mixed peel (chopped)	4 oz
100 g	currants	4 oz
100 g	sultanas	4 oz
100 g	raisins	4 oz
100 g	apples (chopped)	4 oz
100 g	barbados sugar	4 oz
5 g	mixed spice	$\frac{1}{4}$ oz
	1 lemon grated zest and juice	
	1 orange grated zest and juice	
	$\frac{1}{2}$ wineglass rum	
	$\frac{1}{2}$ wineglass brandy	

Mix the ingredients together, place in jars and use as required.

197 Christmas Cake

400 g	butter or margarine	1 lb
	10 eggs	
400 g	currants	1 lb
200 g	raisins	8 oz
100 g	glacé cherries	4 oz
	mixed spice	
100 g	ground almonds	4 oz
400 g	demerara sugar	1 lb
400 g	sultanas	1 lb
200 g	peel	8 oz
100 g	chopped almonds	4 oz
600 g	flour	1 lb 8 oz
185 ml	milk	1$\frac{1}{2}$ gills
	glass of brandy or rum	

Cream the butter and sugar well, mix in the eggs to a smooth cream after adding each egg. Fold in the flour and almonds and add the spice, fruit, rum and correct the consistency with milk.

Line a 20–24 cm (10–12 in) cake tin with paper, place in the mixture, cook in a moderate oven (150°–200°C) approx. 3$\frac{1}{2}$ hr. Remove from the tin and cool.

Brush with boiling apricot glaze, line the side with almond icing and the top.

Cover with Royal Icing and set for 24 hr, give another coat and decorate.

198 Marzipan or Almond Paste

Raw

400 g	ground almonds	1 lb
	3–4 yolks	
600 g	icing sugar	1 lb 8 oz
	vanilla	

Sift the almonds and sugar, make a well and add the egg yolks and flavouring. Knead well.

Cooked

400 g	ground almonds	1 lb
	3 yolks	
250 ml	water	$\frac{1}{2}$ pt
1 kg	castor sugar	2 lb
	almond essence	

Place the water and sugar in a pan and boil. Skim. When the sugar reaches 240°F draw aside and mix in the almonds, then add the yolks and essence and mix in quickly to avoid scrambling. Knead well.

199 Royal Icing

400 g	icing sugar	1 lb
	juice of lemon	
	3 whites of egg	

Mix well together in a basin the sieved icing sugar and the whites of egg, with a wooden spoon. Add a few drops of lemon juice and beat till stiff.

200 Salted Almonds

400 g	almonds	1 lb
50 g	salt	2 oz
	1 egg white	

1   Place the almonds in boiling water for 2–3 min.
2   Strain, cool slightly and remove the skins.
3   Lightly beat the white for 5–6 sec in a bowl. Add the almonds and salt and mix well.
4   Place on a baking sheet and brown carefully in a hot oven, turning the almonds to obtain an even colour.

Salted almonds should always be available on every cocktail bar and at cocktail parties.

201 Petits Fours

These are an assortment of small biscuits, cakes and sweets served with coffee after special meal. There is a wide variety of items that can be prepared and when serving petits fours as large as assortment as possible should be offered.

Basically petits fours fall into two categories—dry and glazed. Dry including all manner of biscuits, macaroons, meringue and marzipan items.

Glazed including fruits dipped in sugar, fondants, chocolates, sweets, and small pieces of neatly cut genoese sponge covered in fondant.

202   Dry Petits Fours

203   Cats Tongues *Langues de chat*

100 g	butter	4 oz
100 g	soft flour	4 oz
150 g	icing sugar	6 oz
	4 egg whites	
	vanilla	

1   Lightly cream sugar and butter, add 3–4 drops of vanilla.
2   Add egg whites one by one continually mixing being careful not to allow the mixture to curdle.
3   Gently fold in the sifted flour and mix lightly.
4   Pipe on to a lightly greased baking sheet using a 3 mm ($\frac{1}{8}$ in) plain tube, 4 cm (2 in) in length.
5   Bake in hot oven at 230°–250°C (450°–475°F) for a few minutes.
6   The outside edges should be light brown and the centres yellow.
7   When cooked, remove on to a cooling rack using a palette knife.

204   Cornets *Cornets*

100 g	butter	4 oz
100 g	soft flour	4 oz
150 g	icing sugar	6 oz
	4 egg whites	
	vanilla	

1   Lightly cream sugar and butter, add 3–4 drops of vanilla.
2   Add egg whites one by one mixing continuously, taking care not to allow the mixture to curdle.
3   Gently fold in the sifted flour and mix lightly.
4   Using a 3 mm ($\frac{1}{8}$ in) plain tube, pipe out the mixture onto a lightly greased baking sheet into rounds approx. 2$\frac{1}{2}$ cm (1$\frac{1}{4}$ in) in diameter.
5   Bake in hot oven 230°–250°C (450°–475°F) until the edges turn brown and the centre remains uncoloured.
6   Remove the tray from the oven.
7   Work quickly while the cornets are hot and twist them into a cornet shape using the point of a cream horn mould. (For a tight cornet shape it will be found best to set the pieces tightly inside the cream horn moulds and to leave them until set.)

205   Piped Biscuits *Sablés à la poche*

200 g	soft flour	$\frac{1}{2}$ lb
150 g	butter	6 oz
100 g	castor sugar	4 oz
	1 egg	
	2 egg yolks	
	vanilla	

1   Cream sugar and butter until light in colour and texture.
2   Add egg and yolks gradually beating continuously, add 3–4 drops vanilla.
3   Gently fold in sifted flour, mix lightly.
4   Pipe on to a lightly greased and floured baking sheet using a medium-sized star tube (a variety of shapes can be used).
5   Some can be left plain, some decorated with half almonds or neatly cut pieces of angelica and glacé cherries.
6   Bake in a moderate oven at 180°–200°C (375°–400°F) for approximately 10 min.
7   When cooked, remove on to a cooling rack using a palette knife.

206 Almond Biscuits

100 g	ground almonds	¼ lb
50 g	castor sugar	2 oz
	1½ egg whites	
	almond essence	
	1 sheet rice paper	
	glacé cherries and angelica	

1   Whisk the egg whites until stiff.
2   Gently stir in the ground almonds, sugar and 3–4 drops almond essence.
3   Place rice paper on a baking sheet.
4   Pipe mixture using a medium star tube into shapes.
5   Decorate with neatly cut diamonds of angelica and glacé cherries.
6   Bake in a moderate oven at 175°–200°C (375°–400°F) for 10–15 min.
7   Trim with small knife to cut through rice paper and place on to a cooling rack using a palette knife.

207 Shortbread Biscuits

100 g	soft flour	4 oz
100 g	rice flour	4 oz
100 g	castor sugar	4 oz
100 g	butter	4 oz
	1 egg (beaten)	

1   Sieve the flour and rice flour into a basin.
2   Rub in the butter until the texture of fine breadcrumbs.
3   Mix in the sugar.
4   Bind the mixture to a stiff paste using the beaten egg.
5   Roll out 3 mm (⅛ in) using castor sugar, prick well with a fork and cut in fancy shapes.
6   Place biscuits on a lightly greased baking sheet.
7   Bake in moderate oven at 175°–200°C (375°–400°F) until golden brown (approx. 15 min).
8   Remove with a palette knife on to a cooling rack.

208 Glazed Fruits

1   Dates stoned, stuffed with marzipan (left yellow or lightly coloured pink or green) and rolled in castor sugar.

2   Grapes (in pairs left on the stalk) ⎱ passed through a syrup
     Tangerines in segments   ⎰ prepared as follows:

400 g	sugar	1 lb
50 g	water	2 oz
50 g	glucose	2 oz
	juice of 1 lemon	

1   Boil sugar, glucose and water to 160°–165°C (310°–315°F).
2   Add lemon juice, shake in thoroughly, remove from heat.
3   Pass fruits through this syrup using a fork and place them on to a lightly oiled marble slab to cool and set.

Marzipan (page 352) can be coloured and moulded into a variety of shapes. They can then be either rolled in castor sugar or glazed by dipping in a syrup as in previous recipe.

209 Praline

Praline is a basic preparation used for flavouring items such as gateaux, soufflés, ice-creams and many other sweets.

60 ml	water	⅛ pt
200 g	sugar	½ lb
100 g	almonds ⎱ peeled	¼ lb
100 g	hazelnuts ⎰	¼ lb

1   Lightly brown the almonds and hazelnuts in an oven.
2   Cook the water and sugar in copper or thick bottomed pan until the caramel stage is reached.
3   Remove the pan from the heat.
4   Mix in the nuts.
5   Turn out the mixture on to a lightly oiled marble slab.
6   Allow to become quite cold.
7   Crush to a coarse texture using a rolling pin.
8   Store in an airtight container.

THE COOKING OF SUGAR

Sugar is boiled for a number of purposes—in pastry work, bakery and sweet-making. Loaf (lump) sugar is generally used, placed in a copper saucepan or sugar boiler and moistened with sufficient cold water to melt the sugar (approx. ⅛ litre per ¼ kg) and allowed to boil steadily without being stirred. Any scum on the surface should be carefully removed, otherwise the sugar is liable to granulate. Once the water has evaporated the sugar begins to cook and it will be noticed that the bubbling in the pan will be slower. It is now necessary to keep the sides of the pan free from crystallised sugar; this can be done either with the fingers or a piece of damp linen. In either case the fingers or linen should be dipped in ice water or cold water, rubbed round the inside of the pan and then quickly dipped back into the water.

The cooking of the sugar then passes through several stages which may be tested with a special sugar thermometer or by the fingers (dip the fingers into ice water, then into the sugar and quickly back into the ice water).

DEGREES OF COOKING SUGAR

Small thread (104°C). When a drop of sugar held between the thumb and forefinger forms small threads when the finger and thumb are drawn apart. Used for stock syrup.

Large thread (110°C). When proceeding as for small thread the threads are more numerous and stronger. Used for crystallising fruits.

Soft ball (116°C). Proceeding as above, the sugar rolls into a soft ball. Used for making fondant.

Hard ball (121°C). As for soft ball, but the sugar rolls into a firmer ball. Used for making sweets.

Small crack (140°C). The sugar lying on the finger peels off in the form of a thin pliable film which sticks to the teeth when chewed. Used for meringue.

Large crack (153°C). The sugar taken from the end of the fingers when chewed breaks clean in between the teeth, like glass. Used for dipping fruits.

Caramel (176°C). Cooking is continued until the sugar is a golden brown colour. Used for crème caramel.

Black-jack. Cooking is continued until the sugar is deeply coloured and almost black. Water is then added and the black sugar is allowed to dissolve over a gentle heat. Used for colouring.

To prevent the granulating of sugar a tablespoon of glucose or a few drops of lemon juice per lb may be added before boiling.

19
Savouries

SERVICE OF SAVOURIES

All savouries should be served on a dish paper on a flat dish with sprigs of parsley. The crusts should always be removed from the bread after toasting.

Savouries must always be served very hot.

1   Anchovies on Toast

50 g	anchovies	2 oz
10 g	butter	½ oz
	2 slices toast	
	cayenne pepper	

Neatly arrange the anchovy fillets on half slices of buttered toast from which the crusts have been removed, reheat slowly under the salamander, sprinkle with a little cayenne pepper.

2   Angels on Horseback   *Anges à Cheval*

	8 live oysters (removed from the shell)	
	2 slices toast	
	cayenne pepper	
	4 rashers of streaky bacon	
10 g	butter	½ oz

1   Wrap each raw oyster in half a rasher of thin streaky bacon.
2   Place on a skewer then on a baking tray.
3   Grill gently on both sides for a few minutes.
4   Sprinkle with cayenne.
5   Cut the trimmed, buttered toast into four neat rectangles.
6   Place two oysters on each and serve.

3   Toast Baron   *Croûte Baron*

50 g	grilling mushrooms	2 oz
50 g	beef marrow	2 oz
10 g	butter	½ oz
	4 rashers streaky bacon	
	2 slices toast	

1   Peel and wash the mushrooms.
2   Brush with a little fat.
3   Season with salt.
4   Place on a baking tray.
5   Grill on both sides for a few minutes.
6   Grill the bacon on both sides.
7   Cut the marrow into ½ cm (¼ in) thick slices.
8   Simmer gently in a little stock or water for a few minutes.
9   Remove and drain.
10   Cut and trim the buttered toast into four neat rectangles.
11   Arrange on top the mushrooms (cut if necessary), bacon and marrow.
12   Sprinkle with cayenne and serve.

4   Devils on Horseback   *Diables à Cheval*

	8 well-soaked or cooked prunes	
50 g	chopped chutney	2 oz
10 g	butter	½ oz
	4 rashers streaky bacon	
	2 slices toast	
	cayenne	

1 Stone the prunes carefully.
2 Stuff with chutney
3 Wrap each one in half a thin rasher of bacon.
4 Place on a skewer and on a baking sheet.
5 Grill on both sides under a salamander.
6 On each rectangle of buttered toast place two prunes.
7 Sprinkle with cayenne and serve.

5 Devilled Kidneys on Toast

Method I

	4 sheep's kidneys	
10 g	butter	$\frac{1}{2}$ oz
	1 tspn Worcester sauce	
	salt	
	2 slices toast	
	1 tbspn English mustard	
	1 tbspn vinegar	
	mill pepper	

1 Remove skin and gristle from kidney.
2 Cut seven-eights of the way across.
3 Secure in an open grilling position on skewers.
4 Season with salt and mill pepper on both sides.
5 Brush with fat and grill for approx. 5 min on each side.
6 Meanwhile make a liquid paste with the mustard, Worcester
   sauce and vinegar.
7 Brush it liberally on both sides of the kidney.
8 Complete the cooking (approx. a further 2 min on each side).
9 Serve on trimmed, buttered rectangles of toast.

Method II

	4 sheep's kidneys	
	2 slices toast	
	salt	
125 ml	sauce diable (p. 24)	$\frac{1}{4}$ pt
50 g	butter	2 oz

1 Prepare kidneys as for sauté.
2 Season and quickly fry in 35 g (1½ oz) butter in a frying-pan.
3 Drain in a colander.
4 Add to the boiling sauce diable.
5 Mix in and serve on buttered rectangles of toast.

6 Mushrooms on Toast

150 g	grilling mushrooms	6 oz
10 g	butter	$\frac{1}{2}$ oz
	2 slices toast	

1 Peel and wash the mushrooms.
2 Place on a baking tray.

3   Season with salt, brush with melted fat.
4   Gently grill on both sides for a few minutes.
5   Cut and trim the buttered toast into rectangles.
6   Neatly arrange the mushrooms on the toast.
7   Sprinkle with cayenne and serve.

7 Curried Shrimps or Prawns on Toast

150 g	pickled shrimps or prawns (peeled)	6 oz
	2 slices toast	
125 ml	curry sauce (p. 27)	$\frac{1}{4}$ pt
10 g	butter	$\frac{1}{2}$ oz

1   Boil the curry sauce.
2   Add the shrimps or prawns.
3   Simmer 2–3 min.
4   Dress on rectangles or round-cut pieces of buttered toast and serve.

8 Curried Shrimp Bouchées   *Bouchée Indienne*

	4 bouchées (1$\frac{1}{2}$ in diameter puff pastry cases)	
150 g	pickled shrimps (peeled)	6 oz
25 g	chopped chutney	1 oz
125 ml	curry sauce (p. 27)	$\frac{1}{4}$ pt

1   Place the shrimps in boiling curry sauce.
2   Simmer 2–3 min.
3   Meanwhile warm the bouchées through in a moderate oven.
4   Fill the bouchées.
5   Place a little chutney on each.
6   Replace the lids and serve.

9 Fried Ham and Cheese Savoury   *Croque Monsieur*

	4 slices cooked ham	
	8 slices thin toast	
	8 slices Gruyère cheese	
50 g	clarified butter	2 oz

1   Place each slice of ham between two slices of cheese, then between two slices of lightly toasted bread.
2   Cut out with a round cutter.
3   Gently fry on both sides in clarified butter and serve.

10 Toast Derby   *Croûte Derby*

100 g	chopped cooked ham	4 oz
	2 pickled walnuts	
10 g	butter	$\frac{1}{2}$ oz
125 ml	béchamel	$\frac{1}{4}$ pt
	2 slices toast	
	cayenne pepper	

Add the ham to the boiling sauce, simmer for 2–3 min, season with a little cayenne, spread on the four rectangles or round-cut pieces of buttered toast. Place half a pickled walnut on each.

11   Chopped Ham on Toast   *Canapé Yorkaise*

100 g	cooked ham	4 oz
	2 slices toast	
	cayenne	
250 ml	béchamel	½ pt
10 g	butter	½ oz

1   Cut eight neat, thin diamonds of ham for decoration.
2   Cut the remainder into small neat dice.
3   Bind with boiling béchamel.
4   Simmer 2–3 min.
5   Season with cayenne.
6   Dress on rectangles or round-cut buttered toast.
7   Place two diamonds of ham on each and serve.

12   Curried Ham on Toast   *Croûte Radjah*

100 g	chopped cooked ham	4 oz
25 g	chopped chutney	1 oz
10 g	butter	½ oz
125 ml	curry sauce (p. 27)	¼ pt
	2 slices toast	

Simmer the ham in the curry sauce for 2–3 min. Dress on buttered rectangles or rounds of toast. Add a little chutney on each and serve.

13   Kippers on Toast   *Canapé Yarmouth*

	2 small kippers	
10 g	butter	½ oz
	2 slices toast	
	cayenne	

1   Remove all skin and bone from the kippers.
2   Trim into four neat even pieces.
3   Place on a baking tray.
4   Grill gently on both sides for a few minutes.
5   Dress on trimmed rectangles of buttered toast.
6   Sprinkle with cayenne and serve.

The kippers may also be cooked whole, the skin and bone removed, the flesh flaked, then piled on the toast.

14   Soft Roes on Toast

	6 soft roes	
10 g	butter	½ oz
	2 slices toast	
	cayenne	

1   Pass the roes through seasoned flour.
2   Shake off all surplus flour.
3   Then either shallow fry on both sides in hot fat or grill.
4   Dress on rectangles of buttered toast and serve.

15   Devilled Soft Roes   *Laitances Méphisto*

150 g	soft roes (herring)	6 oz
	4 short pastry barquettes	
125 ml	sauce diable (p. 24)	$\frac{1}{4}$ pt

The barquettes are warmed through in the oven and filled with the
soft roes cooked as in the previous recipe and mixed with sauce diable
then served.

16   Mushroom and Soft Roes on Toast   *Canapé Quo Vadis*

75 g	grilling mushrooms	3 oz
75 g	soft roes	3 oz
10 g	butter	$\frac{1}{2}$ oz

Cook the mushrooms (Recipe 6) and soft roes (Recipe 14) as
indicated and dress neatly on rectangles of buttered toast, sprinkle
with cayenne and serve.

17   Chicken Liver and Bacon on Toast   *Canapé Diane*

	4 trimmed chicken livers	
	2 slices toast	
	cayenne	
	4 rashers streaky bacon	
10 g	butter	$\frac{1}{2}$ oz

1   Roll each half liver in half a rasher of thin bacon.
2   Place on a skewer, then on a baking tray.
3   Grill gently on both sides for a few minutes.
4   Sprinkle with cayenne.
5   Cut the trimmed, buttered toast into four rectangles.
6   Place two livers on each and serve.

18   Scotch Woodcock

	2–3 eggs	
5 g	anchovy fillets	$\frac{1}{4}$ oz
	2 slices toast	
35 g	butter	$1\frac{1}{2}$ oz
5 g	capers	$\frac{1}{4}$ oz
	salt	
	pepper	

1   Break the eggs into a basin.
2   Season with salt and pepper.
3   Thoroughly mix with a fork or whisk.
4   Place 25 g (1 oz) of butter in a small thick-bottomed pan.

5   Allow to melt over a low heat.
6   Add the eggs and cook slowly, stirring continuously until lightly scrambled.
7   Spread on four rectangles or round-cut pieces of buttered toast.
8   Decorate with two thin fillets of anchovy and four capers on each and serve.

19   Mushroom, Bacon and Olive on Toast   *Canapé Fédora*

	2 rashers streaky bacon	
	4 stoned olives	
10 g	butter	½ oz
75 g	grilling mushrooms	3 oz
	2 slices of toast	

1   Grill the bacon and mushrooms.
2   Dress neatly on four rectangles of buttered toast.
3   Place an olive on each.
4   Sprinkle with cayenne and serve.

20   Mushroom and Bacon on Toast

Proceed as for Canapé Fédora, but without the olive.

21   Haddock on Toast

200 g	trimmed smoked haddock fillet	8 oz
10 g	butter	½ oz
	2 slices toast	
	cayenne	

1   Cut and trim the fish into four neat rectangles.
2   Place on a baking tray with a little butter on top.
3   Grill gently on both sides for a few minutes.
4   Place on the trimmed rectangles of buttered toast.
5   Sprinkle with cayenne and serve.

22   Haddock and Bacon on Toast

150 g	skinned smoked haddock fillet	6 oz
	2 slices toast	
	cayenne	
	4 rashers streaky bacon	
10 g	butter	½ oz

1   Cut and trim the fish into four neat rectangles.
2   Fold each one in a thin rasher of bacon.
3   Place on a baking tray.
4   Grill gently on both sides for a few minutes.
5   Place on a buttered rectangle of toast.
6   Sprinkle with cayenne and serve.

23   Smoked Haddock on Toast

Canapé Hollandaise

200 g	smoked haddock fillet	8 oz
250 ml	milk and water, approx	$\frac{1}{2}$ pt
10 g	butter	$\frac{1}{2}$ oz
	1 hard-boiled egg	
	2 slices toast	
	cayenne	

1   Poach the fish in the milk and water.
2   Flake into small pieces.
3   Remove any skin.
4   Pile on to rectangles or round-cuts of buttered toast.
5   Place two slices of egg on each.
6   Sprinkle with cayenne and serve.

24   Creamed Haddock and Pickled Walnut on Toast

Canapé Ivanhoë

200 g	smoked fillet haddock	8 oz
125 ml	béchamel	$\frac{1}{4}$ pt
	2 slices toast	
	cayenne	
250 ml	milk and water approx.	$\frac{1}{2}$ pt
	4 cooked mushrooms or	
	4 slices pickled walnut	
10 g	butter	$\frac{1}{2}$ oz

1   Poach the fish in the milk and water.
2   Remove all the skin.
3   Mix in the boiling béchamel.
4   Season with cayenne.
5   Spread on rectangles or round-cuts of buttered toast.
6   Place a mushroom or a slice of pickled walnut on each and serve.

25   Creamed Haddock on Toast

Proceed as for Canapé Ivanhoë, but without the mushroom or walnut.

26   Creamed Haddock and Cheese on Toast

Canapé Ritchie

Proceed as for Canapé Ivanhoë, omitting the mushroom or walnut. Instead, sprinkle with grated cheese and lightly brown under the salamander.

27   Marrow on Toast

Moelle sur Croûte

150 g	beef marrow	6 oz
10 g	butter	$\frac{1}{2}$ oz
	2 slices toast	
	cayenne	

1   Cut the marrow in ½ cm (¼ in) thick slices.
2   Simmer gently in water or stock for a few minutes.
3   Drain and place on rectangles of buttered toast.
4   Sprinkle with cayenne and serve.

28   Mushroom, Tomato and Pickled Walnut on Toast   *Canapé Nina*

10 g	butter	½ oz
75 g	grilling mushrooms	3 oz
	2 pickled walnuts	
	2 tomatoes	
	2 slices toast	
	cayenne	

1   Grill the mushrooms.
2   Peel the tomatoes and cut into thick slices.
3   Season and grill gently.
4   Cut the walnuts into thick slices.
5   Dress neatly on rectangles of buttered toast.
6   Sprinkle with cayenne and serve.

29   Sardines on Toast

10 g	butter	½ oz
	8 sardines	
	2 slices toast	
	cayenne	

1   If the sardines are large enough and firm enough, they should be
     skinned and boned.
2   Arrange on rectangles of buttered toast.
3   Reheat carefully under the salamander.
4   Sprinkle with cayenne and serve.

30   Welsh Rarebit

100 g	Cheddar cheese	4 oz
10 g	flour	½ oz
	1 egg yolk	
	2 slices toast	
	salt	
	Worcester sauce	
25 g	margarine	1 oz
125 ml	milk	¼ pt
	4 tbspn beer	
10 g	butter	½ oz
	cayenne	
	English mustard	

1   Melt the margarine in a thick-bottomed pan.
2   Add the flour and mix in with a wooden spoon.
3   Cook on a gentle heat for a few minutes without colouring.

4 Gradually add the cold milk and mix to a smooth sauce.
5 Allow to simmer for a few minutes.
6 Add the grated or finely sliced cheese.
7 Allow to melt slowly over a gentle heat until a smooth mixture is obtained.
8 Add the yolk to the hot mixture, stir in and immediately remove from the heat.
9 Meanwhile, in a separate pan boil the beer and allow it to reduce to $\frac{1}{2}$ tbspn.
10 Add to the mixture with the other seasonings.
11 Allow the mixture to cool.
12 Spread on the four rectangles of buttered toast.
13 Place on a baking sheet and brown gently under the salamander and serve.
14 Cheese contains a large amount of protein which will become tough and stringy if heated for too long or at too high a temperature.

31 Buck Rarebit

Prepare Welsh Rarebit and place a well-drained poached egg on each portion.

32 Cheese Soufflé   *Soufflé au Fromage*

25 g	butter	1 oz
125 ml	milk	$\frac{1}{4}$ pt
	3–4 egg whites	
	salt	
15 g	flour	$\frac{3}{4}$ oz
	3 egg yolks	
50 g	grated cheese	2 oz
	cayenne	

1 Melt the butter in a thick-bottomed pan.
2 Add the flour and mix with a wooden spoon.
3 Cook out for a few seconds without colouring.
4 Gradually add the cold milk and mix to a smooth sauce.
5 Simmer for a few minutes.
6 Add one egg yolk, mix in quickly and immediately remove from the heat.
7 When cool, add remaining yolks.
8 Season with salt and pepper.
9 Add the cheese.
10 Place the egg whites and a pinch of salt in a scrupulously clean bowl, preferably copper, and whisk until stiff.
11 Add one-eighth of the whites to the mixture and mix well.
12 Gently fold in the remaining seven-eights of the mixture, mix as lightly as possible.
13 Place into a buttered soufflé case.

14   Cook in a hot oven (230°–250°C) for approx. 15–20 min.
15   Remove from the oven and place on a round flat silver dish and
      serve *immediately*.

33 Cheese Fritters   *Beignets de Fromage*

125 ml	water	¼ pt
60 g	flour	2½ oz
50 g	grated cheese	2 oz
	cayenne	
50 g	margarine	2 oz
	2 eggs	
	salt	

1   Bring the water and margarine to the boil in a thick-bottomed pan.
2   Remove from the heat.
3   Add the flour, mix with a wooden spoon.
4   Return to a gentle heat and mix well until the mixture leaves the
      sides of the pan.
5   Remove from the heat.
6   Allow to cool slightly.
7   Gradually add the eggs, beating well.
8   Add the cheese and seasoning.
9   Using a spoon, scoop out the mixture in pieces the size of a
      walnut, place into deep hot fat (185°C).
10   Allow to cook with the minimum of handling for approx.
      10 min.
11   Drain and serve on a dish paper on a silver flat.
12   Sprinkle with grated Parmesan cheese.

34 Cheese Straws   *Paillettes au Fromage*

100 g	puff paste or rough paste	¼ lb
	cayenne	
50 g	grated cheese	2 oz

1   Roll out the pastry 48 × 12 cm (24 × 6 in).
2   Sprinkle with cheese and cayenne.
3   Give a single turn, that is, fold the paste one-third the way over
      so that it covers the first fold.
4   Roll out approx. 3 mm (⅛ in) thick.
5   Cut out four circles approx. 4 cm (2 in) diameter.
6   Remove the centre with a smaller cutter leaving a circle approx.
      ½ cm (¼ in) wide.
7   Cut the remaining paste into strips approx. 6 × ½ cm (3 × ¼ in).
8   Twist each once or twice.
9   Place on a lightly greased baking sheet.
10   Bake in a hot oven (230°–250°C) for approx. 10 min until a
      golden brown.
11   To serve place a bundle of straws into each circle.

35   Cheese and Ham Savouries   *Quiche Lorraine*

100 g	rough puff, puff or short pastry	4 oz
	1 egg	
25 g	grated cheese	1 oz
	cayenne	
125 ml	milk	$\frac{1}{4}$ pt
50 g	chopped ham	2 oz
	salt	

1   Lightly grease four good-size barquette or tartlet moulds.
2   Line thinly with pastry.
3   Prick the bottoms of the paste two or three times with a fork.
4   Cook in a hot oven (230°–250°C) for 3–4 min or until the pastry
    is lightly set.
5   Remove from the oven, press the pastry down if it has tended to
    rise.
6   Add the chopped ham and grated cheese.
7   Mix the egg, milk, salt and cayenne thoroughly.
8   Strain into the barquettes.
9   Return to a moderate oven (230°–250°C) and bake gently till
    nicely browned and set, approx. 15–20 min.

36   Savoury Flan

Line a 12 cm (6 in) flan-ring with short paste and proceed as for
Quiche Lorraine, or vary the filling by using lightly fried lardons of
bacon (in place of ham), chopped cooked onion and chopped parsley.

20
Sandwiches

Sandwiches are one of the most varied types of food produced. They may be made from every kind of bread, fresh or toasted, in a variety of shapes and with an almost endless assortment of fillings.

Types of bread	*Types of filling*	
White	Ham	Tomato
Brown	Tongue	Cucumber
Caraway seed	Beef	Cress
Rye	Chicken	Lettuce
	Smoked fish	Watercress
	Tinned fish	Egg
	Fish and meat paste	

Examples of Combination Fillings
Fish and lettuce
Cheese and tomato
Cucumber and egg
Apple and chutney

Seasonings to Flavour Sandwiches
Mayonnaise (egg, salmon, etc)
Vinaigrette (crab, lobster, fish, egg)
English mustard (ham, beef)
French mustard (cheese, tongue)
Chutney (cheese, tinned meat)

Where sandwiches are required in large quantities the usual method is to use large sandwich loaves, remove the crusts from three sides and one end. The bread is then cut in thin slices across the loaf, using a sharp carving knife (the modern type of serrated knife will be found ideal). (The bread may be buttered before being cut.)

The slices of bread are stacked neatly, one on top of the other, resting on a crust of bread. When the bread is cut it is then buttered (unless this has been done) and the prepared fillings are added quickly and efficiently and the complete loaf is made into long sandwiches. If they are to be kept for any length of time the crusts are replaced and wrapped in clean cloth or greaseproof paper. When required for service the sandwiches are easily and quickly cut into any required size or shape, neatly dressed on a doilly on a silver flat dish and spinkled with washed and drained mustard and cress. A typical set of fillings for a loaf could be, ham, tongue, smoked salmon, tomato, cucumber, egg.

Toasted Sandwiches
These are made by inserting a variety of savoury fillings between two slices of hot, freshly buttered toast, e.g. scrambled egg, bacon, fried egg, scrambled egg with chopped ham.

Club Sandwich
This is made by placing between two slices of hot buttered toast a filling of lettuce, grilled bacon, slices of hard-boiled egg, mayonnaise and slices of chicken.

Bookmaker Sandwich
This is an underdone minute steak between two slices of hot buttered toast.

Double-decker and Treble-decker Sandwiches
Toasted and untoasted bread can be made into double-decker sandwiches, using three slices of bread with two separate fillings. Treble- and quadro-decker sandwiches may also be prepared. They may be served hot or cold.

The Open Sandwich or Scandinavian Smorrëbrod
This is prepared from a buttered slice of any bread garnished with any type of meat, fish, eggs, vegetables, salads, etc.
 The varieties of open sandwich can include some of the following:

1   Smoked salmon, lettuce, potted shrimps, slice of lemon.
2   Scrambled egg, asparagus tips, chopped pimento.
3   Grilled bacon, cold fried egg, tomato sauce, mushrooms.
4   Cold sliced beef, sliced tomato, fans of gherkins.
5   Shredded lettuce, sliced hard-boiled egg, mayonnaise, cucumber.
6   Cold boiled rice, cold curried chicken, chutney.
7   Minced raw beef, anchovy fillet, raw egg yolk, chopped horse radish, onion and parsley.
8   Pickled herring, chopped gherkin, capers sieved, hard-boiled egg.

 When serving open sandwiches it is usual to offer a good choice. care should be taken with finishing touches, using parsley, sliced radishes, gherkins, pickles, capers, etc., to give a neat clean look to the dish. Presentation is important.

GINGERBREAD

8 ozs Flour

½ level tsp of salt

2 " " " Ground Ginger

½ " " " Bicarb. of soda

2 ozs Marg / Lard / Butter

4 ozs treacle

2 ozs Soft Brown Sugar

¼ pt milk

METHOD

Sieve dry ingredients together in a bowl. Put fat, sugar and treacle into a pan and warm through. Mix in dry ingredients plus milk. Pour mixture into a greased tin and Bake for 1 hour at 350°F (gas 7-8.)

CHOC SAUCE

3 ozs Soft Brown Sugar

3 ozs Castor Sugar

3 ozs cocoa powder

½ pt milk

1 tsp vanilla essence

1 oz Butter.

Mix all ingredients together in a pan and bring to boil stirring occasionally. Boil for 2 minutes without stirring. Serve Hot or cold.

Index of Recipes